RAND McNALLY

the atlas

MIDSIZE

United States, Canada & Mexico

M000086800

contents

Travel Information 2003

(L) ON INDUSTRIAL PKY 2.7

(R) TO TAKE I-65S 3.1

TOWARDS MOBILE/PRICHARD EXIT 9
I-165 EXIT

WATER ST

I-10 TOWARDS PENSACOLA

Maps and Indexes

U.S. states

U.S. cities

Canada

Canadian provinces

Canadian city maps

México and Puerto Rico

Reproducing or recording maps, tables, text, or any other material that appears in this publication by photocopying, by electronic storage and retrieval, or by any other means is prohibited.

Rand McNally updates this *Midsize Road Atlas* annually, and every effort has been made to provide accurate information. Changes can and do occur, however, and we cannot be legally responsible for any errors, changes, omissions, or any loss, injury, or inconvenience sustained by any person or entity as a result of information or advice contained in this book.

Photo Credits: Images provided by PhotoDisc ©2003 — back cover, ii (bl), iii (tl), v (ml) & (bl), 82 (tm) & (br), 83 (br), 84 (tl) & (tr), 85 (bl), vi (tl) & (tr), vii (tl), 81 (bl) & (tr), viii (bl) & (br), 86 (bl), 87 (br); © Rand McNally — ii (br), iii (bl) & (tr), iv (ml) & (br), v (tl) & (tr) & (mr) & (br); © Janis Maguire iii (mr); © Photonica/ Charles Gullung ii (tl); © Edgecomb Pottery Gallery ii (tr); © Buffalo/Niagara CVB/Angel Art Ltd. iii (br); © Hillebrand Estates Winery iv (tl); © Tammy Love iv (bl); © FoodPix/Steve Mark Needham iv (mr); © FoodPix/ Burke/Triolo Productions iv (tl); FoodPix/ Spencer Jones 83 (tl); © Great Wisconsin Cheese Festival 83 (tl); © FoodPix/Maximilian Stock Ltd. 83 (tr); © Louisiana Shrimp and Petroleum Fetival and Fair Association 84 (bl); © Idaho Potato Commission 85 (tl); © Norsk Høstfest 85 (tr); © San Antonio Convention & Visitors Bureau vi (ml); © Bridlewood Farms vi (m); © Dan Curran, Nebraska Division of Tourism vi (bl); © 2002 Harley-Davidson Motor Company vi (br); © Marilyn Humphries vii (bl); © Replacements, Inc. vii (tr); © Washington, D.C. Convention & Tourism Corporation vii (br); © Stone/Andrea Booher 86 (tl); © The Image Bank/Larry Dale Gordon viii (tm) © The Image Bank/Michael Melford 86 (tr)

Copyright © 2003 by
Rand McNally & Company.
All rights reserved.

For licensing and copyright permissions, contact us at
licensing@randmcnally.com

If you have a comment or suggestion, please call
1-800-333-0136, ext. 6171,
or e-mail us at:
consumeraffairs@randmcnally.com

Made in U.S.A.

10 9 8 7 6 5 4 3 2

2003

2003 Best of the Road™

The best road trips capture more than just pretty scenery. The roadside attractions, the local diners, unique shops, and new takes on well-known spots make it worth the drive. Last year, we launched ***Best of the Road™***, selecting five top drives and designating best stops along the route. This year, the editors of Rand McNally have combed through dozens more great trips to uncover new drives and the tasty dining, unique shopping and attractions, or unusual angles to well-known attractions that we've rated ***Best of the Road™*** for 2003.

For more information on any of these trips – including additional things to see and do along the way – or to explore other ***Best of the Road™*** trips, go to ***www.randmcnally.com*** and type in the Express Access Code ***BR***.

COASTING TO ACADIA

Maine *(see p. 24)*

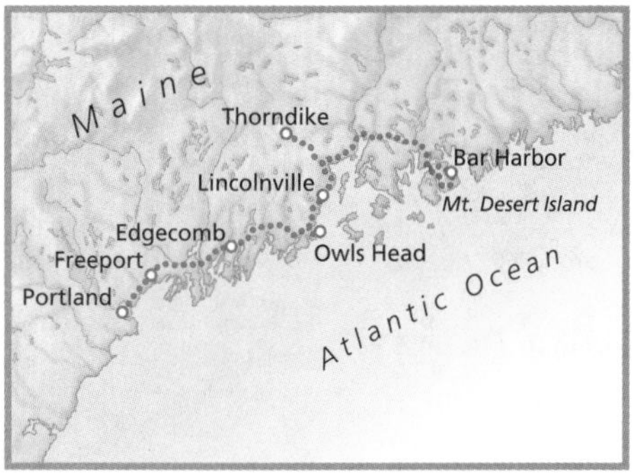

Coastal Maine may well be the ultimate seaside retreat. Think fall foliage drives, cozy B&Bs, roadside artists' studios, and lobster buoys bobbing in harbors. All is not quiet on the eastern front, though. This state's hallmark is generations of fishermen who ***wrangled clawed crustaceans*** and outlasted wicked winters. Maine's Route 1 delivers plenty of hearty adventures and unique discoveries.

Best-known: Roadside lobster roll stands; Portland's Old Port historic district; Freeport's discount shopping; Boothbay Harbor puffin-watching cruises; and Thunder Hole and Cadillac Mountain in Acadia National Park.

catch a puffin watching cruise

Highlights of the drive:

- **L.L. Bean Outdoor Discovery Schools (Freeport)**
Shoppers make the pilgrimage 'round the clock to Bean's flagship store in Freeport, but the Outdoor Discovery Schools (hour-long to week-long) are the best find here. ***Learn fly-casting,*** kayaking, outdoor photography, and other activities in Maine's lush wilderness. Expert-led classes go for as little as $10. *Main St. at Bow St., 888/552-2094*

- **Edgecomb Potters Gallery (Edgecomb)**
Swirled peacock colors and crystalline patterns grace vases, bowls, and hundreds of one-of-a-kind items at this pottery studio. Function meets style in each piece made by local artists. Serving bowls run $45-$75 and mugs are $22-$28. *727 Boothbay Rd., 207/882-9493*

- **Owls Head Transportation Museum (Owls Head)**

Amazingly, most of the 100 planes, trains, and automobiles in this museum actually run. Every other weekend from May through October you can hitch a free ride in a Model T or ***see antique airplanes fly.*** Mechanics repair and restore classics in the museum's Auto Works shop. *On ME 73 adjacent to Knox County Airport, 207/594-4418*

- **Lobster Pound (Lincolnville)**
Possibly the best new-shell lobster (and butter!) on Route 1. Servers tie bibs on diners before presenting a lobster that's sweet, tender, and easy to coax from the shell. Get a 1½-pounder for $20, a 2-pounder for $25. *US 1, 207/789-5550*

- **Bryant Stove and Music (Thorndike)**
Nowhere is there such a kitschy yet historically important accumulation of antique stoves, mechanical music devices, and dolls. Visitors who ask the owner to show his favorite pieces will get an earful of interesting stories, maybe even a little ditty at the player piano.
27 Stovepipe Alley, 207/568-3665

- **Acadia National Park's Wildwood Stable (Seal Harbor, near Bar Harbor)**
Traverse some of the park's remote roads and hear about its interesting history (including stories of ***"Rockefeller's teeth"***) on a horse-drawn carriage ride. Guides at Wildwood Stable halt horses to point out hawks overhead or panoramic views and explain how John D. Rockefeller Jr.'s team constructed the park's carriage roads in the early 1900s. Rides run mid-June through early October. *Park Loop Rd., 1 mile south of Jordan Pond House Restaurant, 207/276-3622 or 207/288-3338*

FROM PACIFIC TO PALMS

California (see p. 9)

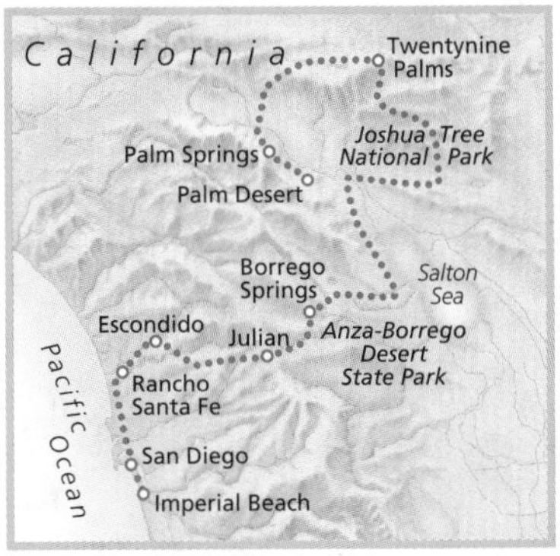

The only problem with starting a trip in temperate, attraction-packed San Diego is ... it's hard to leave. Then again, the same is true of much along this route. Like the apple pie haven of Julian, or the cactus-flanked trails of Anza-Borrego Desert State Park, or the shops and sunshine of Palm Springs. This slice of Southern California is made for vacations.

Best-known: In San Diego, the zoo, Old Town's Mexican food, Shamu at SeaWorld, Balboa Park museums; San Diego Wild Animal Park; Julian's gold mines and apple orchards; the resorts, spas, and golf courses of Palm Springs and Borrego Springs; and lots of sunshine.

Highlights of the drive:

- **Tijuana Slough National Wildlife Refuge (Imperial Beach)**

Serious birdwatchers from all over the continent flock to this avian haven. A recent count registered more than 370 species, from hummingbirds to hawks to herons. Pick up a map and a bird list at the Visitor Center, then head out onto the eight miles of trails that meander across a broad, flat expanse of wetland.
301 Caspian Way, 619/575-2704

- **The Vegetable Shop (Rancho Santa Fe)**

This is not your run-of-the-mill farm stand. On a typical day, the offerings might include 15 varieties of tomatoes, small Mara des Bois strawberries, delicate little carrots in five different colors, and a dozen types of melons. Top California restaurants such as Chez Panisse and Spago buy their vegetables and fruit here, so you might have to fight with Wolfgang Puck for that last pint of blackberries. *6123 Calzada del Bosque, 858/756-3184*

- **Borrego Palm Canyon Trail (Anza-Borrego Desert State Park)**

After a mile-and-a-half scramble over rocky, sun-baked terrain dotted with agave, cholla, and barrel cactuses,

you'll reach a green, shady oasis where ***hundreds of fan palms*** tower over a tumbling stream. "Borrego" is a Spanish word for bighorn sheep; keep your eyes peeled and you might spot some of these timid, graceful creatures on the rocky slopes above the trail.
200 Palm Canyon Dr., Borrego Springs, 760/767-5311 (park headquarters)

- **Palapas of Araby Cove (Palm Springs)**

Clustered in a shady garden setting are roughly 30 palapas, or palm frond-thatched huts, each serving as studio and gallery for a different artist. Wander around and check out the hand-blown glass ornaments ($15 to $25), colorfully painted rocks ($15 to $100), Raku pottery ($35 to $150), handmade paper ($10 to $20), and etched gourds ($35 to $75). Artists are happy to talk about their work even as they're creating it. *3255 East Palm Canyon Dr., 760/416-1818*

- **The Living Desert (Palm Desert)**

Desert tortoises, big-eared fennec foxes, meerkats, Arabian oryxes, and cinereous vultures are just a few of the 134 species of desert-dwellers you'll find at this 1,200-acre zoological park and botanical garden. At the state-of-the-art Tennity Wildlife Hospital, you can ***watch live and videotaped surgeries*** while veterinarians provide running narrative.
47-900 Portola Ave., 760/346-5694

BEYOND NIAGARA FALLS

New York, Ontario (see pp. 60-61)

Niagara Falls is a tough act to follow, but there's way more to see all along this stunning shoreline meander. There are walking tours highlighting Buffalo's architecture, icewine specialties in Niagara's wine country, and exotic culinary and cultural adventures in Toronto. The route through rolling country wraps around tiny hamlets, sprawling farms, pick-your-own-fruit orchards, artists' studios, and stores peddling antiques and esoteric books.

the route wraps around tiny ***hamlets***

Best-known: Niagara Falls; the Shaw Festival in Niagara-on-the-Lake; the Blossom Festival; Toronto's CN Tower; antiquing along Hwy 2; fall foliage tours; bird-watching in Presqu'ile Provincial Park; Kingston's historic downtown; and Thousand Islands' boat cruises.

(continued on the next page)

Highlights of the drive:

• Duff's (Amherst, NY, near Buffalo)

Locals have been flocking here for Buffalo wings since 1969. More than 5,000 pounds of these chicken wings are served each week, slathered in Frank's original *red-hot cayenne pepper sauce.* Select from seven levels, plain to super-hot (high-intensity heat is $1 extra). *3651 Sheridan Dr., 716/834-6234*

• Hillebrand Estates Winery (Niagara-on-the-Lake, ON)

The ins and outs of winemaking and the secret of why Ontario's freezing winters are ideal for producing icewine are all revealed during a Hillebrand tour. Afterward, visitors can *enjoy vineyard vistas* while tasting award-winning wines and sampling from a tantalizing menu at the Vineyard Café. Extra special: lemon mousse with Riesling-marinated berries ($8). *1249 Niagara Stone Rd., 905/468-7123 or 800/582-8412*

• Ten Ren Tea (Toronto, ON)

Stay for a cuppa, enjoying the gentle ambiance of this long-established Chinese teahouse, one of six in Canada. It's a tea connoisseur's hangout, with more than 100 varieties of high-quality tea, loose and Ten Ren's own packaged brands: Tung Ting oolong, orange-ginger chai, and Delicious Plum herbal tea. *454 Dundas St. W., 416/598-7872*

• Hand Works (Bloomfield, ON)

Tammy Love's striking paintings adorn the walls of her gallery, while unusual handmade pieces, created by artists far and wide, beg to be touched and used. Selections include gleaming mango-wood rice dishes from India ($20), bright colored Roman-mosaic-styled earrings (from $15 to $195), fragrant hand-milled soaps ($10), striking multi-colored baskets made from telephone wire, and sturdy cast-aluminum sculptured cookware — all for $50 to $65. *246 Main St., 613/393-3888*

• The Penitentiary Museum (Kingston, ON)

Leg shackles, cat-o'-nine tails, and an ice-cold water bath are some early examples of "restraint equipment" used by Canada's penitentiary system, which began in the 1830s. Inmates' inventiveness in creating weapons included a cannon made from plumbing pipes and a crossbow *fashioned out of toothbrushes.* Former correctional officers conduct the tours, offering personal insider tales. *555 King St. W., 613/530-3122*

Canadian goods in approximate US dollars.

LET THE GOOD TIMES ROLL!

Louisiana *(see p. 23)*

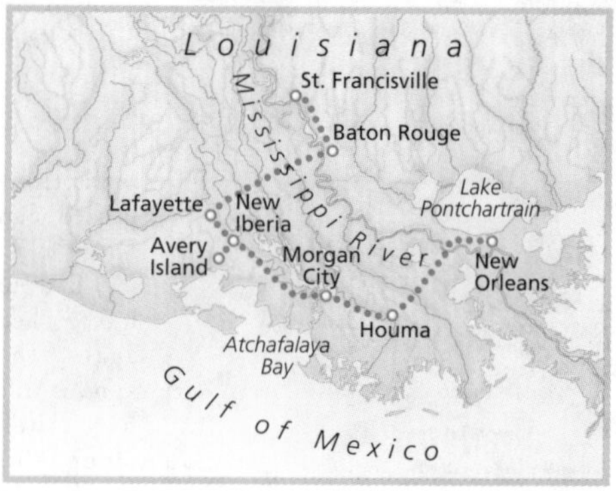

If you're looking for revelry, Louisiana is the place to party. Flamboyant parades, 24/7 entertainment, and the locals' laid-back attitude make for a carefree escape in both the city and the country. But there's more to Bayou Country than Mardi Gras. The snaky path through lowland Louisiana promises *swampy alligator encounters,* surprising museums, and plenty of creepy ghost stories — not to mention a gastronomic bonanza of Cajun eats.

Best-known: In New Orleans, beignets and café au lait at Café du Monde and streetcar tours through the Garden District; ***buckets of Cajun-spiced crawfish*** in Morgan City (no utensils required); living Acadian history at Vermilionville in Lafayette; Huey Long history at the Old Governor's Mansion in Baton Rouge; and antebellum plantation tours along the Great River Road.

Highlights of the drive:

• Johnny's Po Boys (New Orleans)

This joint brags that even its mistakes are edible, and after a bite or two you'll understand why. Locals stand in long lines for huge, flaky rolls literally dripping with fried oysters and a huge dousing of mayo. And with almost everything on the menu ringing in under $6, it's a diet for the wallet — just maybe not for you. *511 St. Louis St., 504/524-8129*

• Pharmacy Museum (New Orleans)

Travel back in time to the 19th century when bloodletting, leeches, snake oil, and voodoo concoctions were all legitimate medical remedies. For just $2, poke through the musty jars of powders and "magical" elixirs, then creak up the winding stairs for a peek at the museum's collection of historic — and rather painful looking — dental devices. *514 Chartres St., 504/565-8027*

- **Tabasco Factory and Country Store (Avery Island)**
Bland doesn't cut it in Louisiana cuisine, so it's no surprise that Tabasco pepper sauce has been produced here for 130 years. Learn how particular peppers are picked, mashed, salted, and aged to make the peppery red stuff, then take a free spin around the factory to watch up close as workers bottle the final product. Try a sample (or two or three) at the Country Store, where mini bottles of red or green sauce are 50 cents each, and the popular hot sauce 4-pack of red, green, garlic, and habañero in a wooden crate is $18. The shop offers t-shirts, aprons, towels — all with the Tabasco label.
LA 14 to LA 329, 800/634-9599

- **Atchafalaya Experience Swamp Tour (Lafayette)**
Shoot an alligator (with a camera, of course!) on a two-hour guided boat tour of the Atchafalaya Basin, the largest river delta on the continent. ***Reptiles not your thing?*** Beavers, foxes, black bears, raccoons, nutria, and more than 300 species of birds complete the swamp's waterlogged menagerie. *338 N. Sterling St., 337/233-7816*

- **Myrtles Plantation (St. Francisville)**
Believe in ghosts or not, this place just feels scary. Revisit the sordid past of this 200-year-old house on a candlelit nighttime mystery tour, complete with cringe-worthy tales of the many active ghosts haunting the mansion. The fainter-of-heart should try a daytime history tour, which details the plantation's beautiful plaster friezework and Aubusson tapestries. But beware — the spirits *don't* only come out at night.
7747 US 61, 225/635-6277

HILLS & ARCHITECTURE

Indiana *(see p. 18)*

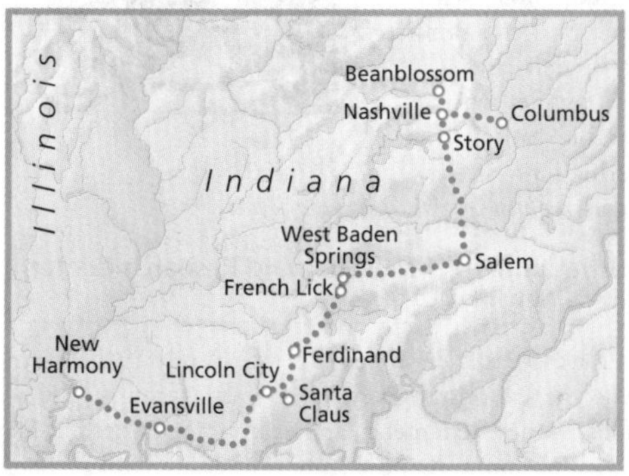

The folks are friendly, the vittles homemade. And a trip through the wooded hills and forests of southern Indiana has many cultured surprises in store, too. Columbus ranks among the country's top 10 architecturally significant cities. In tiny towns like Gnaw Bone, Nashville, and Beanblossom, sorghum, ***fried biscuits, and bluegrass music prevail.*** Other highlights include spa waters in French Lick and historic sites of New Harmony. From the down-home to the sublime, southern Indiana shines.

Best-known: Nashville's crafts; Marengo Cave; Bedford limestone; geodes along the roadsides; Holiday World roller coasters; and Lincoln Boyhood National Memorial.

Highlights of the drive:

- **Columbus Architectural Tour (Columbus)**
Less than $10 buys a two-hour tour past nearly 70 eye-popping churches, commercial buildings, schools, and a hospital that dot this community of 39,000. Even the city jail has style, with a domed rooftop exercise area for inmates. *506 Fifth St., 800/468-6564 (visitors center)*

even the city jail has style

- **Covered Bridge (Beanblossom)**
Drive through a sturdy, authentic covered bridge, built in 1880. The remote wooded setting makes it picture perfect. (Another bridge is at the northeast gate to Brown Co. State Park, off IN 46.) *Covered Bridge Rd., off IN 135, 812/988-7303 (Brown Co. Visitors Center)*

- **West Baden Springs Hotel (West Baden Springs)**
A stroll through the partially restored 1902 domed wonder offers a glimpse of grandeur that once attracted personages like Al Capone and Helen Keller. A 70-minute tour is $10 for adults. ***Arrive in style*** by taking the trolley ($2 roundtrip) from the Indiana Railway Museum.
IN 56, 317/639-4534

- **Pluto Bath (French Lick)**
Until you've "taken the waters," you haven't really experienced French Lick. The Spa at the French Lick Springs Resort offers a half-hour soak in the warm, dark, frothy, and, shall we say, fragrant baths of the mineral-rich spring waters for $20. *8670 W. IN 56, 800/457-4042*

- **Buffalo Run Grill (Lincoln City)**
Ride herd on hunger at Buffalo Run Grill by gobbling down a buffalo burger for just $3.50 (add 15 cents for cheese). Buffalo and ostrich are raised on the ranch behind the restaurant. Check out the buffalo hides, hair, and even teeth (about $4 each) at the gift shop.
IN 162, 812/937-2799

- **Historic New Harmony (New Harmony)**
Founded in 1814, this town's been both a spiritual community and a utopian experiment. It still draws the contemplative and artistic. Many buildings from the early days remain, creating a kind of time warp. Meditate while you ***walk the labyrinth,*** shop at art galleries, or splurge on a gourmet meal at the Red Geranium. A must-do: breakfast at the Main Cafe, where local farmers gather to gossip and sip coffee.
IN 66, west of IN 69, 800/231-2168

Land of the Free

25 great things to see and do for free

The Alamo
San Antonio, Texas *(p. 47, F-8)*

Walk through the old mission and Long Barrack where, in 1836, Davy Crockett and a small band of Texans held out for 13 days before falling to Mexican troops. View a flintlock rifle used in the battle and the actual buckskin vest worn by the King of the Wild Frontier. *210/225-1391, www.thealamo.org*

Battleship *Wisconsin*
Norfolk, Virginia *(p. 49, H-12)*

Weighing 50,000 tons, the *Wisconsin* is 887 feet long (that's nearly three football fields) and 108 feet wide (just two feet narrower than the Panama Canal locks). See the ship's *Tomahawk missile launchers,* 15-ton anchors, and towering guns capable of launching 2.5-ton shells a distance of 23 nautical miles.
800/664-1080, www.battleshipwisconsin.org

Bridlewood Farms
Bell Buckle, Tennessee *(p. 20, H-7, near Shelbyville)*

Several former World Champions stand at stud on this Tennessee Walking Horse breeding farm. Learn about the breed, see newborn foals, and get a firsthand look at the entire breeding operation. *931/389-9388, www.bridlewood-farm.com*

Canyon de Chelly National Monument
Chinle, Arizona *(p. 6, B-7)*

a close-up look at Anasazi rock art

The sheer sandstone walls of this canyon are pocked with notches and caves containing ruins of Indian dwellings more than 700 years old. Scenic drives along the North and South Rims offer views of the ruins and *stunning canyon scenery.* In summer, ranger-led hikes offer a close-up look at Anasazi rock art and spectacular ruins. *928/674-5500, www.nps.gov/cach*

Carhenge
Alliance, Nebraska *(p. 30, B-2)*

Here on the plains of western Nebraska is a faithful recreation of England's Stonehenge ... sort of. Vintage American autos, painted gray and planted trunk-down, represent all 38 of the major stones that compose the original. *308/762-1520, www.carhenge.com*

Cliff Walk
Newport, Rhode Island *(p. 11, G-8)*

This 3.5-mile National Recreation Trail winds past grand *Gilded Age mansions* built as summer homes by wealthy New Yorkers like Cornelius Vanderbilt and Caroline Astor. The walk offers panoramic views along Newport's rocky coastline.
401/849-8098, www.cliffwalk.com

Family History Library
Salt Lake City, Utah *(p. 50, C-4)*

If you're curious about your roots, there's no better place to start digging than the world's largest family history library. Here you can search 2.3 million rolls of microfilm, create a family search website, and e-mail your newly discovered kin. *801/240-2331, www.familysearch.org*

Frank Lloyd Wright architecture at FSC
Lakeland, Florida *(p. 14, E-4)*

The West Campus of Florida Southern College represents the ***largest single-site collection*** of Frank Lloyd Wright buildings in the world. Grab a free map at the Visitor Center, then set off on a self-guided walking tour of 12 Wright-designed structures, including two chapels and a planetarium. *863/680-4110, www.flsouthern.edu/fllwctr*

Hallmark Visitors Center
Kansas City, Missouri *(p. 28, C-2)*

Watch greeting cards roll off printing presses, reminisce over tear-jerking Hallmark commercials, and browse through an exhibit of more than 250 Hallmark Keepsake Ornaments. Then marvel as a machine transforms 42 inches of ribbon into a souvenir gift bow in seconds.
816-274-3613, www.hallmarkvisitorscenter.com

Harley-Davidson Final Assembly Plant
York, Pennsylvania *(p. 45, H-9)*

Six hundred Harleys roll off this plant's assembly lines each day, and visitors can see it all happen. Guided tours begin with a short film, then move on to the shop floor where giant presses stamp out fenders and gas tanks while workers assemble Softail and Touring motorcycles. *717/852-6590, www.yorkonline.org/visit_york/harleytour.htm*

International UFO Museum and Research Center
Roswell, New Mexico *(p. 33, F-6)*

Did a UFO really crash near Roswell in July 1947? Learn about the notorious Roswell Incident through photographs, witness statements, and exhibits. See what's inside the manual on U.S. presidential procedures for dealing with UFOs, and check out a *UFO-sighting map.*
505/625-9495, www.iufomrc.org

Joe Hogan State Fish Hatchery
Lonoke, Arkansas *(p. 7, D-5)*

This hatchery — one of the country's largest — annually produces more than 6 million largemouth bass, crappie, catfish, and other big ones that might get away. It's also home to ducks, great blue herons, sandpipers, and other wildlife. A watchtower provides panoramic views of the hatchery's 57 fish-filled ponds. *501/676-6963*

John Day Fossil Beds National Monument
Near Fossil, Oregon (p. 43, C-5)

Scenery meets paleontology in the deeply eroded volcanic deposits of this National Monument. Visitors can view rainbow-hued claystone hills and **hike over volcanic lavas,** ashfall, and mudflows. The museum at Sheep Rock displays animal and plant fossils dating back 54 million years. *541/987-2333, www.nps.gov/joda*

The Las Vegas Strip
Las Vegas, Nevada (p. 9, H-9)

After dusk, spectacular shows fire up every 30 minutes outside several casinos. Take a stroll down the Strip to see pirates battling the British Navy at Treasure Island, more than **1,000 synchronized fountains** dancing in front of the Bellagio, and, outside the Mirage, a volcano spewing smoke and fire 100 feet into the air.
702/892-7575, www.lasvegas24hours.com

Lincoln Park Zoo
Chicago, Illinois (p. 17, B-6)

This is one of the last free zoos in the United States. With the magnificent Chicago skyline as a backdrop, visitors can watch river otters frolicking, lions prowling, and penguins waddling. The little ones will love the Children's Zoo, with its hedgehogs, owls, lizards, and even a tarantula.
312/742-2000, www.lpzoo.org

Mount Rushmore
Keystone, South Dakota (p. 39, D-2)

Prepare to be awestruck by the 60-foot granite profiles of George Washington, Thomas Jefferson, Theodore Roosevelt, and Abraham Lincoln. At the Sculptor's Studio you'll find the **original 1/12 scale model** created by Rushmore artist Gutzon Borglum. (Note: Free parking is limited.) *605/574-2523, www.nps.gov/moru*

National Braille Press
Boston, Massachusetts (p. 11, D-9)

Examine a huge Braille printing press or **spell out your name** in the raised-dot language while taking a guided tour.* Housed in a converted piano factory, this is one of only a few U.S. companies that mass-produce Braille materials. *888/965-8965, www.nbp.org*

National Radio Astronomy Observatory
Green Bank, West Virginia (p. 48, E-7)

Scientists listen and learn about "the final frontier" at this observatory, home to the world's largest fully steerable satellite dish. Experience a close encounter of the solar kind when you look at sunspots through an eight-inch radio telescope. *304/456-2011, www.gb.nrao.edu*

Pleasant Hawaiian Hula Show
Honolulu, O'ahu, Hawaii (p. 5, J-3)

Keep pace with these hip swingers and you might hurt yourself. Since its origin as "The Kodak Hula Show" more than six decades ago, this must-see spectacle has entertained more than 17 million visitors. *808/945-1851, www.hoganfoundation.org/programs/kodak.htm*

Replacements, Ltd.
Greensboro, North Carolina (p. 36, C-7)

This mammoth warehouse holds more than 8 million pieces of china, crystal, and silver in more than 160,000 discontinued patterns. The sheer volume here will inspire you to register your own patterns with the company — just in case.
800/737-5223, www.replacements.com

San Francisco Cable Car Museum
San Francisco, California (p. 8, F-2)

Descend the basement stairs to see a maze of tunnels filled with humming motors, gears, cables, and pulleys. This isn't just a museum — it's the actual powerhouse for the city's famous cable cars. A 15-minute video explains how the cable car system works.
415/474-1887, www.cablecarmuseum.com

The Smithsonian Institution
Washington, D.C. (p. 13, C-6)

Not one, but 15 fabulous freebie attractions, including the Museum of Natural History, the Air and Space Museum, and the Museum of American History. Together, the Smithsonian's family of museums house more than 140 million artifacts, from the Hope Diamond to Muhammad Ali's boxing gloves to George Washington's false teeth. *202/357-2700, www.si.edu*

South Carolina Botanical Garden
Clemson, South Carolina (p. 36, E-3)

Some 2,200 varieties of ornamental plants thrive here. Stroll the colorful **azalea and camellia trails** or explore the wildflower, fern, and bog gardens. At the Bob Campbell Geology Museum you'll find such curiosities as glow-in-the-dark minerals and "alien rocks from space."
864/656-4470, virtual.clemson.edu/groups/scbg

U.S. Air Force Museum
Dayton, Ohio (p. 41, H-2)

No badge or special-op assignment is required to gain access to the presidential hangar here, where nine retired Air Force One planes reside. With 300 aircraft and missiles, WWII artifacts, and the Apollo 15 capsule, the USAF museum is the oldest and largest military aviation museum in the world. 937/255-3286, *www.wpafb.af.mil/museum*

U.S. Olympic Training Center
Colorado Springs, Colorado (p. 12, D-6)

One look at this super-sized, high-tech equipment and your neighborhood gym will seem positively puny. Take a guided tour and **see athletes honing their skills** on the parallel bars, in the swimming flume, or at the shooting center. Also check out the interactive kiosks and Hall of Fame. *719/578-4618, www.usolympicteam.com*

look at this super-sized high-tech equipment

**Reservations required.*

Call ahead for reservations

Hotel and rental car resources

Hotels

Adam's Mark Hotels & Resorts
800/444-2326
www.adamsmark.com

AmericInn
800/634-3444
www.americinn.com

Baymont Inns & Suites
800/301-0200 or
877/229-6668
www.baymontinn.com

Best Inns Suites Hotels
800/237-8466
www.bestinn.com

Best Western
800/528-1234 or
800/937-8376
www.bestwestern.com

Budget Host
800/283-4678
www.budgethost.com

Clarion Hotels
800/252-7466
www.clarioninn.com

Coast Hotels & Resorts
800/663-1144
www.coasthotels.com

Comfort Inns
800/228-5150
www.comfortinn.com

Comfort Suites
800/517-4000
www.comfortsuites.com

Country Hearth Inn
800/848-5767
www.countryhearth.com

Courtyard by Marriott
800/321-2211
www.courtyard.com

Crowne Plaza Hotel & Resorts
800/227-6963
www.crowneplaza.com

Days Inn
800/329-7466
www.daysinn.com

Delta Hotels & Resorts
800/268-1133
www.deltahotels.com

Doubletree Hotels & Guest Suites
800/222-8733
www.doubletree.com

Drury Hotels
800/378-7946
(U.S.& Canada)
800/325-8300 (Mexico)
www.drury-inn.com

Econo Lodge
800/553-2666
www.econolodge.com

Embassy Suites Hotels
800/362-2779
www.embassy-suites.com

Exel Inns of America
800/367-3935
www.exelinns.com

Extended StayAmerica
800/398-7829
www.extstay.com

Fairfield Inn by Marriott
800/228-2800
www.fairfieldinn.com

Fairmont Hotels & Resorts
800/441-1414
www.fairmont.com

Four Points Hotels by Sheraton
800/325-3535
www.fourpoints.com

Four Seasons Hotels & Resorts
800/332-3442 (U.S.)
800/268-6282 (Canada)
www.fourseasons.com

Hampton Inn
800/426-7866
www.hampton-inn.com

Hilton Hotels
800/445-8667
www.hilton.com

Holiday Inn/Holiday Inn Express/Holiday Inn Select
800/465-4329
www.holiday-inn.com

Homewood Suites
800/225-5466
www.homewood-suites.com

Howard Johnson Lodges
800/446-4656
www.hojo.com

Hyatt Hotels & Resorts
800/233-1234
www.hyatt.com

Inter-Continental Hotels & Resorts
800/327-0200
www.intercontinental.com

Knights Inn
800/843-5644
www.knightsinn.com

La Quinta Inn & Suites
800/531-5900
www.laquinta.com

Le Meridien Hotels
800/543-4300
www.lemeridien-hotels.com

Loews Hotels
800/235-6397
www.loewshotels.com

MainStay Suites
800/660-6246
www.mainstaysuites.com

Marriott International
800/228-9290
www.marriott.com

Microtel Inns & Suites
888/771-7171
www.microtelinn.com

Motel 6
800/466-8356
www.motel6.com

Omni Hotels
800/843-6664
www.omnihotels.com

Park Inn/Park Plaza
800/670-7275
www.parkhtls.com

Preferred Hotels & Resorts
800/323-7500
www.preferredhotels.com

Quality Inns & Suites
800/228-5151
www.qualityinn.com

Radisson Hotels Worldwide
800/333-3333
www.radisson.com

Ramada Inn/Ramada Limited/Ramada Plaza Hotels
800/272-6232
www.ramada.com

Red Roof Inns
800/733-7663
www.redroof.com

Renaissance Hotels & Resorts
800/468-3571
www.renaissancehotels.com

Residence Inn by Marriott
800/331-3131
www.residenceinn.com

The Ritz-Carlton
800/241-3333
www.ritzcarlton.com

Rodeway Inn
800/228-2000
www.rodeway.com

Sheraton Hotels & Resorts
800/325-3535
www.sheraton.com

Signature Inns
800/822-5252
www.signature-inns.com

Sleep Inn
800/753-3746
www.sleepinn.com

Super 8 Motels
800/800-8000
www.super8.com

Thriftlodge
800/525-9055
www.thriftlodge.com

Travelodge Hotels
800/578-7878
www.travelodge.com

Villager
800/328-7829
www.villager.com

WestCoast Hotels
800/426-0670 or
800/325-4000
www.westcoasthotels.com

Westin Hotels & Resorts
800/228-3000 or
800/937-8461
www.westin.com

Wyndham International
800/996-3426
www.wyndham.com

To find a Bed & Breakfast at your destination, contact the National Bed & Breakfast Association at 203/847-6196 or www.nbba.com.

Car Rental

AAPEX Rent-a-Car
800/327-9106
www.aapexrentals.com
AAPEX is only in Florida

Advantage Rent-a-Car
800/777-5000
www.arac.com

Alamo
800/327-9633
(U.S., Canada & Mexico)
www.goalamo.com

Avis
800/331-1212 (U.S.)
800/879-2847 (Canada)
01/288-8888 (Mexico)
800/331-1084 (Int'l)
www.avis.com

Brooks Rent-a-Car
800/634-6721
www.brookscarrental.com

Budget Rent-a-Car
800/527-0700
(U.S. & Canada)
800/268-8900 (Int'l)
www.budget.com

Dollar Rent-a-Car
800/800-4000
(U.S., Canada & Mexico)
www.dollar.com

Enterprise Rent-a-Car
800/325-8007
www.enterprise.com

Hertz
800/654-3131
800/654-3001 (Int'l)
www.hertz.com

National Car Rental
800/227-7368
www.nationalcar.com

Payless Car Rental
800/729-5377
(U.S., Canada & Mexico)
www.800-payless.com

Thrifty Car Rental
800/367-2277
(U.S., Canada & Mexico)
www.thrifty.com

*NOTE: All toll-free reservation numbers are for the U.S. and Canada unless otherwise noted. These numbers were accurate at press time, but are subject to change. Find more listings or book a hotel online at **randmcnally.com**.*

red means go

randmcnally.com
Express Access Code FL

Each map and editorial feature in this atlas has its own unique **Express Access Code**. These codes give you quick and easy access to tons of useful trip-planning information at **randmcnally.com**.

Here's how to use them:

1. Look for the red Express Access Code box FL located in the top corner of state and province map pages, or **Miami** FL4 next to the city name on city inset maps. You'll also find Express Access Codes on the mileage chart, mileage & driving times map, and editorial feature pages.

2. Go to **www.randmcnally.com**.

3. Look for the Road Atlas Express Access Code window on the **randmcnally.com** home page, type in a code from the atlas, and click "go."

4. Begin exploring! Road construction updates, driving directions, fun things to see and do, mileages, and expanded editorial features are all right at your fingertips.

Rand McNally.
The road continues online.

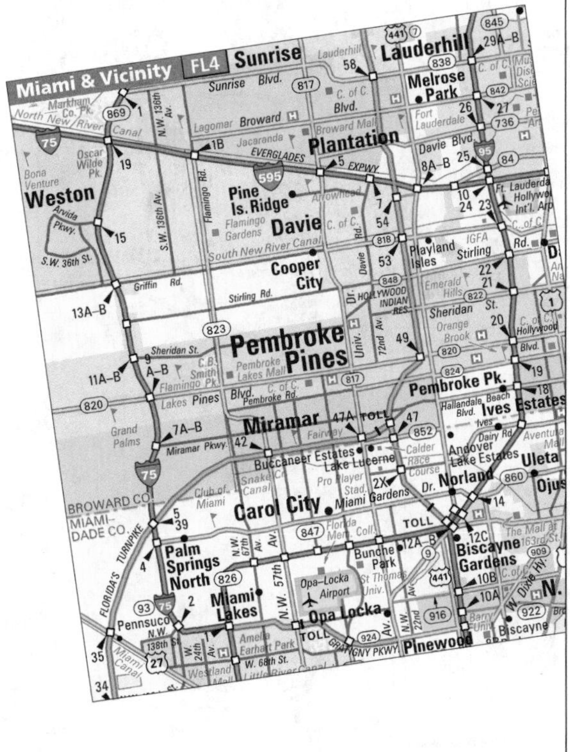

road atlas
express access code

Look for the Express Access Code listed on all the maps in the 2003 Road Atlas!

randmcnally.com
Express Access Code FL

Enter your Road Atlas Express Access Code here for instant access to lots of useful travel information.

go

Tell me more about this feature.

Map Legend

Roads and related symbols

	Free limited-access highway
	New — under construction
	Toll limited-access highway
	New — under construction
	Other multilane highway
	Principal highway
	Other through highway
	Other road (conditions vary — local inquiry suggested)
	Unpaved road (conditions vary — local inquiry suggested)
90 190 80/90	Interstate highway
ALT 17 183 18	U.S. highway
8 18 14/83	State or provincial highway
4 43 147	Secondary state, provincial, or county highway
N NM	County trunk highway
⊓ 15	Trans-Canada highway; Canadian autoroute
1	Mexican or Central American highway
9	Miles between arrows
	One mile or less not shown
2 10	Interchanges and interchange numbers (For most states, mileages between interchanges may be determined by subtracting one number from the other.)
	Tunnel
TOLL	Service area; toll booth or fee booth

Cities and towns

	Urbanized area — state or province map
	Urbanized area — city map
	Separate cities within metro area
⊛ ⊛	National capital; state capital
● ○ ○	City, town, or recognized place; county seat; neighborhood (size of type indicates relative population of cities and towns)

Parks, recreation areas, points of interest

	U.S. or Canadian National Park
	U.S. or Canadian National Monument; other National Park Service facility; State/Provincial Park or Recreation Area
▲ ♠	Park with camping facilities; without camping facilities
▲	Campsite
	National Forest or Grassland, city park
	Wildlife Refuge
	Indian reservation or rancheria
■	Point of interest, area of interest, historic site or monument
⌐	Golf course or country club

Other symbols

randmcnally.com **Express Access Code** FL	Express Access Code for use on randmcnally.com (These codes provide direct access to online travel information and road construction updates.)
Miami FL4	Express Access Code for city maps
?	Information Center, Tourist Information Center (T.I.C.)
⛱	Wayside, roadside park
⊞	Hospital, medical center
✈ ⊞	Airport; military installation
✈	Major airport outside map area
/	Dam
▲▲ ▲	Mountain peak; highest point in state
⟡	Port of entry
☼	Great River Road
	Swamp
	Desert
	Ferry
	Time zone boundary
	Continental divide

Comparative distances

1 mile = 1.609 kilometers 1 kilometer = .621 miles

U.S. population figures are from Devonshire Associates Ltd. and Scan/US, Inc. 2001. Canadian and Mexican population figures are from the latest available census.

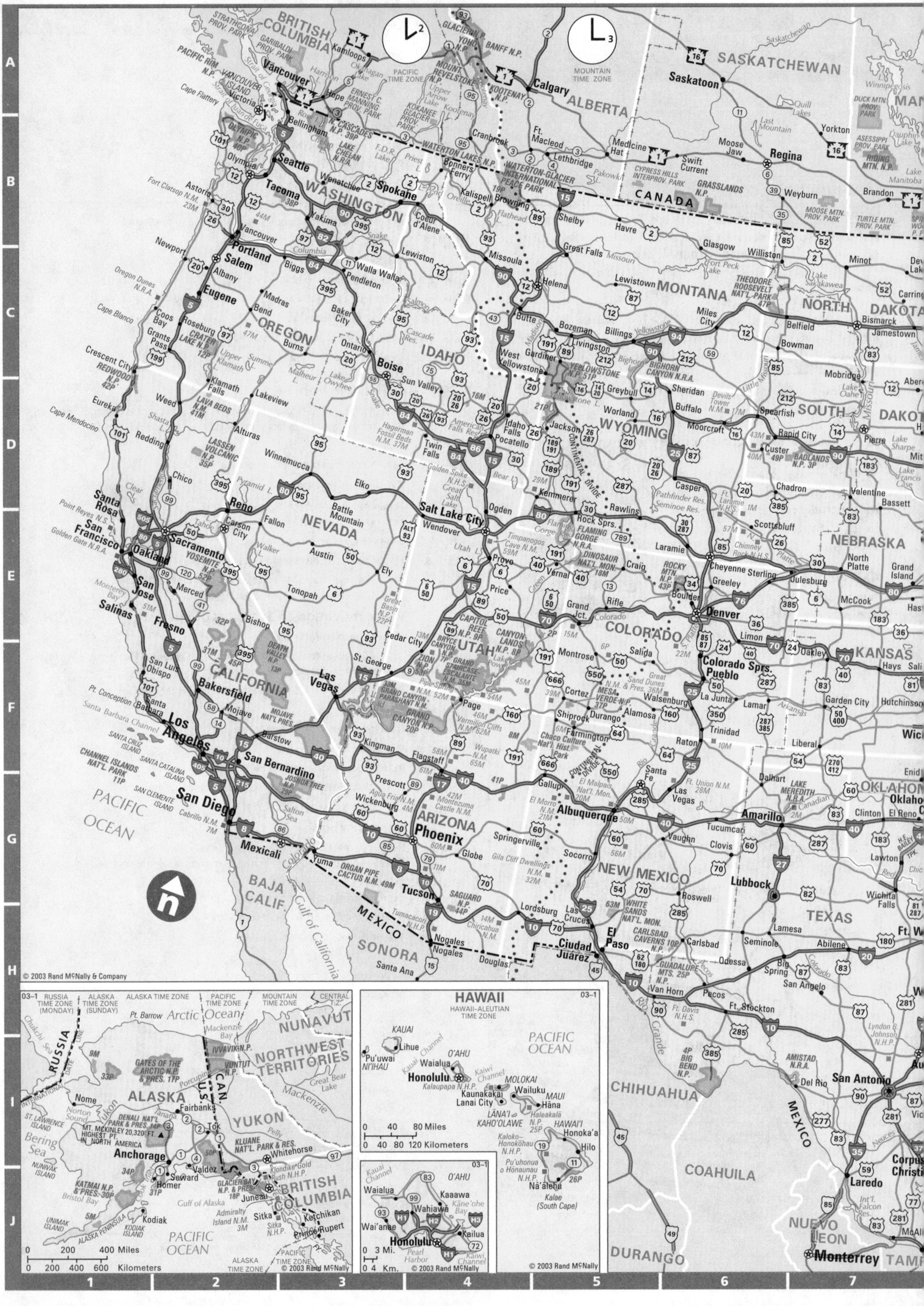

BRITISH COLUMBIA
ALBERTA
SASKATCHEWAN
CANADA
PACIFIC TIME ZONE
MOUNTAIN TIME ZONE
Kamloops
Vancouver
Victoria
Calgary
Saskatoon
Regina
Medicine Hat
Lethbridge
Swift Current
Moose Jaw
Yorkton
Brandon
Weyburn
WASHINGTON
Seattle
Tacoma
Olympia
Bellingham
Spokane
Wenatchee
Yakima
Walla Walla
Vancouver
Portland
Salem
Eugene
OREGON
Pendleton
Bend
Baker City
Burns
Medford
Klamath Falls
Coos Bay
Roseburg
Grants Pass
Astoria
Newport
IDAHO
Boise
Lewiston
Coeur d'Alene
Idaho Falls
Pocatello
Twin Falls
Sun Valley
MONTANA
Missoula
Helena
Great Falls
Butte
Bozeman
Billings
Kalispell
Shelby
Havre
Glasgow
Miles City
Lewistown
Livingston
WYOMING
Cheyenne
Casper
Sheridan
Laramie
Rock Sprs.
Jackson
Rawlins
Gillette
Worland
Cody
NORTH DAKOTA
Bismarck
Minot
Williston
Jamestown
Dickinson
SOUTH DAKOTA
Pierre
Rapid City
Spearfish
Mobridge
Aberdeen
NEBRASKA
North Platte
Grand Island
Scottsbluff
McCook
Valentine
Chadron
KANSAS
Hays
Garden City
Hutchinson
Liberal
Wichita
Dodge City
COLORADO
Denver
Boulder
Colorado Sprs.
Pueblo
Grand Jct.
Durango
Alamosa
Trinidad
La Junta
Lamar
Limon
Sterling
Julesburg
UTAH
Salt Lake City
Ogden
Provo
Moab
St. George
Cedar City
Vernal
Price
NEVADA
Reno
Carson City
Las Vegas
Elko
Ely
Winnemucca
Tonopah
Austin
Fallon
Wendover
CALIFORNIA
San Francisco
Oakland
Sacramento
San Jose
Fresno
Bakersfield
Los Angeles
San Diego
San Bernardino
Santa Barbara
San Luis Obispo
Salinas
Merced
Redding
Chico
Eureka
Crescent City
Santa Rosa
Barstow
Mojave
Bishop
ARIZONA
Phoenix
Tucson
Flagstaff
Yuma
Kingman
Prescott
Page
Globe
Nogales
Douglas
NEW MEXICO
Albuquerque
Santa Fe
Gallup
Farmington
Las Cruces
Roswell
Carlsbad
Clovis
Tucumcari
Socorro
Raton
Las Vegas
Lordsburg
TEXAS
El Paso
Amarillo
Lubbock
Odessa
Midland
Abilene
San Angelo
San Antonio
Laredo
Corpus Christi
Del Rio
Pecos
Van Horn
OKLAHOMA
MEXICO
BAJA CALIF.
SONORA
CHIHUAHUA
COAHUILA
NUEVO LEON
DURANGO
Mexicali
Ciudad Juárez
Monterrey
PACIFIC OCEAN
Gulf of California
Rio Grande
Colorado
Missouri
Snake
Columbia
Platte
Arkansas
YELLOWSTONE N.P.
GRAND CANYON N.P.
YOSEMITE N.P.
DEATH VALLEY N.P.
GLACIER N.P.
OLYMPIC N.P.
CRATER LAKE N.P.
ROCKY MTN. N.P.
BIG BEND N.P.
CONTINENTAL DIVIDE
© 2003 Rand McNally & Company
ALASKA
RUSSIA
YUKON
NORTHWEST TERRITORIES
NUNAVUT
BRITISH COLUMBIA
Anchorage
Fairbanks
Juneau
Nome
Kodiak
Whitehorse
Valdez
Seward
Homer
Sitka
Ketchikan
Prince Rupert
Arctic Ocean
Bering Sea
Gulf of Alaska
PACIFIC OCEAN
ALASKA TIME ZONE
DENALI NAT'L PARK & PRES.
MT. MCKINLEY 20,320 FT. HIGHEST PT. IN NORTH AMERICA
0 200 400 Miles
0 200 400 600 Kilometers
© 2003 Rand McNally
HAWAII
HAWAII–ALEUTIAN TIME ZONE
KAUAI
NI'IHAU
O'AHU
MOLOKAI
LANA'I
MAUI
KAHO'OLAWE
HAWAI'I
Honolulu
Lihue
Hilo
Kailua
Wahiawa
Waialua
Wai'anae
PACIFIC OCEAN
0 40 80 Miles
0 40 80 120 Kilometers
© 2003 Rand McNally

National Parks

1P	Acadia	C-14
2P	Arches	E-5
3P	Badlands	D-7
4P	Big Bend	I-6
5P	Biscayne	J-13
6P	Black Canyon	F-5
7P	Bryce Canyon	F-4
8P	Canyonlands	F-4
9P	Capitol Reef	E-4
10P	Carlsbad Caverns	H-6
11P	Channel Islands	F-1
12P	Crater Lake	C-2
13P	Death Valley	F-2
14P	Denali	I-2
15P	Dry Tortugas	J-12
16P	Everglades	J-12
17P	Gates of the Arctic	I-1
18P	Glacier Bay	J-2
19P	Glacier	B-4
20P	Grand Canyon	F-4
21P	Grand Teton	D-5
22P	Great Basin	E-3
23P	Great Smoky Mts.	G-11
24P	Guadalupe Mts.	H-5
25P	Haleakalā	I-4
26P	Hawai'i Volcanoes	J-5
27P	Hot Springs	G-8
28P	Isle Royale	C-9
29P	Joshua Tree	G-3
30P	Katmai	J-1
31P	Kenai Fjords	J-2
32P	Kings Canyon	E-2
33P	Kobuk Valley	I-1
34P	Lake Clark	J-1
35P	Lassen Volcanic	D-2
36P	Mammoth Cave	F-10
37P	Mesa Verde	F-5
38P	Mt. Rainier	B-3
39P	North Cascades	B-3
40P	Olympic	B-2
41P	Petrified Forest	G-4
42P	Redwood	C-1
43P	Rocky Mountain	E-6
44P	Saguaro	H-4
45P	Sequoia	F-2
46P	Shenandoah	E-12
47P	Theodore Roosevelt	C-6
48P	Voyageurs	C-8
49P	Wind Cave	D-6
50P	Wrangell-St. Elias	I-2
51P	Yellowstone	C-5
52P	Yosemite	E-2
53P	Zion	F-4

Nat'l Monuments and Memorials

1M	Agate Fossil Beds	E-6
2M	Alibates Flint Quarries	G-7
3M	Admiralty Island	J-3
4M	Agua Fria	G-4
5M	Aniakchak	J-1
6M	Aztec Ruins	F-5
7M	Cabrillo	G-2
8M	Canyon de Chelly	F-4
9M	Cape Krusenstern	I-1
10M	Capulin Volcano	F-6
11M	Casa Grande Ruins	G-4
12M	Castillo de San Marcos	H-12
13M	Cedar Breaks	F-4
14M	Chiricahua	H-4
15M	Colorado	E-5
16M	Craters of the Moon	D-4
17M	Devils Tower	D-6
18M	Dinosaur	E-5
19M	Effigy Mounds	D-9
20M	El Malpais	G-5
21M	El Morro	G-5
22M	Florissant Fossil Beds	F-6
23M	Fort Clatsop	B-2
24M	Fort Frederica	H-12
25M	Fort Mantanzas	H-12
26M	Fort Pulaski	H-12
27M	Fort Sumter	G-12
28M	Fort Union	G-6
29M	Fossil Butte	D-5
30M	George Washington Carver	F-8
31M	Giant Sequoia	F-2
32M	Gila Cliff Dwellings	G-5
33M	Grand Canyon-Parashant	F-3
34M	Grand Portage	C-9
35M	Grand Staircase-Escalante	F-4
36M	Great Sand Dunes	F-6
37M	Hagerman Fossil Beds	D-4
38M	Homestead	E-8
39M	Hovenweep	F-5
40M	Jewel Cave	D-6
41M	Lava Beds	D-2
42M	Montezuma Castle	G-4
43M	Mount Rushmore	D-6
44M	Mount St. Helens	B-2
45M	Natural Bridges	F-4
46M	Navajo	F-4
47M	Newberry Volcanic	C-2
48M	Ocmulgee	H-11
49M	Organ Pipe Cactus	G-3
50M	Petroglyph	G-5
51M	Pinnacles	E-1
52M	Pipe Spring	F-4
53M	Pipestone	D-8
54M	Rainbow Bridge	F-4
55M	Russell Cave	G-10
56M	Salinas Pueblo Missions	G-5
57M	Scotts Bluff	E-6
58M	Sunset Crater Volcano	F-4
59M	Timpanogos Cave	E-4
60M	Tonto	G-4
61M	Tuzigoot	G-4
62M	Vermillion Cliffs	F-4
63M	White Sands	H-5
64M	Wright Brothers	F-13
65M	Wupatki	F-4

Alabama

Population:
4,495,300 (1/1/01 estimate)

Land Area: 50,750 sq. mi.

Capital: Montgomery

Cities and Towns

Abbeville	H-6
Alabaster	D-3
Albertville	B-4
Alexander City	E-5
Aliceville	E-1
Andalusia	H-4
Anniston	C-5
Arab	B-4
Ashland	D-5
Ashville	C-4
Athens	A-3
Atmore	I-2
Attalla	C-4
Auburn	F-6
Bay Minette	I-2
Bessemer	D-3
Birmingham	D-3
Boaz	B-4
Brent	E-3
Brewton	H-3
Bridgeport	A-5
Brundidge	G-5
Butler	G-1
Calera	E-3
Camden	G-3
Carbon Hill	C-2
Carrollton	D-1
Centre	C-5
Centreville	E-3
Chatom	H-1
Childersburg	D-4
Citronelle	H-1
Clanton	E-4
Clayton	G-6
Columbiana	D-4
Cottondale	D-2
Cullman	C-3
Dadeville	E-5
Daleville	H-5
Decatur	B-3
Demopolis	F-2
Dothan	H-6
Double Springs	C-2
East Brewton	H-3
Elba	H-5
Enterprise	H-5
Eufaula	G-6
Eutaw	E-2
Evergreen	H-3
Fairfield	D-3
Fairhope	J-1
Fayette	C-2
Florala	I-4
Florence	A-2
Foley	J-2
Fort Payne	B-5
Gadsden	C-5
Geneva	I-5
Greensboro	E-2
Greenville	G-4
Grove Hill	G-2
Guin	C-2
Gulf Shores	J-2
Guntersville	B-4
Haleyville	B-2
Hamilton	C-1
Hanceville	C-3
Hartford	H-5
Hartselle	B-3
Hayneville	F-4
Hazel Green	A-4
Headland	H-6
Heflin	D-5
Homewood	D-3
Hoover	D-3
Huntsville	A-4
Jackson	H-2
Jacksonville	C-5
Jasper	C-3
Lafayette	E-6
Lanett	E-6
Leeds	D-4
Lincoln	D-4
Linden	F-2
Lineville	D-5
Livingston	F-1
Luverne	G-4
Marion	E-2
Mobile	I-1
Monroeville	H-2
Montevallo	E-3
Montgomery	F-4
Moulton	B-3
Mountain Brook	D-4
Muscle Shoals	A-2
Northport	D-2
Oneonta	C-4
Opelika	E-6
Opp	H-4
Orange Beach	J-2
Oxford	D-5
Ozark	H-5
Pell City	D-4
Phenix City	F-6
Piedmont	C-5
Point Clear	J-1
Prattville	F-4
Prichard	I-1
Rainbow City	C-5
Rainsville	B-5
Red Bay	B-1
Reform	D-1
Roanoke	D-6
Robertsdale	J-2
Russellville	B-2
Samson	H-5
Saraland	I-1
Scottsboro	B-5
Selma	F-3
Sheffield	A-2
Spanish Fort	I-1
Stevenson	A-5
Sumiton	C-3
Sylacauga	E-4
Talladega	D-4
Tallassee	F-5
Tarrant	D-3
Theodore	J-1
Thomasville	G-2
Troy	G-5
Tuscaloosa	D-2
Tuscumbia	A-2
Tuskegee	F-5
Union Springs	F-5
Valley	E-6
Vernon	C-1
Warrior	C-3
Wedowee	D-5
Wetumpka	F-4
Winfield	C-2
York	F-1

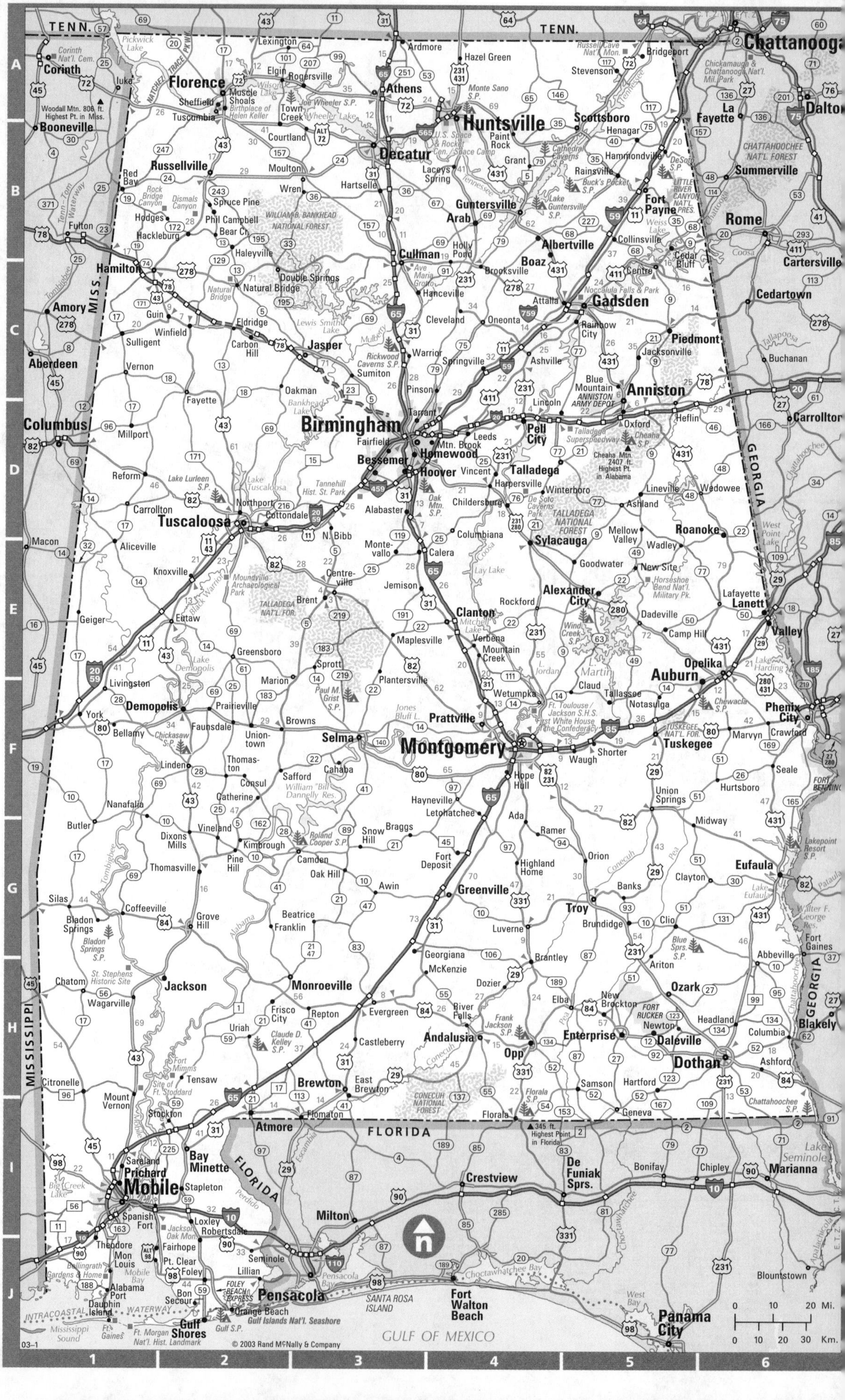

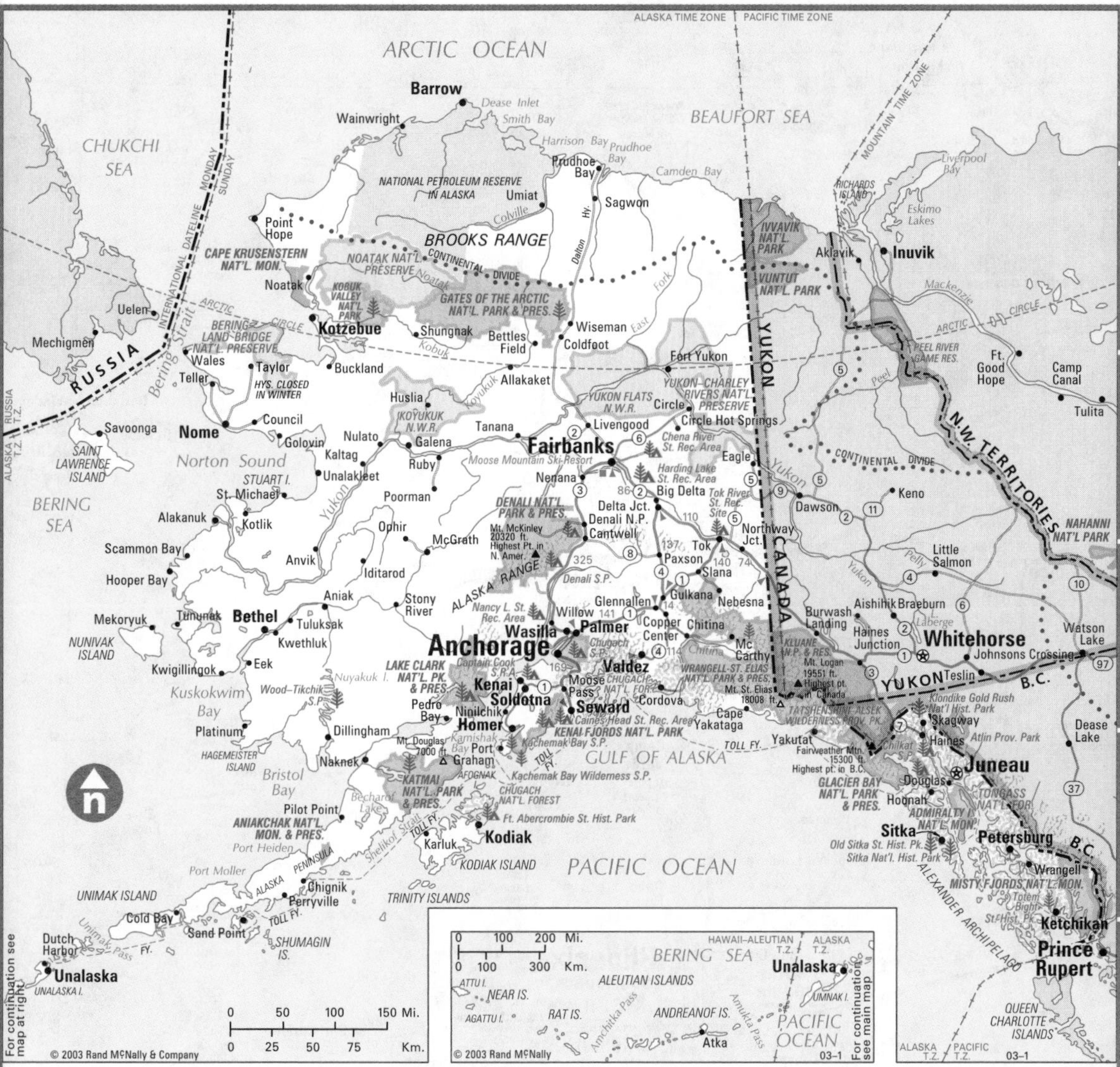

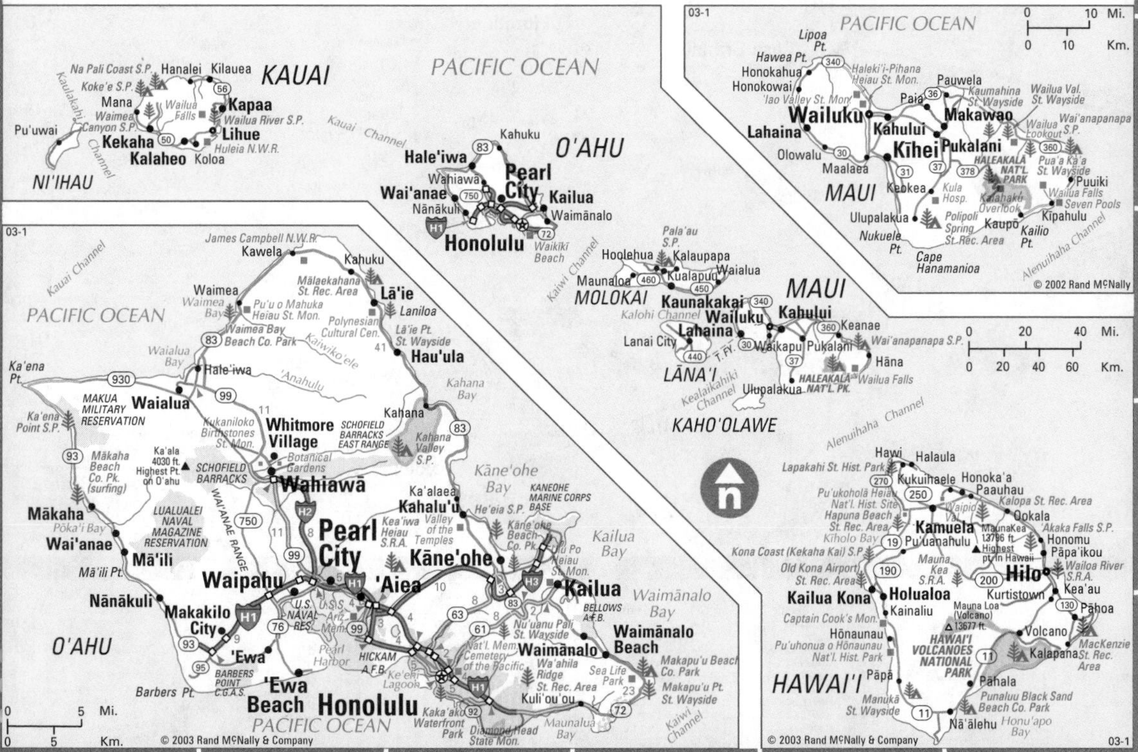

Alaska

Population: 636,900 (1/1/01 estimate)
Land Area: 570,374 sq. mi.
Capital: Juneau

Cities and Towns

Alakanuk	C-2
Allakaket	C-3
Anchorage	D-4
Barrow	A-3
Bethel	D-2
Big Delta	C-4
Cantwell	D-4
Chignik	E-2
Circle	C-4
Circle Hot Springs	C-4
Cold Bay	F-1
Cordova	D-4
Delta Junction	C-4
Dillingham	E-2
Douglas	E-6
Eagle	C-5
Eek	D-2
Fairbanks	C-4
Fort Yukon	C-4
Glennallen	D-4
Haines	E-5
Homer	D-3
Hoonah	E-5
Hooper Bay	D-1
Iditarod	D-2
Juneau	E-6
Kaltag	C-2
Karluk	E-3
Kenai	D-3
Ketchikan	E-6
Kodiak	E-3
Kotzebue	B-2
Kwethluk	D-2
Kwigillingok	D-2
Livengood	C-4
McGrath	D-3
Nenana	C-4
Noatak	B-2
Nome	C-2
Palmer	D-4
Perryville	E-2
Petersburg	E-6
Port Graham	E-3
Point Hope	B-2
Prudhoe Bay	B-4
Ruby	C-3
Saint Michael	C-2
Sand Point	F-2
Savoonga	C-1
Scammon Bay	D-1
Seward	D-4
Shungnak	B-3
Sitka	E-6
Skagway	D-5
Soldotna	D-3
Tanana	C-3
Taylor	C-2
Thorne Bay	I-12
Tok	D-4
Umiat	B-3
Unalaska	F-1
Valdez	D-4
Wainwright	A-3
Wasilla	D-4
Willow	D-3
Wrangell	E-6
Yakutat	E-5

Hawaii

Population: 1,224,500 (1/1/01 estimate)
Land Area: 6,423 sq. mi.
Capital: Honolulu

Cities and Towns

'Aiea	J-2
'Ewa	J-2
'Ewa Beach	J-2
Halaula	I-5
Hale'iwa	H-2
Hāna	H-5
Hau'ula	H-3
Hilo	I-6
Holualoa	J-5
Hōnaunau	J-5
Honoka'a	I-6
Honolulu	J-3
Honomu	I-6
Hoolehua	H-4
Kahalu'u	I-3
Kahana	I-3
Kahuku	H-2
Kahului	G-5
Kailua	I-3
Kailua Kona	I-5
Kailiu	J-5
Kalaheo	G-1
Kalaupapa	H-4
Kamuela	I-5
Kāne'ohe	I-3
Kapaa	G-2
Kaunakakai	H-4
Kea'au	I-6
Kekaha	G-1
Kīhei	G-5
Kilauea	G-2
Kīpahulu	G-6
Koloa	G-1
Kukuihaele	I-6
Kurtistown	J-6
Lahaina	G-5
Lā'ie	H-2
Lanai City	H-4
Lihue	G-2
Maalaea	G-5
Mā'ili	I-1
Makakilo City	J-2
Mākaha	I-1
Makawao	G-6
Maunaloa	H-4
Nā'ālehu	J-6
Nānākuli	J-1
Ookala	I-6
Pāhala	J-6
Pāhoa	J-6
Pāpa'ikou	I-6
Pauwela	G-6
Pearl City	I-2
Pukalani	G-5
Volcano	J-6
Wahiawā	I-2
Waialua	H-1
Wai'anae	I-1
Wailuku	G-5
Waimānalo	J-4
Waimānalo Beach	J-4
Waimea	H-2
Waipahu	J-2
Whitmore Village	I-2

randmcnally.com
Express Access Code: AZ

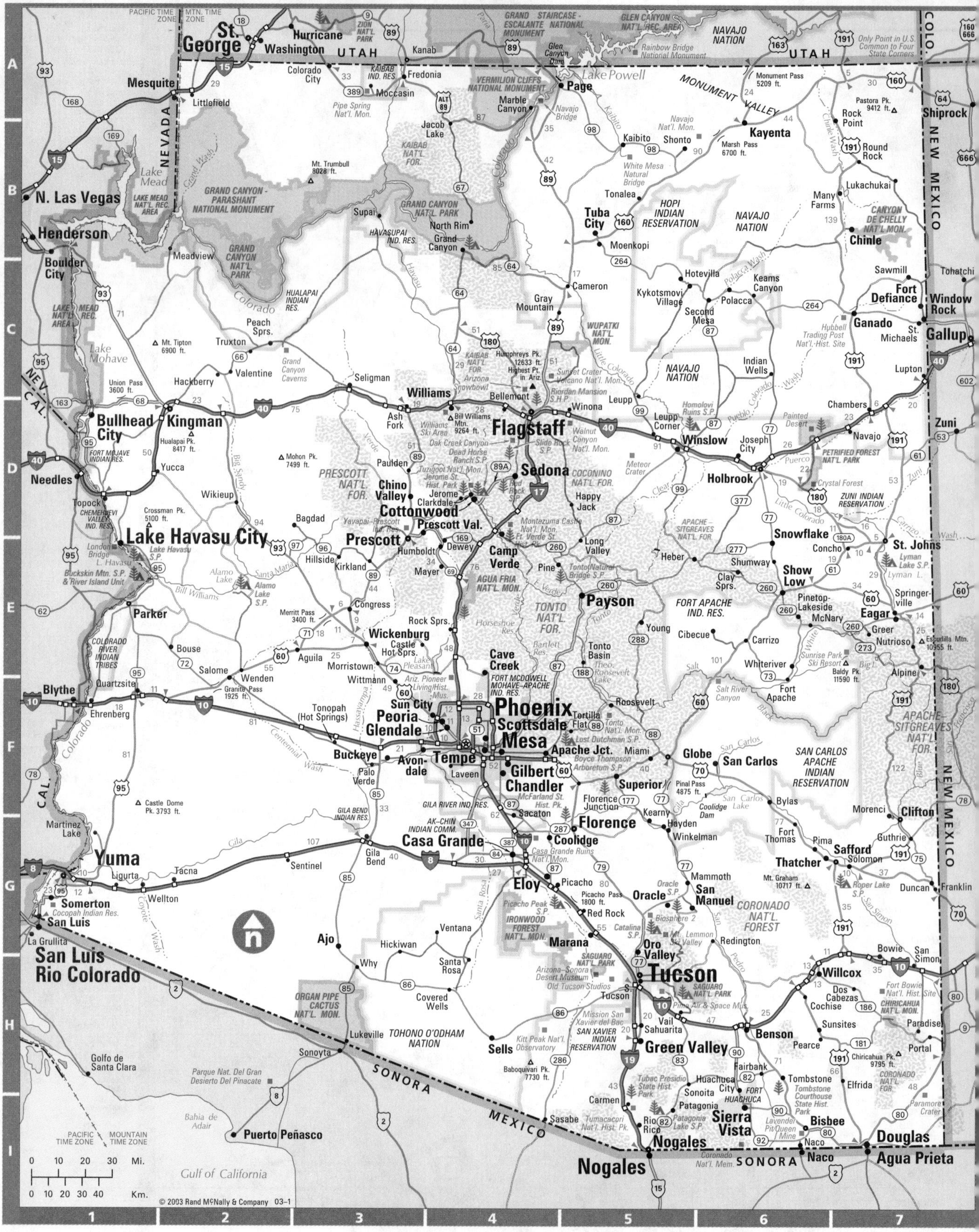

Arizona

Population: 5,312,900 (1/1/01 estimate)
Land Area: 113,642 sq. mi.
Capital: Phoenix

Cities and Towns

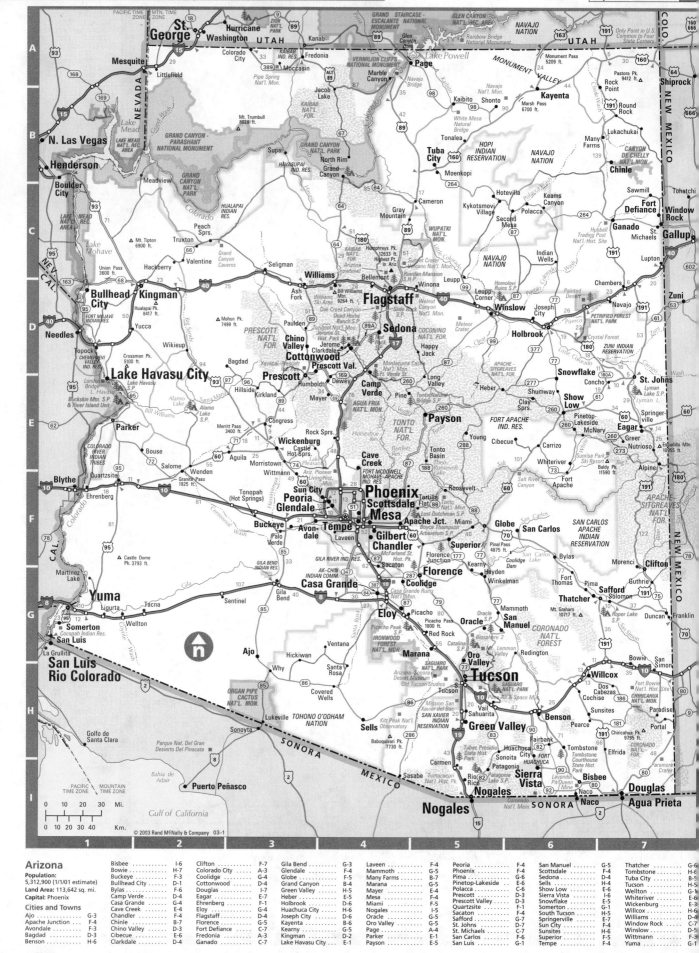

Arkansas

Population: 2,712,300 (1/1/01 estimate)
Land Area: 52,075 sq. mi.
Capital: Little Rock

Cities and Towns

Arkadelphia	E-3
Arkansas City	F-6
Ash Flat	A-6
Ashdown	F-2
Augusta	C-6
Bald Knob	C-6
Batesville	B-6
Beebe	C-5
Bella Vista	A-1
Benton	D-4
Bentonville	A-2
Berryville	A-3
Blytheville	B-8
Booneville	C-2
Brinkley	D-6
Bull Shoals	A-4
Cabot	D-5
Camden	F-4
Charleston	C-2
Clarendon	D-6
Clarksville	C-3
Clinton	B-4
Conway	C-4
Corning	A-7
Crossett	G-5
Danville	C-3
Dardanelle	C-3
De Queen	E-1
De Valls Bluff	D-6
De Witt	E-6
Des Arc	D-6
Dumas	F-6
El Dorado	G-4
Eureka Springs	A-2
Evening Shade	A-6
Fayetteville	A-2
Fordyce	F-4
Forrest City	D-7
Fort Smith	C-1
Greenwood	C-1
Hamburg	G-5
Hampton	F-4
Harrisburg	B-7
Harrison	A-3
Heber Springs	C-5
Helena	D-7
Hope	F-2
Hot Springs	D-3
Huntsville	A-2
Jacksonville	D-5
Jasper	B-3
Jonesboro	B-7
Lake City	B-7
Lake Village	G-6
Lewisville	G-2
Little Rock	D-4
Lonoke	D-5
Magnolia	G-3
Malvern	E-4
Marianna	D-7
Marion	C-8
Marshall	B-4
McGehee	F-6
Melbourne	A-5
Mena	D-1
Monticello	F-5
Morrilton	C-4
Mount Ida	D-2
Mountain Home	A-4
Mountain View	B-5
Murfreesboro	E-2
Nashville	F-2
Newport	B-6
North Little Rock	D-5
Osceola	B-8
Ozark	C-2
Paragould	A-7
Paris	C-2
Perryville	D-4
Piggott	A-8
Pine Bluff	E-5
Pocahontas	A-7
Prescott	F-3
Rison	F-5
Rogers	A-2
Russellville	C-3
Salem	A-5
Searcy	C-5
Sheridan	E-4
Siloam Springs	A-1
Springdale	A-2
Star City	F-5
Stuttgart	D-6
Texarkana	G-2
Trumann	B-7
Van Buren	C-1
Viola	A-5
Waldron	D-2
Walnut Ridge	A-7
Warren	F-5
West Helena	D-7
West Memphis	C-8
Wynne	C-7
Yellville	A-4

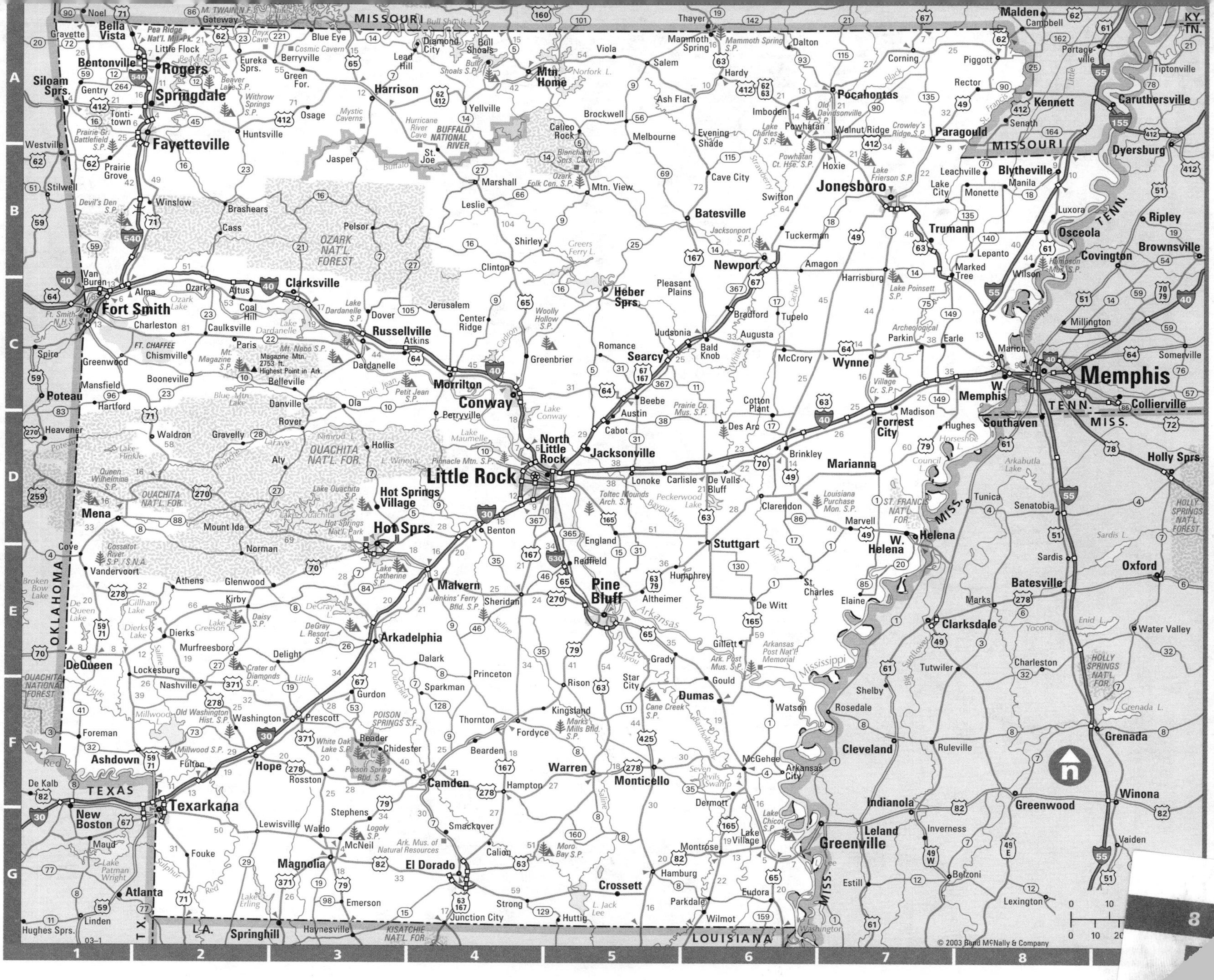

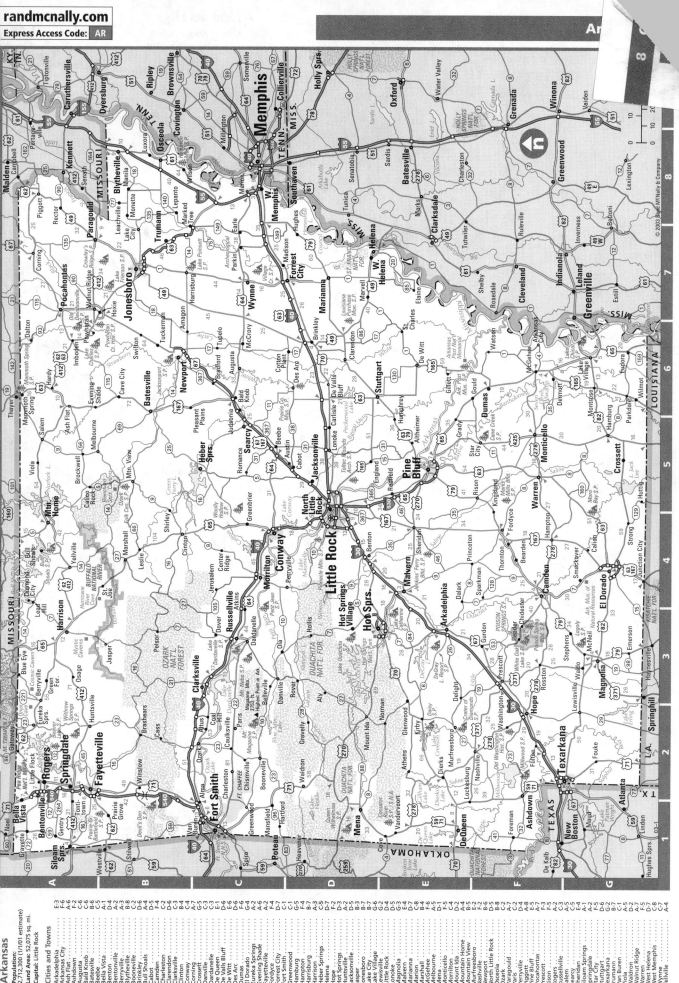

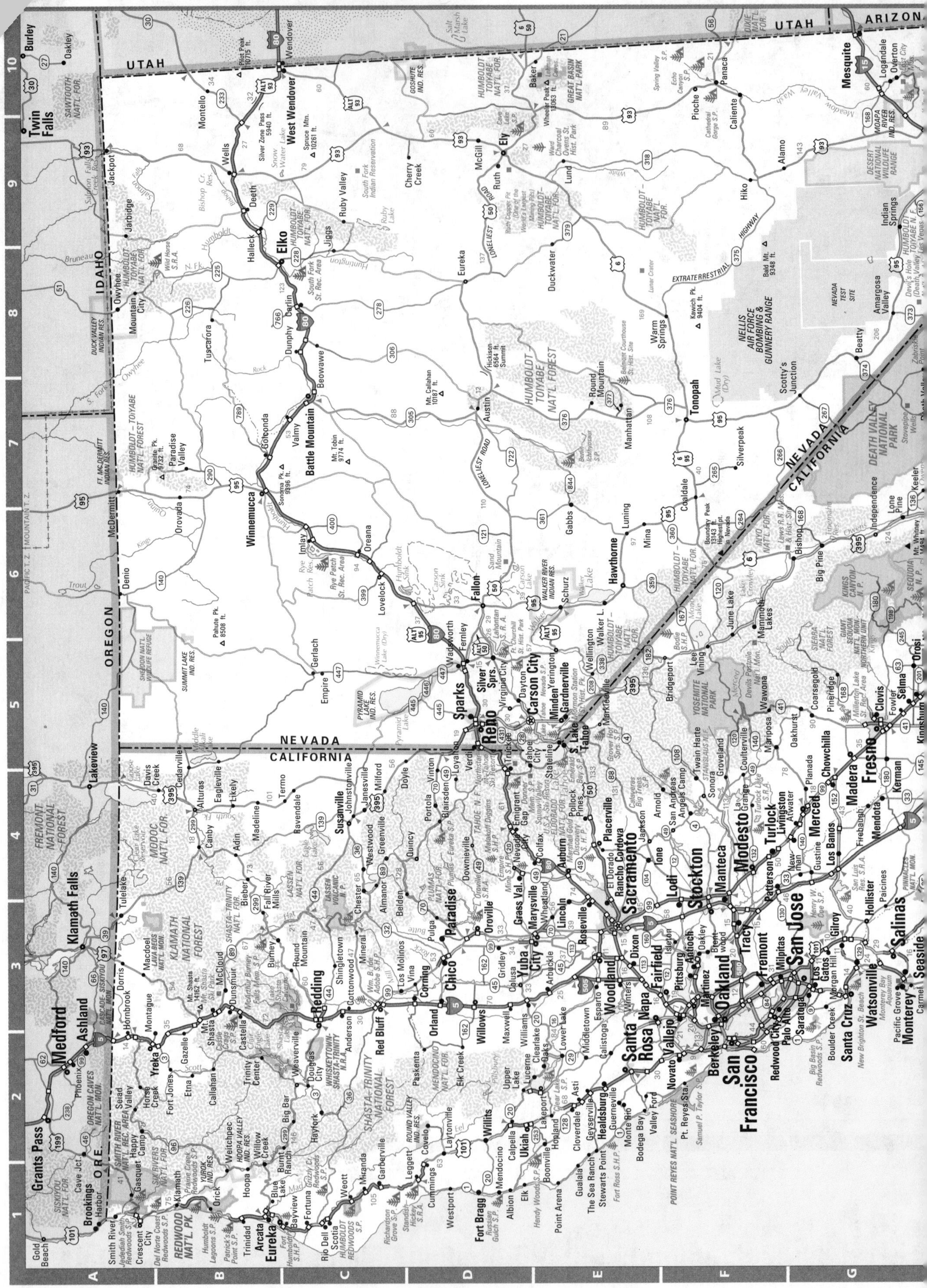
OREGON
IDAHO
UTAH
ARIZONA
NEVADA
CALIFORNIA
Medford
Ashland
Grants Pass
Klamath Falls
Lakeview
Twin Falls
Burley
Jackpot
Wendover
West Wendover
Wells
Elko
Carlin
Battle Mountain
Winnemucca
Lovelock
Fallon
Reno
Sparks
Carson City
Ely
Eureka
Austin
Tonopah
Hawthorne
Mesquite
Redding
Red Bluff
Chico
Eureka
Arcata
Crescent City
Sacramento
Stockton
Modesto
Merced
Fresno
Madera
San Francisco
Oakland
San Jose
Santa Rosa
Salinas
Monterey
Santa Cruz
LASSEN VOLCANIC N.P.
YOSEMITE NATIONAL PARK
DEATH VALLEY NATIONAL PARK
NELLIS AIR FORCE BOMBING & GUNNERY RANGE
NEVADA TEST SITE
GREAT BASIN NAT'L PARK
REDWOOD NAT'L PK.
POINT REYES NAT'L SEASHORE
SHASTA-TRINITY NATIONAL FOREST
HUMBOLDT-TOIYABE NAT'L FOREST
LONELIEST ROAD
EXTRATERRESTRIAL HIGHWAY

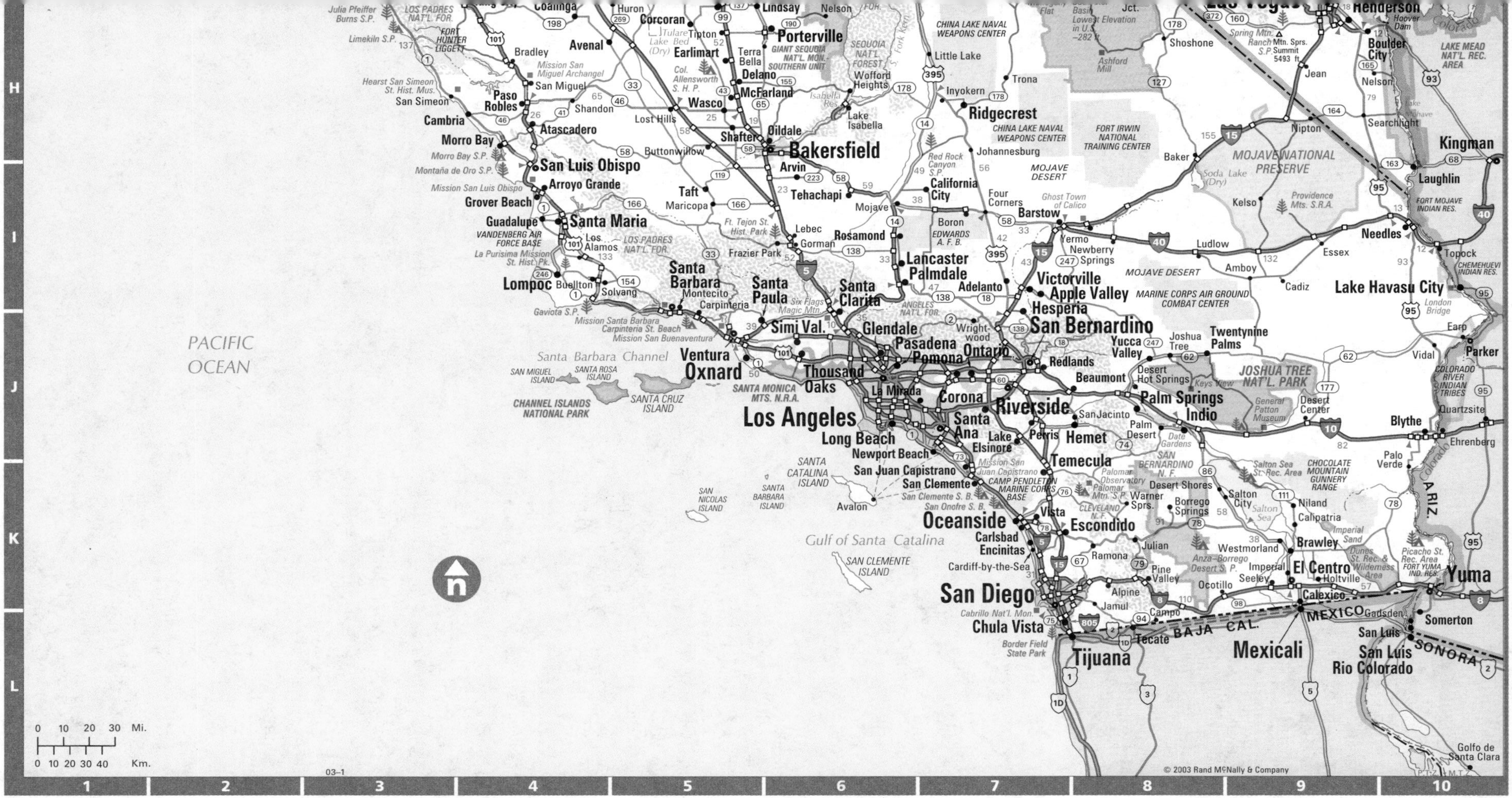

California

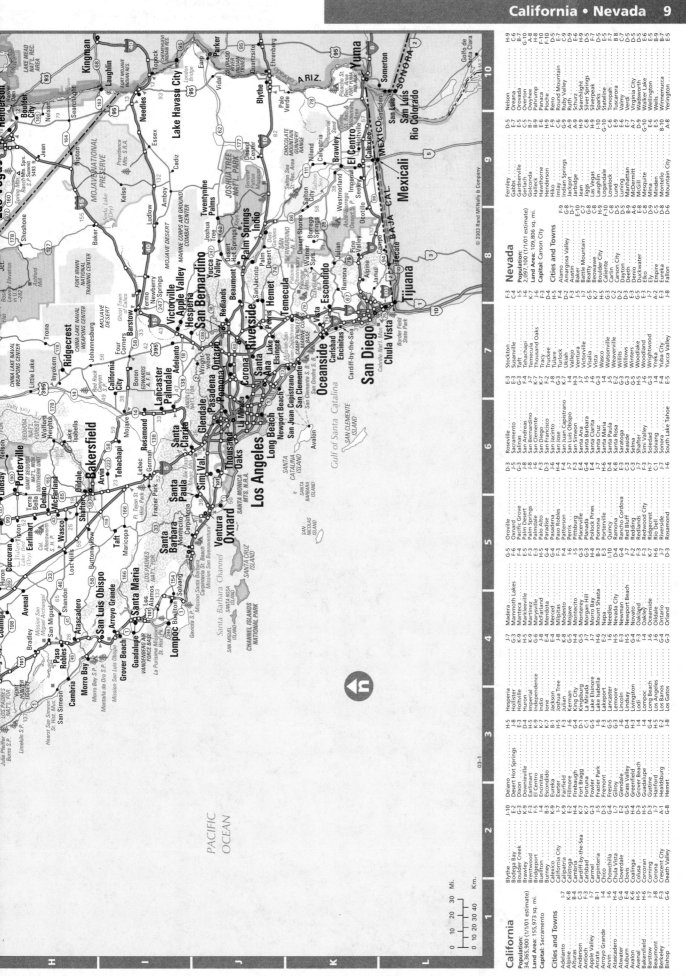

Population: 34,365,900 (1/1/01 estimate)

Land Area: 155,973 sq. mi.

Capital: Sacramento

Cities and Towns

Adelanto I-7
Alpine K-8
Alturas B-4
Anderson C-3
Antioch F-3
Apple Valley I-7
Arcata B-1
Arroyo Grande I-4
Arvin I-6
Atascadero H-4
Atwater G-4
Auburn E-4
Avalon K-6
Avenal H-5
Bakersfield H-6
Barstow I-7
Beaumont J-8
Berkeley F-3
Bishop G-6
Blythe J-10
Bodega Bay E-2
Boulder Creek G-3
Brawley K-9
Brentwood F-3
Bridgeport F-5
Buellton I-4
Burney B-3
Calexico K-9
California City I-7
Calipatria K-9
Calistoga E-2
Cambria H-4
Cardiff-by-the-Sea K-7
Carlsbad K-7
Carmel G-3
Carpinteria J-5
Chico D-3
Chowchilla G-4
Chula Vista L-7
Cloverdale E-2
Clovis G-5
Coalinga H-4
Colusa D-3
Corcoran H-5
Corning D-3
Corona J-7
Crescent City A-1
Death Valley G-8
Delano H-5
Desert Hot Springs J-8
Dixon E-3
Downieville D-4
Earlimart H-5
El Centro K-9
Encinitas K-7
Escondido K-7
Eureka B-1
Exeter H-5
Fairfield F-3
Fillmore J-6
Firebaugh G-4
Fort Bragg D-1
Fortuna C-1
Fowler G-5
Frazier Park I-6
Fremont F-3
Fresno G-5
Gilroy G-3
Glendale J-6
Grass Valley D-4
Greenfield H-3
Grover Beach I-4
Guadalupe I-4
Gustine G-4
Hanford H-5
Healdsburg E-2
Hemet J-8
Hesperia J-7
Hollister G-3
Holtville K-9
Huron H-5
Imperial K-9
Independence G-6
Indio J-8
Ione E-4
Jackson E-4
Joshua Tree J-8
Julian K-8
Kerman G-5
King City H-4
Kingsburg G-5
La Mirada J-7
Lake Elsinore J-7
Lake Isabella H-6
Lakeport E-2
Lancaster I-6
Lemoore H-5
Lincoln E-3
Lindsay H-5
Livingston G-4
Lodi F-3
Lompoc I-4
Long Beach J-6
Los Angeles J-6
Los Banos G-4
Los Gatos G-3
Madera G-5
Mammoth Lakes F-6
Manteca F-4
Markleeville E-5
Martinez F-3
Marysville E-3
McFarland H-5
Mendota G-4
Merced G-4
Milpitas F-3
Modesto F-4
Mojave I-6
Montecito I-5
Monterey G-3
Morgan Hill G-3
Morro Bay H-4
Mount Shasta B-3
Napa E-3
Needles I-10
Nevada City D-4
Newman G-4
Newport Beach J-7
Novato F-2
Oakland F-3
Oakley F-3
Oceanside K-7
Oildale H-6
Ontario J-7
Orland D-3
Oroville D-3
Oxnard J-5
Pacific Grove G-3
Palm Desert J-8
Palm Springs J-8
Palmdale I-6
Palo Alto F-3
Paradise D-3
Pasadena J-6
Paso Robles H-4
Patterson F-4
Perris J-7
Pittsburg F-3
Placerville E-4
Planada G-4
Pollock Pines E-4
Pomona J-7
Porterville H-6
Quincy D-4
Ramona K-8
Rancho Cordova E-3
Red Bluff C-3
Redding C-3
Redlands J-7
Redwood City F-3
Ridgecrest H-7
Rio Dell C-1
Riverside J-7
Rosamond I-6
Roseville E-3
Sacramento E-3
Salinas G-3
San Andreas F-4
San Bernardino J-7
San Clemente K-7
San Diego K-7
San Francisco F-2
San Jacinto J-8
San Jose G-3
San Juan Capistrano K-7
San Luis Obispo I-4
San Simeon H-3
Santa Ana J-7
Santa Barbara I-5
Santa Clarita J-6
Santa Cruz G-3
Santa Maria I-4
Santa Paula J-5
Santa Rosa E-2
Saratoga G-3
Seaside G-3
Selma G-5
Shafter H-5
Simi Valley J-6
Soledad G-3
Solvang I-4
Sonora F-4
South Lake Tahoe E-5
Stockton F-3
Susanville C-4
Taft I-5
Tehachapi I-6
Temecula K-7
Thousand Oaks J-6
Tracy F-3
Truckee D-4
Tulare H-5
Turlock F-4
Ukiah D-2
Vallejo F-3
Ventura J-5
Victorville I-7
Visalia G-5
Vista K-7
Wasco H-5
Watsonville G-3
Weaverville C-2
Willits D-2
Willows D-3
Winters E-3
Woodlake G-5
Woodland E-3
Wrightwood J-7
Yreka A-2
Yuba City E-3
Yucca Valley J-8

Nevada

Population: 2,097,100 (1/1/01 estimate)

Land Area: 109,806 sq. mi.

Capital: Carson City

Cities and Towns

Alamo F-9
Amargosa Valley G-8
Austin D-7
Baker E-10
Battle Mountain C-7
Beatty G-8
Beowawe C-8
Boulder City H-9
Caliente F-10
Carlin C-8
Carson City D-5
Dayton D-5
Deeth B-9
Denio A-6
Duckwater E-8
Elko C-8
Ely D-9
Empire C-5
Eureka D-8
Fallon D-6
Fernley D-5
Gabbs E-7
Gardnerville E-5
Gerlach C-5
Golconda B-7
Halleck B-9
Hawthorne E-6
Henderson H-9
Hiko F-9
Imlay C-6
Indian Springs G-9
Jackpot A-9
Jarbidge A-9
Jean H-9
Jiggs C-8
Las Vegas H-9
Laughlin I-10
Logandale G-10
Lovelock C-6
Lund E-9
Luning E-6
Manhattan E-7
McDermitt A-7
McGill D-9
Mesquite G-10
Mina E-6
Minden E-5
Montello B-10
Mountain City A-8
Nelson H-9
Oreana C-6
Orovada B-7
Overton G-10
Owyhee A-8
Pahrump H-8
Panaca F-10
Pioche F-10
Reno D-5
Round Mountain E-7
Ruby Valley C-9
Ruth D-9
Schurz E-6
Searchlight H-9
Silver Springs D-5
Silverpeak F-7
Sparks D-5
Stateline E-5
Tonopah F-7
Tuscarora .... B 8
Valmy C-7
Verdi D-5
Virginia City D-5
Wadsworth D-5
Walker Lake E-6
Wellington E-5
Wells B-9
Winnemucca B-7
Yerington E-5

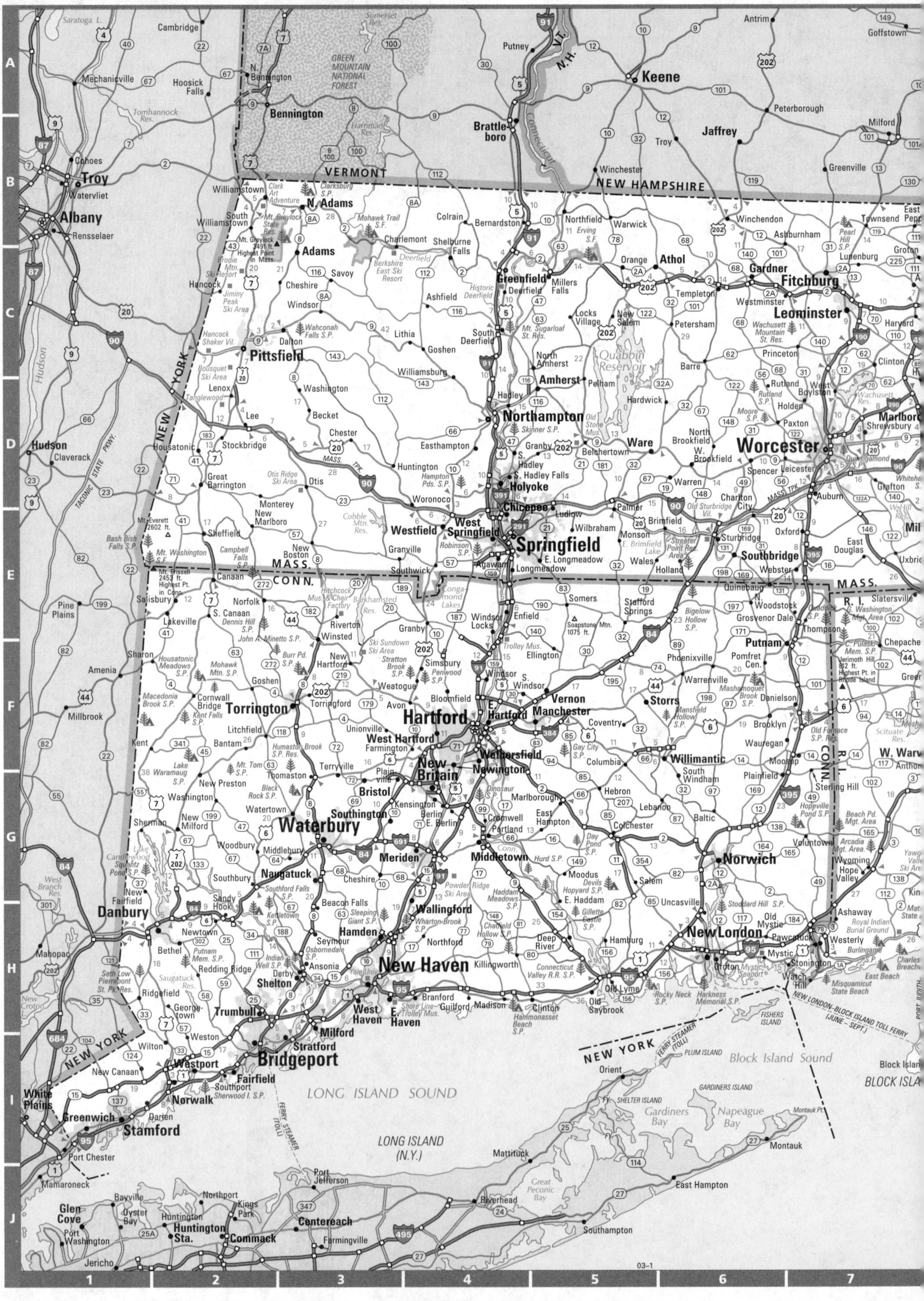
VERMONT
NEW HAMPSHIRE
NEW YORK
MASS.
CONN.
R.I.
GREEN MOUNTAIN NATIONAL FOREST
Quabbin Reservoir
LONG ISLAND SOUND
LONG ISLAND (N.Y.)
Block Island Sound
Gardiners Bay
Napeague Bay
Great Peconic Bay
Albany
Troy
Pittsfield
Springfield
Worcester
Fitchburg
Leominster
Keene
Hartford
New Britain
Waterbury
New Haven
Bridgeport
Stamford
Danbury
Norwich
New London
Torrington
Northampton
Holyoke
Chicopee
Bristol
Meriden
Middletown
Manchester
Norwalk
Greenwich
White Plains
NEW LONDON–BLOCK ISLAND TOLL FERRY (JUNE – SEPT.)
FERRY STEAMER (TOLL)
03-1

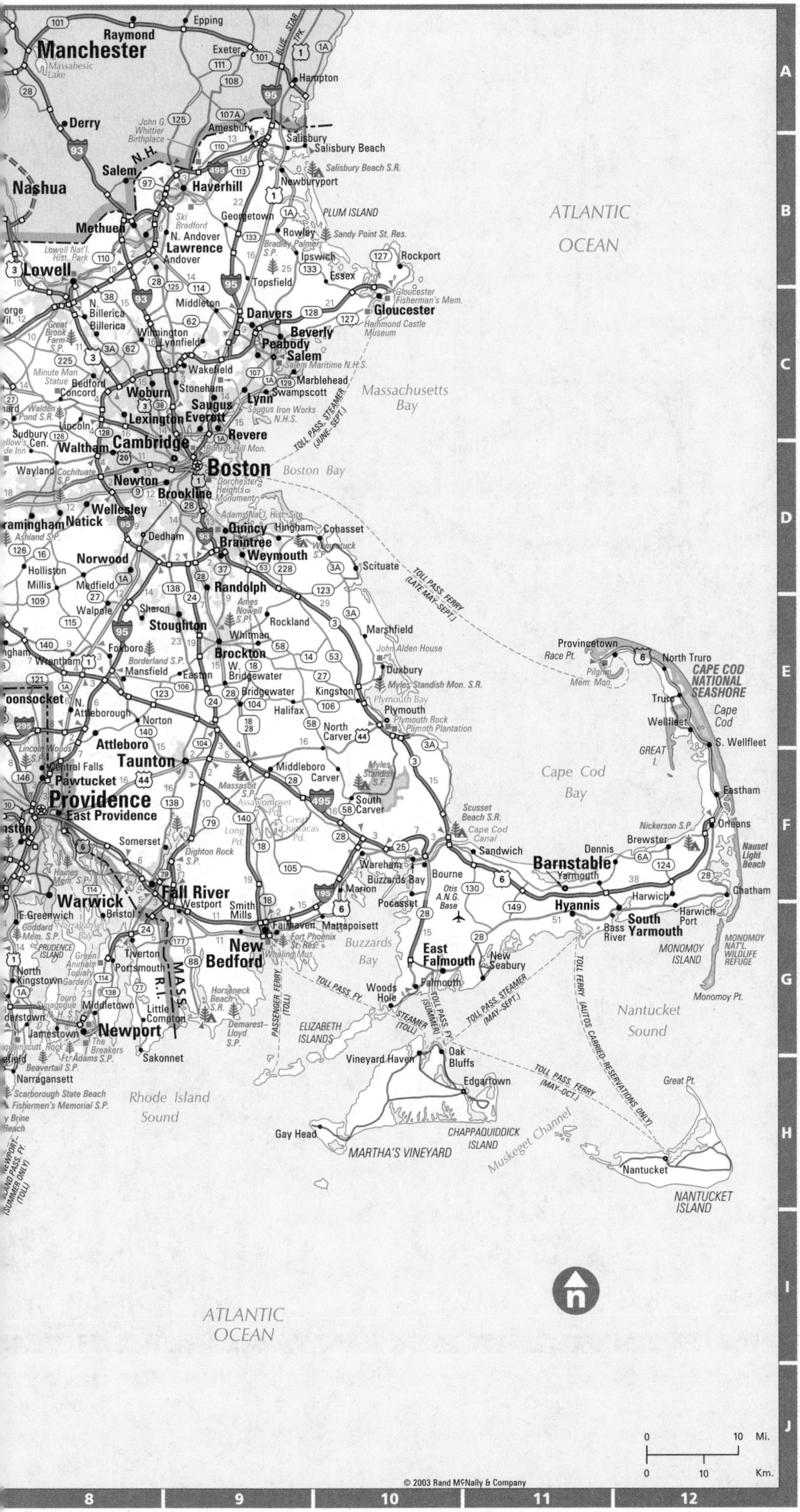

Connecticut

Population: 3,419,700 (1/1/01 estimate)

Land Area: 4,845 sq. mi.

Capital: Hartford

Cities and Towns

Ansonia	H-3
Avon	F-4
Beacon Falls	H-3
Bethel	H-2
Bloomfield	F-4
Bridgeport	I-2
Bristol	G-3
Brooklyn	F-6
Canaan	E-2
Clinton	H-5
Colchester	G-5
Cromwell	G-4
Danbury	H-2
Danielson	F-7
Deep River	H-5
Derby	H-3
East Hartford	F-4
East Haven	H-3
Enfield	E-4
Fairfield	I-2
Farmington	F-4
Georgetown	H-2
Goshen	F-2
Granby	E-4
Greenwich	I-1
Groton	H-6
Guilford	H-4
Hamden	H-3
Hartford	F-4
Litchfield	F-2
Manchester	F-5
Marlborough	G-5
Meriden	G-4
Middlebury	G-3
Middletown	G-4
Milford	H-3
Moodus	G-5
Moosup	F-7
Mystic	H-6
Naugatuck	G-3
New Britain	G-4
New Canaan	I-1
New Fairfield	H3
New Hartford	F-3
New Haven	H-3
New London	H-6
New Milford	G-2
New Preston	G-2
Newington	F-4
Northford	H-4
Norwalk	I-2
Norwich	G-6
Old Lyme	H-5
Old Saybrook	H-5
Pawcatuck	H-7
Plainfield	G-6
Plainville	G-3
Portland	G-4
Putnam	F-7
Ridgefield	H-1
Salisbury	E-2
Sandy Hook	H-2
Seymour	H-3
Shelton	H-3
Simsbury	F-4
Somers	E-5
South Windsor	F-4
Southbury	G-2
Southington	G-3
Stafford Springs	E-5
Stamford	I-1
Storrs	F-5
Stratford	I-3
Terryville	G-3
Thomaston	G-3
Torrington	F-3
Trumbull	H-2
Unionville	F-3
Vernon	F-5
Wallingford	G-4
Waterbury	G-3
Watertown	G-3
West Hartford	F-4
West Haven	H-3
Westport	I-2
Wethersfield	F-4
Willimantic	F-6
Wilton	I-2
Windsor	F-4
Windsor Locks	E-4
Winsted	E-3

Massachusetts

Population: 6,390,700 (1/1/01 estimate)

Land Area: 7,838 sq. mi.

Capital: Boston

Cities and Towns

Adams	C-3
Agawam	E-4
Amesbury	B-9
Amherst	D-5
Andover	B-8
Athol	C-5
Attleboro	E-8
Auburn	D-7
Ayer	C-7
Barnstable	F-11
Bedford	C-8
Beverly	C-9
Billerica	C-8
Boston	D-9
Braintree	D-9
Brewster	F-12
Bridgewater	E-9
Brockton	E-9
Brookline	D-9
Buzzards Bay	F-10
Cambridge	D-9
Chatham	F-12
Chicopee	E-4
Clinton	C-7
Cohasset	D-10
Concord	C-8
Dalton	C-3
Danvers	C-9
Dedham	D-8
Deerfield	C-4
Duxbury	E-10
East Falmouth	G-10
East Longmeadow	E-5
East Pepperell	B-7
Eastham	F-12
Easthampton	D-4
Edgartown	H-11
Everett	C-9
Fairhaven	G-9
Fall River	F-8
Falmouth	G-10
Fitchburg	C-7
Foxboro	E-8
Framingham	D-8
Gardner	C-6
Gloucester	C-10
Grafton	D-7
Great Barrington	D-2
Greenfield	C-4
Harwich Port	G-12
Haverhill	B-9
Hingham	D-9
Holliston	D-8
Holyoke	D-4
Housatonic	D-2
Hudson	D-7
Hyannis	G-11
Ipswich	B-9
Lawrence	B-8
Lenox	D-2
Leominster	C-7
Lexington	C-8
Longmeadow	E-4
Lowell	B-8
Ludlow	D-5
Lynn	C-9
Lynnfield	C-9
Mansfield	E-8
Marblehead	C-9
Marion	F-10
Marlborough	D-7
Marshfield	E-10
Mattapoisett	G-10
Maynard	C-8
Methuen	B-8
Middleboro	F-9
Middleton	C-9
Milford	E-8
Nantucket	H-12
Natick	D-8
New Bedford	G-9
Newburyport	B-9
Newton	D-8
North Adams	B-3
North Andover	B-8
North Attleborough	E-8
Northampton	D-4
Northfield	B-5
Norwood	D-8
Oak Bluffs	G-10
Orange	C-5
Oxford	E-7
Palmer	E-5
Peabody	C-9
Petersham	C-6
Pittsfield	C-2
Plymouth	E-10
Princeton	C-7
Provincetown	E-12
Quincy	D-9
Randolph	D-9
Revere	C-9
Rockland	E-9
Rockport	B-10
Rutland	D-6
Salem	C-9
Salisbury	B-9
Sandwich	F-11
Saugus	C-9
Sharon	E-8
Shelburne Falls	C-4
Shrewsbury	D-7
Smith Mills	G-9
Somerset	F-9
South Hadley	D-4
South Yarmouth	G-12
Southbridge	E-6
Spencer	D-6
Springfield	E-4
Stoneham	C-9
Stoughton	E-9
Sturbridge	E-6
Sudbury Center	D-8
Swampscott	C-9
Taunton	F-9
Townsend	B-7
Truro	E-12
Uxbridge	E-7
Vineyard Haven	G-10
Wakefield	C-9
Walpole	E-8
Waltham	D-8
Ware	D-5
Wareham	F-10
Webster	E-7
Wellesley	D-8
Wellfleet	E-12
West Boylston	D-7
West Bridgewater	E-9
West Brookfield	D-6
West Springfield	E-4
Westfield	E-4
Westminster	C-6
Weymouth	D-9
Whitman	E-9
Wilmington	C-8
Winchendon	B-6
Woburn	C-8
Woods Hole	G-10
Worcester	D-7
Wrentham	E-8

Rhode Island

Population: 1,053,900 (1/1/01 estimate)

Land Area: 1,045 sq. mi.

Capital: Providence

Cities and Towns

Anthony	F-7
Bristol	G-8
Central Falls	F-8
Cranston	F-8
East Greenwich	G-8
East Providence	F-8
Jamestown	G-8
Kingston	G-8
Middletown	G-8
Narragansett	H-8
Newport	G-8
North Kingstown	G-8
Pawtucket	F-8
Portsmouth	G-8
Providence	F-8
Slatersville	E-7
Tiverton	G-8
Wakefield	H-8
Warwick	F-8
West Warwick	F-7
Westerly	H-7
Woonsocket	E-8

Colorado

Population: 4,426,500 (1/1/01 estimate)
Land Area: 103,729 sq. mi.
Capital: Denver

Cities and Towns

City	Grid
Akron	B-8
Alamosa	F-5
Arvada	C-6
Aspen	D-4
Aurora	C-6
Boulder	C-5
Breckenridge	C-4
Brighton	C-6
Brush	B-7
Buena Vista	D-4
Burlington	D-9
Cañon City	E-5
Carbondale	D-3
Castle Rock	D-6
Center	F-4
Central City	C-5
Cheyenne Wells	D-9
Clifton	D-2
Colorado Springs	D-6
Conejos	G-4
Cortez	G-1
Craig	B-3
Creede	F-3
Cripple Creek	E-5
Del Norte	F-4
Delta	D-2
Denver	C-6
Dove Creek	F-1
Durango	G-2
Eads	E-8
Eagle	C-4
Eaton	B-6
Englewood	C-6
Estes Park	B-5
Evans	B-6
Evergreen	C-5
Fairplay	D-4
Florence	E-6
Fort Collins	B-6
Fort Lupton	C-6
Fort Morgan	B-7
Fountain	E-6
Fowler	E-7
Fruita	D-1
Fruitvale	D-2
Georgetown	C-5
Glenwood Springs	C-3
Golden	C-5
Grand Junction	D-1
Greeley	B-6
Gunnison	E-3
Holyoke	B-9
Hot Sulphur Sprs.	C-4
Hugo	D-7
Idaho Springs	C-5
Julesburg	A-9
Kiowa	D-6
La Junta	F-7
Lafayette	C-6
Lake City	F-3
Lamar	E-8
Las Animas	F-8
Leadville	D-4
Limon	D-7
Lincoln Park	E-5
Littleton	C-6
Longmont	B-6
Loveland	B-6
Lyons	B-5
Manitou Springs	D-6
Meeker	C-2
Monte Vista	F-4
Montrose	E-2
Ordway	E-7
Ouray	F-2
Pagosa Springs	G-3
Palisade	D-2
Parker	C-6
Platteville	B-6
Pueblo	E-6
Rangely	B-1
Rifle	C-2
Rocky Ford	F-7
Saguache	F-4
Salida	E-4
San Luis	G-5
Silverton	F-2
Springfield	G-9
Steamboat Sprs.	B-4
Sterling	B-8
Telluride	F-2
Trinidad	G-6
Vail	C-4
Walden	B-4
Walsenburg	F-6
Wellington	B-6
Westcliffe	E-5
Windsor	B-6
Winter Park	C-5
Woodland Park	D-6
Wray	B-9
Yuma	B-8

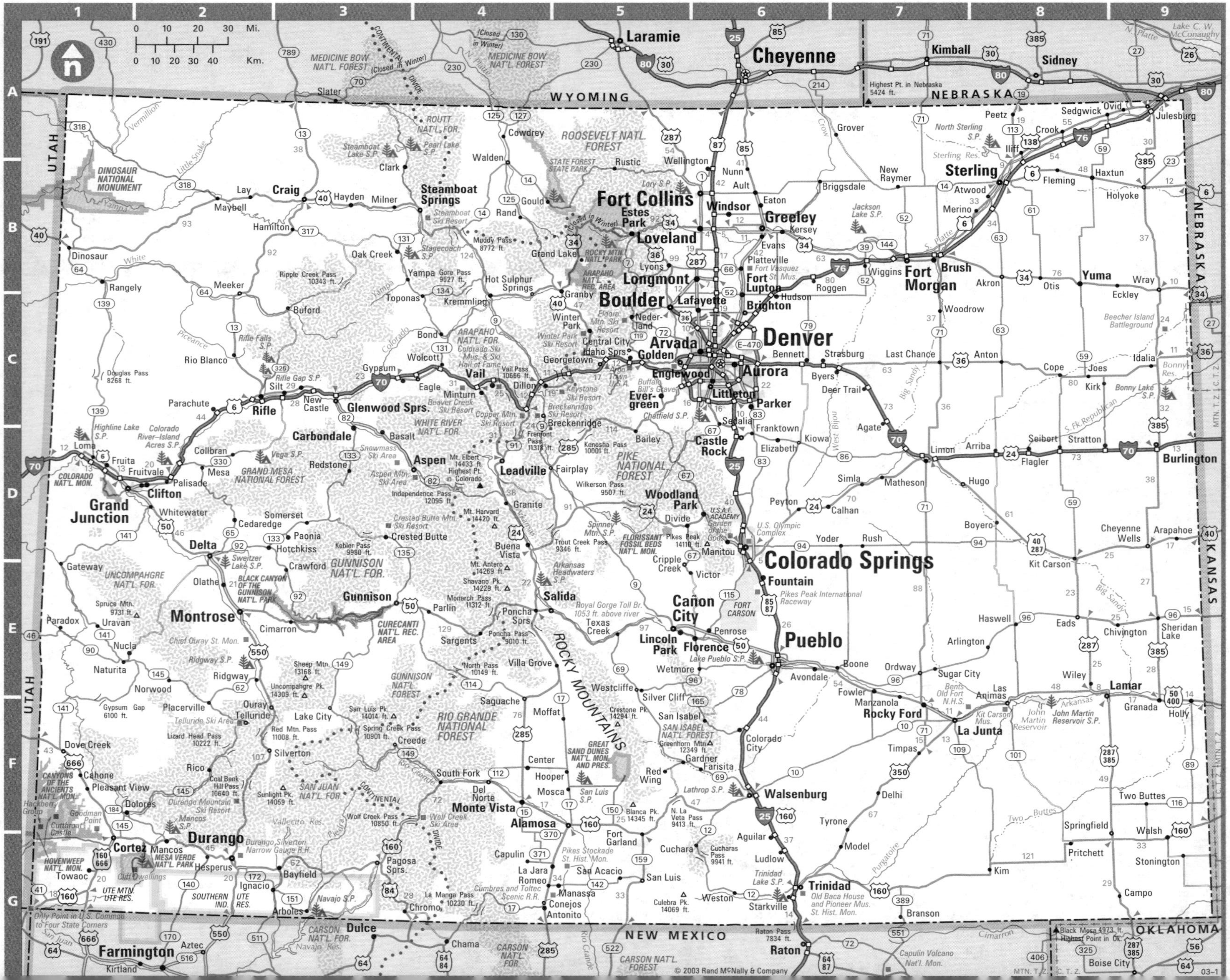

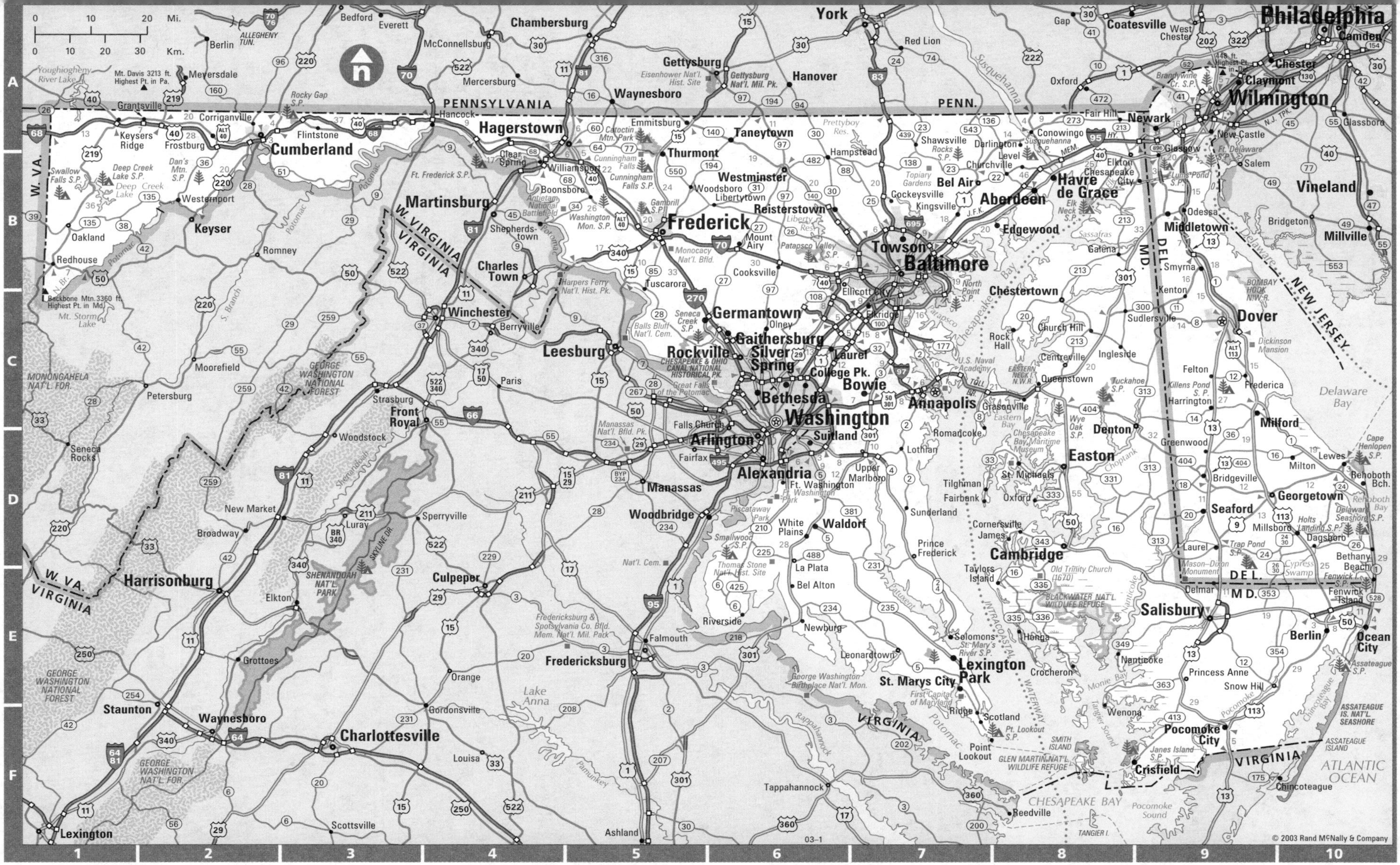

Delaware

Population: 797,700 (1/1/01 estimate)
Land Area: 1,955 sq. mi.
Capital: Dover

Cities and Towns

Bridgeville	D-9
Claymont	A-9
Delmar	E-9
Dover	C-9
Georgetown	D-9
Harrington	C-9
Laurel	D-9
Lewes	D-10
Middletown	B-9
Milford	C-9
Millsboro	D-10
Milton	D-10
New Castle	A-9
Newark	A-9
Rehoboth Bch.	D-10
Seaford	D-9
Smyrna	B-9
Wilmington	A-9

District of Columbia

Population: 568,800 (1/1/01 estimate)
Land Area: 61 sq. mi.

City

Washington	C-6

Maryland

Population: 5,358,400 (1/1/01 estimate)
Land Area: 9,775 sq. mi.
Capital: Annapolis

Cities and Towns

Aberdeen	B-8
Annapolis	C-7
Baltimore	B-7
Bel Air	B-7
Bel Alton	E-6
Berlin	E-10
Bethesda	C-6
Boonsboro	B-5
Bowie	C-7
Cambridge	D-8
Centreville	C-8
Chesapeake City	B-9
Chestertown	C-8
Church Hill	C-8
Churchville	B-8
Clear Spring	A-4
College Park	C-6
Conowingo	A-8
Cooksville	B-6
Cornersville	D-8
Corriganville	A-2
Crisfield	F-8
Crocheron	E-8
Cumberland	A-2
Darlington	A-8
Denton	C-9
Easton	D-8
Edgewood	B-8
Elkridge	C-7
Elkton	B-8
Ellicott City	B-6
Emmitsburg	A-5
Fair Hill	A-8
Flintstone	A-3
Frederick	B-5
Frostburg	A-2
Gaithersburg	C-6
Galena	B-8
Grantsville	A-2
Grasonville	C-8
Hagerstown	A-5
Hampstead	B-6
Hancock	A-4
Havre de Grace	B-8
Honga	E-8
Ingleside	C-8
Kingsville	B-7
La Plata	D-6
Laurel	C-6
Leonardtown	E-7
Level	B-8
Lexington Park	E-7
Libertytown	B-6
Lothian	D-7
Mount Airy	B-6
Nanticoke	E-8
Newburg	E-6
Oakland	B-1
Ocean City	E-10
Olney	C-6
Oxford	D-8
Pocomoke City	F-9
Point Lookout	F-7
Prince Frederick	D-7
Princess Anne	E-9
Queenstown	C-8
Reisterstown	B-6
Ridge	F-7
Rock Hall	C-8
Rockville	C-6
Romancoke	D-7
St. Marys City	E-7
St. Michaels	D-8
Salisbury	E-9
Scotland	F-7
Shawsville	A-7
Silesia	D-6
Silver Spring	C-6
Snow Hill	E-9
Solomons	E-7
Sudlersville	C-8
Suitland	D-6
Sunderland	D-7
Taneytown	A-6
Taylors Island	E-8
Thurmont	B-5
Tilghman	D-7
Towson	B-7
Tuscarora	B-5
Upper Marlboro	D-6
Waldorf	D-6
Wenona	F-8
Westernport	B-2
Westminster	B-6
White Plains	D-6
Williamsport	B-4
Woodsboro	B-5

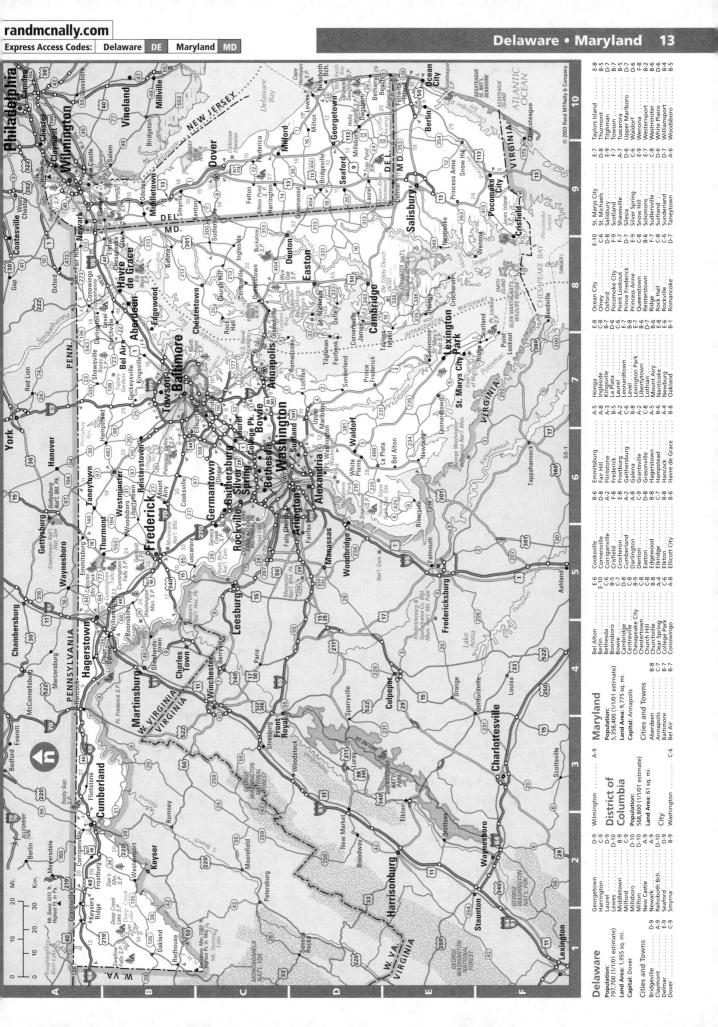

Florida

Population: 16,351,900 (1/1/01 estimate)
Land Area: 53,937 sq. mi.
Capital: Tallahassee

Cities and Towns

Altamonte Sprs.	D-4
Apalachicola	J-4
Arcadia	F-4
Atlantic Beach	B-4
Avon Park	F-4
Bartow	E-4
Belle Glade	G-5
Big Pine Key	J-5
Blountstown	I-4
Boca Raton	G-6
Bonifay	I-3
Bradenton	F-3
Brandon	E-3
Brooksville	D-3
Bunnell	C-5
Bushnell	D-4
Cape Canaveral	E-5
Cape Coral	G-4
Chipley	I-3
Clearwater	E-3
Clermont	D-4
Cocoa Beach	E-5
Coral Gables	H-6
Crawfordville	B-1
Crestview	I-2
Cross City	C-2
Dade City	E-3
Dania Beach	H-6
Daytona Beach	D-5
Debary	D-4
De Funiak Springs	I-2
DeLand	D-4
Deerfield Beach	G-6
Delray Beach	G-6
Dunedin	E-3
East Naples	H-4
Edgewater	D-5
Englewood	F-3
Eustis	D-4
Fort Lauderdale	H-6
Fort Myers	G-4
Fort Myers Beach	G-4
Fort Pierce	F-6
Fort Walton Beach	I-2
Gainesville	C-3
Green Cove Sprs.	C-4
Haines City	E-4
Hallandale Beach	H-6
Hialeah	H-6
Holly Hill	C-5
Hollywood	H-6
Homestead	H-6
Hudson	E-3
Immokalee	G-4
Inverness	D-3
Jacksonville	B-4
Jacksonville Bch.	B-4
Jasper	B-3
Jensen Beach	F-6
Jupiter	F-6
Key Largo	I-6
Key West	J-4
Kissimmee	E-4
La Belle	G-4
Lady Lake	D-4
Lake Butler	B-3
Lake City	B-3
Lake Wales	E-4
Lake Worth	G-6
Lakeland	E-4
Largo	E-3
Leesburg	D-4
Lehigh Acres	G-4
Live Oak	B-3
Lutz	E-3
Macclenny	B-4
Madeira Beach	E-3
Madison	B-2
Marathon	I-5
Marco	H-4
Marianna	I-3
Mayo	B-2
Melbourne	E-5
Miami	H-6
Miami Beach	H-6
Milton	I-1
Monticello	B-2
Moore Haven	G-5
Mount Dora	D-4
Naples	H-4
New Port Richey	E-3
New Smyrna Bch.	D-5
North Palm Beach	G-6
Ocala	D-4
Okeechobee	F-5
Orlando	D-4
Ormond Beach	C-5
Palatka	C-4
Palm Bay	E-5
Palm Beach	G-6
Palmetto	F-3
Panama City	J-3
Pensacola	I-1
Perrine	H-6
Perry	B-2
Plant City	E-4
Pompano Beach	G-6
Port Charlotte	F-4
Port Orange	D-5
Port St. Joe	J-3
Port St. Lucie	F-6
Punta Gorda	G-4
Quincy	B-1
St. Augustine	C-4
St. Cloud	E-5
St. Petersburg	E-3
St. Petersburg Bch.	E-3
Sanford	D-5
Sanibel	G-4
Sarasota	F-3
Sebastian	E-5
Sebring	F-4
Starke	C-4
Stuart	F-6
Tallahassee	B-1
Tampa	E-3
Tarpon Springs	E-3
Tavares	D-4
The Villages	D-4
Titusville	D-5
Treasure Island	E-3
Trenton	C-3
Venice	F-3
Vero Beach	F-6
Warrington	I-1
Wauchula	F-4
West Palm Beach	G-6
Winter Garden	D-4
Winter Haven	E-4
Yulee	B-4
Zephyrhills	E-3

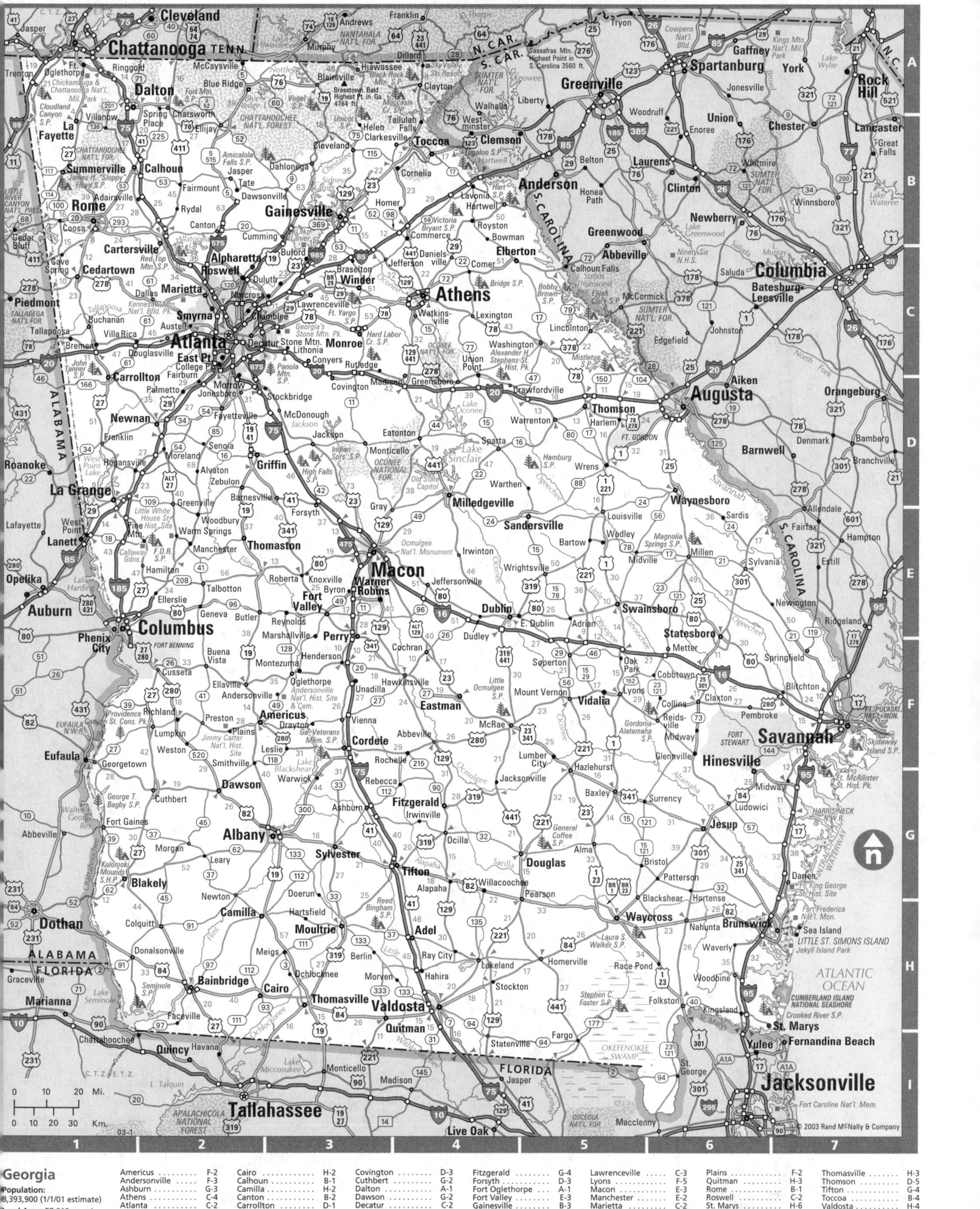

Georgia

Population: 8,393,900 (1/1/01 estimate)

Land Area: 57,919 sq. mi.

Capital: Atlanta

Cities and Towns

City	Grid
Adel	H-4
Albany	G-3
Alma	G-5
Alpharetta	C-2
Americus	F-2
Andersonville	F-3
Ashburn	G-3
Athens	C-4
Atlanta	C-2
Augusta	D-6
Austell	C-2
Bainbridge	H-2
Barnesville	D-3
Baxley	G-5
Blakely	G-1
Bremen	C-1
Brunswick	H-7
Buford	C-3
Cairo	H-2
Calhoun	B-1
Camilla	H-2
Canton	B-2
Carrollton	D-1
Cartersville	B-2
Cedartown	C-1
Chamblee	C-2
Cochran	F-4
College Park	C-2
Columbus	E-1
Commerce	B-4
Conyers	C-3
Cordele	F-3
Covington	D-3
Cuthbert	G-2
Dalton	A-1
Dawson	G-2
Decatur	C-2
Douglas	G-5
Douglasville	C-2
Dublin	E-4
Duluth	C-3
Eastman	F-4
Eatonton	D-4
Elberton	C-4
Fairburn	D-2
Fayetteville	D-2
Fitzgerald	G-4
Forsyth	D-3
Fort Oglethorpe	A-1
Fort Valley	E-3
Gainesville	B-3
Griffin	D-2
Hartwell	B-4
Hazlehurst	F-5
Hinesville	G-6
Jackson	D-3
Jesup	G-6
Kingsland	H-6
La Fayette	B-1
La Grange	D-1
Lawrenceville	C-3
Lyons	F-5
Macon	E-3
Manchester	E-2
Marietta	C-2
Metter	F-6
Milledgeville	D-4
Millen	E-6
Monroe	C -3
Montezuma	F-3
Moultrie	H-3
Newnan	D-2
Norcross	C-3
Perry	E-3
Plains	F-2
Quitman	H-3
Rome	B-1
Roswell	C-2
St. Marys	H-6
St. Simons Island	H-7
Sandersville	E-5
Savannah	F-7
Statesboro	E-6
Stone Mountain	C-3
Summerville	B-1
Swainsboro	E-5
Sylvester	G-3
Thomaston	E-2
Thomasville	H-3
Thomson	D-5
Tifton	G-4
Toccoa	B-4
Valdosta	H-4
Vidalia	F-5
Villa Rica	C-1
Warm Springs	E-2
Warner Robins	E-3
Washington	C-5
Waycross	H-5
Waynesboro	D-6
West Point	E-1
Winder	C-3

Idaho

Population:
1,328,800 (1/1/01 estimate)

Land Area: 82,751 sq. mi.

Capital: Boise

Cities and Towns

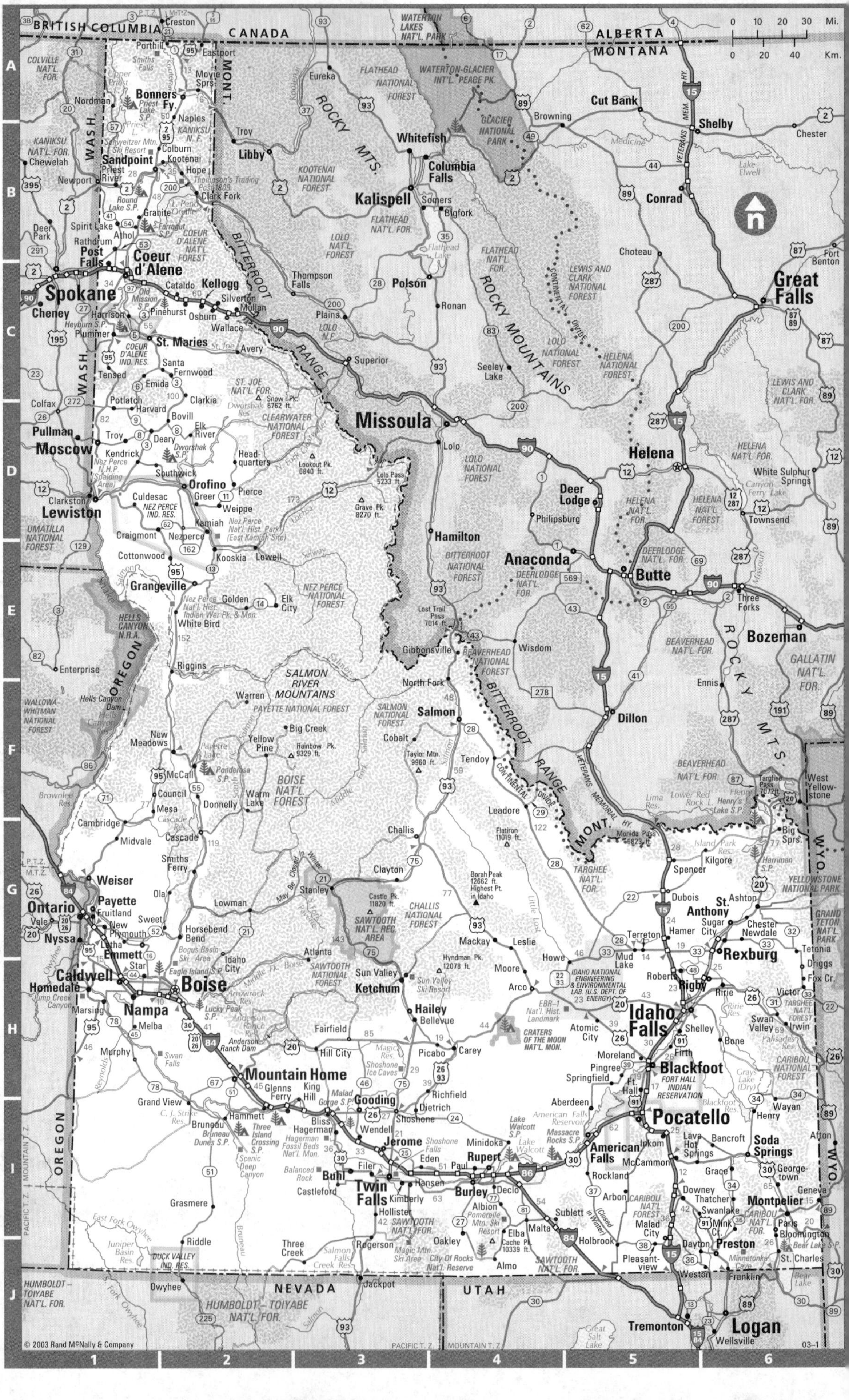

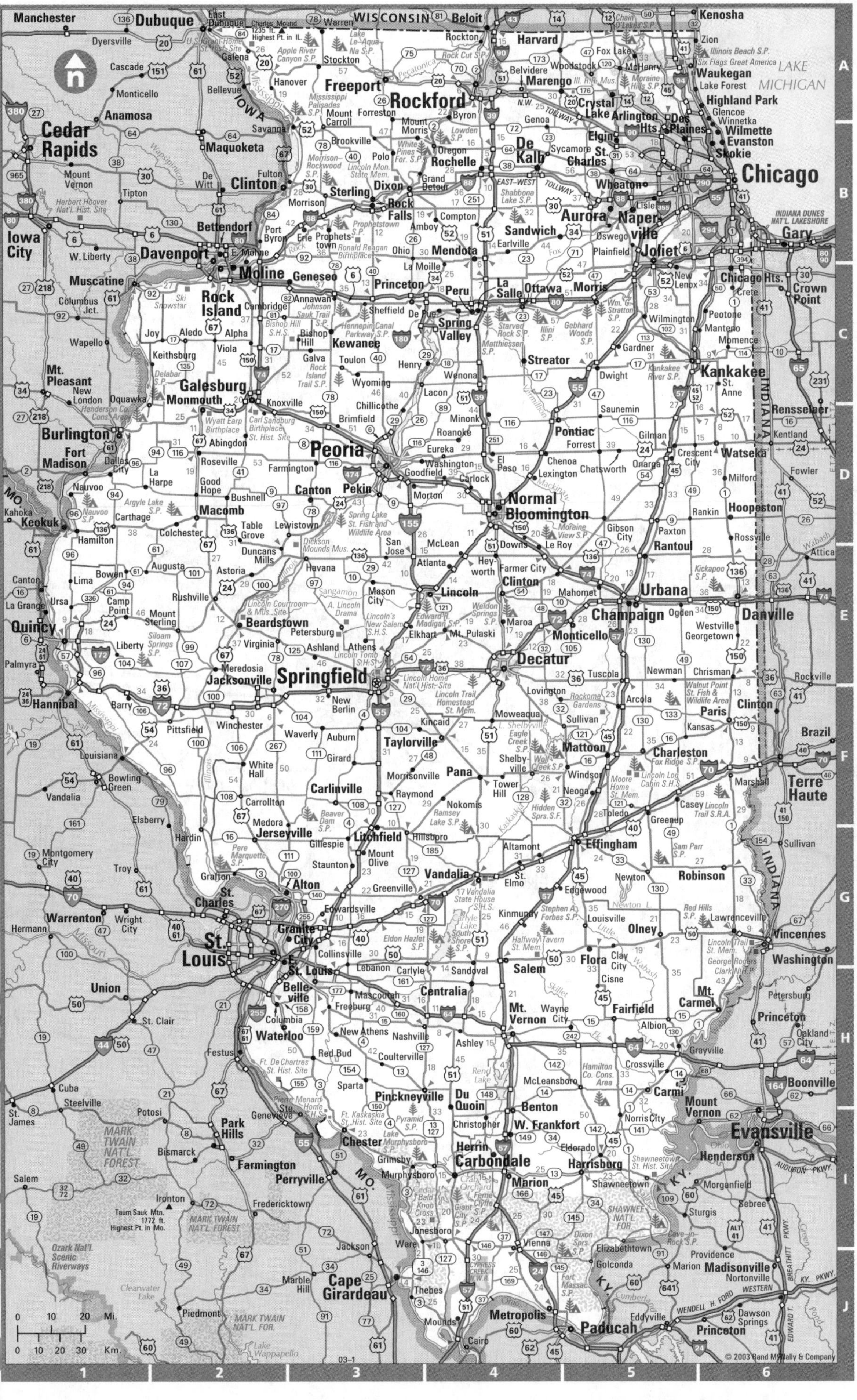
WISCONSIN
IOWA
MO.
INDIANA
KY.
LAKE MICHIGAN
Chicago
Rockford
Peoria
Springfield
Decatur
Champaign
Urbana
Bloomington
Normal
Joliet
Aurora
Naperville
Elgin
Waukegan
Kankakee
Danville
Galesburg
Moline
Rock Island
Davenport
Quincy
Alton
St. Louis
East St. Louis
Belleville
Carbondale
Cairo
Paducah
Evansville
Terre Haute
Cedar Rapids
Dubuque
Gary
MARK TWAIN NAT'L. FOREST
SHAWNEE NAT'L. FOR.
Charles Mound 1235 ft. Highest Pt. in IL.
Taum Sauk Mtn. 1772 ft. Highest Pt. in Mo.
0 10 20 Mi.
0 10 20 30 Km.
03-1
© 2003 Rand McNally & Company
A B C D E F G H I J
1 2 3 4 5 6

Illinois

Population:
12,539,700 (1/1/01 estimate)

Land Area: 55,593 sq. mi.

Capital: Springfield

Cities and Towns

Albion	H-5
Aledo	C-2
Alton	G-3
Arlington Heights	B-5
Aurora	B-5
Belleville	H-3
Belvidere	A-4
Bishop Hill	C-3
Bloomington	D-4
Cairo	J-4
Cambridge	C-2
Canton	D-3
Carbondale	I-4
Carlinville	F-3
Carlyle	G-4
Carmi	H-5
Carrollton	F-2
Carthage	D-1
Centralia	H-4
Champaign	E-5
Charleston	F-5
Chester	I-3
Chicago	B-6
Chicago Heights	C-6
Clinton	E-4
Collinsville	G-3
Crystal Lake	A-5
Danville	E-6
De Kalb	B-4
Decatur	E-4
Dixon	B-3
Du Quoin	H-4
Dwight	C-5
East Moline	B-2
East St. Louis	G-2
Edwardsville	G-3
Effingham	G-5
Elgin	B-5
Eureka	D-4
Evanston	B-6
Fairfield	H-5
Freeport	A-3
Galena	A-2
Galesburg	C-2
Granite City	G-3
Greenville	G-3
Hardin	G-2
Harrisburg	I-5
Havana	E-3
Herrin	I-4
Highland Park	A-6
Hillsboro	G-3
Jacksonville	F-2
Jerseyville	G-2
Joliet	B-5
Jonesboro	I-4
Kankakee	C-5
Kewanee	C-3
La Salle	C-4
Lacon	C-3
Lake Forest	A-6
Lawrenceville	G-6
Lewistown	D-3
Lincoln	E-4
Lisle	B-5
Louisville	G-5
Macomb	D-2
Marion	I-4
Marshall	F-6
Mattoon	F-5
McHenry	A-5
McLeansboro	H-5
Meredosia	E-2
Metropolis	J-4
Moline	C-2
Monmouth	D-2
Monticello	E-5
Morris	C-5
Morrison	B-3
Morton	D-3
Mount Carmel	H-6
Mount Carroll	B-3
Mount Pulaski	E-4
Mount Sterling	E-2
Mount Vernon	H-4
Murphysboro	I-4
Naperville	B-5
Nashville	H-4
Nauvoo	D-1
Newton	G-5
Normal	D-4
Olney	G-5
Oquawka	D-2
Oregon	B-4
Ottawa	C-4
Pana	F-4
Paris	F-6
Paxton	D-5
Pekin	D-3
Peoria	D-3
Peru	C-4
Petersburg	E-3
Pinckneyville	H-4
Pittsfield	F-2
Pontiac	D-4
Princeton	C-3
Quincy	E-1
Rantoul	E-5
Robinson	G-6
Rock Island	C-2
Rockford	A-4
Rushville	E-2
St. Charles	B-5
Salem	G-4
Shawneetown	I-5
Shelbyville	F-4
Skokie	B-6
Springfield	E-3
Sterling	B-3
Streator	C-4
Sullivan	F-5
Sycamore	B-4
Taylorville	F-4
Toledo	F-5
Toulon	C-3
Tuscola	E-5
Urbana	E-5
Vandalia	G-4
Vienna	I-4
Viola	C-2
Virginia	E-2
Washington	D-3
Waterloo	H-2
Watseka	D-6
Waukegan	A-5
Wheaton	B-5
Wilmette	B-6
Winchester	F-2
Winnetka	B-6
Woodstock	A-5
Zion	A-6

randmcnally.com
Express Access Code: IN

Indiana

Population: 6,145,700 (1/1/01 estimate)
Land Area: 35,870 sq. mi.
Capital: Indianapolis

Cities and Towns

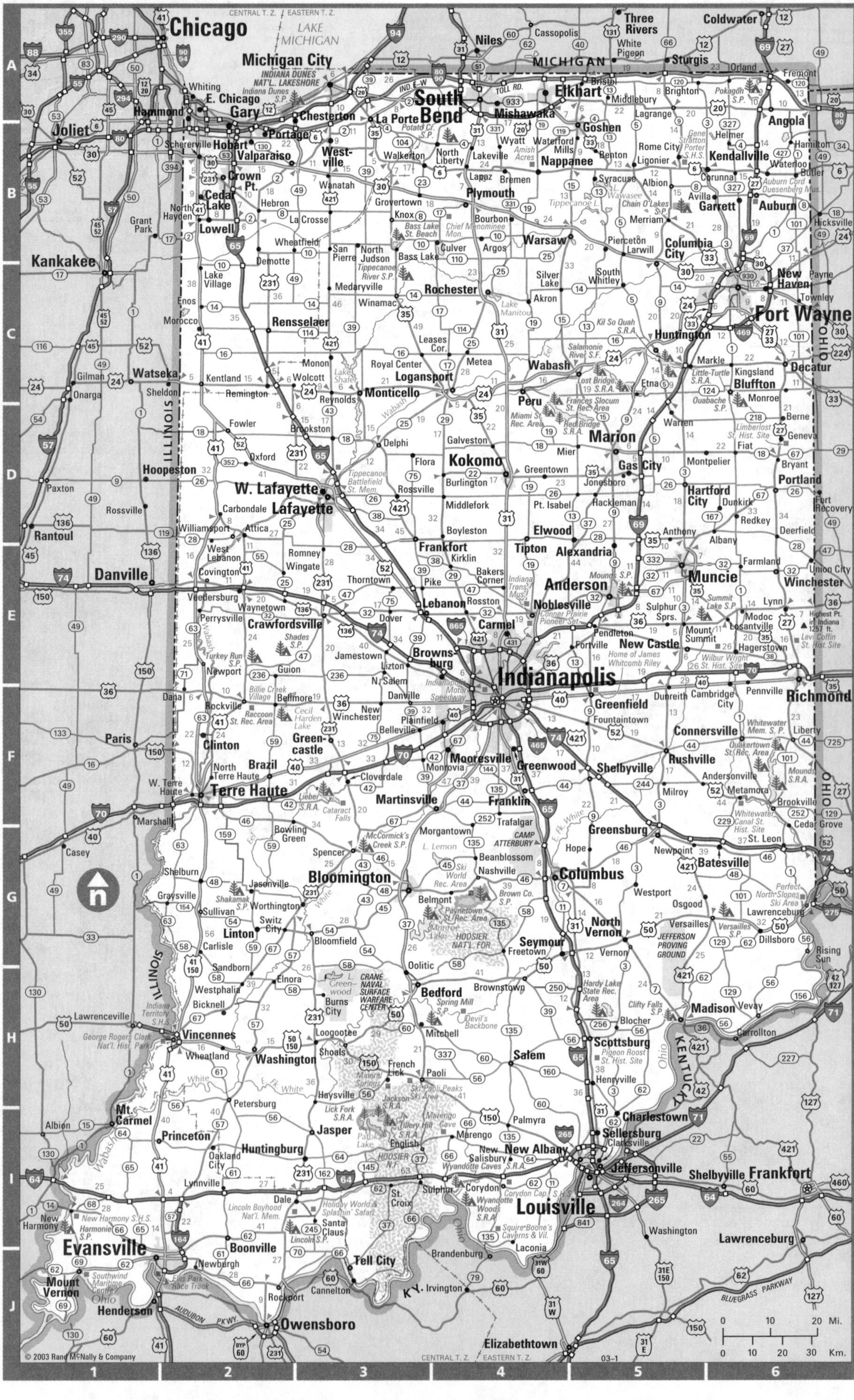

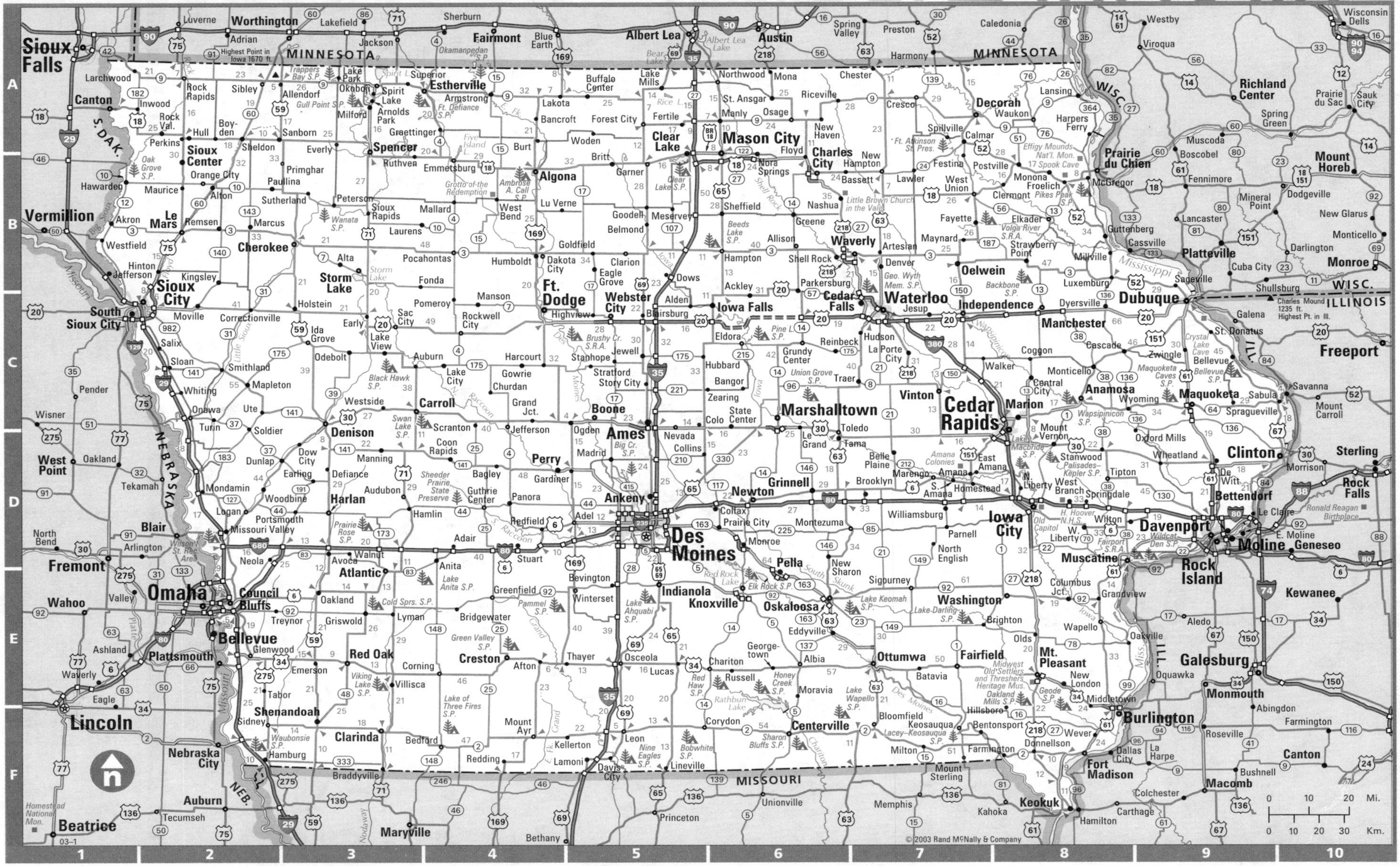

Iowa

Population: 2,944,600 (1/1/01 estimate)

Land Area: 55,875 sq. mi.

Capital: Des Moines

Cities and Towns

Adel	D-5
Albia	E-6
Algona	B-4
Allison	B-6
Amana	D-7
Ames	C-5
Anamosa	C-8
Ankeny	D-5
Atlantic	E-3
Audubon	D-3
Bedford	F-4
Belle Plaine	D-7
Bettendorf	D-9
Bloomfield	F-7
Boone	C-5
Burlington	F-8
Carroll	C-3
Cedar Falls	C-7
Cedar Rapids	D-8
Centerville	F-6
Chariton	E-6
Charles City	B-6
Cherokee	B-3
Clarinda	F-3
Clarion	B-5
Clear Lake	B-5
Clinton	D-10
Coon Rapids	D-4
Corning	E-4
Corydon	F-5
Council Bluffs	E-2
Cresco	A-7
Creston	E-4
Dakota City	B-4
Davenport	D-9
De Witt	D-9
Decorah	A-7
Denison	C-3
Des Moines	D-5
Dubuque	C-9
Dyersville	C-8
Eagle Grove	B-5
Eldora	C-6
Elkader	B-8
Emmetsburg	B-4
Estherville	A-4
Fairfield	E-7
Forest City	A-5
Fort Dodge	C-4
Garner	B-5
Glenwood	E-2
Greenfield	E-4
Grinnell	D-6
Griswold	E-3
Grundy Center	C-6
Guthrie Center	D-4
Guttenberg	B-8
Hamburg	F-2
Hampton	B-6
Harlan	D-3
Humboldt	B-4
Ida Grove	C-3
Independence	C-7
Indianola	E-5
Iowa City	D-8
Iowa Falls	C-6
Jefferson	C-4
Keokuk	F-8
Keosauqua	F-7
Knoxville	E-6
Le Claire	D-9
Le Mars	B-2
Leon	F-5
Logan	D-2
Manchester	C-8
Maquoketa	C-9
Marengo	D-7
Marion	C-8
Marshalltown	C-6
Mason City	B-6
McGregor	B-8
Missouri Valley	D-2
Montezuma	D-7
Monticello	C-8
Mount Ayr	F-4
Mount Pleasant	E-8
Mount Vernon	D-8
Muscatine	D-8
Nashua	B-6
Nevada	C-5
New Hampton	B-7
Newton	D-6
North Liberty	D-8
Northwood	A-6
Oelwein	B-7
Onawa	C-2
Orange City	B-2
Osage	A-6
Osceola	E-5
Oskaloosa	E-6
Ottumwa	E-7
Pella	E-6
Perry	D-4
Pocahontas	B-4
Primghar	B-3
Red Oak	E-3
Rock Rapids	A-2
Rockwell City	C-4
Sac City	C-3
Sheldon	A-2
Shenandoah	F-3
Sibley	A-2
Sidney	F-2
Sigourney	E-7
Sioux Center	B-2
Sioux City	C-2
Spencer	A-3
Spirit Lake	A-3
State Center	C-6
Storm Lake	B-3
Story City	C-5
Tama	D-6
Tipton	D-8
Toledo	D-6
Vinton	C-7
Wapello	E-8
Washington	E-8
Waterloo	C-7
Waukon	A-8
Waverly	B-7
Webster City	C-5
West Branch	D-8
West Liberty	D-8
West Union	B-7
Wilton	D-8
Winterset	E-5

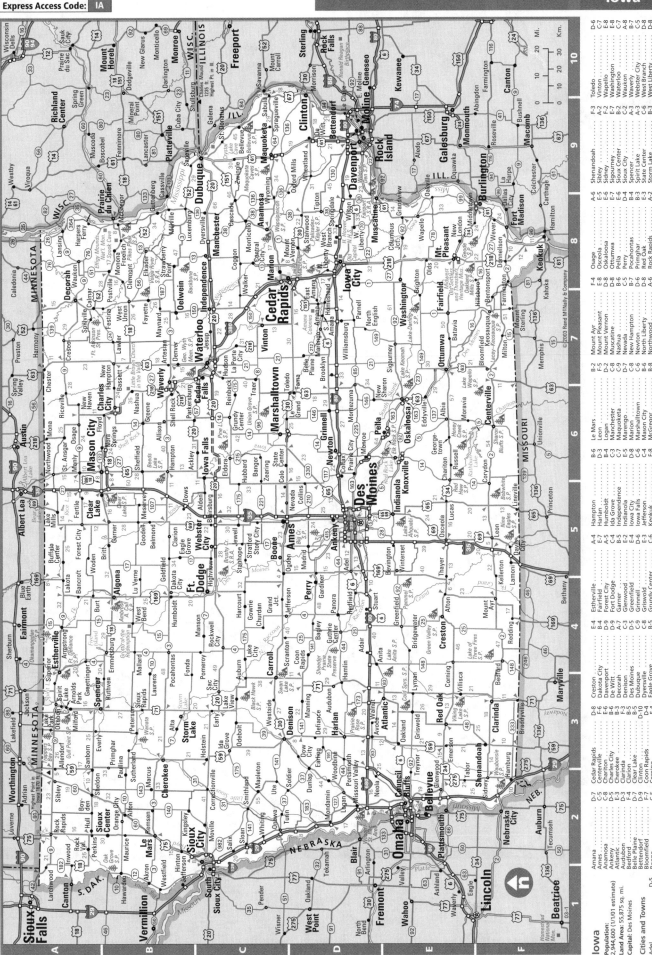

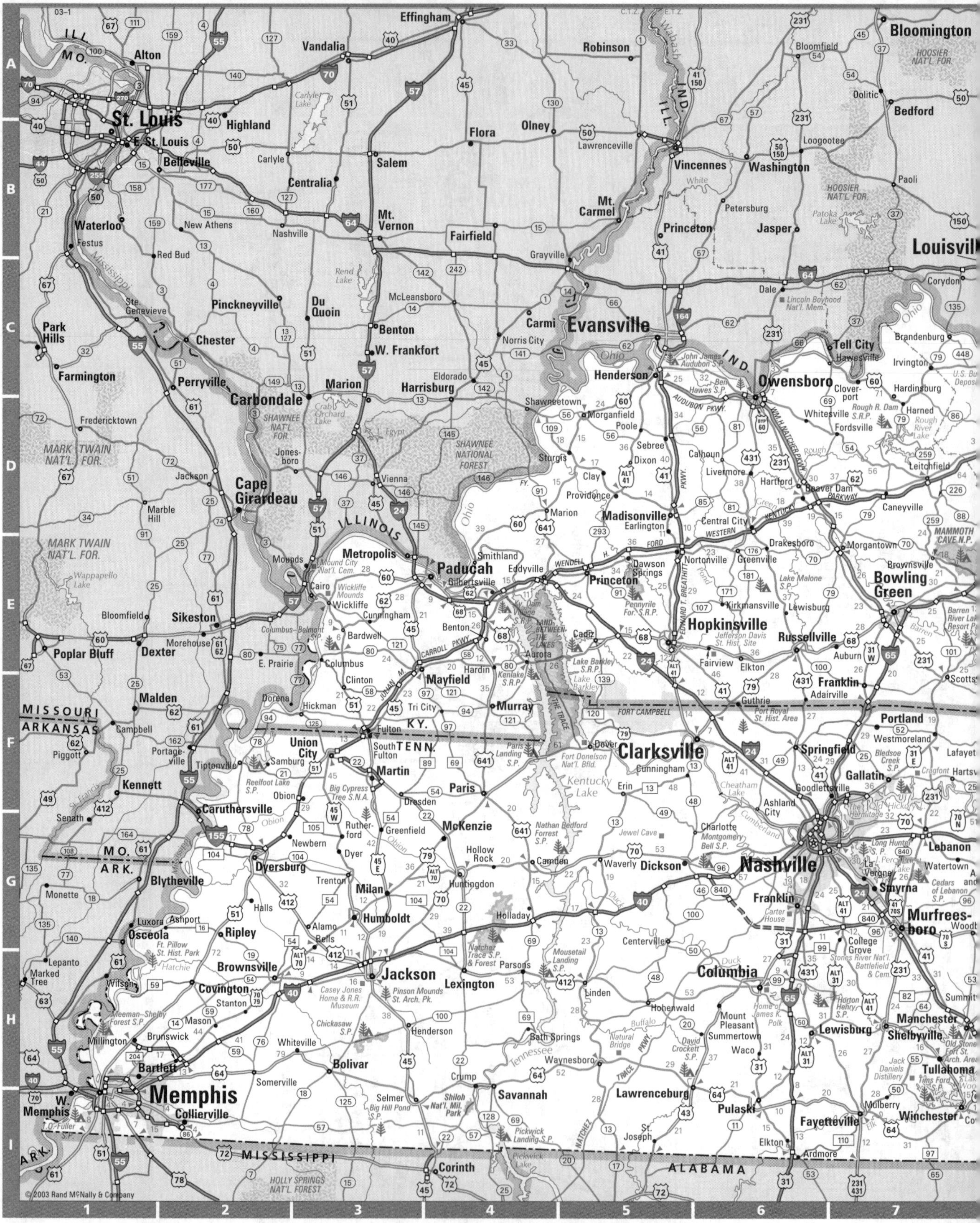

Kentucky

Population: 4,085,300 (1/1/01 estimate)

Land Area: 39,732 sq. mi.

Capital: Frankfort

Cities and Towns

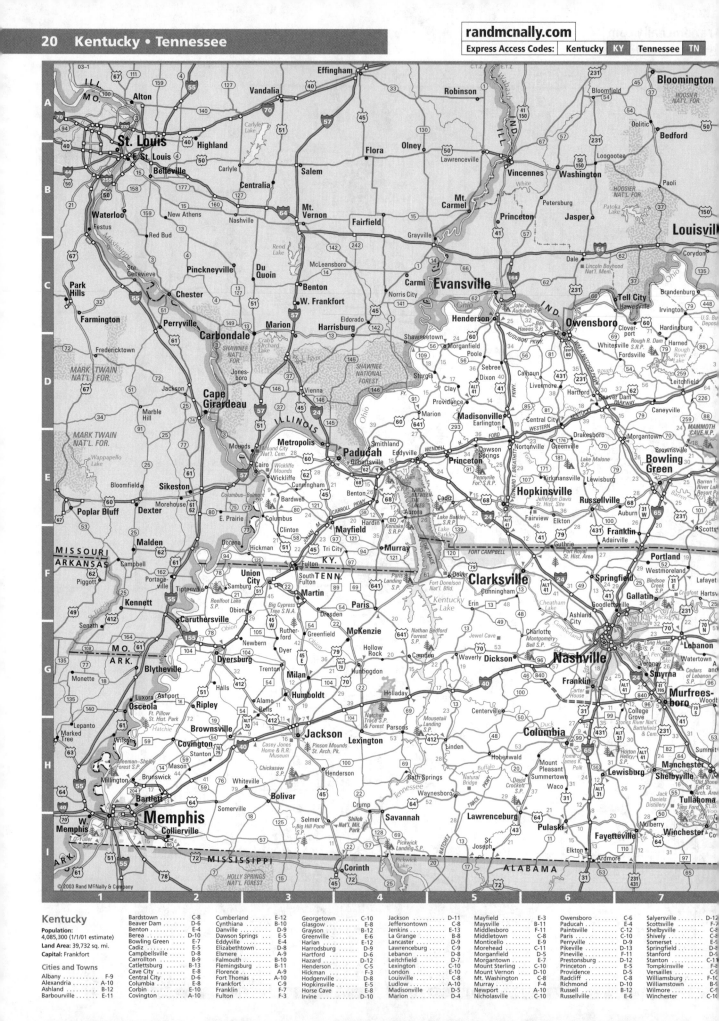

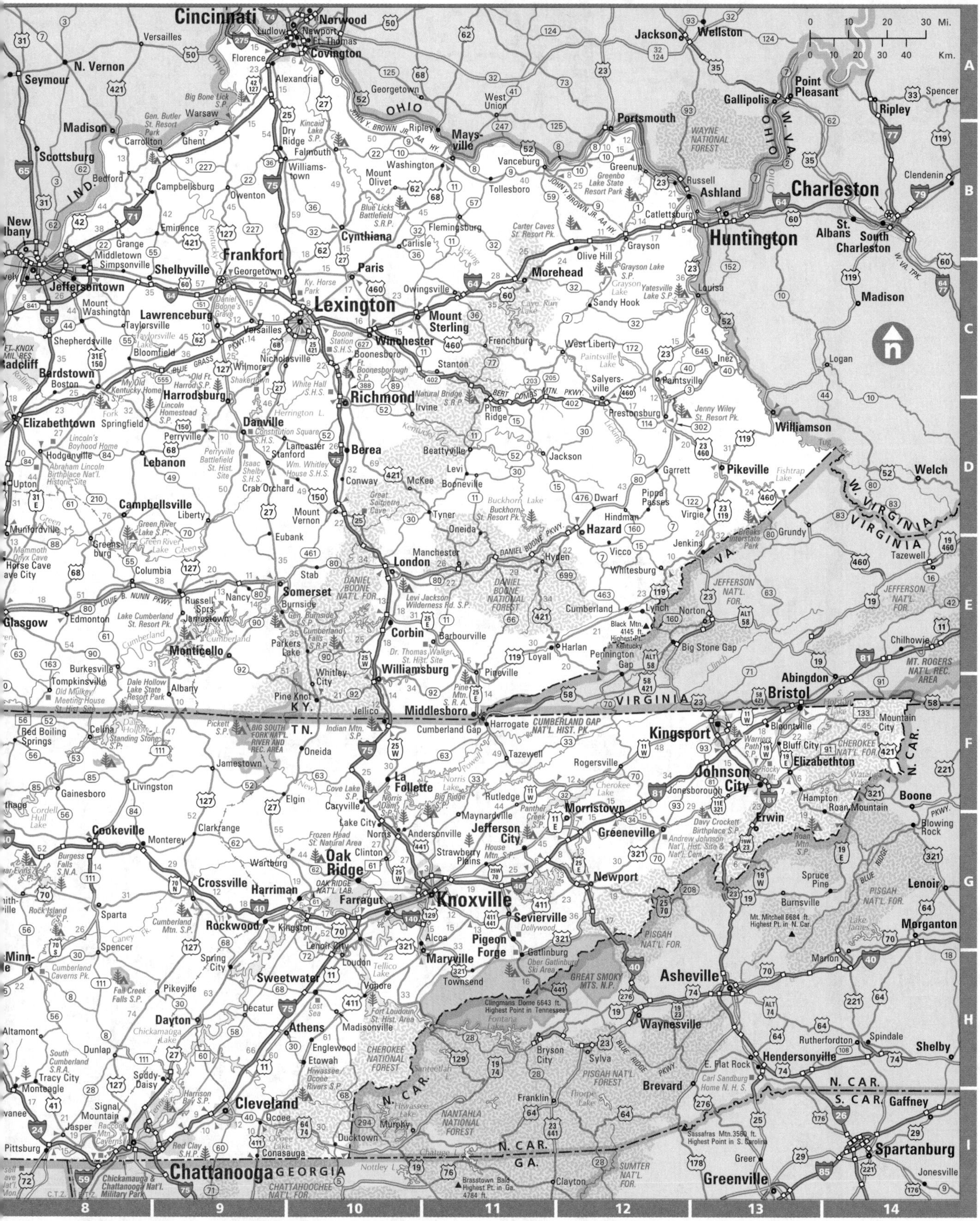

Tennessee

Population: 5,789,700 (1/1/01 estimate)

Land Area: 41,219 sq. mi.

Capital: Nashville

Cities and Towns

Alamo	G-3
Alcoa	G-10
Ashland City	F-6
Athens	H-10
Bartlett	H-1
Bolivar	H-3
Bristol	F-13
Brownsville	H-2
Camden	G-4
Carthage	G-8
Centerville	G-5
Chattanooga	I-8
Clarksville	F-6
Cleveland	I-9
Clinton	G-10
Collierville	I-2
Columbia	H-6
Cookeville	G-8
Covington	H-2
Crossville	G-9
Dayton	H-9
Dickson	G-5
Dresden	F-3
Dunlap	H-8
Dyersburg	G-2
Elizabethton	F-13
Erwin	G-13
Etowah	H-10
Fayetteville	I-7
Franklin	G-6
Gallatin	F-7
Gatlinburg	H-11
Goodlettsville	F-7
Greeneville	G-12
Halls	G-2
Harriman	G-10
Henderson	H-3
Humboldt	G-3
Huntingdon	G-4
Jackson	H-3
Jasper	I-8
Jefferson City	G-11
Jellico	F-10
Johnson City	F-13
Jonesborough	F-13
Kingsport	F-13
Kingston	G-10
Knoxville	G-11
La Follette	F-10
La Vergne	G-7
Lafayette	F-7
Lake City	G-10
Lawrenceburg	H-5
Lebanon	G-7
Lenoir City	G-10
Lewisburg	H-6
Lexington	H-4
Livingston	F-8
Loudon	H-10
Madisonville	H-10
Manchester	H-7
Martin	F-3
Maryville	H-11
McKenzie	G-4
McMinnville	H-8
Memphis	I-1
Milan	G-3
Millington	H-1
Monterey	G-8
Morristown	G-12
Mount Pleasant	H-6
Murfreesboro	G-7
Nashville	G-6
Newport	G-12
Oak Ridge	G-10
Oneida	F-10
Paris	F-4
Pigeon Forge	G-11
Portland	F-7
Pulaski	I-6
Ripley	G-2
Rockwood	G-9
Rogersville	F-12
Savannah	H-4
Selmer	I-3
Sevierville	G-11
Shelbyville	H-7
Signal Mountain	I-8
Smithville	G-8
Smyrna	G-7
Soddy-Daisy	H-9
South Fulton	F-3
South Pittsburg	I-8
Sparta	G-8
Springfield	F-6
Sweetwater	H-10
Trenton	G-3
Tullahoma	H-7
Union City	F-3
Waverly	G-5
Winchester	I-7
Woodbury	G-7

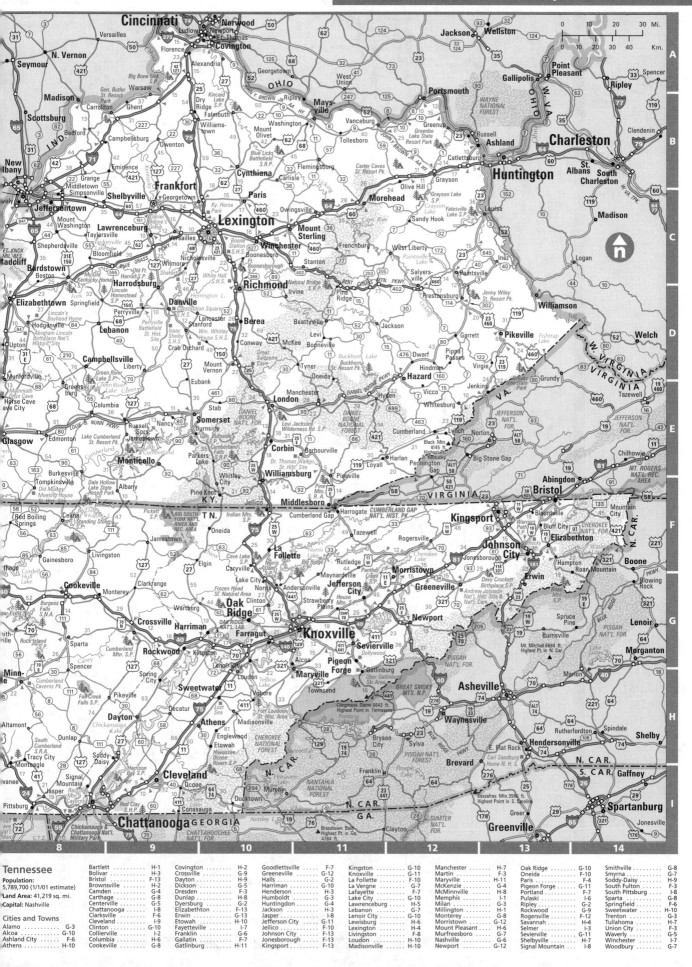

Kansas

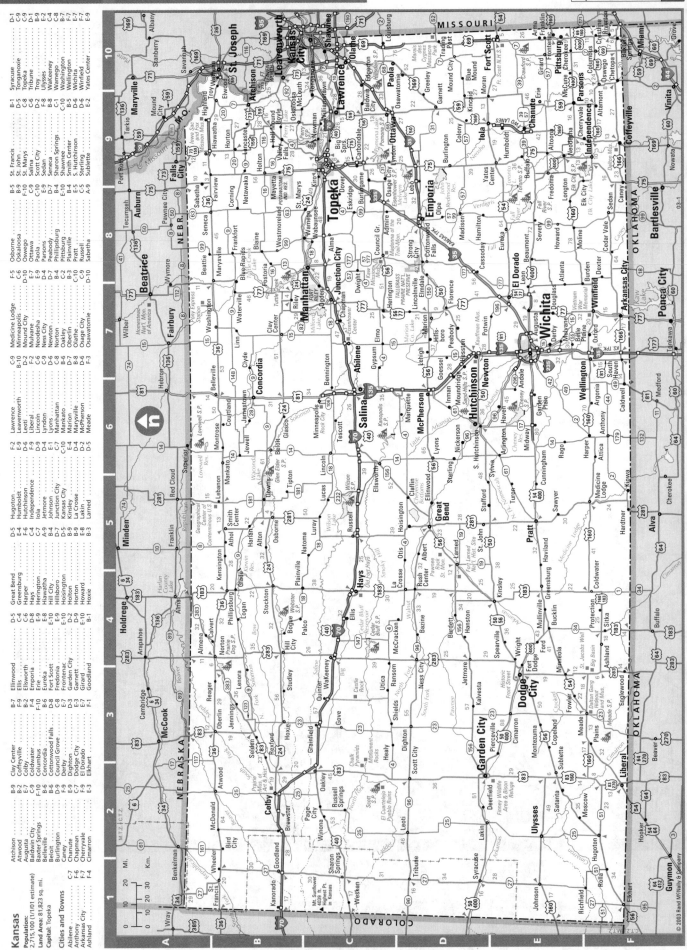

Population: 2,715,100 (1/1/01 estimate)
Land Area: 81,823 sq. mi.
Capital: Topeka

Cities and Towns

Abilene C-7
Anthony F-6
Arkansas City F-7
Ashland F-4
Atchison B-9
Atwood B-2
Augusta E-7
Baldwin City C-9
Baxter Springs F-10
Belleville B-6
Beloit B-6
Burlington D-9
Caney F-9
Chanute E-9
Chapman C-7
Cherryvale F-9
Cimarron E-3
Clay Center B-7
Coffeyville F-9
Colby B-2
Coldwater F-4
Columbus F-10
Concordia B-6
Cottonwood Falls D-8
Council Grove C-8
Derby E-7
Dighton D-3
Dodge City E-3
El Dorado E-7
Elkhart F-1
Ellinwood D-5
Ellis C-4
Ellsworth C-6
Emporia D-8
Erie E-9
Eureka E-8
Fort Scott E-10
Fredonia E-9
Frontenac E-10
Garden City D-2
Garnett D-9
Girard E-10
Goodland B-1
Great Bend D-5
Greensburg E-4
Harper F-6
Hays C-4
Herington C-7
Hiawatha A-9
Hill City B-4
Hillsboro D-7
Hoisington D-5
Holton B-9
Horton B-9
Howard E-8
Hoxie B-3
Hugoton F-2
Humboldt E-9
Hutchinson D-6
Independence F-9
Iola D-9
Jetmore D-4
Johnson E-1
Junction City C-7
Kansas City C-10
Kinsley E-4
La Crosse D-4
Lakin D-2
Larned D-5
Lawrence C-9
Leavenworth B-10
Leoti D-2
Liberal F-2
Lincoln C-6
Lyndon C-9
Lyons D-6
Manhattan C-8
Mankato B-6
Marion D-7
Marysville B-8
McPherson D-6
Meade F-3
Medicine Lodge F-5
Minneapolis C-6
Mound City D-10
Mulvane E-7
Neodesha E-9
Ness City D-4
Newton D-7
Norton B-4
Oakley C-2
Oberlin B-3
Olathe C-10
Osage City C-9
Osawatomie D-10
Osborne B-5
Oskaloosa B-9
Oswego F-10
Ottawa C-9
Paola C-10
Parsons E-9
Peabody D-7
Phillipsburg B-4
Pittsburg E-10
Plainville B-4
Pratt E-5
Russell C-5
Sabetha A-9
St. Francis B-1
St. John D-5
St. Marys C-8
Salina C-6
Scott City D-2
Sedan F-8
Seneca B-8
Sharon Springs C-1
Shawnee C-10
Smith Center B-5
S. Hutchinson D-6
Sterling D-6
Sublette E-2
Syracuse D-1
Tonganoxie C-9
Topeka C-8
Tribune D-1
Troy B-9
Ulysses E-2
WaKeeney C-4
Wamego C-8
Washington B-7
Wellington F-7
Wichita E-7
Winfield F-7
Yates Center E-9

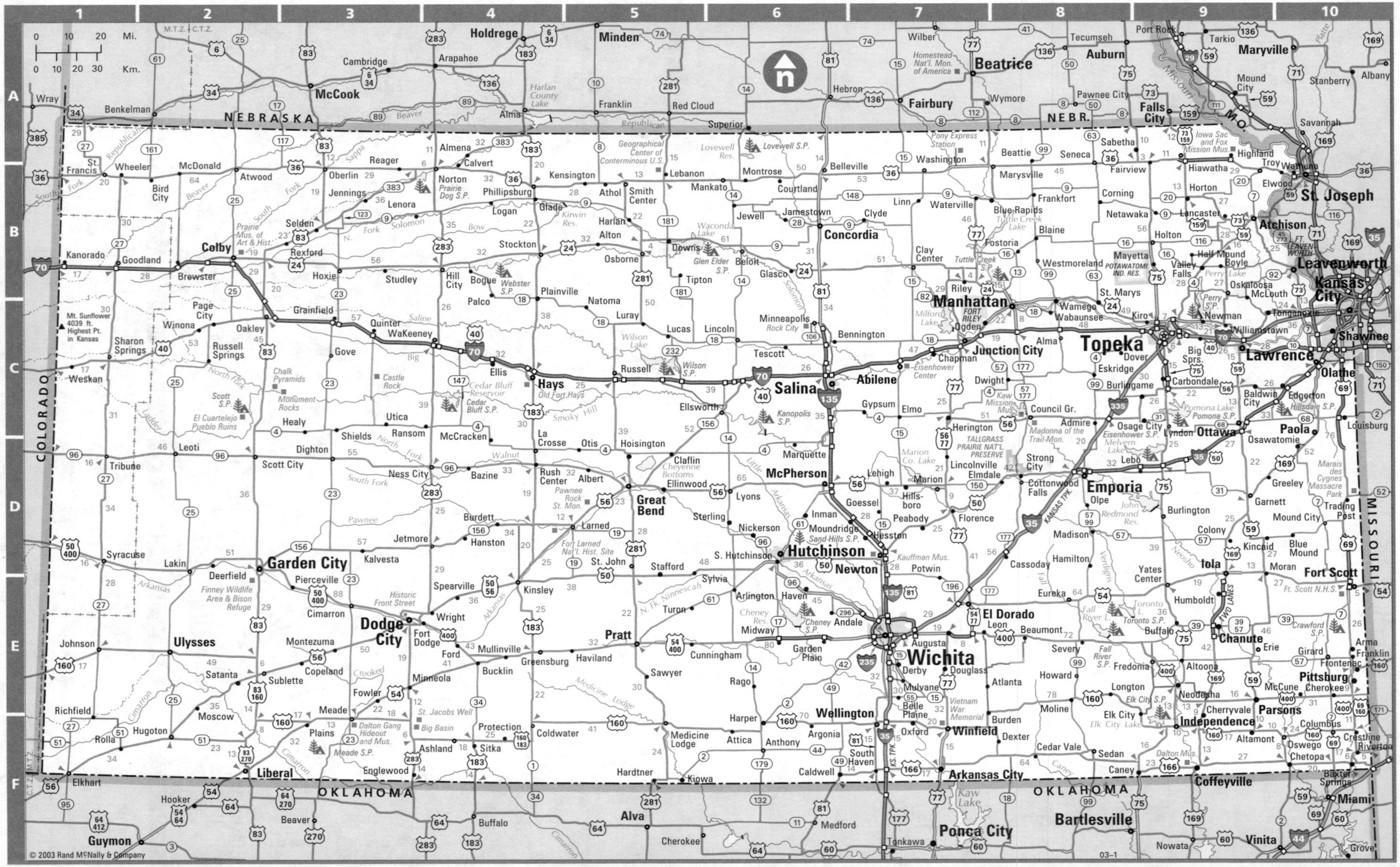

randmcnally.com
Express Access Code: KS

Louisiana

Population: 4,498,400 (1/1/01 estimate)
Land Area: 43,566 sq. mi.
Capital: Baton Rouge

Cities and Towns

Abbeville F-4
Alexandria D-4
Amite E-7
Arcadia A-3
Baldwin F-5
Bastrop A-5
Baton Rouge E-6
Benton A-2
Bogalusa D-8
Bossier City A-2
Breaux Bridge E-5
Bunkie D-4
Chalmette F-7
Clinton D-6
Colfax C-3
Columbia B-4
Coushatta B-2
Covington E-7
Crowley E-4
De Quincy E-2
De Ridder D-2
Delhi B-5
Denham Springs E-6
Donaldsonville F-6
Erath F-4
Eunice E-4
Farmerville A-4
Ferriday C-5
Franklin F-5
Franklinton D-7
Gramercy F-6
Grand Isle G-7
Greensburg D-6
Gretna F-7
Hahnville F-7
Hammond E-7
Harrisonburg C-5
Haynesville A-3
Homer A-3
Houma F-6
Iowa E-3
Jackson D-6
Jeanerette F-5
Jena C-4
Jennings E-3
Jonesboro B-3
Kaplan F-4
Kentwood D-7
Kinder E-3
La Place F-7
Lafayette E-4
Lake Arthur F-3
Lake Charles E-3
Lake Providence A-6
Leesville D-2
Livingston E-6
Mamou E-4
Mandeville E-7
Mansfield B-2
Many C-2
Marksville D-4
Metairie F-7
Minden A-3
Monroe A-4
Morgan City F-6
Napoleonville F-6
Natchitoches C-3
New Iberia F-5
New Orleans F-7
New Roads E-5
Oak Grove A-5
Oakdale D-3
Oberlin E-3
Opelousas E-4
Patterson F-5
Plaquemine E-6
Ponchatoula E-7
Port Allen E-6
Port Sulphur G-8
Raceland F-7
Rayne E-4
Rayville B-5
Ruston A-3
St. Francisville D-5
St. Joseph B-6
St. Martinville F-5
Scotlandville E-6
Shreveport A-2
Slidell E-8
Springhill A-2
Sulphur E-2
Tallulah B-6
Thibodaux F-6
Vidalia C-5
Ville Platte E-4
Vivian A-1
Walker E-6
Welsh E-3
West Monroe A-4
Winnfield B-3
Winnsboro B-5

ARKANSAS
MISSISSIPPI
TEXAS
GULF OF MEXICO
Shreveport
Bossier City
Monroe
Alexandria
Lafayette
Lake Charles
Baton Rouge
New Orleans
Metairie
Houma
Jackson
Vicksburg
Natchez
Hattiesburg
Biloxi
Gulfport
Beaumont
Port Arthur
Meridian
Laurel
0 10 20 Mi.
0 10 20 30 Km.
© 2003 Rand McNally & Company
03-1

Maine

Population:
1,281,100 (1/1/01 estimate)

Land Area: 30,865 sq. mi.

Capital: Augusta

Cities and Towns

Andover	F-1
Ashland	C-4
Auburn	H-2
Augusta	G-2
Bailey Island	H-2
Bangor	F-4
Bar Harbor	G-5
Bath	H-2
Belfast	G-4
Bethel	G-1
Biddeford	I-1
Bingham	F-2
Blue Hill	G-4
Boothbay Harbor	H-3
Brewer	F-4
Bridgewater	C-5
Bridgton	H-1
Brownville Jct.	E-3
Brunswick	H-2
Bucksport	G-4
Calais	E-6
Camden	G-3
Caribou	B-5
Castine	G-4
Chebeague Island	H-2
Corinna	F-3
Cornish	H-1
Damariscotta	H-3
Danforth	D-5
Deer Isle	G-4
Dexter	F-3
Dixfield	G-1
Dover-Foxcroft	E-3
Eagle Lake	B-4
East Corinth	F-3
East Machias	F-6
East Millinocket	E-4
Eastport	F-6
Ellsworth	G-4
Fairfield	G-3
Falmouth	H-2
Farmington	F-2
Fort Fairfield	B-5
Fort Kent	A-4
Freeport	H-2
Frenchville	A-4
Friendship	H-3
Fryeburg	H-1
Gardiner	G-2
Gorham	H-1
Gray	H-2
Greenville	E-3
Guilford	E-3
Hampden	F-4
Harrington	G-5
Harrison	H-1
Houlton	D-5
Howland	E-4
Jackman	E-2
Jonesport	G-6
Kennebunk	I-1
Kennebunkport	I-1
Kingfield	F-2
Kittery	J-1
Lewiston	H-2
Limestone	B-5
Lincoln	E-4
Livermore Falls	G-2
Lubec	F-6
Machias	F-6
Madawaska	A-4
Madison	F-2
Mars Hill	C-5
Mattawamkeag	E-4
Medway	E-4
Mexico	G-1
Milbridge	G-5
Millinocket	D-4
Milo	E-4
Monson	E-3
Monticello	C-5
Naples	H-1
Newport	F-3
Norridgewock	F-2
North Anson	F-2
North Berwick	I-1
North Bridgton	H-1
Northeast Harbor	G-5
Norway	G-1
Ogunquit	I-1
Old Town	F-4
Orono	F-4
Patten	D-4
Phillips	F-2
Pine Point	I-2
Pittsfield	F-3
Poland	H-2
Port Clyde	H-3
Portage	B-4
Portland	H-2
Presque Isle	B-5
Princeton	E-6
Rangeley	F-1
Rockland	H-3
Rumford	G-1
Saco	I-1
Sanford	I-1
Searsport	G-4
Sebago Lake	H-1
Sherman Station	D-4
Skowhegan	F-3
Solon	F-2
South China	G-3
South Paris	G-1
Standish	H-1
Stockton Springs	G-4
Stonington	G-4
Stratton	E-2
Thomaston	H-3
Turner	G-2
Union	G-3
Unity	G-3
Van Buren	B-5
Vinalhaven	H-4
Waldoboro	H-3
Washburn	B-5
Waterville	G-3
Wells	I-1
West Enfield	E-4
Westbrook	H-2
Wilton	G-2
Windham	H-1
Winslow	G-3
Winterport	F-4
Winthrop	G-2
Woodland	E-6
Yarmouth	H-2
York Beach	I-1
York Harbor	I-1

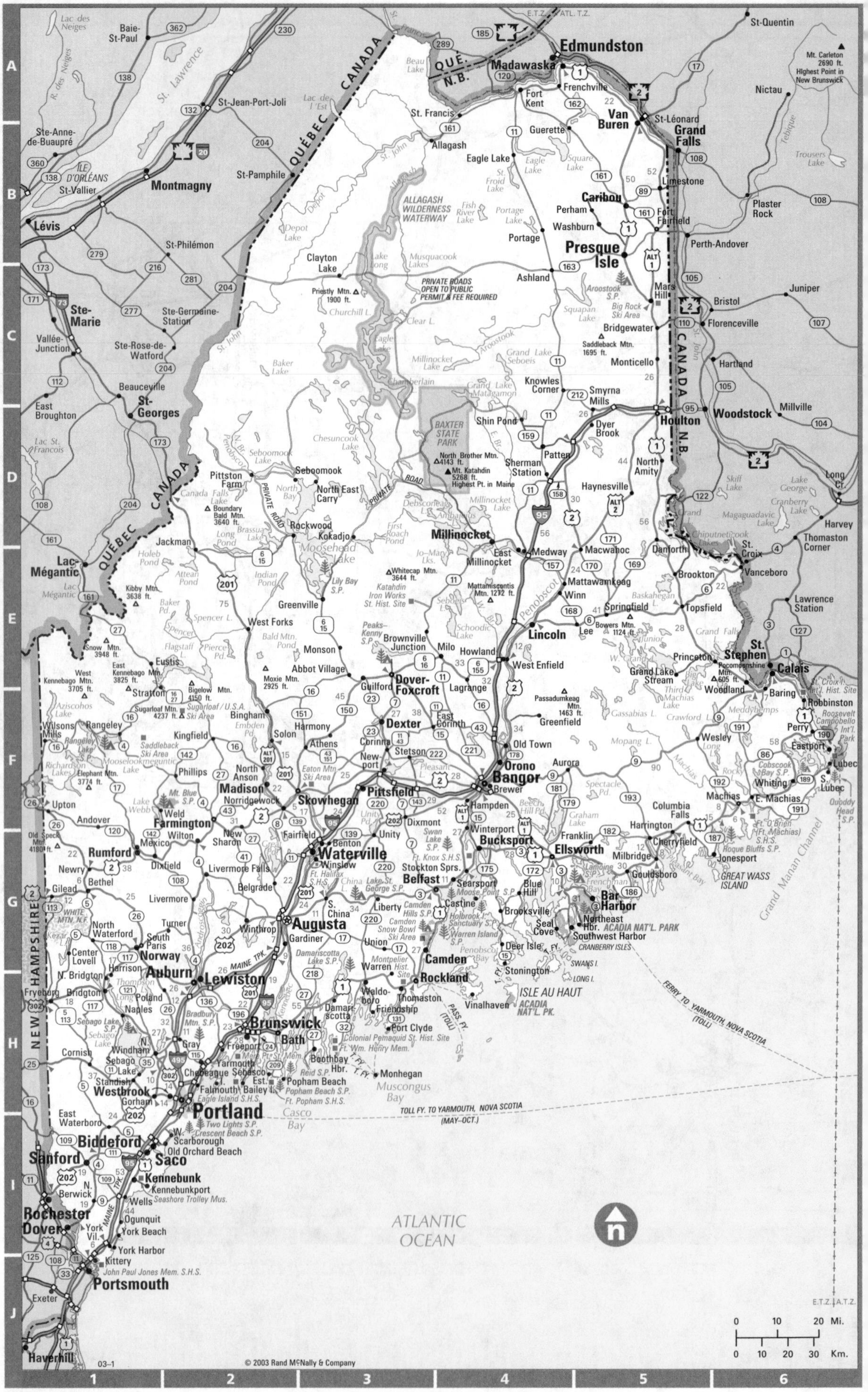

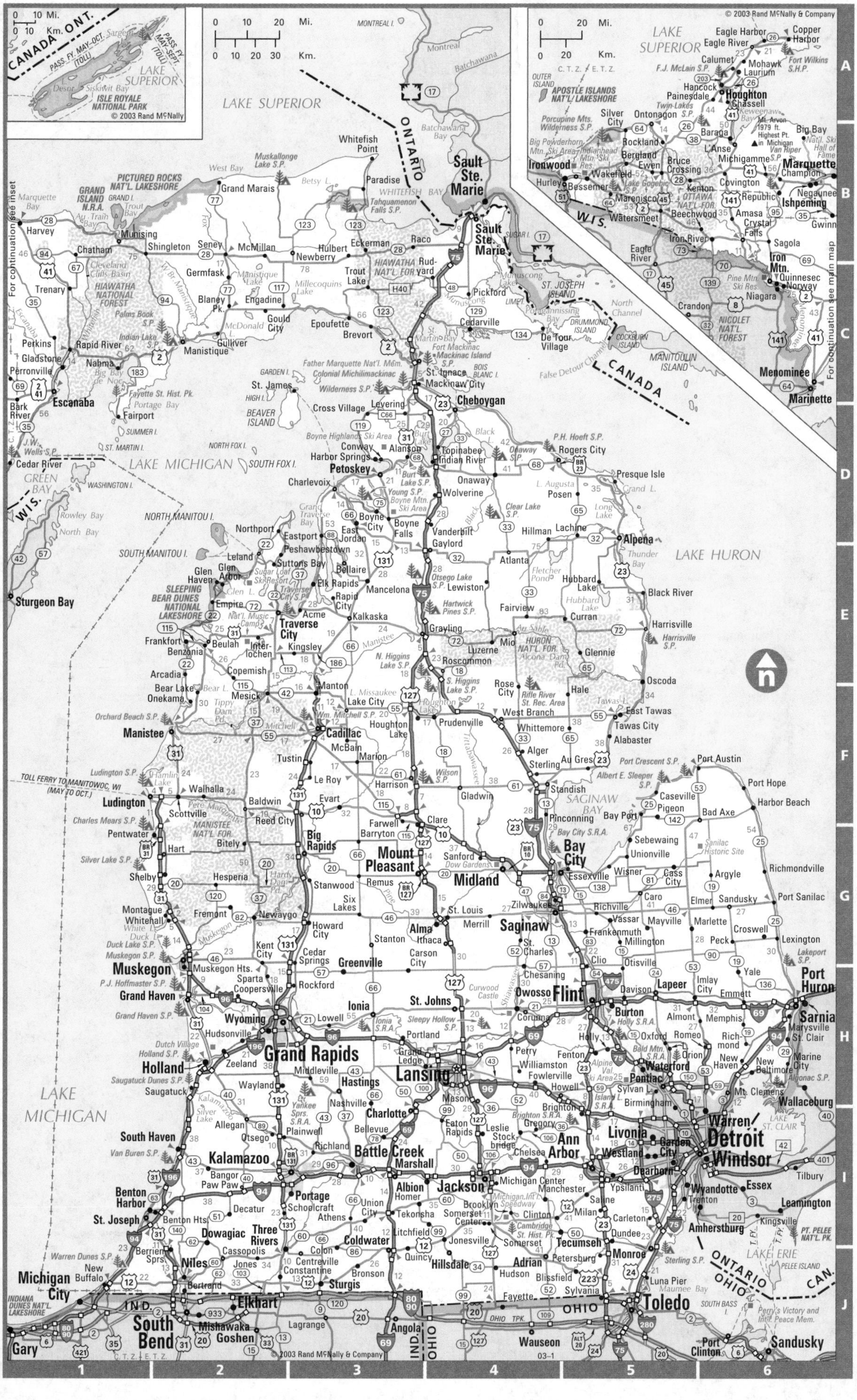
CANADA ONT.
LAKE SUPERIOR
ISLE ROYALE NATIONAL PARK
© 2003 Rand McNally
ONTARIO
Sault Ste. Marie
Whitefish Point
Paradise
Grand Marais
PICTURED ROCKS NAT'L. LAKESHORE
Munising
Newberry
Manistique
Escanaba
Gladstone
St. Ignace
Mackinaw City
Cheboygan
Rogers City
Petoskey
Charlevoix
Presque Isle
Gaylord
Alpena
LAKE HURON
LAKE MICHIGAN
Sturgeon Bay
SLEEPING BEAR DUNES NATIONAL LAKESHORE
Traverse City
Grayling
Oscoda
Cadillac
Manistee
Ludington
East Tawas
Mount Pleasant
Midland
Bay City
Saginaw
SAGINAW BAY
Port Austin
Harbor Beach
Muskegon
Grand Haven
Grand Rapids
Holland
Lansing
Flint
Port Huron
Sarnia
Kalamazoo
Battle Creek
Jackson
Ann Arbor
Detroit
Windsor
LAKE ST. CLAIR
LAKE ERIE
Toledo
Sandusky
Benton Harbor
St. Joseph
Michigan City
South Bend
Elkhart
Gary
IND.
OHIO
ONTARIO
CAN.
WIS.
LAKE SUPERIOR
Houghton
Marquette
Ishpeming
Ironwood
Iron Mtn.
Menominee
Marinette
CANADA
For continuation see inset
For continuation see main map
© 2003 Rand McNally & Company
A
B
C
D
E
F
G
H
I
J
1
2
3
4
5
6

Michigan

Population: 10,015,000 (1/1/01 estimate)

Land Area: 56,809 sq. mi.

Capital: Lansing

Cities and Towns

Adrian	J-4
Albion	I-4
Allegan	I-2
Alma	G-4
Alpena	D-5
Ann Arbor	I-5
Bad Axe	F-6
Baldwin	F-2
Battle Creek	I-3
Bay City	G-4
Bellaire	E-3
Benton Harbor	I-1
Benton Heights	I-2
Berrien Springs	J-2
Bessemer	B-5
Big Rapids	G-3
Birmingham	I-5
Boyne City	D-3
Brighton	I-5
Burton	H-5
Cadillac	F-3
Caro	G-5
Cass City	G-5
Cassopolis	J-2
Cedar Springs	G-3
Centreville	J-3
Charlevoix	D-3
Charlotte	I-3
Cheboygan	D-4
Chelsea	I-4
Clare	F-3
Clio	H-5
Coldwater	J-3
Corunna	H-4
Croswell	G-6
Crystal Falls	B-6
Davison	H-5
Dearborn	I-5
Detroit	I-5
Dowagiac	I-2
East Tawas	F-5
Escanaba	C-1
Evart	F-3
Fenton	H-5
Flint	H-5
Frankenmuth	G-5
Frankfort	E-2
Fremont	G-2
Garden City	I-5
Gaylord	E-4
Gladstone	C-1
Gladwin	F-4
Grand Haven	H-2
Grand Ledge	H-4
Grand Rapids	H-2
Grayling	E-3
Greenville	H-3
Hancock	A-6
Harbor Beach	F-6
Harbor Springs	D-3
Harrison	F-3
Hart	G-2
Hastings	H-3
Hillsdale	J-4
Holland	H-2
Holly	H-5
Houghton	A-6
Howell	H-4
Hudson	J-4
Hudsonville	H-2
Imlay City	H-5
Ionia	H-3
Iron Mountain	C-6
Iron River	B-6
Ironwood	B-5
Ishpeming	B-6
Ithaca	G-4
Jackson	I-4
Jonesville	I-4
Kalamazoo	I-3
Kalkaska	E-3
L'Anse	B-6
Lake City	F-3
Lansing	H-4
Lapeer	H-5
Livonia	I-5
Ludington	F-1
Mackinaw City	C-3
Manistee	F-2
Manistique	C-2
Marlette	G-5
Marquette	B-6
Marshall	I-3
Marysville	H-6
Mason	H-4
Menominee	C-6
Midland	G-4
Monroe	J-5
Mount Clemens	H-6
Mount Pleasant	G-3
Munising	B-1
Muskegon	G-2
Muskegon Heights	H-2
Negaunee	B-6
New Buffalo	J-1
Newberry	B-3
Niles	J-2
Norway	C-6
Ontonagon	B-5
Owosso	H-4
Paw Paw	I-2
Petoskey	D-3
Plainwell	I-2
Pontiac	H-5
Port Huron	H-6
Portage	I-3
Reed City	F-3
Rockford	H-3
Rogers City	D-4
Saginaw	G-4
St. Clair	H-6
St. Ignace	C-3
St. Johns	H-4
St. Joseph	I-1
Saline	I-5
Sandusky	G-6
Sault Ste. Marie	B-4
South Haven	I-2
Sparta	H-2
Standish	F-4
Sturgis	J-3
Tawas City	F-5
Tecumseh	I-4
Three Rivers	J-2
Traverse City	E-2
Trenton	I-5
Vassar	G-5
Wakefield	B-5
Warren	I-6
West Branch	F-4
Westland	I-5
Wyandotte	I-5
Wyoming	H-2
Ypsilanti	I-5
Zeeland	H-2

Minnesota

Population: 4,985,800 (1/1/01 estimate)
Land Area: 79,617 sq. mi.
Capital: St. Paul

Cities and Towns

Ada	E-1
Aitkin	F-4
Albert Lea	J-4
Alexandria	G-2
Anoka	H-4
Aurora	D-5
Austin	J-5
Bagley	D-2
Barnesville	F-1
Baudette	C-3
Belle Plaine	H-4
Bemidji	D-3
Benson	G-2
Big Lake	G-4
Biwabik	D-5
Blooming Prairie	J-5
Blue Earth	J-3
Brainerd	F-3
Breckenridge	F-1
Buffalo	H-4
Caledonia	J-6
Cambridge	G-4
Cannon Falls	I-5
Chaska	H-4
Chatfield	J-5
Chisholm	D-5
Cloquet	E-5
Cokato	H-3
Crookston	D-1
Crosby	F-4
Delano	H-4
Detroit Lakes	E-2
Duluth	E-5
East Grand Forks	D-1
Elbow Lake	G-2
Elk River	H-4
Ely	D-6
Eveleth	D-5
Fairmont	J-3
Faribault	I-4
Farmington	H-4
Fergus Falls	F-2
Foley	G-4
Forest Lake	H-5
Gaylord	I-3
Glencoe	H-3
Glenwood	G-2
Grand Marais	B-6
Grand Rapids	E-4
Granite Falls	H-2
Hallock	C-1
Hastings	H-5
Hawley	E-1
Hutchinson	H-3
International Falls	C-4
Ivanhoe	I-1
Jackson	J-3
Jordan	H-4
Kasson	I-5
La Crescent	J-6
Lake City	I-5
Lake Crystal	I-3
Lakeland	H-5
Le Sueur	I-4
Litchfield	H-3
Little Falls	G-3
Long Prairie	G-3
Luverne	J-1
Madelia	I-3
Madison	H-1
Mahnomen	E-2
Mankato	I-4
Marshall	I-2
Milaca	G-4
Minneapolis	H-4
Montevideo	H-2
Montgomery	I-4
Monticello	G-4
Moorhead	E-1
Moose Lake	F-5
Mora	G-4
Nashwauk	E-4
New Prague	I-4
New Ulm	I-3
Northfield	I-4
Olivia	H-3
Ortonville	G-1
Owatonna	I-4
Park Rapids	E-3
Paynesville	G-3
Perham	F-2
Pine City	G-5
Pine Island	I-5
Pipestone	I-1
Plainview	I-5
Preston	J-6
Princeton	G-4
Red Lake Falls	D-1
Red Wing	I-5
Redwood Falls	I-2
Rochester	I-5
Roseau	B-2
St. Cloud	G-3
St. James	I-3
St. Joseph	G-3
St. Paul	H-5
St. Peter	I-4
Sandstone	F-5
Sauk Centre	G-3
Sauk Rapids	G-3
Savage	H-4
Shakopee	H-4
Silver Bay	E-6
Slayton	I-2
Sleepy Eye	I-3
Spring Valley	J-5
Springfield	I-3
Staples	F-3
Stewartville	J-5
Stillwater	H-5
Thief River Falls	D-2
Tracy	I-2
Two Harbors	E-6
Tyler	I-1
Virginia	D-5
Wabasha	I-6
Wadena	F-2
Walker	E-3
Warren	C-1
Waseca	I-4
Wells	J-4
Wheaton	G-1
White Bear Lake	H-5
Willmar	H-3
Windom	J-2
Winona	I-6
Worthington	J-2
Zimmerman	G-4

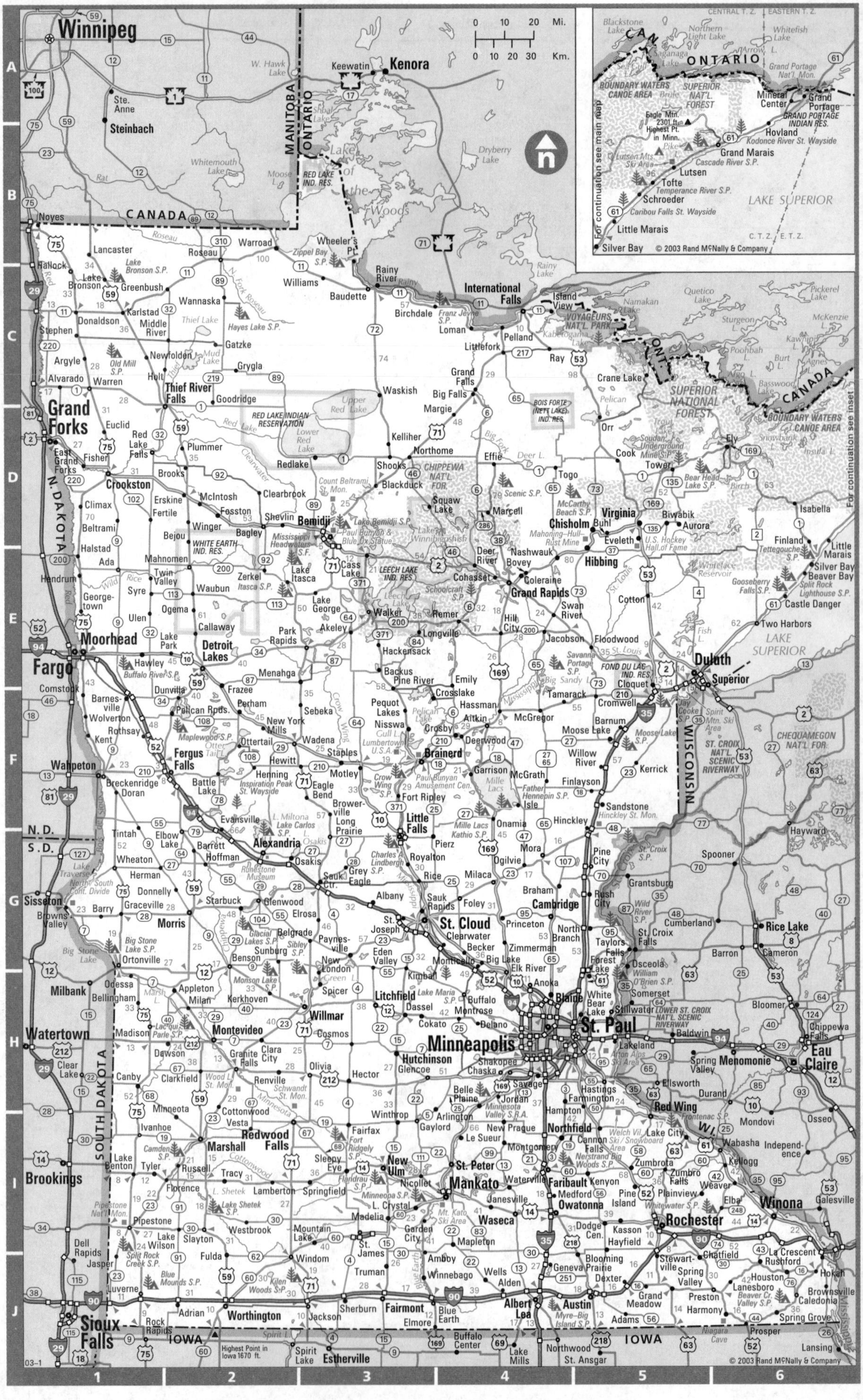

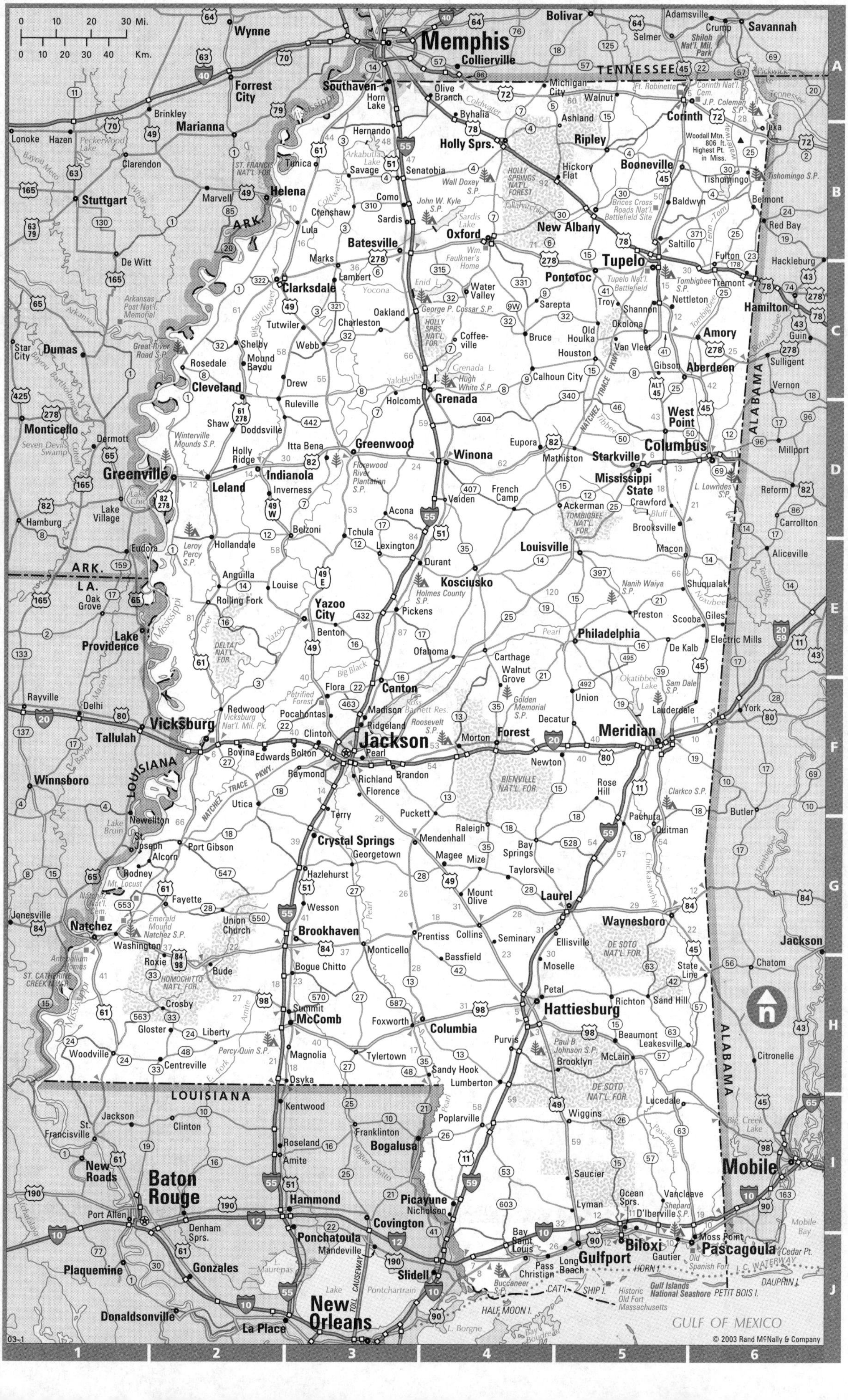

Mississippi

Population: 2,876,200 (1/1/01 estimate)
Land Area: 46,914 sq. mi.
Capital: Jackson

Cities and Towns

Missouri

Population: 5,653,400 (1/1/01 estimate)
Land Area: 68,898 sq. mi.
Capital: Jefferson City

Cities and Towns

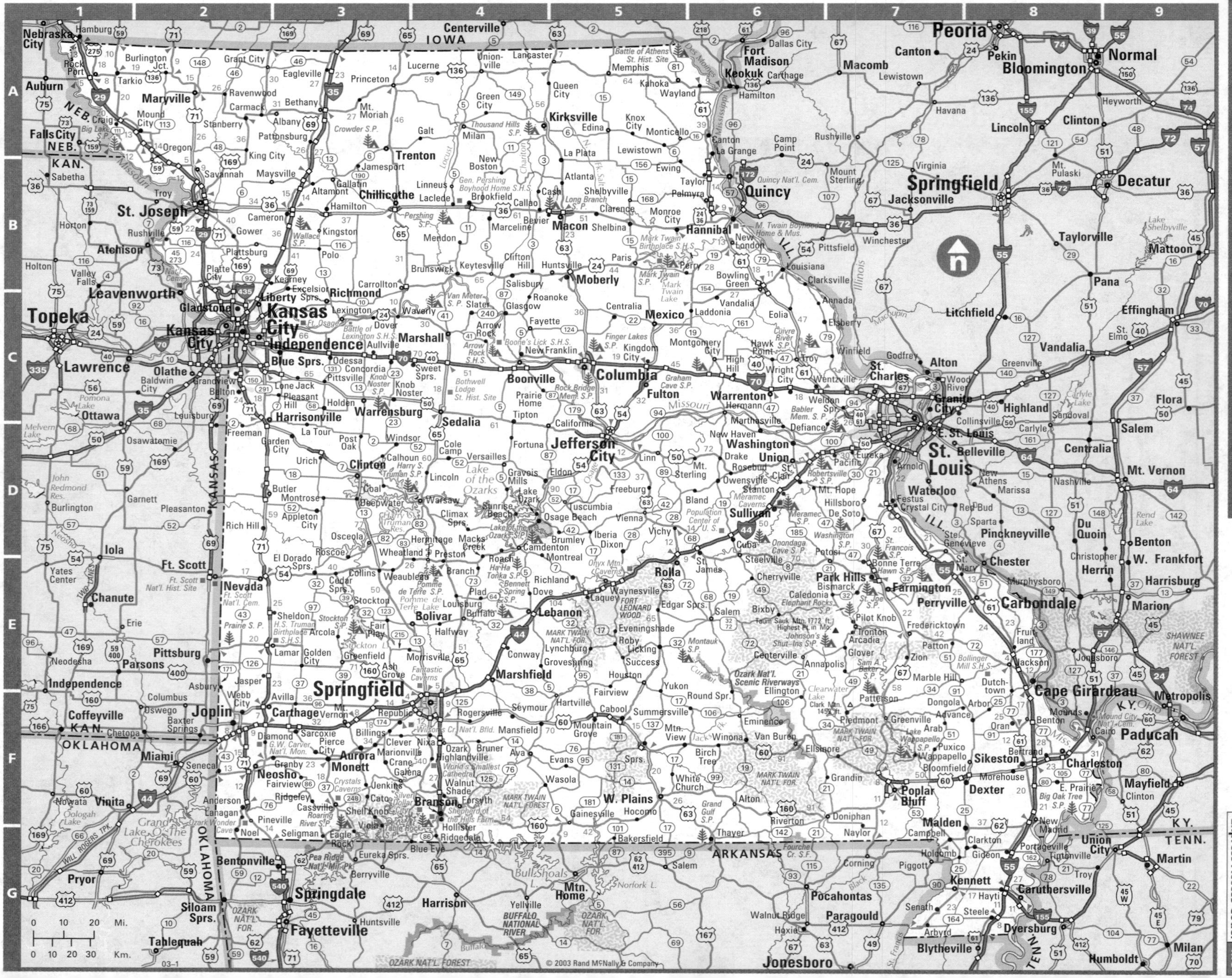

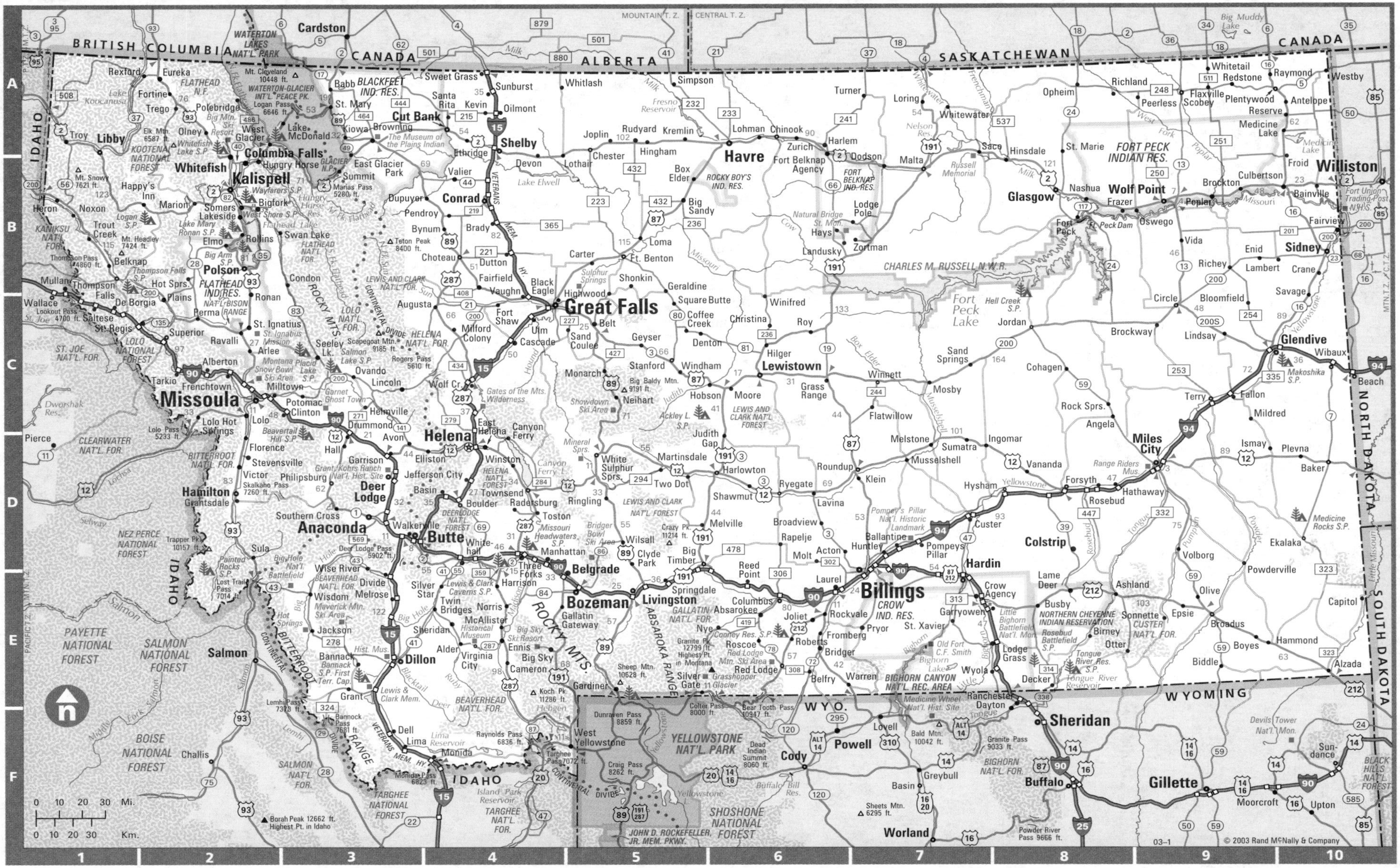

Montana

Population: 915,500 (1/1/01 estimate)
Land Area: 145,556 sq. mi.
Capital: Helena

Cities and Towns

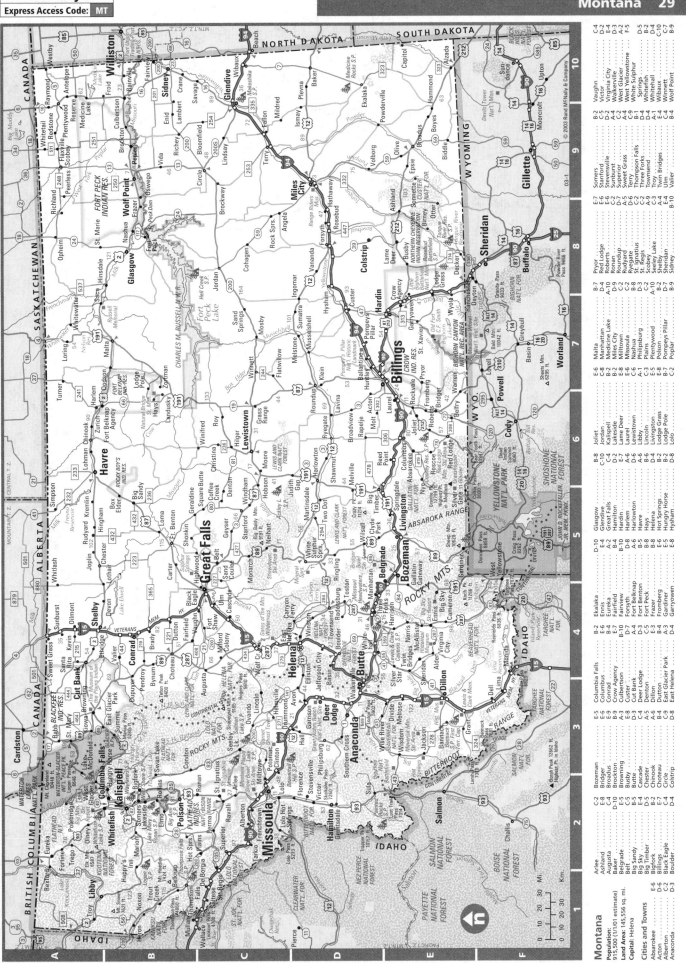

randmcnally.com
Express Access Code: NE

Nebraska

Population: 1,727,700 (1/1/01 estimate)
Land Area: 76,878 sq. mi.
Capital: Lincoln

Cities and Towns

Ainsworth B-5
Albion C-7
Alliance B-2
Alma E-6
Arapahoe E-5
Arthur C-3
Ashland D-9
Atkinson B-6
Auburn E-10
Aurora D-7
Bartlett C-7
Bassett B-6
Bayard C-2
Beatrice E-9
Beaver City E-5
Bellevue D-9
Benkelman E-3
Blair C-9
Bloomfield B-8
Brewster C-5
Bridgeport C-2
Broken Bow C-5
Burwell C-6
Butte A-6
Cambridge E-5
Center B-7
Central City D-7
Chadron A-2
Chappell D-3
Clay Center E-7
Columbus C-8
Cozad D-5
Crawford B-2
Crete D-8
Dakota City B-9
David City D-8
Eagle D-9
Elwood E-5
Fairbury E-8
Falls City E-10
Franklin E-6
Fremont C-9
Friend D-8
Fullerton C-7
Geneva E-8
Genoa C-8
Gering C-1
Gibbon D-6
Gordon A-3
Gothenburg D-5
Grand Island D-7
Grant D-3
Greeley C-7
Harrisburg C-1
Harrison B-1
Hartington B-8
Hastings E-7
Hayes Center E-4
Hebron E-8
Holdrege E-6
Hyannis C-3
Imperial E-3
Kearney D-6
Kimball D-1
Laurel B-8
Lexington D-5
Lincoln D-9
Louisville D-9
Loup City D-6
Lyons C-9
Madison C-8
McCook E-4
Milford D-8
Minden E-6
Mitchell C-1
Mullen C-4
Nebraska City D-10
Neligh B-7
Nelson E-7
Norfolk C-8
North Bend C-9
North Platte D-4
O'Neill B-7
Oakland C-9
Ogallala D-3
Omaha D-9
Ord C-6
Osceola D-8
Oshkosh C-3
Papillion D-9
Pawnee City E-9
Pender B-9
Peru E-10
Pierce B-8
Plainview B-7
Plattsmouth D-9
Ponca B-9
Randolph B-8
Ravenna D-6
Red Cloud E-7
Rushville B-3
St. Paul D-7
Schuyler C-8
Scottsbluff C-1
Scribner C-9
Seward D-8
Sidney D-2
South Sioux City B-9
Springview A-5
Stanton C-8
Stapleton C-5
Stockville E-5
Stromsburg D-8
Superior E-7
Sutherland D-4
Sutton E-7
Syracuse D-9
Taylor C-6
Tecumseh E-9
Tekamah C-9
Thedford C-5
Trenton E-4
Tryon C-4
Valentine A-5
Valley D-9
Waverly D-9
Wayne B-8
West Point C-9
Wilber E-8
Wisner C-8
Wood River D-7
Wymore E-9
York D-8

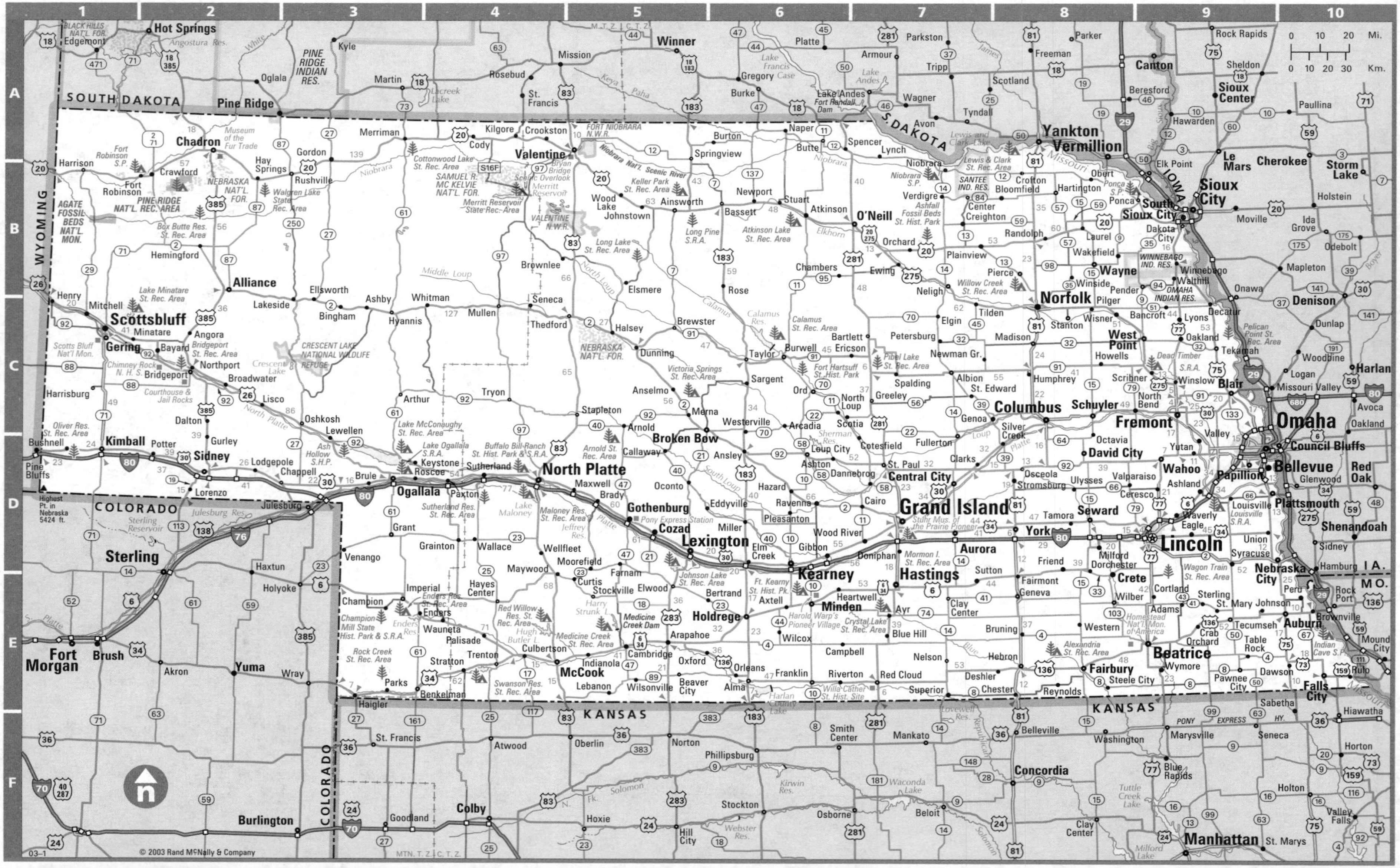

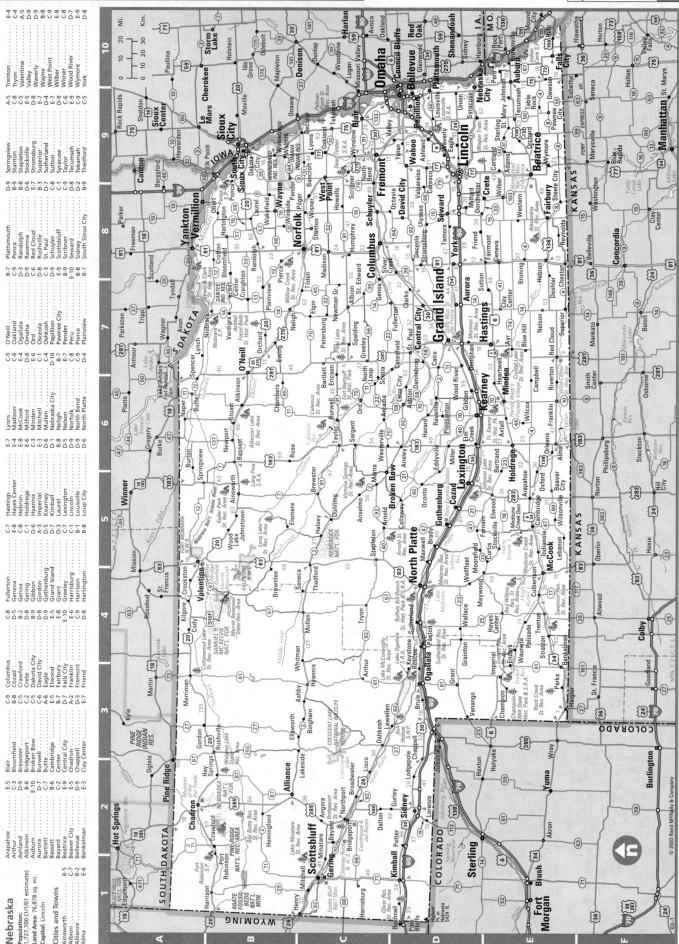

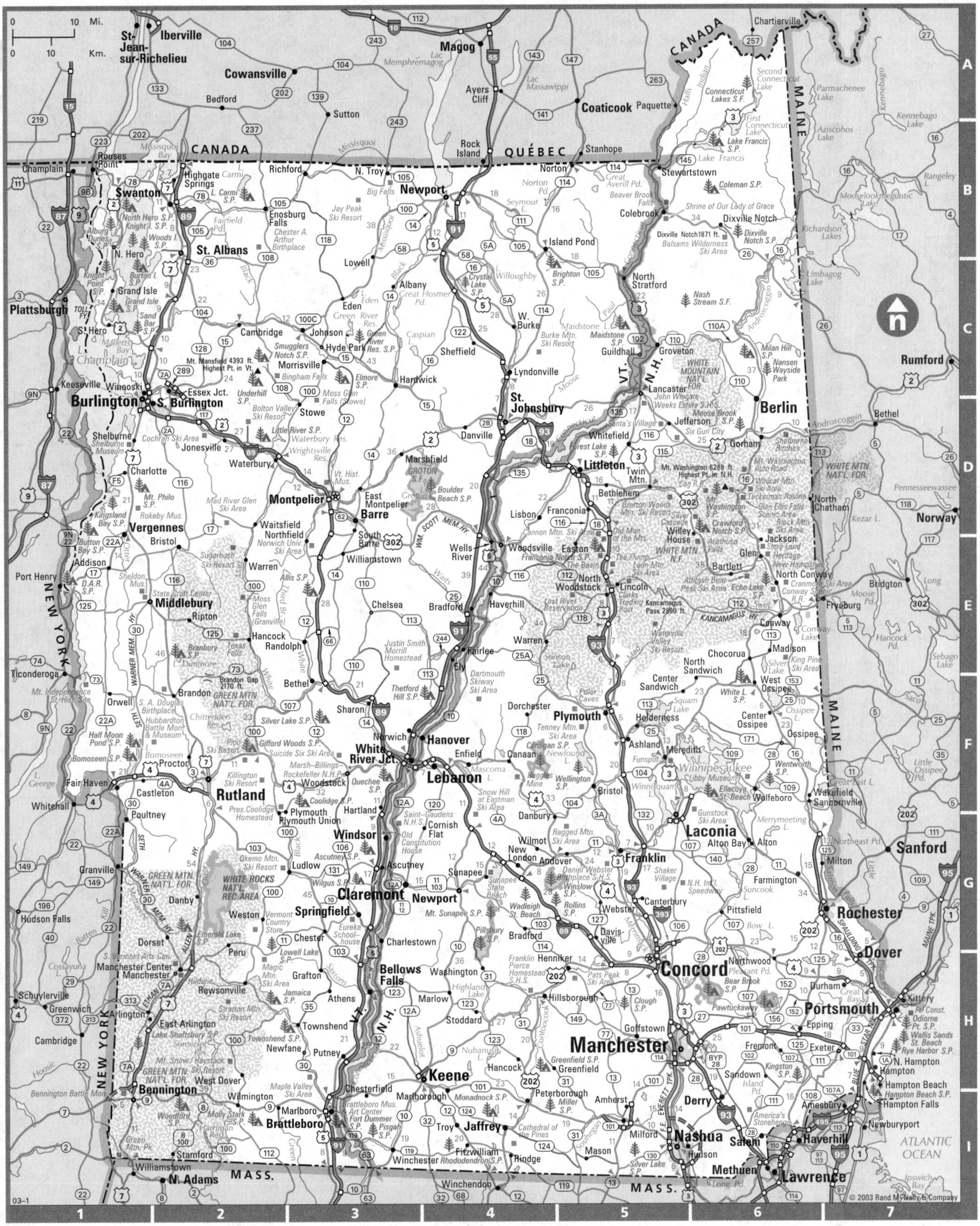

New Hampshire

Population: 1,251,300 (1/1/01 estimate)

Land Area: 8,969 sq. mi.

Capital: Concord

Cities and Towns

Ashland F-5
Berlin D-6
Bristol F-5
Charlestown G-3
Claremont G-3
Concord H-5
Conway E-6
Derry I-6
Dover H-7
Durham H-7
Enfield F-4
Epping H-6
Exeter H-7
Farmington G-6
Franklin G-5
Goffstown H-5
Gorham D-6
Groveton C-5
Hampton H-7
Hampton Beach H-7
Hanover F-4
Henniker H-5
Hillsboro H-4
Hudson I-6
Jaffrey I-4
Keene H-4
Laconia G-5
Lancaster C-5
Lebanon F-4
Lisbon D-4
Littleton D-5
Manchester H-5
Marlborough H-4
Meredith F-5
Milford I-5
Nashua I-5
New London G-4
Newport G-4
North Conway E-6
Ossipee F-6
Peterborough I-4
Pittsfield G-6
Plymouth F-5
Portsmouth H-7
Rochester G-7
Salem I-6
Troy I-4
Whitefield D-5
Winchester I-3
Wolfeboro F-6
Woodsville E-4

Vermont

Population: 614,600 (1/1/01 estimate)

Land Area: 9,249 sq. mi.

Capital: Montpelier

Cities and Towns

Barre D-3
Bellows Falls H-3
Bennington I-1
Brandon F-2
Brattleboro I-3
Bristol E-2
Burlington C-1
Chelsea E-3
Enosburg Falls B-2
Essex Junction C-2
Fair Haven F-1
Guildhall C-5
Hardwick C-3
Hyde Park C-3
Island Pond B-4
Johnson C-3
Ludlow G-3
Lyndonville C-4
Manchester H-2
Manchester Cen. H-2
Middlebury E-2
Montpelier D-3
Newfane H-3
Newport B-4
North Hero B-1
Northfield E-3
Poultney G-1
Proctor F-2
Putney H-3
Richford B-3
Rutland F-2
St. Albans B-2
St. Johnsbury D-4
South Barre D-3
South Burlington D-2
Springfield G-3
Swanton B-2
Vergennes D-1
Waterbury D-2
White River Jct. F-3
Windsor G-3
Winooski C-1
Woodstock F-3

randmcnally.com
Express Access Code: NJ

New Jersey

Population: 8,495,500 (1/1/01 estimate)
Land Area: 7,419 sq. mi.
Capital: Trenton

Cities and Towns

Absecon	H-4
Asbury Park	E-5
Atlantic City	I-4
Atlantic Highlands	E-5
Audubon	G-2
Barnegat Light	G-5
Bayonne	D-5
Beach Haven	H-5
Beachwood	F-5
Belleville	C-5
Belvidere	C-2
Berlin	G-3
Bernardsville	C-4
Blackwood	G-2
Bloomfield	C-5
Boonton	C-4
Bordentown	F-3
Bound Brook	D-4
Bridgeton	H-2
Bridgewater	D-4
Brigantine	H-4
Browns Mills	F-4
Budd Lake	C-3
Buena	H-3
Burlington	F-3
Butler	B-4
Caldwell	C-5
Camden	F-2
Cape May	J-3
Cape May Court House	J-3
Cherry Hill	F-3
Clark	D-4
Clifton	C-5
Cranford	D-4
Denville	C-4
Dover	C-4
Dumont	C-5
East Orange	C-5
Eatontown	E-5
Edison	D-4
Egg Harbor City	H-4
Elizabeth	D-5
Englewood	C-5
Ewing	E-3
Flemington	D-3
Franklin	B-4
Freehold	E-5
Glassboro	G-2
Gloucester City	G-2
Hackensack	C-5
Hackettstown	C-3
Hammonton	G-3
High Bridge	D-3
Highlands	E-5
Hightstown	E-4
Hopatcong	C-3
Irvington	C-5
Iselin	D-4
Jamesburg	E-4
Jersey City	C-5
Keansburg	D-5
Lakehurst	F-5
Lakewood	F-5
Lambertville	E-3
Lawrenceville	E-3
Linden	D-5
Little Silver	E-5
Long Branch	E-5
Madison	C-4
Mahwah	B-5
Manville	D-4
Margate City	I-4
Matawan	E-5
Mays Landing	H-3
Metuchen	D-4
Millville	H-2
Morris Plains	C-4
Morristown	C-4
Mount Holly	F-3
Neptune City	E-5
Netcong	C-3
New Brunswick	D-4
New Providence	C-4
Newark	C-5
Newfoundland	B-4
Newton	B-3
North Bergen	C-5
Oakland	B-5
Ocean City	I-4
Ocean Grove	E-5
Old Bridge	E-4
Palisades Park	C-5
Paramus	B-5
Passaic	C-5
Paterson	C-5
Paulsboro	G-2
Penns Grove	G-1
Pennsauken	F-2
Pennsville	G-1
Perth Amboy	D-5
Phillipsburg	C-2
Plainfield	D-4
Pleasantville	H-4
Point Pleasant	F-5
Princeton	E-3
Rahway	D-5
Ramsey	B-5
Raritan	D-4
Red Bank	E-5
Ridgewood	B-5
Salem	H-1
Sayreville	D-4
Scotch Plains	D-4
Sea Bright	E-5
Sea Isle City	I-3
Seaside Park	F-5
Ship Bottom	G-5
Somerdale	G-2
Somers Point	I-4
Somerville	D-4
South River	D-4
Sparta	B-4
Spring Lake	E-5
Stratford	G-2
Toms River	F-5
Trenton	E-3
Tuckerton	H-4
Union	C-5
Ventnor City	I-4
Villas	J-3
Vineland	H-2
Waldwick	B-5
Wanaque	B-5
Washington	C-3
West Orange	C-5
Wildwood	J-3
Williamstown	G-3
Willingboro	F-3
Woodbury	G-2
Woodstown	G-2
Wrightstown	F-4
Wyckoff	B-5

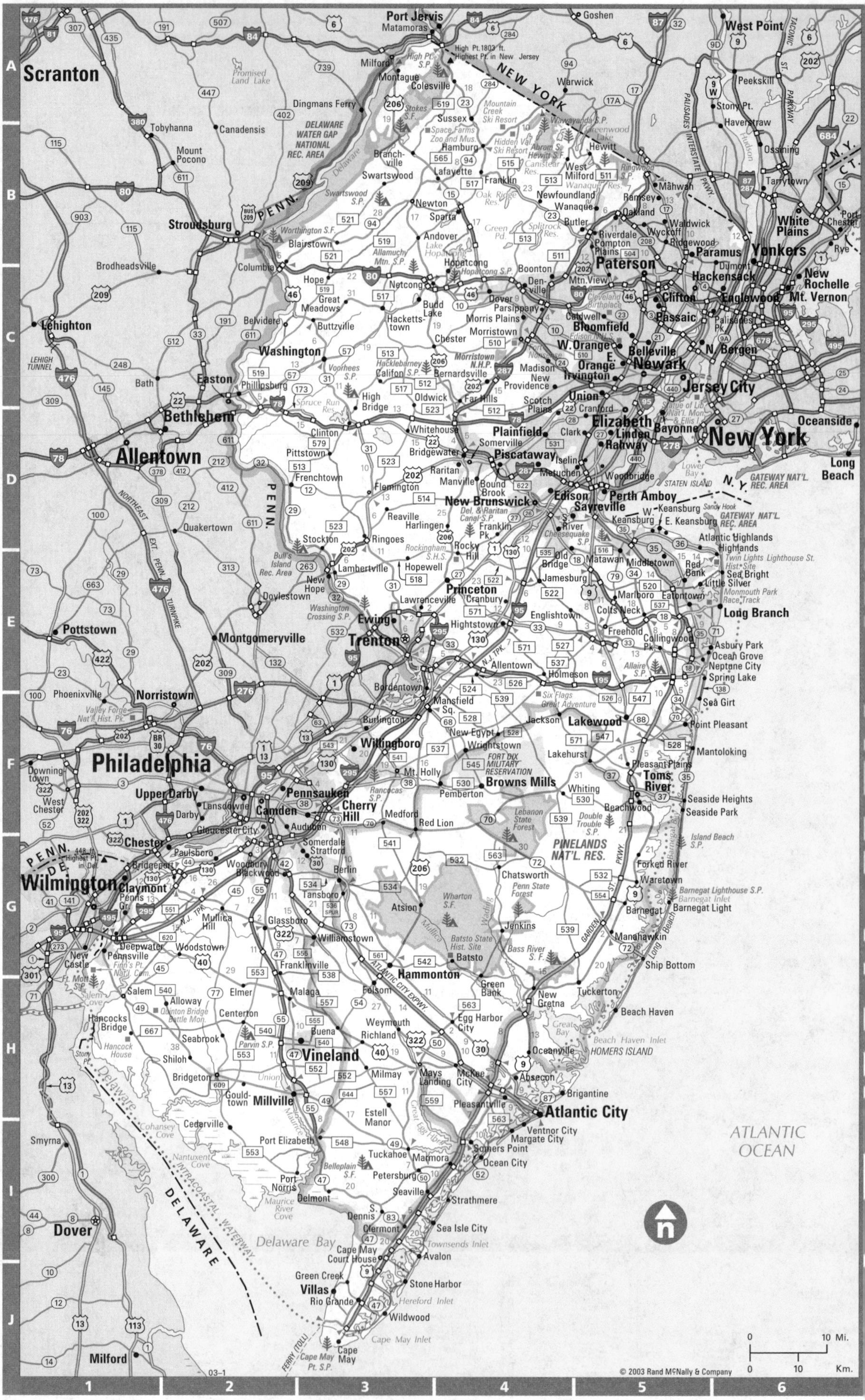

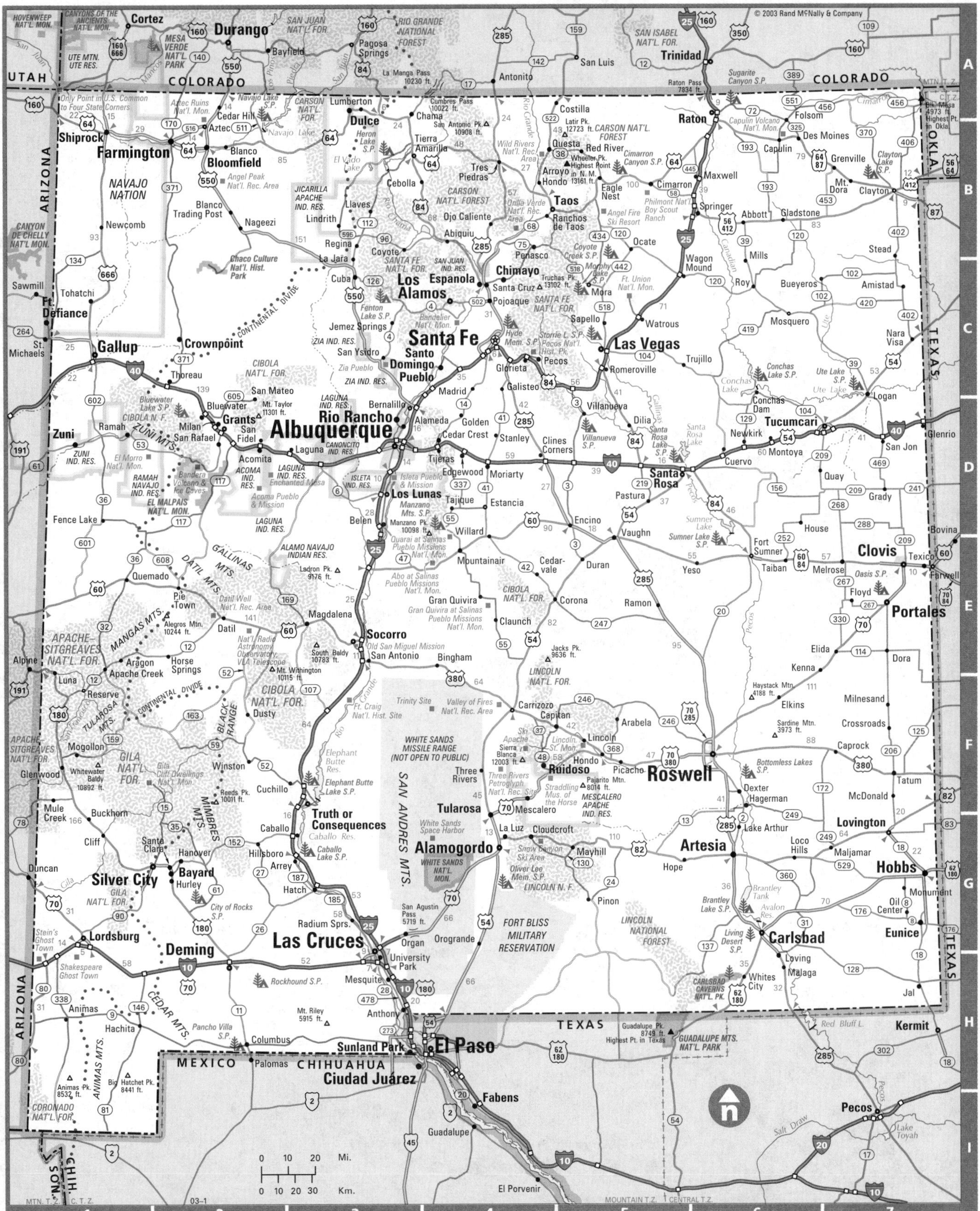

New Mexico

Population: 1,856,500 (1/1/01 estimate)
Land Area: 121,364 sq. mi.
Capital: Santa Fe

Cities and Towns

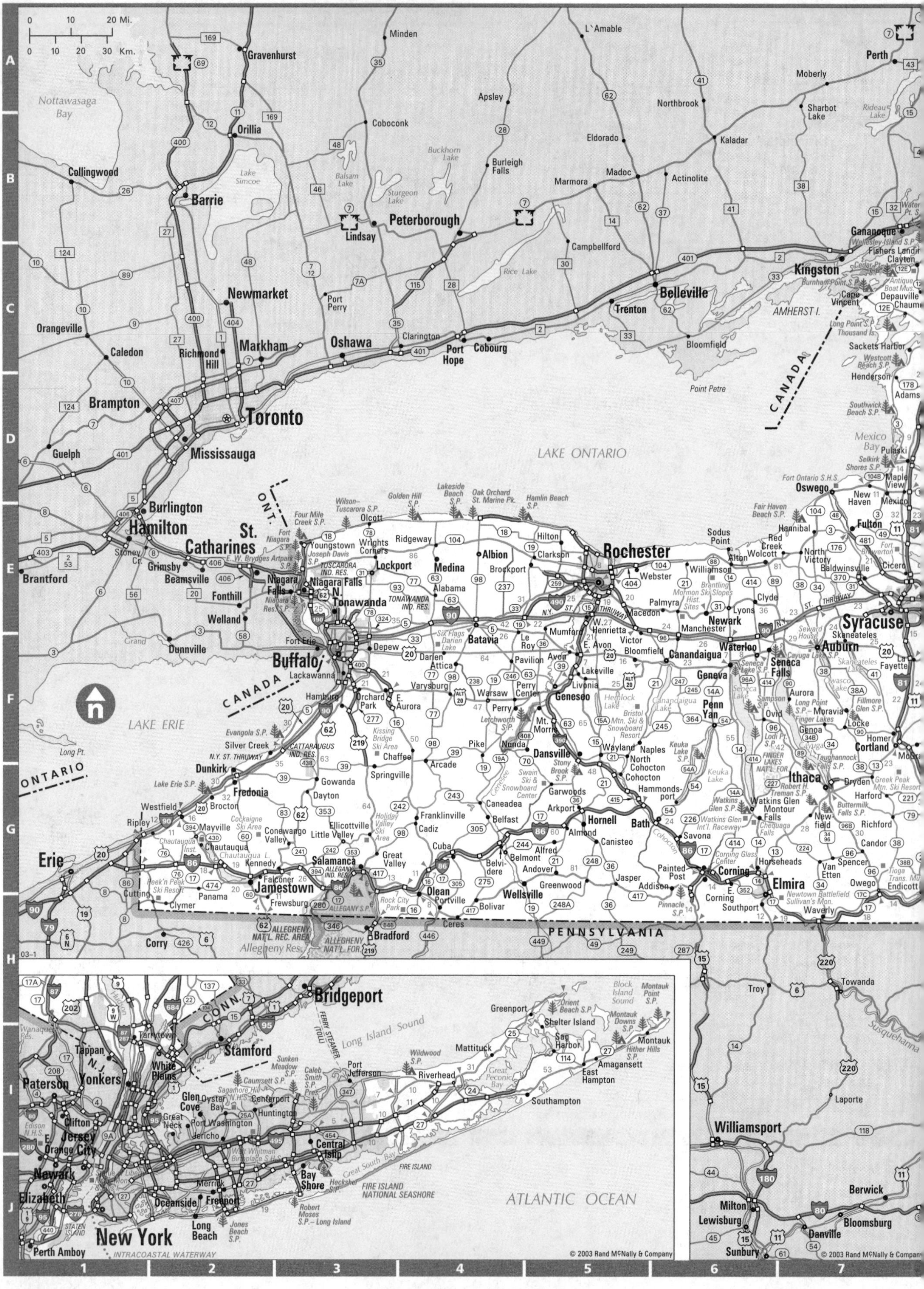
0 10 20 Mi.
0 10 20 30 Km.
Nottawasaga Bay
Gravenhurst
Minden
L'Amable
Perth
Moberly
Apsley
Northbrook
Sharbot Lake
Rideau Lake
Orillia
Coboconk
Eldorado
Kaladar
Buckhorn Lake
Burleigh Falls
Collingwood
Lake Simcoe
Balsam Lake
Madoc
Actinolite
Marmora
Barrie
Sturgeon Lake
Peterborough
Lindsay
Campbellford
Gananoque
Kingston
Belleville
Trenton
Rice Lake
Newmarket
Port Perry
Orangeville
Oshawa
Clarington
Port Hope
Cobourg
Bloomfield
AMHERST I.
Cape Vincent
Caledon
Richmond Hill
Markham
Sackets Harbor
Henderson
Adams
Point Petre
Brampton
Toronto
Mississauga
Guelph
CANADA
LAKE ONTARIO
Mexico Bay
Pulaski
Oswego
Burlington
Hamilton
St. Catharines
Grimsby
Beamsville
Fonthill
Welland
Dunnville
Brantford
ONT.
Niagara Falls
Youngstown
Olcott
Lockport
N. Tonawanda
Medina
Albion
Brockport
Rochester
Hilton
Clarkson
Webster
Sodus Point
Wolcott
Williamson
Palmyra
Macedon
Newark
Lyons
Clyde
Fulton
Baldwinsville
Syracuse
Skaneateles
Auburn
Seneca Falls
Waterloo
Geneva
Canandaigua
Victor
Henrietta
Batavia
Le Roy
Avon
Mumford
Buffalo
Lackawanna
Depew
Darien
Attica
Varysburg
Warsaw
Perry
Geneseo
Livonia
Lakeville
Penn Yan
Fort Erie
Hamburg
Orchard Park
E. Aurora
LAKE ERIE
Long Pt.
ONTARIO
Evangola S.P.
Silver Creek
Dunkirk
Fredonia
Brocton
Westfield
Ripley
Mayville
Chautauqua
Erie
Gowanda
Dayton
Springville
Chaffee
Arcade
Pike
Nunda
Dansville
Wayland
Naples
North Cohocton
Cohocton
Hammondsport
Ithaca
Cortland
Homer
Dryden
Watkins Glen
Montour Falls
Horseheads
Elmira
Corning
Painted Post
Bath
Hornell
Almond
Canisteo
Arkport
Alfred
Belmont
Andover
Wellsville
Belfast
Caneadea
Cuba
Olean
Portville
Bolivar
Salamanca
Ellicottville
Little Valley
Great Valley
Conewango Valley
Jamestown
Falconer
Frewsburg
Panama
Clymer
Kennedy
Bradford
Ceres
Corry
Waverly
Owego
Endicott
Newfield
Richford
Candor
Spencer
Van Etten
Jasper
Addison
Southport
PENNSYLVANIA
Troy
Towanda
Susquehanna
Laporte
Williamsport
Milton
Lewisburg
Sunbury
Danville
Bloomsburg
Berwick
Bridgeport
Stamford
Tarrytown
White Plains
Yonkers
Tappan
N.J.
CONN.
Paterson
Clifton
Jersey City
Newark
Elizabeth
Perth Amboy
New York
Long Beach
Oceanside
Freeport
Merrick
Bay Shore
Central Islip
Jericho
Port Washington
Great Neck
Glen Cove
Oyster Bay
Huntington
Centerport
Port Jefferson
Long Island Sound
Riverhead
Mattituck
Greenport
Shelter Island
Sag Harbor
Montauk
Amagansett
East Hampton
Southampton
FIRE ISLAND
FIRE ISLAND NATIONAL SEASHORE
ATLANTIC OCEAN
INTRACOASTAL WATERWAY
Block Island Sound
Montauk Point S.P.
© 2003 Rand McNally & Company

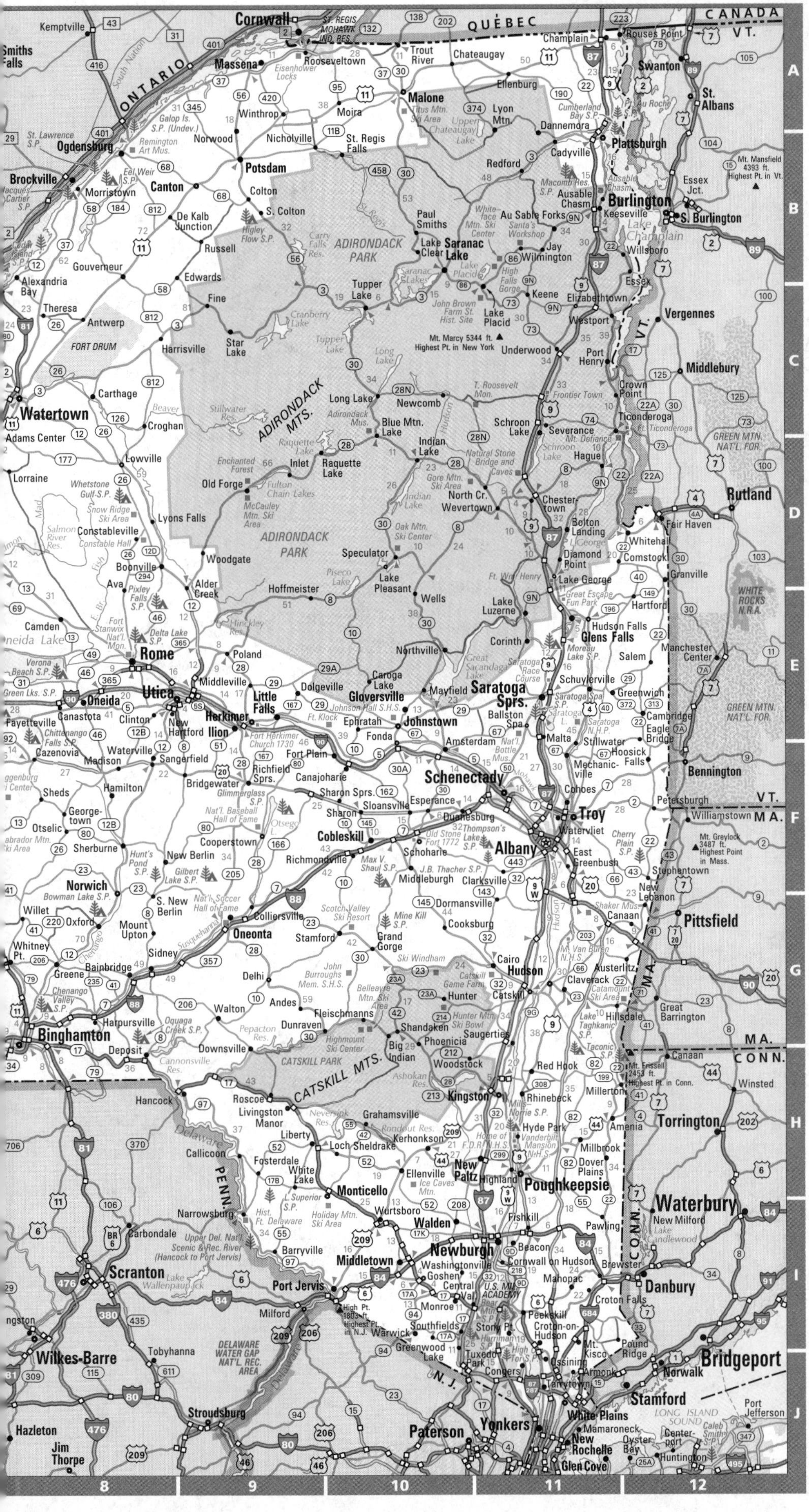

New York

Population: 19,097,000 (1/1/01 estimate)

Land Area: 47,224 sq. mi.

Capital: Albany

Cities and Towns

Adams	D-7
Adams Center	D-8
Addison	G-6
Albany	F-11
Albion	E-4
Alexandria Bay	B-8
Alfred	G-5
Amagansett	I-5
Amenia	H-11
Amsterdam	F-10
Andover	G-5
Antwerp	C-8
Arcade	F-4
Attica	F-4
Au Sable Forks	B-11
Auburn	F-7
Avon	F-5
Bainbridge	G-8
Baldwinsville	E-7
Ballston Spa	E-11
Batavia	E-4
Bath	G-6
Bay Shore	J-3
Beacon	I-11
Belfast	G-4
Belmont	G-4
Binghamton	G-8
Blue Mountain Lake	C-10
Bolivar	H-4
Bolton Landing	D-11
Boonville	D-8
Brewster	I-11
Brockport	E-5
Brocton	G-2
Buffalo	F-3
Cadyville	B-11
Cairo	G-11
Cambridge	E-12
Camden	E-8
Canajoharie	F-10
Canandaigua	F-6
Canastota	E-8
Candor	G-7
Canisteo	G-5
Canton	B-9
Cape Vincent	C-7
Carthage	C-8
Catskill	G-11
Cazenovia	F-8
Centerport	J-12
Central Islip	I-3
Central Valley	I-10
Champlain	A-11
Chateaugay	A-10
Chaumont	C-7
Chautauqua	G-2
Cicero	E-7
Claverack	G-11
Clayton	C-7
Clinton	E-8
Clyde	E-6
Cobleskill	F-10
Cohocton	G-5
Cohoes	F-11
Congers	J-11
Cooperstown	F-9
Corinth	E-11
Corning	G-6
Cornwall on Hudson	I-11
Cortland	F-7
Croton Falls	I-11
Croton-on-Hudson	I-11
Crown Point	C-11
Cuba	G-4
Dannemora	B-11
Dansville	F-5
Delhi	G-9
Depew	F-3
Deposit	H-8
Dolgeville	E-9
Dover Plains	H-11
Downsville	H-9
Dryden	G-7
Dunkirk	G-2
East Aurora	F-3
East Greenbush	F-11
East Hampton	I-5
Elizabethtown	C-11
Ellenville	H-10
Elmira	H-6
Endicott	G-7
Falconer	G-2
Fayetteville	E-8
Fishkill	I-11
Fonda	F-10
Fort Plain	F-10
Franklinville	G-4
Fredonia	G-2
Freeport	J-2
Frewsburg	H-2
Fulton	E-7
Geneseo	F-5
Geneva	F-6
Glen Cove	J-11
Glens Falls	E-11
Gloversville	E-10
Goshen	I-10
Gouverneur	B-8
Gowanda	G-3
Grand Gorge	G-10
Granville	D-12
Great Neck	I-2
Greene	G-8
Greenport	H-5
Greenwich	E-11
Greenwood Lake	I-0
Hamburg	F-3
Hamilton	F-8
Hammondsport	G-6
Hancock	H-9
Herkimer	E-9
Highland	H-11
Hilton	E-5
Homer	F-7
Hoosick Falls	F-12
Hornell	G-5
Horseheads	G-6
Hudson	G-11
Hudson Falls	E-11
Huntington	J-12
Hyde Park	H-11
Ilion	E-9
Ithaca	G-7
Jamestown	G-2
Jericho	I-2
Johnstown	E-10
Keeseville	B-11
Kerhonkson	H-10
Kingston	H-11
Lackawanna	F-3
Lake George	D-11
Lake Luzerne	E-11
Lake Placid	C-11
Lake Pleasant	D-10
Lakeville	F-5
Le Roy	E-4
Liberty	H-9
Little Falls	E-9
Little Valley	G-3
Livingston Manor	H-9
Livonia	F-5
Loch Sheldrake	H-10
Lockport	E-3
Long Beach	J-2
Lowville	D-8
Lyon Mountain	A-11
Lyons	E-6
Macedon	E-6
Mahopac	I-11
Malone	A-10
Mamaroneck	J-11
Manchester	F-6
Massena	A-9
Mattituck	I-4
Mayfield	E-10
Mayville	G-2
Mechanicville	F-11
Medina	E-4
Merrick	J-2
Mexico	D-7
Middleburgh	F-10
Middletown	I-10
Millbrook	H-11
Millerton	H-11
Monroe	I-10
Montauk	I-5
Monticello	H-10
Montour Falls	G-6
Moravia	F-7
Mount Kisco	I-11
Mount Morris	F-5
Naples	F-5
New Berlin	F-8
New Hartford	E-8
New Paltz	H-11
New Rochelle	J-11
New York	J-1
Newark	E-6
Newburgh	I-11
Niagara Falls	E-3
North Tonawanda	E-3
Northville	E-10
Norwich	F-8
Norwood	A-9
Nunda	F-5
Oceanside	J-2
Ogdensburg	B-8
Olcott	E-3
Old Forge	D-9
Olean	H-4
Oneida	E-8
Oneonta	G-9
Orchard Park	F-3
Ossining	J-11
Oswego	D-7
Owego	G-7
Oxford	G-8
Oyster Bay	J-12
Painted Post	G-6
Palmyra	E-6
Paul Smiths	B-10
Pawling	I-11
Peekskill	I-11
Penn Yan	F-6
Perry	F-4
Plattsburgh	B-11
Port Henry	C-11
Port Jefferson	J-12
Port Jervis	I-10
Port Washington	I-2
Portville	H-4
Potsdam	B-9
Poughkeepsie	H-11
Pulaski	D-7
Red Hook	H-11
Rhinebeck	H-11
Richfield Springs	F-9
Ripley	G-2
Riverhead	I-4
Rochester	E-5
Rome	E-8
Roscoe	H-9
Rouses Point	A-12
Sackets Harbor	C-7
Sag Harbor	I-5
St. Regis Falls	B-10
Salamanca	G-3
Salem	E-12
Saranac Lake	B-10
Saratoga Springs	E-11
Saugerties	G-11
Schenectady	F-11
Schoharie	F-10
Schroon Lake	C-11
Schuylerville	E-11
Seneca Falls	F-6
Shelter Island	I-5
Sherburne	F-8
Sidney	G-8
Silver Creek	F-2
Skaneateles	F-7
Sodus Point	E-6
Southampton	I-5
Southport	H-6
Springville	G-3
Stamford	G-10
Star Lake	C-9
Stillwater	F-11
Stony Point	I-11
Syracuse	E-7
Tarrytown	J-11
Theresa	C-8
Ticonderoga	C-11
Troy	F-11
Tupper Lake	C-10
Utica	E-9
Victor	E-5
Walden	I-10
Walton	G-9
Warsaw	F-4
Warwick	I-10
Washingtonville	I-10
Waterloo	F-6
Watertown	C-8
Waterville	F-8
Watervliet	F-11
Watkins Glen	G-6
Waverly	H-7
Wayland	F-5
Webster	E-5
Wellsville	G-4
Westfield	G-2
White Plains	J-11
Whitehall	D-12
Whitney Point	G-8
Williamson	E-6
Wolcott	E-6
Woodstock	H-10
Wurtsboro	I-10
Yonkers	J-11
Youngstown	E-3

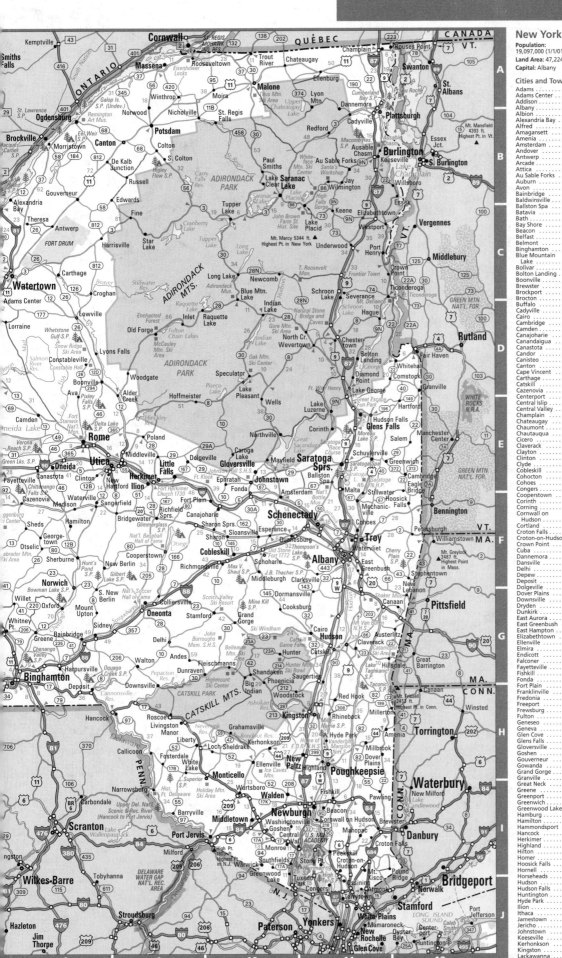

randmcnally.com

Express Access Codes: N. Carolina NC S. Carolina SC

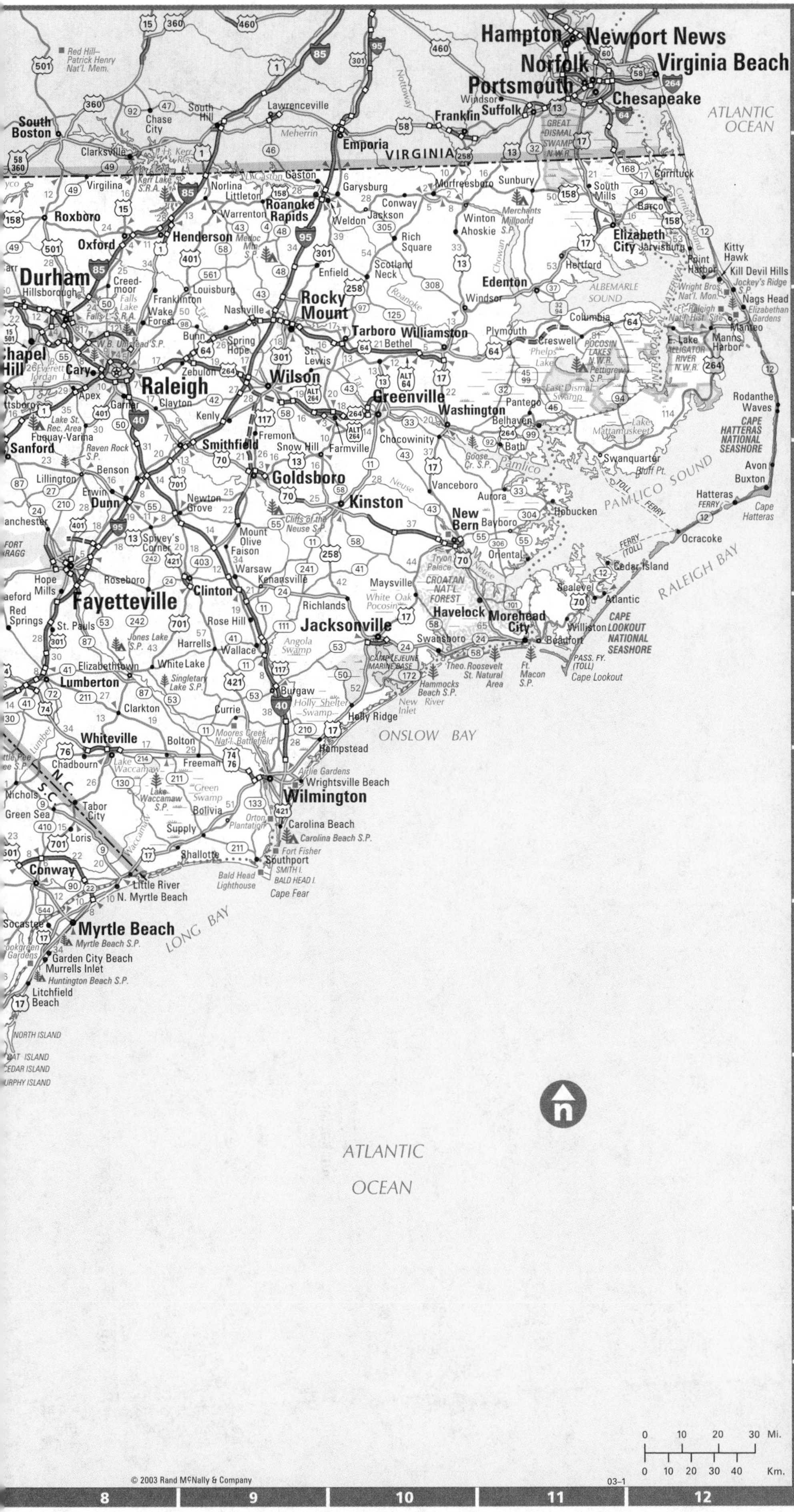

Hampton
Newport News
Norfolk
Virginia Beach
Portsmouth
Chesapeake
ATLANTIC OCEAN
VIRGINIA
Emporia
Franklin
Suffolk
Roanoke Rapids
Henderson
Oxford
Roxboro
Durham
Chapel Hill
Cary
Raleigh
Rocky Mount
Wilson
Tarboro
Williamston
Edenton
Elizabeth City
Greenville
Washington
Goldsboro
Kinston
New Bern
Jacksonville
Havelock
Morehead City
Fayetteville
Lumberton
Whiteville
Wilmington
Wrightsville Beach
Carolina Beach
Southport
Myrtle Beach
Conway
PAMLICO SOUND
ALBEMARLE SOUND
RALEIGH BAY
ONSLOW BAY
LONG BAY
CAPE HATTERAS NATIONAL SEASHORE
CAPE LOOKOUT NATIONAL SEASHORE
Cape Hatteras
Cape Lookout
Cape Fear
Ocracoke
Kill Devil Hills
Kitty Hawk
Nags Head
Manteo
0 10 20 30 Mi.
0 10 20 30 40 Km.
03-1
8
9
10
11
12
A
B
C
D
E
F
G
H
I
J

© 2003 Rand McNally & Company

North Carolina

Population: 8,224,600 (1/1/01 estimate)

Land Area: 48,718 sq. mi.

Capital: Raleigh

Cities and Towns

Aberdeen D-7
Ahoskie B-10
Albemarle D-6
Apex C-8
Asheboro C-7
Asheville C-3
Bayboro D-11
Beaufort E-11
Belhaven C-11
Benson D-8
Black Mtn. C-3
Bolivia F-9
Boone B-4
Brevard D-3
Burgaw E-9
Burlington C-7
Burnsville C-3
Canton C-3
Carolina Beach F-9
Carthage D-7
Cary C-8
Chapel Hill C-8
Charlotte D-6
Cherryville D-5
Clayton C-8
Clinton D-9
Columbia C-11
Columbus D-4
Concord D-6
Dobson B-6
Dunn D-8
Durham C-8
East Flat Rock D-3
Eden B-7
Edenton C-11
Elizabeth City B-11
Elizabethtown E-8
Elkin B-5
Enfield B-9
Erwin D-8
Fairplains B-5
Farmville C-10
Fayetteville D-8
Forest City D-4
Franklin D-2
Fuquay-Varina C-8
Garner C-8
Gastonia D-5
Goldsboro D-9
Graham C-7
Granite Falls C-5
Greensboro C-7
Greenville C-10
Hamlet E-7
Hatteras D-12
Havelock E-11
Henderson B-8
Hendersonville D-3
Hertford B-11
Hickory C-5
High Point C-7
Hillsborough C-8
Hope Mills E-8
Jackson B-10
Jacksonville E-10
Jefferson B-5
Kannapolis D-6
Kenansville D-9
Kernersville C-6
Kill Devil Hills C-12
Kings Mountain D-5
Kinston D-10
Kitty Hawk B-12
Laurinburg E-7
Lenoir C-5
Lexington C-6
Liberty C-7
Lillington D-8
Lincolnton D-5
Long View C-5
Louisburg C-9
Lumberton E-8
Madison B-7
Maiden C-5
Manteo C-12
Marion C-4
Mars Hill C-3
Matthews D-6
Mayodan B-7
Mocksville C-6
Monroe D-6
Mooresville C-6
Morehead City E-11
Morganton C-4
Mount Airy B-6
Mount Gilead D-7
Mount Holly D-5
Mount Olive D-9
Murfreesboro B-10
Murphy D-1
Nags Head C-12
Nashville C-9
Newton C-5
New Bern D-10
North Wilkesboro B-5
Ocracoke D-12
Oxford B-8
Pilot Mountain B-6
Pinehurst D-7
Pineville D-5
Pittsboro C-8
Plymouth C-11
Raeford D-8
Raleigh C-8
Red Springs E-8
Reidsville B-7
Rich Square B-10
Roanoke Rapids B-9
Robbinsville D-1
Rockingham E-7
Rocky Mount C-9
Roxboro B-8
Rutherfordton D-4
Salisbury C-6
Sanford D-8
Scotland Neck B-10
Shelby D-4
Siler City C-7
Smithfield D-9
Snow Hill D-9
Southern Pines D-7
Southport F-9
Sparta B-5
Spruce Pine C-4
Statesville C-5
Swanquarter D-11
Swansboro E-10
Sylva D-2
Tabor City F-8
Tarboro C-10
Taylorsville C-5
Thomasville C-7
Troy D-7
Valdese C-4
Wadesboro D-7
Wake Forest C-8
Wallace E-9
Warrenton B-9
Warsaw D-9
Washington C-10
Waynesville D-2
Whiteville F-8
Wilkesboro B-5
Williamston C-10
Wilmington F-9
Wilson C-9
Windsor C-10
Winston-Salem C-6
Winton B-10
Wrightsville Bch. F-9
Yadkinville B-6
Yanceyville B-7
Zebulon C-9

South Carolina

Population: 4,075,500 (1/1/01 estimate)

Land Area: 30,111 sq. mi.

Capital: Columbia

Cities and Towns

Abbeville F-3
Aiken G-4
Allendale H-5
Anderson E-3
Andrews G-7
Bamberg G-5
Barnwell G-5
Batesburg F-4
Beaufort I-6
Beech Island G-4
Belton E-3
Bennettsville E-7
Bishopville F-6
Blackville G-5
Branchville G-5
Calhoun Falls F-3
Camden F-6
Charleston H-7
Cheraw E-7
Chesnee D-4
Chester E-5
Chesterfield E-7
Clemson E-3
Clinton E-4
Columbia F-5
Conway F-8
Cowpens D-4
Darlington F-7
Denmark G-5
Dillon E-7
Easley E-3
Eastover F-6
Edgefield F-4
Estill H-5
Fairfax H-5
Florence F-7
Folly Beach H-7
Fountain Inn E-4
Gaffney D-4
Garden City Bch. G-8
Georgetown G-7
Goose Creek H-7
Great Falls E-5
Greenville E-3
Greenwood F-4
Greer D-4
Hampton H-5
Hardeeville I-5
Hartsville E-7
Hemingway G-7
Hilton Head Island I-6
Holly Hill G-6
Honea Path E-3
Irmo F-5
Isle of Palms H-7
Jackson G-4
Johnston F-4
Jonesville E-4
Kershaw E-6
Kingstree G-7
Lake City F-7
Lancaster E-6
Landrum D-4
Latta F-7
Laurens E-4
Lexington F-5
Liberty E-3
Little River F-8
Loris F-8
Manning G-6
Marion F-7
Mauldin E-3
McColl E-7
McCormick F-3
Moncks Corner G-7
Mount Pleasant H-7
Murrells Inlet G-8
Myrtle Beach G-8
Newberry F-4
North Augusta G-4
North Charleston H-7
North Myrtle Bch. F-8
Oak Grove F-5
Orangeburg G-5
Pageland E-6
Pickens E-3
Port Royal I-6
Ridgeland I-5
Rock Hill E-5
St. George H-6
St. Matthews G-6
St. Stephen G-7
Saluda F-4
Seneca E-2
Simpsonville E-3
Socastee G-8
Spartanburg D-4
Summerville H-6
Sumter F-6
Timmonsville F-7
Travelers Rest D-3
Union E-4
Varnville H-5
Walhalla E-2
Walterboro H-6
Ware Shoals E-3
Westminster E-2
Whitmire E-4
Williston G-5
Winnsboro E-5
Woodruff E-4
York D-5

North Dakota

Population: 642,900 (1/1/01 estimate)
Land Area: 68,994 sq. mi.
Capital: Bismarck

Cities and Towns

Abercrombie E-10
Amidon E-2
Anamoose C-6
Arthur D-9
Ashley F-7
Beach D-1
Belcourt A-6
Belfield D-2
Berthold B-4
Beulah D-4
Bisbee A-7
Bismarck E-5
Bottineau A-5
Bowbells A-3
Bowman F-2
Burlington B-4
Cando B-7
Cannon Ball E-5
Carrington C-7
Carson E-4
Casselton D-9
Cavalier A-9
Center D-4
Cooperstown C-8
Crosby A-2
Devils Lake B-7
Dickinson D-3
Drake C-6
Drayton B-9
Dunseith A-6
Edgeley E-7
Edmore B-8
Elgin E-4
Ellendale F-8
Enderlin E-9
Fairmount F-10
Fargo D-10
Fessenden C-6
Finley C-8
Flasher E-5
Forman F-9
Fort Totten C-7
Fort Yates F-5
Gackle E-7
Garrison C-4
Gilby B-9
Glen Ullin E-4
Glenburn B-5
Grafton B-9
Grand Forks C-9
Gwinner E-9
Halliday D-3
Hankinson F-10
Harvey C-6
Hatton C-9
Hazen D-4
Hebron D-4
Hettinger F-3
Hillsboro C-9
Hunter D-9
Jamestown D-7
Kenmare B-4
Killdeer D-3
Kindred E-9
Kulm E-7
Lakota B-8
Lamoure E-8
Langdon A-8
Larimore C-9
Leeds B-7
Leonard E-9
Lidgerwood F-9
Lincoln E-5
Linton E-6
Lisbon E-9
Maddock C-6
Mandan E-5
Manning D-3
Manvel B-9
Max C-4
Mayville C-9
McVille C-8
Mcclusky C-5
Medina D-7
Medora D-2
Michigan B-8
Milnor E-9
Minnewaukan B-7
Minot B-4
Minto B-9
Mohall A-4
Mott E-3
Munich A-7
Napoleon E-6
Neche A-9
New England E-3
New Leipzig E-4
New Rockford C-7
New Salem D-4
New Town C-3
Northwood C-9
Oakes F-8
Park River B-9
Parshall C-4
Powers Lake B-3
Ray B-2
Richardton D-3
Rolette A-6
Rolla A-6
Rugby B-6
St. Thomas A-9
Scranton F-2
Sherwood A-4
Stanley B-3
Stanton D-4
Steele D-6
Strasburg F-6
Surrey B-5
Thompson C-9
Tioga B-3
Towner B-5
Turtle Lake C-5
Underwood C-5
Valley City D-8
Wahpeton E-10
Walhalla A-8
Washburn D-5
Watford City C-2
West Fargo D-10
Westhope A-5
Williston B-2
Willow City A-6
Wilton D-5
Wishek E-6
Wyndmere E-9

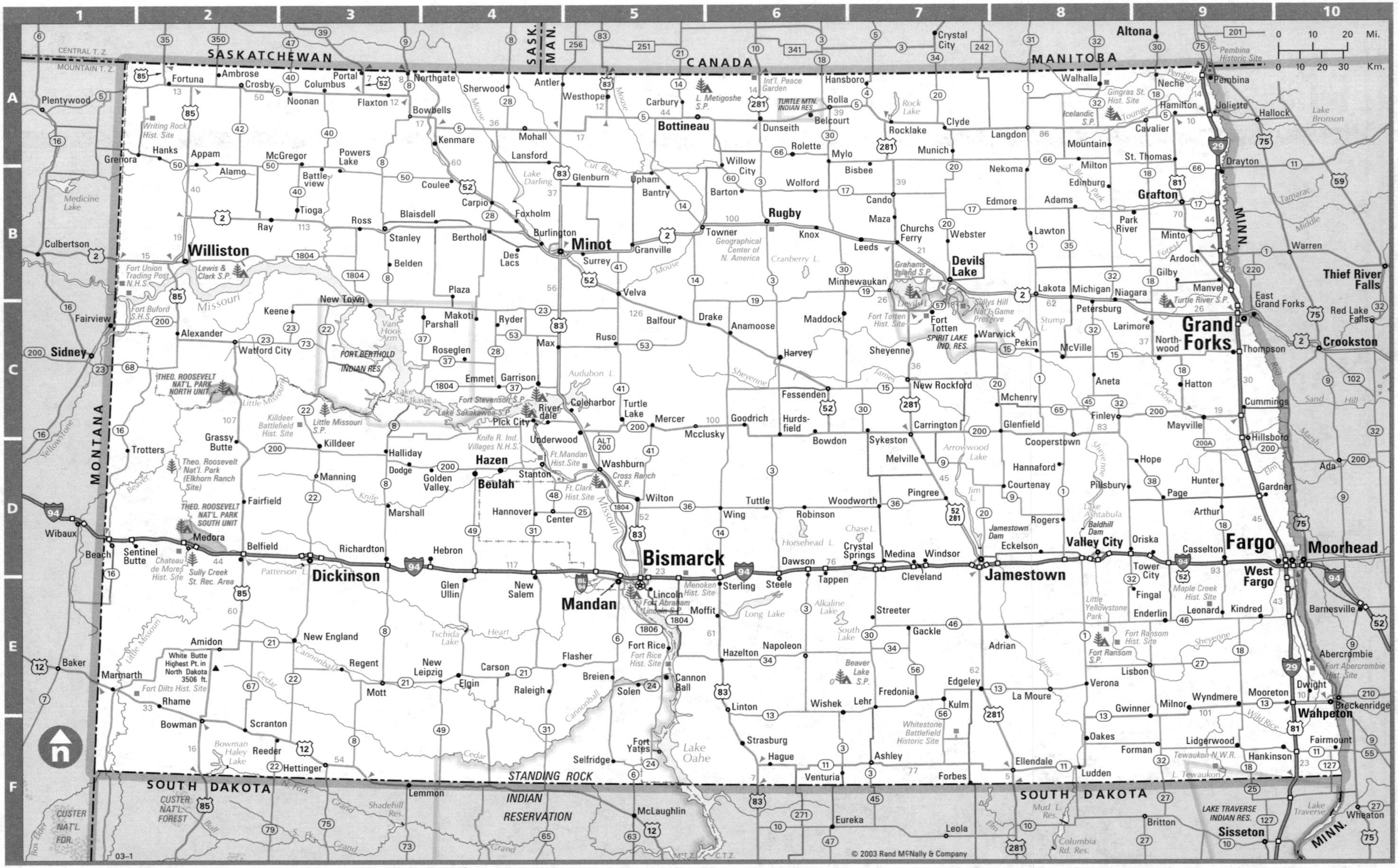

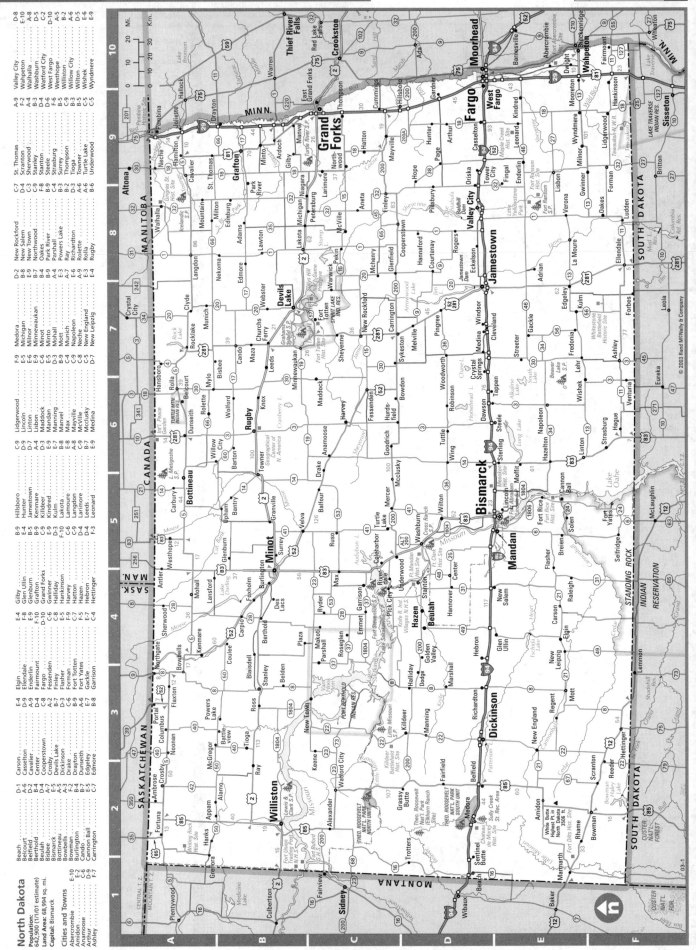

SASKATCHEWAN
CANADA
MANITOBA
MONTANA
SOUTH DAKOTA
MINN.
Williston
Minot
Bismarck
Mandan
Dickinson
Jamestown
Fargo
Grand Forks
Devils Lake
Valley City
Wahpeton
Rugby
Bottineau
STANDING ROCK INDIAN RESERVATION
Lake Sakakawea
Lake Oahe
Missouri
© 2003 Rand McNally & Company

randmcnally.com
Express Access Code: ND

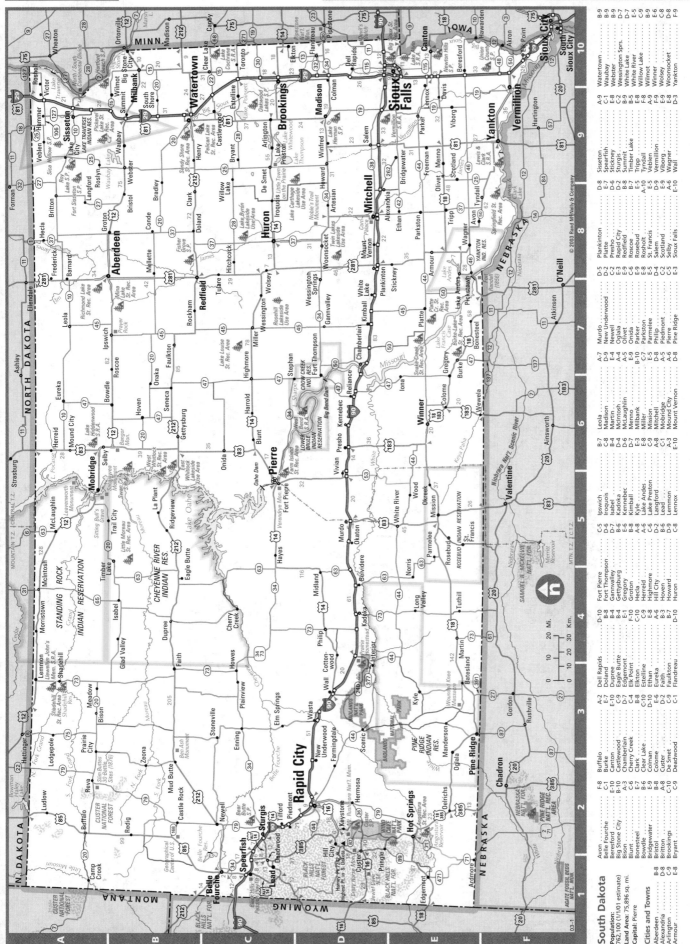

randmcnally.com
Express Access Code: SD

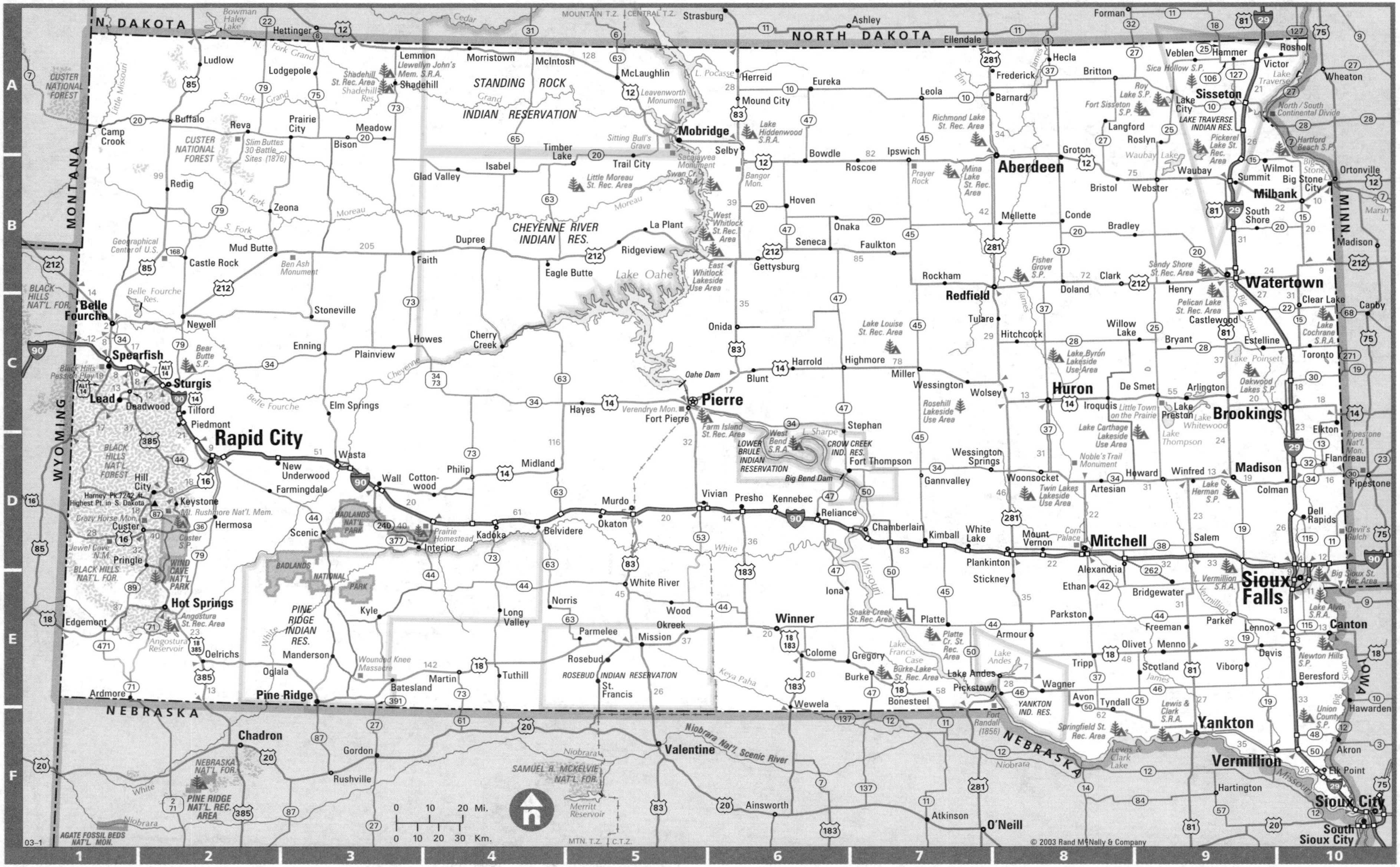
NORTH DAKOTA
NEBRASKA
WYOMING
MONTANA
MINN.
IOWA
Aberdeen
Rapid City
Sioux Falls
Pierre
Watertown
Mitchell
Brookings
Huron
Yankton
Vermillion
Mobridge
Spearfish
Sturgis
Belle Fourche
Winner
Madison
Redfield
Sisseton
Milbank
Hot Springs
Pine Ridge
Lake Oahe
STANDING ROCK INDIAN RESERVATION
CHEYENNE RIVER INDIAN RES.
PINE RIDGE INDIAN RES.
ROSEBUD INDIAN RESERVATION
LAKE TRAVERSE INDIAN RES.
CROW CREEK IND. RES.
LOWER BRULE INDIAN RESERVATION
YANKTON IND. RES.
BLACK HILLS NAT'L FOREST
CUSTER NATIONAL FOREST
BADLANDS NATIONAL PARK
WIND CAVE NAT'L PARK
Chadron
Valentine
O'Neill
Sioux City
© 2003 Rand McNally & Company
03-1

South Dakota

Population: 762,100 (1/1/01 estimate)
Land Area: 75,896 sq. mi.
Capital: Pierre

Cities and Towns

Aberdeen . . . B-8
Alexandria . . . D-8
Arlington . . . C-9
Armour . . . E-8
Avon . . . F-8
Belle Fourche . . . C-1
Beresford . . . E-10
Big Stone City . . . B-10
Bison . . . A-3
Blunt . . . C-6
Bonesteel . . . E-7
Bowdle . . . B-6
Bridgewater . . . E-9
Bristol . . . B-8
Britton . . . A-8
Brookings . . . C-10
Bryant . . . C-9
Buffalo . . . A-2
Burke . . . E-7
Canton . . . E-10
Castlewood . . . C-9
Chamberlain . . . D-7
Cherry Creek . . . C-4
Clark . . . B-8
Clear Lake . . . C-10
Colman . . . D-10
Colome . . . E-6
Custer . . . D-2
De Smet . . . C-9
Deadwood . . . C-1
Dell Rapids . . . D-10
Doland . . . B-8
Dupree . . . B-4
Eagle Butte . . . B-4
Edgemont . . . E-1
Elk Point . . . F-10
Elkton . . . C-10
Estelline . . . C-9
Ethan . . . E-8
Eureka . . . A-6
Faith . . . B-3
Faulkton . . . B-7
Flandreau . . . D-10
Fort Pierre . . . C-5
Fort Thompson . . . D-6
Gannvalley . . . D-7
Gettysburg . . . B-6
Gregory . . . E-6
Groton . . . B-8
Hecla . . . A-8
Herreid . . . A-6
Highmore . . . C-6
Hill City . . . D-2
Hoven . . . B-6
Howard . . . D-9
Huron . . . C-8
Ipswich . . . B-7
Iroquois . . . C-8
Isabel . . . B-4
Kadoka . . . D-4
Kennebec . . . D-6
Kimball . . . D-7
Kyle . . . E-3
Lake Andes . . . E-8
Lake Preston . . . C-9
Langford . . . A-8
Lead . . . C-1
Lemmon . . . A-3
Lennox . . . E-10
Leola . . . A-7
Madison . . . D-9
Martin . . . E-4
McIntosh . . . A-4
McLaughlin . . . A-5
Menno . . . E-9
Milbank . . . B-10
Miller . . . C-7
Mission . . . E-5
Mitchell . . . D-8
Mobridge . . . A-5
Mound City . . . A-6
Mount Vernon . . . D-8
Murdo . . . D-5
New Underwood . . . D-2
Newell . . . C-2
Oglala . . . E-3
Olivet . . . E-9
Onida . . . C-6
Parker . . . E-9
Parkston . . . E-8
Parmelee . . . E-5
Philip . . . D-4
Piedmont . . . C-2
Pierre . . . C-5
Pine Ridge . . . E-3
Plankinton . . . D-8
Platte . . . E-7
Presho . . . D-6
Rapid City . . . D-2
Redfield . . . B-8
Roscoe . . . B-7
Rosebud . . . E-5
Rosholt . . . A-10
St. Francis . . . E-5
Salem . . . D-9
Scotland . . . E-9
Selby . . . A-6
Sioux Falls . . . E-10
Sisseton . . . A-9
Spearfish . . . C-1
Stickney . . . D-8
Sturgis . . . C-2
Summit . . . B-9
Timber Lake . . . B-5
Tripp . . . E-8
Tyndall . . . F-8
Veblen . . . A-9
Vermillion . . . F-9
Viborg . . . E-9
Wagner . . . E-8
Wall . . . D-3
Watertown . . . B-9
Waubay . . . B-9
Webster . . . B-9
Wessington Sprs. . . . D-7
White Lake . . . D-7
White River . . . E-5
Willow Lake . . . C-9
Wilmot . . . B-9
Winner . . . E-6
Wolsey . . . C-8
Woonsocket . . . D-8
Yankton . . . F-9

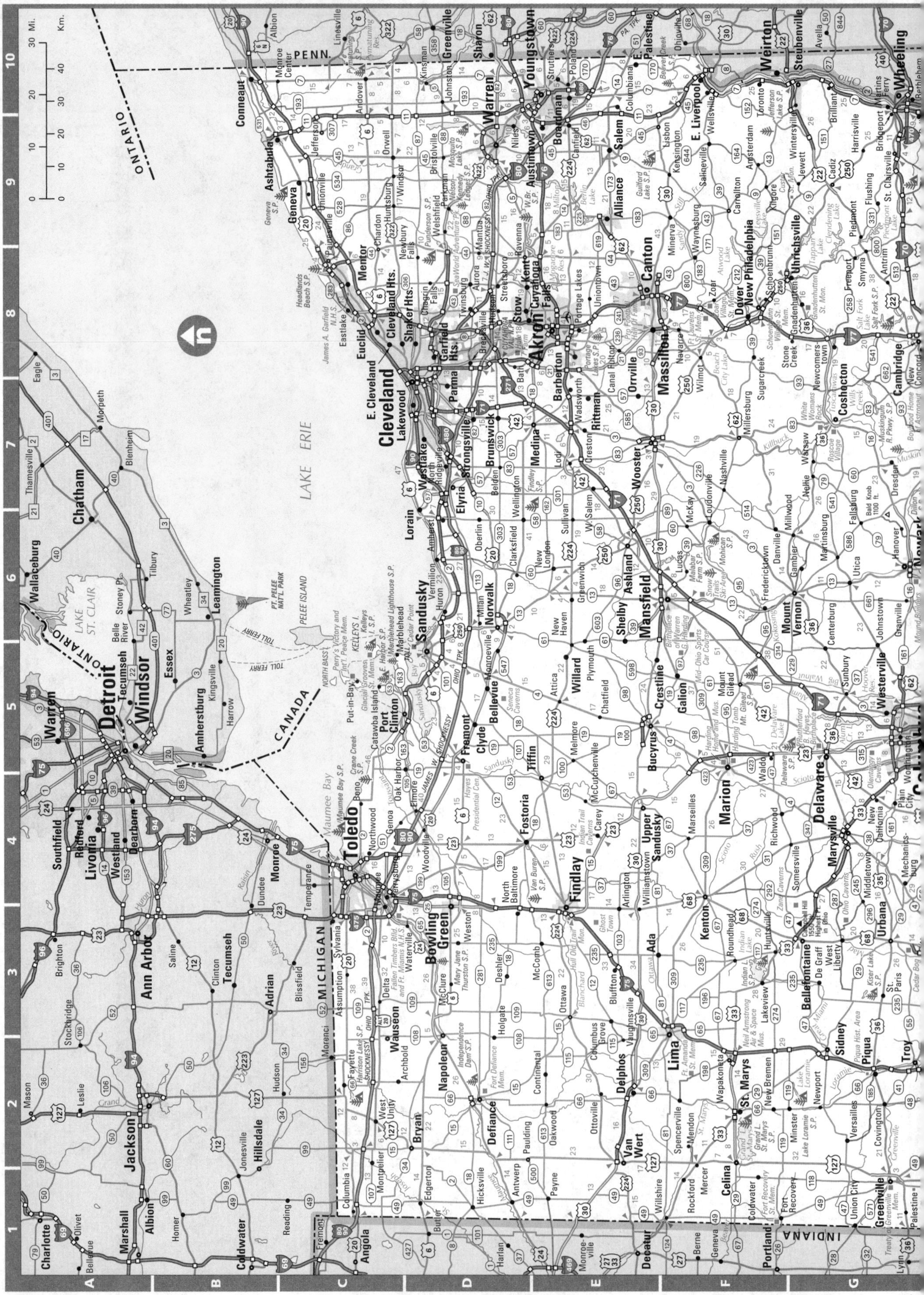
LAKE ERIE
LAKE ST. CLAIR
ONTARIO
CANADA
MICHIGAN
PENN.
INDIANA
Detroit
Windsor
Toledo
Cleveland
Akron
Canton
Youngstown
Warren
Sandusky
Lorain
Elyria
Mansfield
Findlay
Lima
Marion
Delaware
Bowling Green
Fremont
Norwalk
Ashtabula
Conneaut
Massillon
Wooster
Ann Arbor
Jackson
Monroe
Chatham
Leamington
Wheeling
Steubenville
Weirton
New Philadelphia
Coshocton
Cambridge
Defiance
Napoleon
Van Wert
Sidney
Piqua
Troy
Bellefontaine
Kenton
Bucyrus
Tiffin
Fostoria
Ashland
Medina
Kent
Alliance
Salem
Zanesville
Dover
Mount Vernon
Marysville
Greenville
Celina
Wapakoneta
St. Marys
Urbana
Westerville
Newark
Port Clinton
Put-in-Bay
PELEE ISLAND
TOLL FERRY
Scale: 0 10 20 30 Mi.; 0 10 20 30 40 Km.

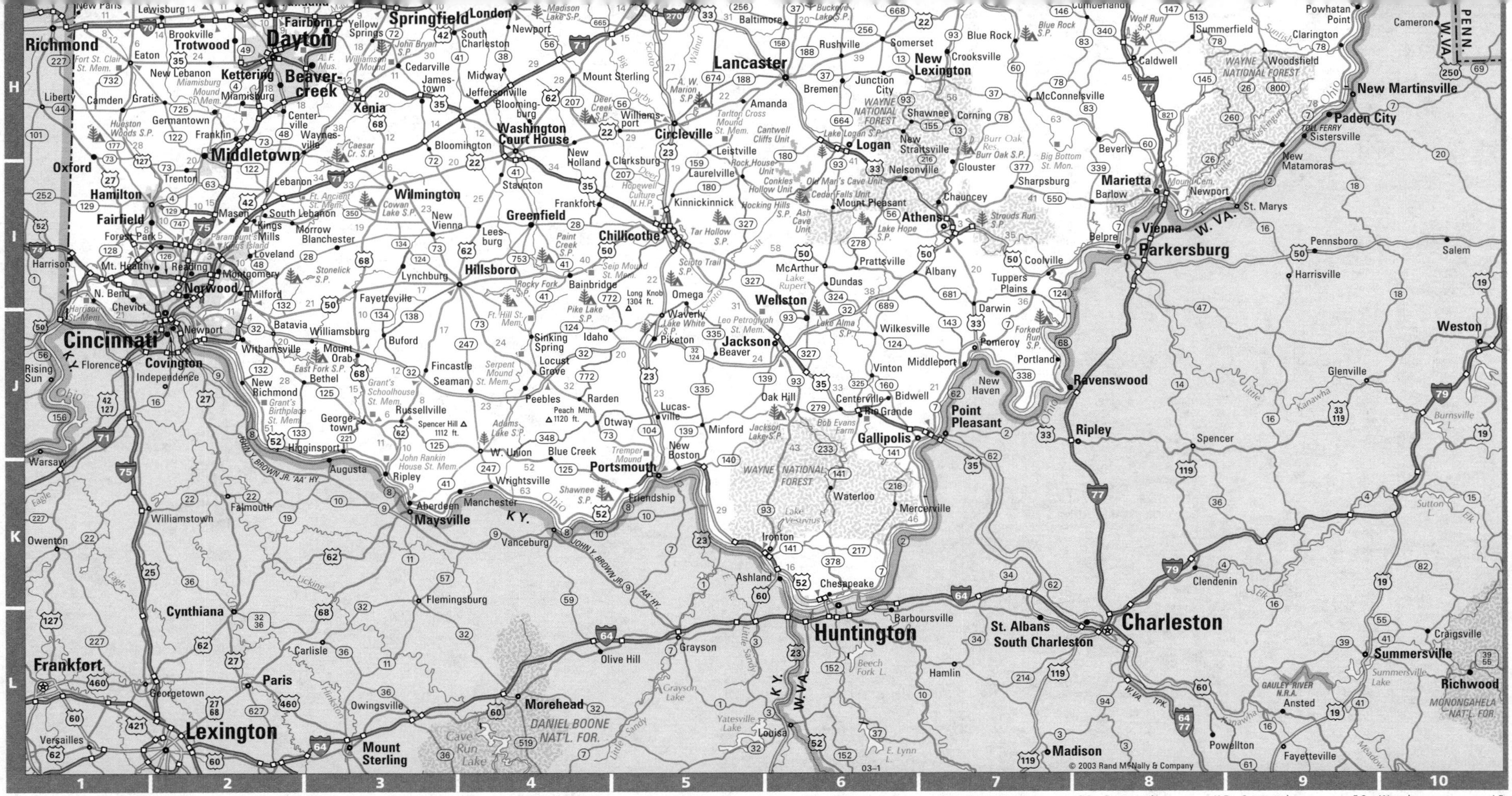

Ohio

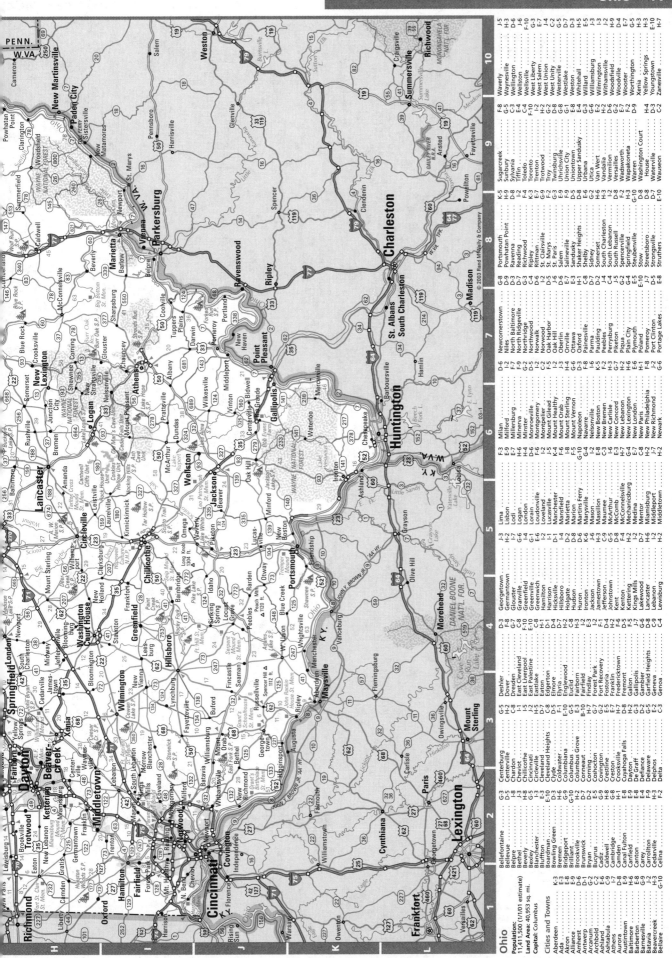

Population: 11,411,500 (1/1/01 estimate)
Land Area: 40,953 sq. mi.
Capital: Columbus

Cities and Towns

Aberdeen	K-3
Ada	E-3
Akron	E-8
Alliance	E-9
Amherst	D-6
Antwerp	D-1
Arcanum	G-2
Archbold	C-2
Ashland	E-6
Ashtabula	C-9
Athens	I-7
Aurora	D-8
Austintown	E-9
Baltimore	H-6
Barberton	E-8
Barnesville	G-9
Batavia	J-2
Beavercreek	H-3
Bellaire	G-10
Bellefontaine	G-3
Bellevue	D-5
Belpre	I-8
Bethel	J-3
Beverly	H-8
Bexley	G-5
Blanchester	I-3
Bluffton	E-3
Boardman	E-10
Bowling Green	D-3
Bremen	H-6
Bridgeport	G-9
Brilliant	G-10
Brookville	H-2
Brunswick	D-7
Bryan	D-2
Bucyrus	E-5
Cadiz	G-9
Caldwell	H-8
Cambridge	G-8
Camden	H-1
Canal Fulton	E-8
Canfield	E-9
Canton	E-8
Carey	E-4
Carrollton	F-9
Cedarville	H-3
Celina	F-2
Centerburg	G-5
Centerville	H-2
Chardon	C-8
Cheviot	I-1
Chillicothe	I-5
Cincinnati	J-2
Circleville	H-5
Cleveland	D-7
Cleveland Heights	C-8
Clyde	D-5
Coldwater	F-1
Columbiana	E-10
Columbus	G-5
Columbus Grove	E-3
Conneaut	B-10
Corning	H-7
Coshocton	G-7
Covington	G-2
Crestline	E-5
Creston	E-7
Crooksville	H-7
Cuyahoga Falls	D-8
Dayton	H-2
De Graff	G-3
Defiance	D-2
Delaware	G-5
Delphos	E-2
Delta	C-3
Deshler	D-3
Dover	F-8
Dresden	G-7
East Cleveland	C-8
East Liverpool	F-10
East Palestine	E-10
Eastlake	C-8
Eaton	H-1
Edgerton	D-1
Elmore	D-4
Elyria	D-7
Englewood	H-2
Euclid	C-8
Fairborn	H-3
Fairfield	I-2
Findlay	E-3
Forest Park	I-2
Fort Recovery	F-1
Fostoria	D-4
Franklin	H-2
Fredericktown	F-6
Fremont	D-5
Galion	F-5
Gallipolis	J-7
Gambier	G-6
Garfield Heights	D-8
Geneva	C-9
Genoa	C-4
Georgetown	J-3
Germantown	H-2
Glouster	I-7
Granville	G-6
Greenfield	I-4
Greenville	G-1
Greenwich	E-6
Hamilton	I-2
Harrison	I-1
Hicksville	D-1
Hillsboro	I-4
Holgate	D-2
Hudson	D-8
Huron	D-6
Ironton	K-6
Jackson	J-6
Jamestown	H-3
Jefferson	C-9
Johnstown	G-5
Kent	D-8
Kenton	F-4
Kettering	H-2
Kings Mills	I-2
Lakewood	D-7
Lancaster	H-6
Lebanon	I-2
Lewisburg	H-2
Lima	F-3
Lisbon	E-9
Lodi	E-7
Logan	H-6
London	H-4
Lorain	D-6
Loudonville	F-6
Loveland	I-2
Lucasville	J-5
Manchester	K-4
Mansfield	F-6
Marietta	I-8
Marion	F-5
Martins Ferry	G-10
Marysville	G-4
Mason	I-2
Massillon	E-8
Maumee	C-3
McArthur	I-6
McComb	E-3
McConnelsville	H-7
Mechanicsburg	G-4
Medina	E-7
Mentor	C-8
Miamisburg	H-2
Middleport	J-7
Middletown	H-2
Milan	D-6
Milford	I-2
Millersburg	F-7
Minerva	F-9
Minster	G-2
Monroeville	D-5
Montgomery	I-2
Montpelier	C-2
Mount Gilead	F-5
Mount Healthy	I-2
Mount Orab	J-3
Mount Sterling	H-4
Mount Vernon	G-6
Napoleon	D-3
Navarre	F-8
Nelsonville	I-6
New Boston	K-5
New Bremen	F-2
New Carlisle	H-3
New Concord	G-7
New Lebanon	H-2
New Lexington	H-6
New London	E-6
New Paris	H-1
New Philadelphia	F-8
New Richmond	J-2
Newark	G-6
Newcomerstown	G-8
Niles	D-9
North Baltimore	D-3
North Ridgeville	D-7
Northridge	G-3
Northwood	C-4
Norwalk	D-6
Norwood	I-2
Oak Harbor	D-5
Oak Hill	J-6
Oberlin	D-6
Orrville	E-7
Ottawa	E-3
Oxford	H-1
Painesville	C-8
Parma	D-7
Paulding	D-2
Peebles	J-4
Perrysburg	C-4
Piketon	J-5
Piqua	G-2
Plain City	G-4
Plymouth	E-5
Poland	E-10
Pomeroy	J-7
Port Clinton	D-5
Portage Lakes	E-8
Portsmouth	K-5
Powhatan Point	H-9
Ravenna	D-8
Reading	I-2
Richwood	F-4
Ripley	K-3
Rittman	E-7
St. Clairsville	G-9
St. Marys	F-2
St. Paris	G-3
Salem	E-9
Salineville	F-9
Sandusky	D-5
Shaker Heights	D-8
Shelby	E-6
Sidney	G-2
Somerset	H-6
South Charleston	H-3
South Lebanon	I-2
South Russell	D-8
Spencerville	F-2
Springfield	H-3
Steubenville	G-10
Stow	D-8
Streetsboro	D-8
Strongsville	D-7
Struthers	E-10
Sugarcreek	F-8
Sunbury	G-5
Sylvania	C-3
Tiffin	E-4
Toledo	C-4
Toronto	F-10
Trenton	I-2
Trotwood	H-2
Troy	G-2
Twinsburg	D-8
Uhrichsville	G-8
Union City	G-1
Uniontown	E-8
Upper Sandusky	E-4
Urbana	G-3
Utica	G-6
Van Wert	E-2
Vandalia	H-2
Vermilion	D-6
Versailles	G-2
Wadsworth	E-7
Wapakoneta	F-2
Warren	D-9
Washington Court House	H-4
Waterville	D-3
Wauseon	C-2
Waverly	J-5
Waynesville	H-3
Wellington	D-6
Wellston	J-6
Wellsville	F-10
West Liberty	G-3
West Salem	E-7
West Union	J-4
West Unity	C-2
Westerville	G-5
Westlake	D-7
Weston	D-3
Whitehall	H-5
Willard	E-5
Williamsburg	J-3
Wilmington	I-3
Withamsville	J-2
Woodsfield	H-9
Woodville	D-4
Wooster	E-7
Worthington	G-5
Xenia	H-3
Yellow Springs	H-3
Youngstown	E-10
Zanesville	H-7

Oklahoma

Population: 3,487,100 (1/1/01 estimate)
Land Area: 68,679 sq. mi.
Capital: Oklahoma City

Cities and Towns

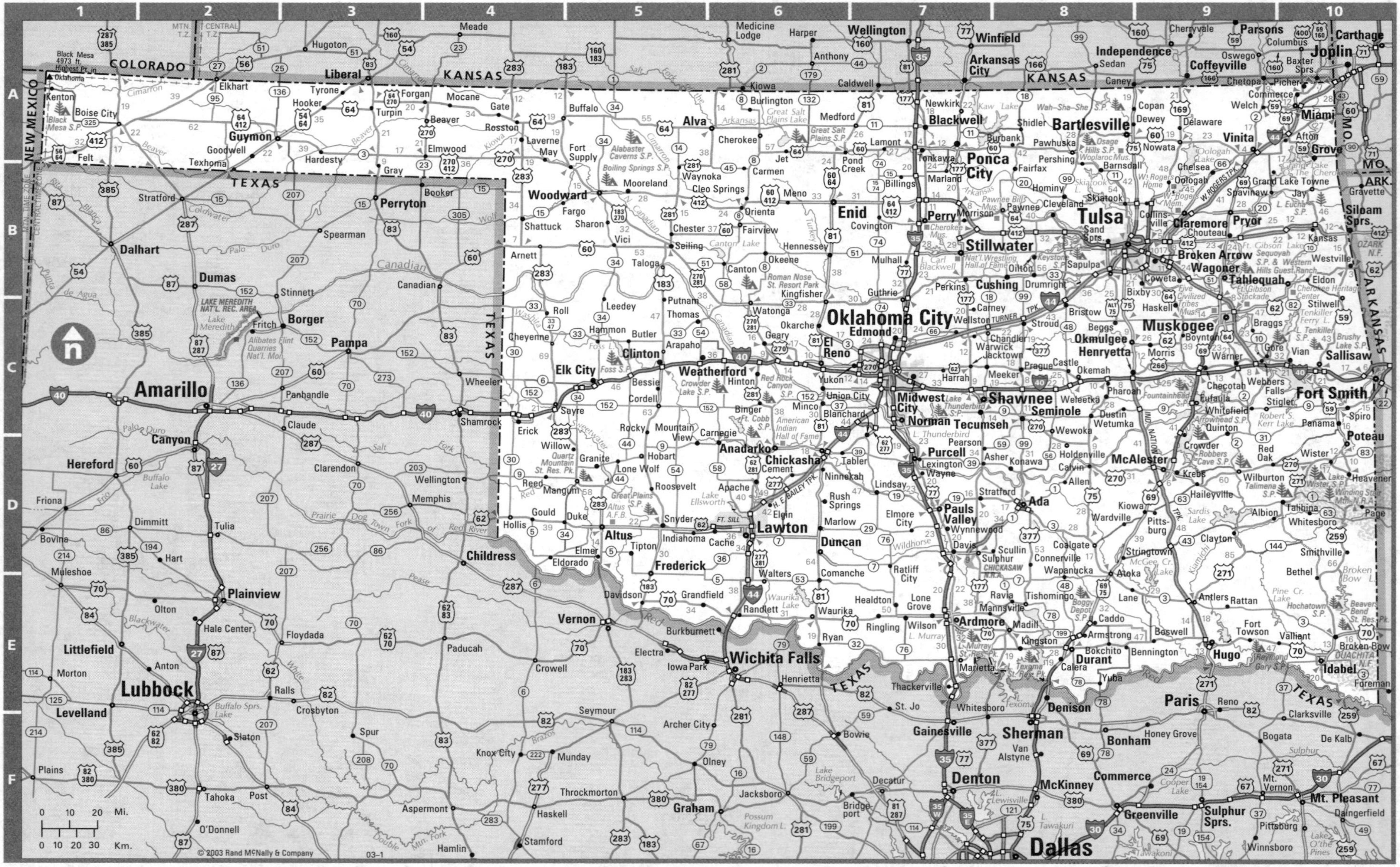

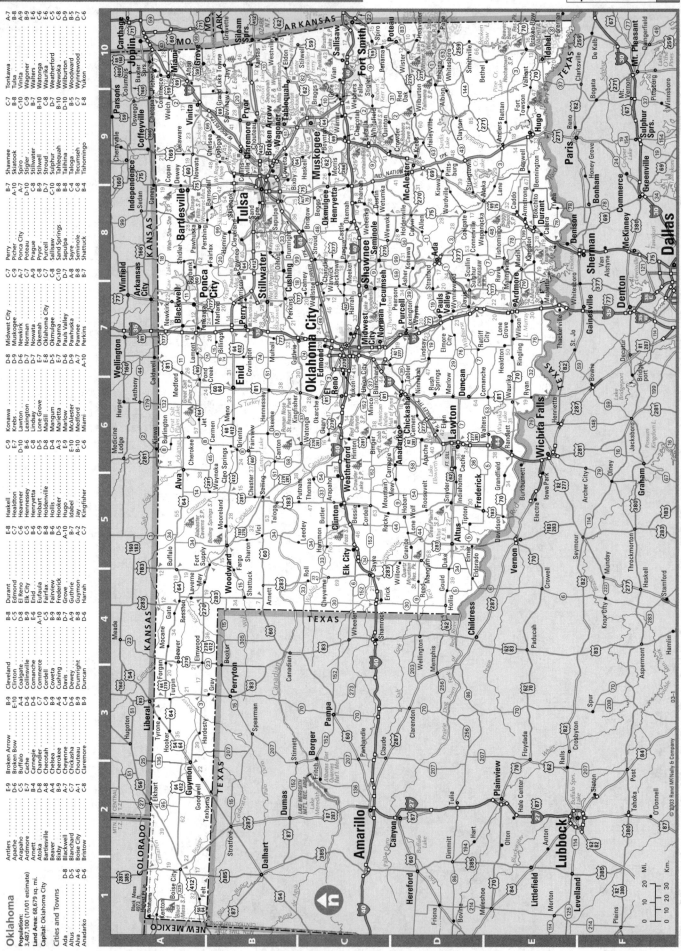

Oregon

Population: 3,492,100 (1/1/01 estimate)
Land Area: 96,002 sq. mi.
Capital: Salem

Cities and Towns

Albany	C-2
Aloha	B-3
Amity	C-2
Ashland	G-3
Astoria	A-2
Baker City	C-8
Bandon	E-1
Bay City	B-2
Beaverton	B-3
Bend	D-4
Boardman	A-6
Brookings	G-1
Bunker Hill	E-1
Burns	E-7
Cannon Beach	A-2
Canyon City	D-7
Canyonville	F-2
Cave Junction	G-2
Central Point	G-2
Clatskanie	A-2
Condon	B-5
Coos Bay	E-1
Coquille	E-1
Corvallis	C-2
Cottage Grove	D-2
Dallas	C-2
Drain	E-2
Eagle Point	F-3
Elgin	B-8
Enterprise	B-8
Estacada	B-3
Eugene	D-2
Florence	D-1
Fossil	C-5
Gold Beach	F-1
Grants Pass	F-2
Heppner	B-6
Hermiston	A-6
Hillsboro	B-3
Jacksonville	G-2
John Day	D-7
Joseph	B-8
Junction City	D-2
Klamath Falls	G-4
La Grande	B-8
Lakeside	E-1
Lakeview	G-5
Lebanon	C-3
Lincoln City	C-1
Madras	C-4
McMinnville	B-2
Medford	G-3
Mill City	C-3
Milton-Freewater	A-7
Molalla	C-3
Monmouth	C-2
Moro	B-5
Myrtle Creek	F-2
Myrtle Point	F-1
Newberg	B-3
Newport	C-1
North Bend	E-1
Nyssa	D-9
Oakridge	E-3
Ontario	D-9
Oregon City	B-3
Pendleton	B-7
Phoenix	G-3
Pilot Rock	B-7
Port Orford	F-1
Portland	B-3
Prospect	F-3
Rainier	A-3
Redmond	D-4
Reedsport	E-1
Roseburg	E-2
St. Helens	A-3
Salem	C-2
Sandy	B-3
Scappoose	B-3
Seaside	A-2
Silverton	C-3
Springfield	D-2
Stayton	C-3
Sublimity	C-3
Sutherlin	E-2
Sweet Home	D-3
The Dalles	B-4
Tillamook	B-2
Toledo	C-2
Umatilla	A-6
Union	B-8
Vale	D-9
Veneta	D-2
Vernonia	A-2
Waldport	D-1
Warm Springs	C-4
Warrenton	A-2
Winston	E-2
Woodburn	C-3

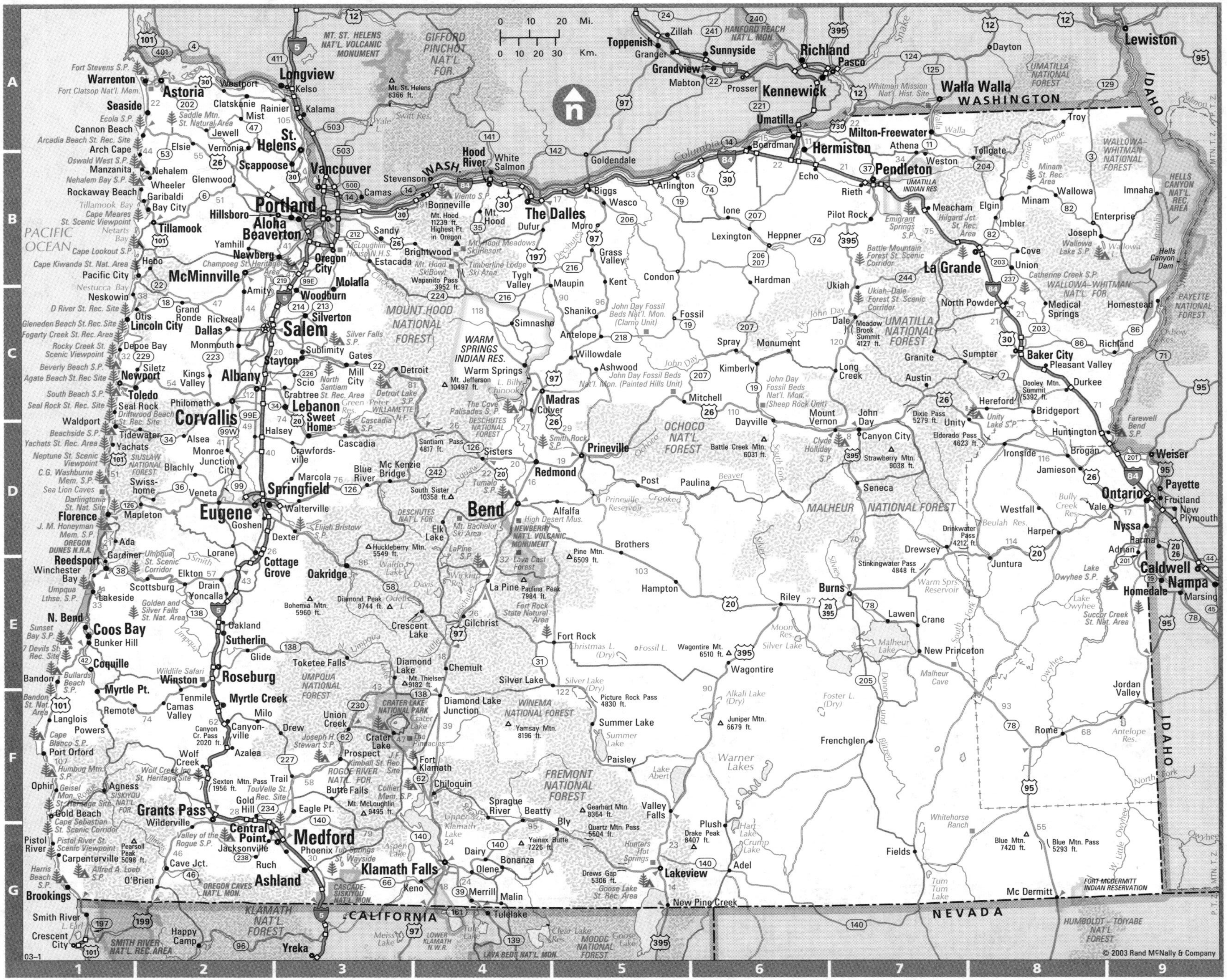

© 2003 Rand McNally & Company

randmcnally.com
Express Access Code: PA

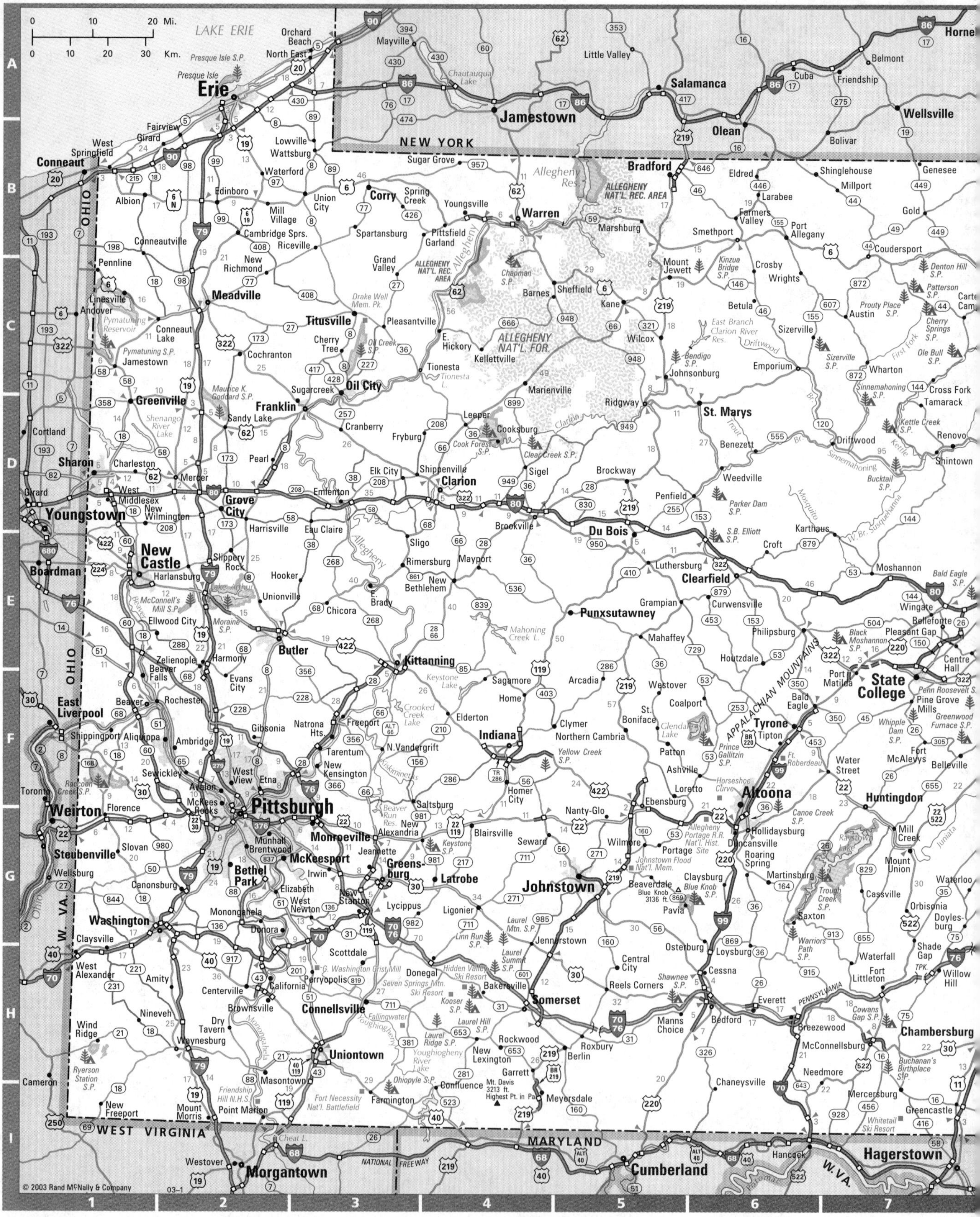

Pennsylvania

Population: 12,320,600 (1/1/01 estimate)

Land Area: 44,820 sq. mi.

Capital: Harrisburg

Cities and Towns

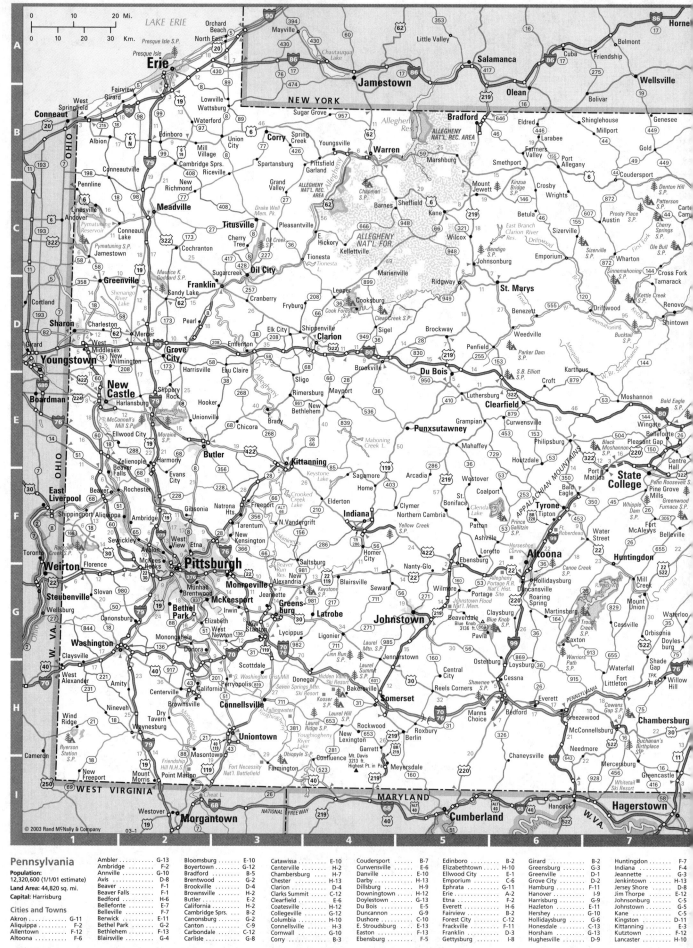

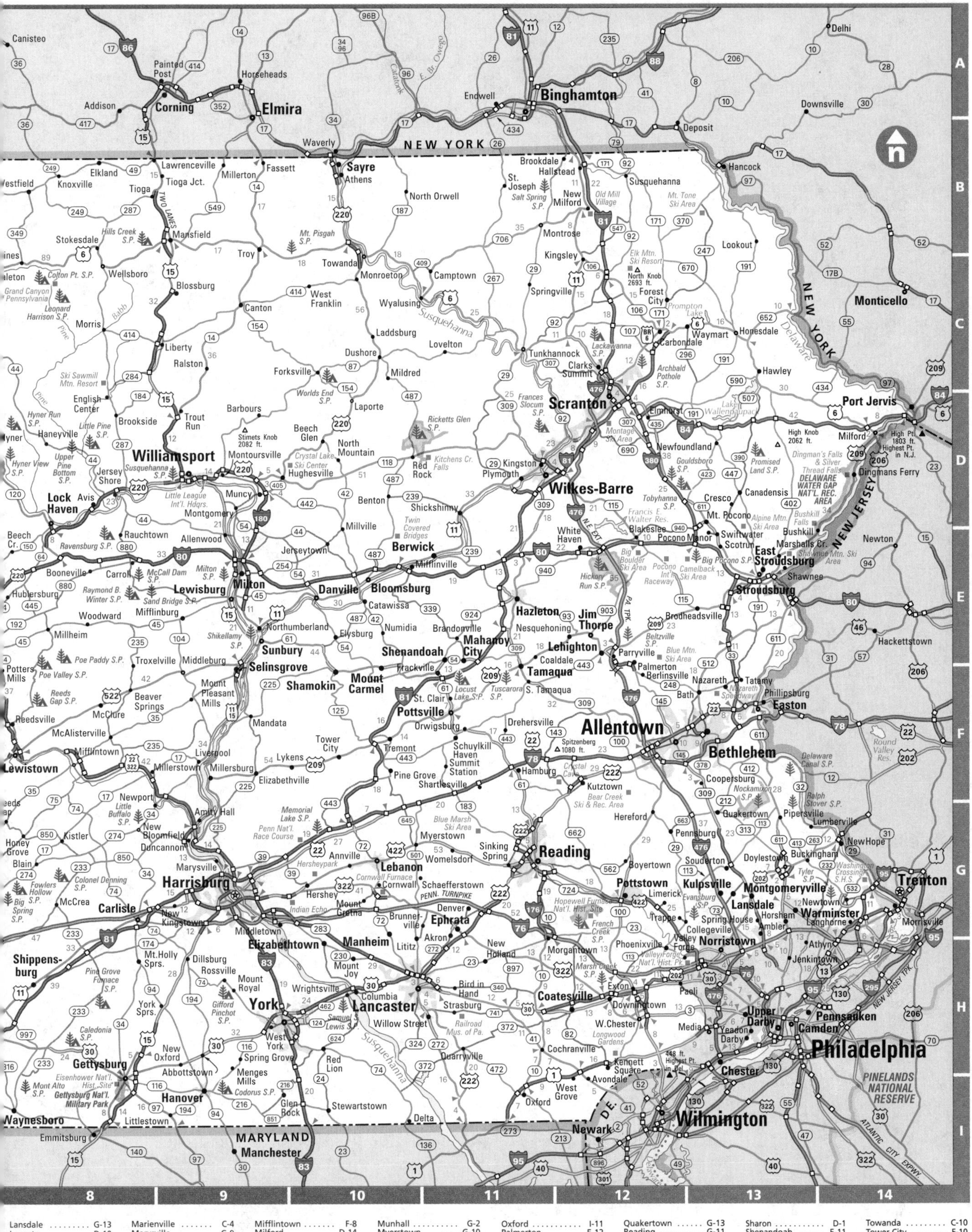

NEW YORK
Binghamton
Elmira
Corning
Monticello
Port Jervis
Sayre
Towanda
Williamsport
Lock Haven
Scranton
Wilkes-Barre
Hazleton
Jim Thorpe
Berwick
Bloomsburg
Danville
Milton
Lewisburg
Sunbury
Selinsgrove
Shamokin
Mount Carmel
Shenandoah
Mahanoy City
Pottsville
Tamaqua
Lehighton
East Stroudsburg
Stroudsburg
Easton
Bethlehem
Allentown
Reading
Lebanon
Harrisburg
Carlisle
Shippensburg
Elizabethtown
Manheim
Ephrata
Lancaster
York
Hanover
Gettysburg
Coatesville
Pottstown
Norristown
Kulpsville
Lansdale
Montgomeryville
Warminster
Trenton
Upper Darby
Camden
Pennsauken
Philadelphia
Chester
Wilmington
Newark
PINELANDS NATIONAL RESERVE
NEW JERSEY
MARYLAND
Manchester
DE.
8
9
10
11
12
13
14
A
B
C
D
E
F
G
H
I

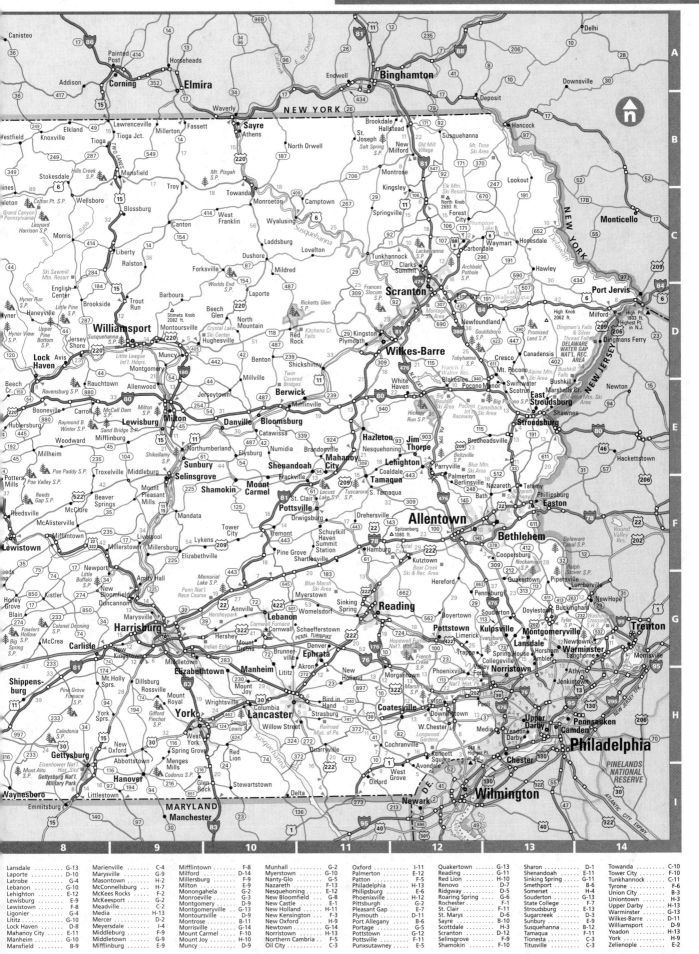

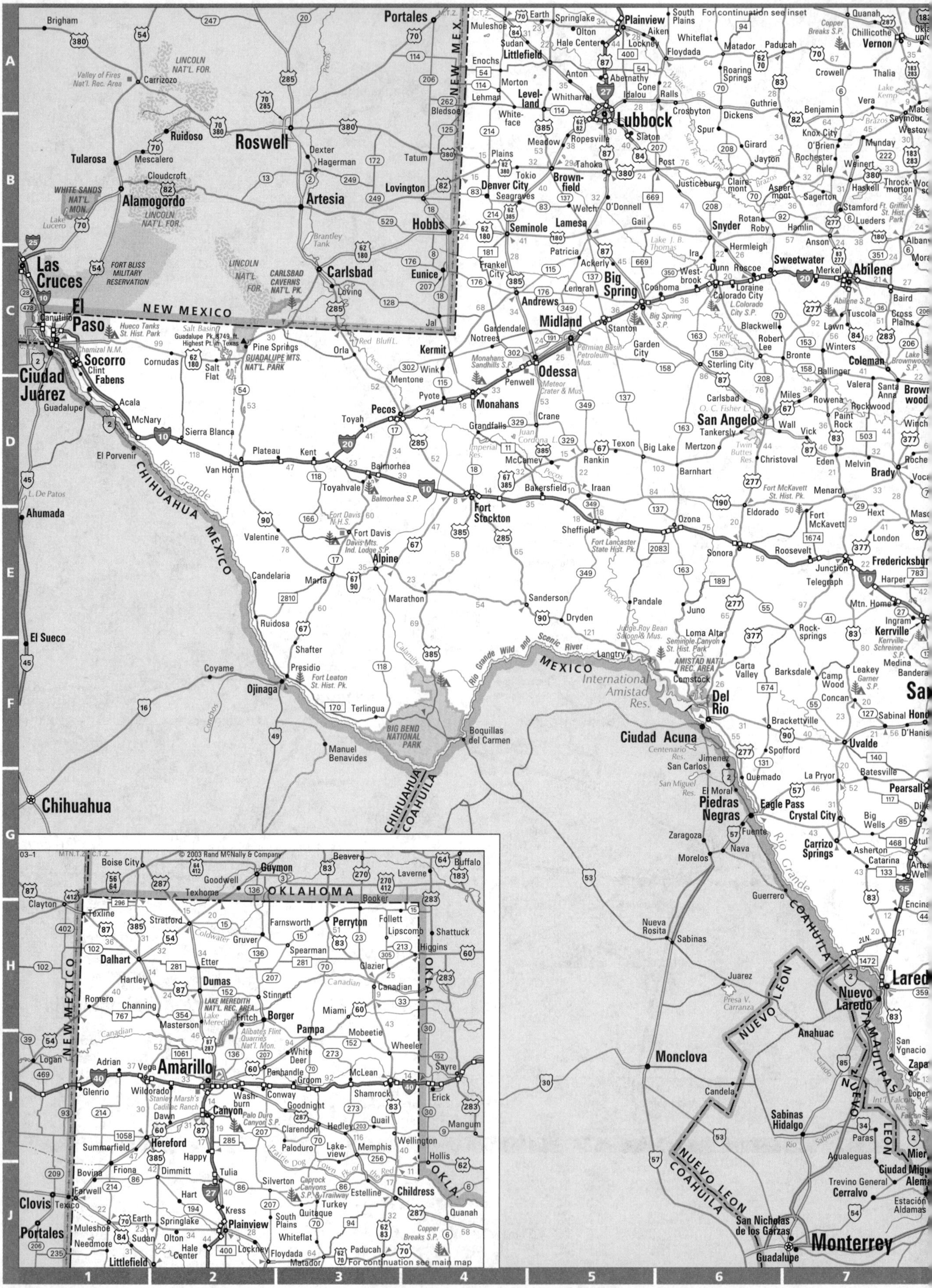
NEW MEXICO
Roswell
Alamogordo
Las Cruces
Artesia
Carlsbad
Hobbs
Portales
Lovington
Ruidoso
Tularosa
Carrizozo
LINCOLN NAT'L. FOR.
WHITE SANDS NAT'L. MON.
FORT BLISS MILITARY RESERVATION
CARLSBAD CAVERNS NAT'L. PK.
El Paso
Ciudad Juarez
Socorro
Fabens
Plainview
Lubbock
Levelland
Littlefield
Brownfield
Lamesa
Seminole
Denver City
Andrews
Big Spring
Midland
Odessa
Monahans
Kermit
Pecos
Fort Stockton
Alpine
Marfa
Presidio
Ojinaga
Van Horn
Sierra Blanca
GUADALUPE MTS. NAT'L. PARK
BIG BEND NATIONAL PARK
Rio Grande
CHIHUAHUA
MEXICO
COAHUILA
Chihuahua
Snyder
Sweetwater
Abilene
San Angelo
Ozona
Sonora
Junction
Kerrville
Fredericksburg
Del Rio
Ciudad Acuna
Amistad Res.
Eagle Pass
Piedras Negras
Uvalde
Crystal City
Carrizo Springs
Laredo
Nuevo Laredo
Monclova
Monterrey
NUEVO LEON
TAMAULIPAS
Vernon
Quanah
Coleman
Brady
Pearsall
OKLAHOMA
Amarillo
Canyon
Hereford
Borger
Pampa
Dumas
Dalhart
Perryton
Childress
Clovis
Portales
Plainview
Guymon
© 2003 Rand McNally & Company
For continuation see inset
For continuation see main map

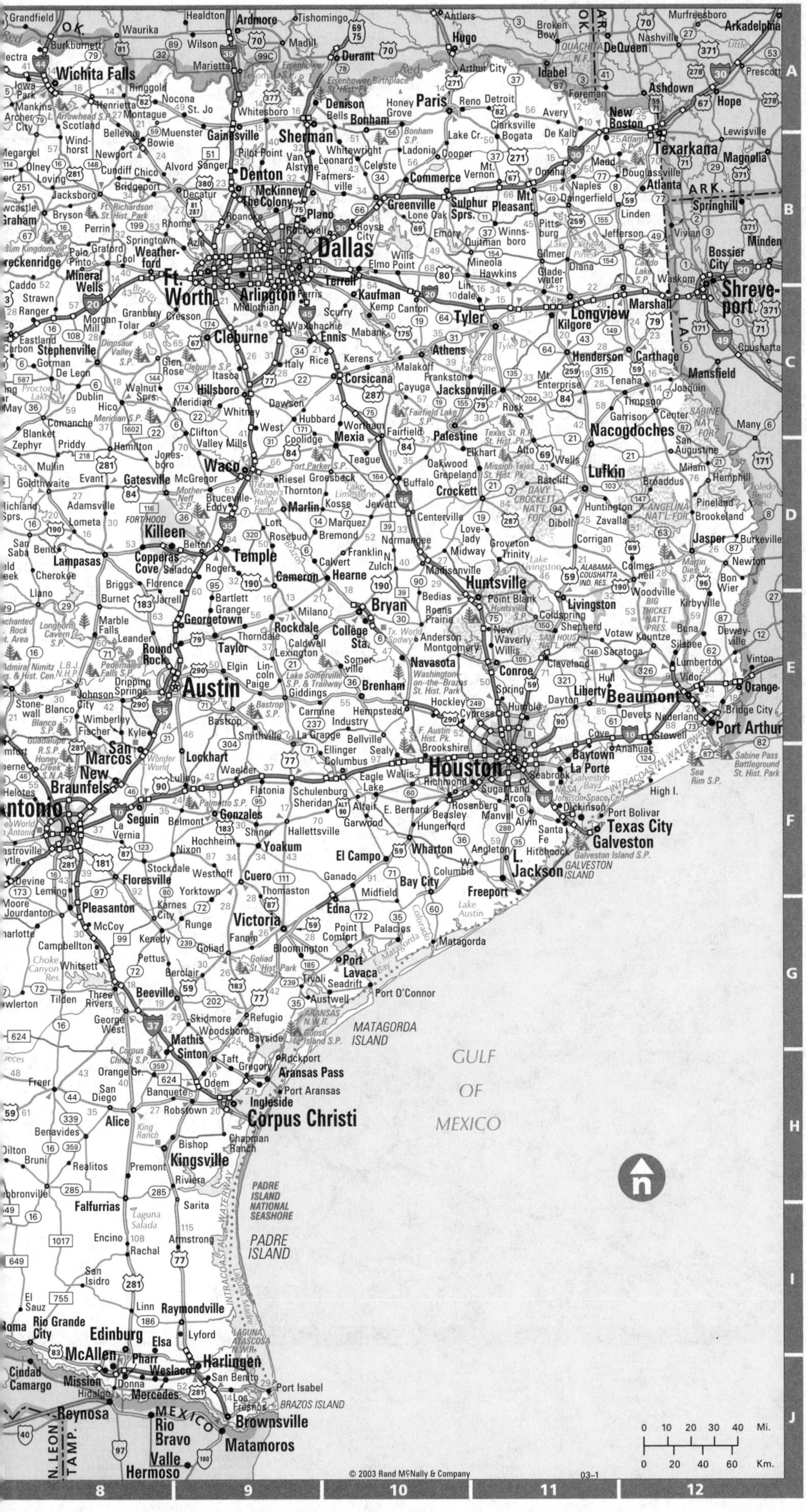

Texas

Population: 21,319,300 (1/1/01 estimate)

Land Area: 261,914 sq. mi.

Capital: Austin

Cities and Towns

Abilene	C-7
Albany	B-7
Alice	H-8
Alpine	E-3
Alvin	F-11
Amarillo	I-2
Anahuac	F-11
Andrews	C-4
Angleton	F-11
Anson	B-7
Archer City	B-8
Arlington	B-9
Aspermont	B-7
Athens	C-10
Austin	E-9
Baird	C-7
Ballinger	D-7
Bandera	F-7
Bastrop	E-9
Baytown	F-11
Bay City	F-10
Beaumont	E-12
Beeville	G-9
Bellville	E-10
Belton	D-9
Big Lake	D-5
Big Spring	C-5
Boerne	F-8
Bonham	A-10
Borger	H-2
Brackettville	F-6
Brady	D-7
Breckenridge	B-8
Brenham	E-10
Brownfield	B-5
Brownsville	J-9
Brownwood	D-8
Bryan	E-10
Burkburnett	A-8
Burnet	E-8
Caldwell	E-9
Cameron	D-9
Canadian	H-3
Canton	C-10
Canyon	I-2
Carrizo Springs	G-7
Carthage	C-12
Center	C-12
Centerville	D-10
Childress	J-3
Clarendon	I-3
Clarksville	A-11
Cleburne	C-9
Coldspring	E-11
Coleman	C-7
College Station	E-10
Colorado City	C-6
Columbus	F-10
Comanche	C-8
Conroe	E-11
Cooper	B-10
Copperas Cove	D-8
Corpus Christi	H-9
Corsicana	C-10
Cotulla	G-7
Crane	D-5
Crockett	D-11
Crosbyton	A-6
Crowell	A-7
Crystal City	G-7
Cuero	F-9
Daingerfield	B-11
Dalhart	H-1
Dallas	B-9
Decatur	B-9
Del Rio	F-6
Denison	A-9
Denton	B-9
Denver City	B-4
Dimmitt	J-2
Donna	J-8
Dumas	H-2
Eagle Pass	G-6
Eastland	C-8
Edinburg	I-8
Edna	G-10
El Campo	F-10
El Paso	C-1
Eldorado	D-6
Emory	B-10
Ennis	C-9
Fairfield	C-10
Falfurrias	H-8
Farwell	J-1
Floresville	F-8
Floydada	A-6
Fort Davis	E-3
Fort Stockton	D-4
Fort Worth	B-9
Franklin	D-10
Fredericksburg	E-8
Freeport	F-11
Friona	J-1
Gainesville	A-9
Galveston	F-11
Garden City	C-5
Gatesville	D-9
George West	G-8
Georgetown	E-9
Gilmer	B-11
Glen Rose	C-8
Goldthwaite	D-8
Goliad	G-9
Gonzales	F-9
Graham	B-8
Granbury	C-8
Greenville	B-10
Groesbeck	D-10
Groveton	D-11
Hallettsville	F-9
Hamilton	D-8
Harlingen	J-9
Haskell	B-7
Hebbronville	H-8
Hemphill	D-12
Hempstead	E-10
Henderson	C-11
Henrietta	A-8
Hereford	I-1
Hillsboro	C-9
Hondo	F-7
Houston	F-11
Humble	E-11
Huntsville	E-11
Jacksboro	B-8
Jacksonville	C-11
Jasper	D-12
Jayton	B-6
Jefferson	B-12
Johnson City	E-8
Jourdanton	G-8
Junction	E-7
Karnes City	G-8
Kaufman	C-10
Kermit	C-4
Kerrville	E-7
Kilgore	C-11
Killeen	D-9
Kingsville	H-8
Kountze	E-12
La Grange	E-9
La Porte	F-11
Lake Jackson	F-11
Lamesa	B-5
Lampasas	D-8
Laredo	H-7
Leakey	F-7
Levelland	A-5
Liberty	E-11
Linden	B-12
Littlefield	A-5
Livingston	E-11
Llano	E-8
Lockhart	F-9
Longview	C-11
Lubbock	B-5
Lufkin	D-11
Madisonville	A-1
Marfa	E-3
Marlin	D-9
Marshall	C-11
Mason	E-7
Matador	A-6
McAllen	J-8
McKinney	B-9
Memphis	I-3
Menard	D-7
Mercedes	I-8
Meridian	C-9
Mertzon	D-6
Miami	H-3
Midland	C-5
Mineral Wells	B-8
Mission	J-8
Monahans	D-4
Montague	A-8
Morton	A-4
Mount Pleasant	B-11
Mount Vernon	B-11
Muleshoe	A-4
Nacogdoches	D-11
Nederland	E-12
New Braunfels	F-8
Newton	D-12
Odessa	C-5
Orange	E-12
Ozona	E-6
Paducah	A-6
Paint Rock	D-7
Palestine	C-10
Palo Pinto	B-8
Pampa	I-3
Panhandle	I-2
Paris	A-10
Pearsall	G-7
Pecos	D-3
Perryton	H-3
Pharr	J-8
Pittsburg	B-11
Plains	B-4
Plainview	A-5
Plano	B-9
Pleasanton	G-8
Port Lavaca	G-10
Post	B-6
Quanah	A-7
Quitman	B-11
Rankin	D-5
Raymondville	I-9
Refugio	G-9
Richmond	F-10
Rio Grande City	I-8
Robert Lee	C-6
Robstown	H-9
Roby	B-6
Rockport	H-9
Rocksprings	E-7
Rockwall	B-10
Rosenberg	F-10
Round Rock	E-9
Rusk	C-11
San Angelo	D-6
San Antonio	F-8
San Augustine	D-12
San Benito	J-9
San Diego	H-8
San Marcos	F-8
San Saba	D-8
Sanderson	E-4
Seguin	F-8
Seminole	B-4
Seymour	A-7
Sherman	A-9
Sierra Blanca	D-2
Silverton	J-2
Sinton	H-9
Snyder	B-6
Socorro	C-1
Sonora	E-6
Spearman	H-3
Stamford	B-7
Stanton	C-5
Stephenville	C-8
Sterling City	C-6
Stinnett	H-2
Stratford	H-2
Sugar Land	F-11
Sulphur Springs	B-10
Sweetwater	C-6
Tahoka	B-5
Taylor	E-9
Temple	D-9
Terrell	B-10
Texarkana	B-12
Texas City	F-11
The Colony	B-9
Three Rivers	G-8
Throckmorton	B-7
Tilden	G-8
Tulia	J-2
Tyler	C-11
Uvalde	F-7
Van Horn	D-2
Vega	I-1
Vernon	A-7
Victoria	G-9
Vidor	E-12
Waco	D-9
Waxahachie	C-9
Weatherford	B-8
Wellington	I-3
Weslaco	J-8
Wharton	F-10
Wheeler	I-3
Wichita Falls	A-8
Woodville	D-12
Zapata	I-7

randmcnally.com
Express Access Codes: Virginia VA | West Virginia WV

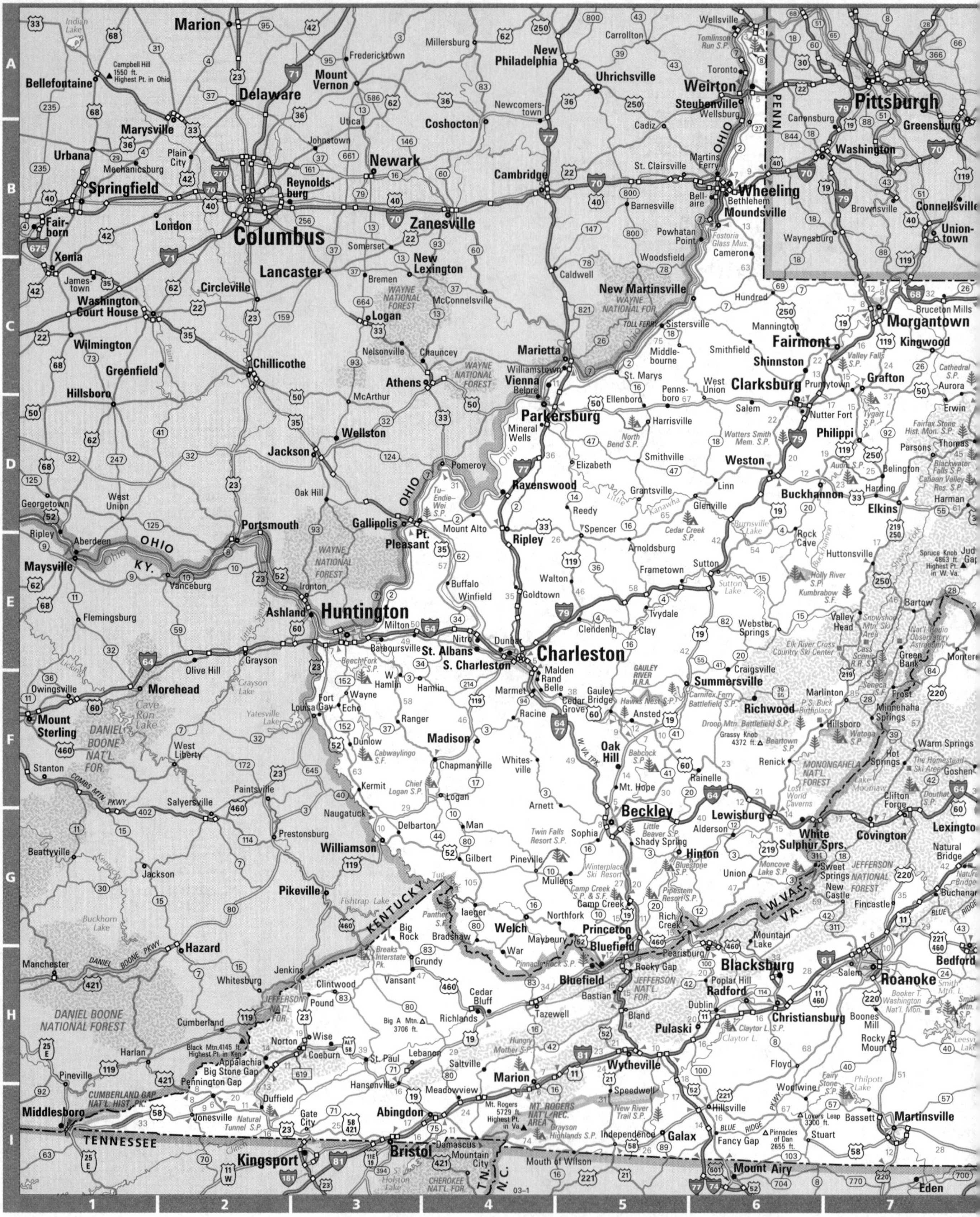

Virginia

Population: 7,187,100 (1/1/01 estimate)

Land Area: 39,598 sq. mi.

Capital: Richmond

Cities and Towns

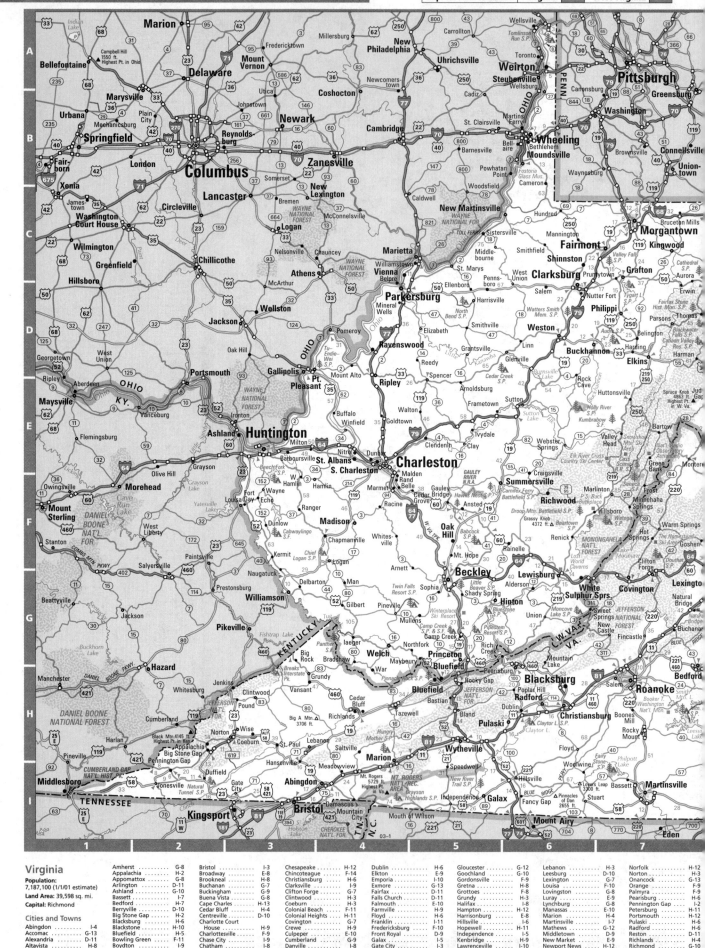

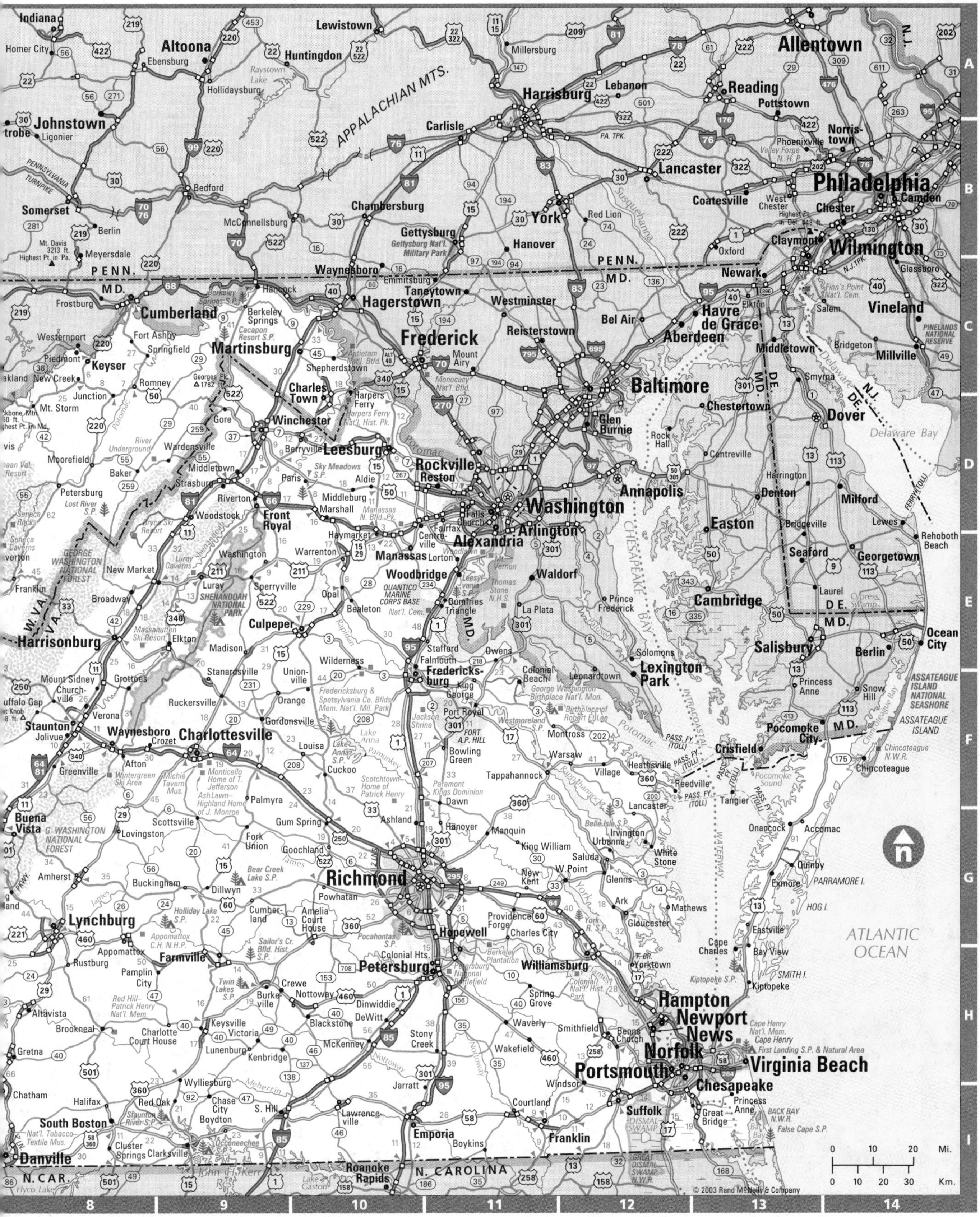

Roanoke	H-7
Rocky Mount	H-7
St. Paul	H-3
Salem	H-7
Saltville	H-4
Saluda	G-12
Smithfield	H-12
South Boston	I-8
South Hill	I-9
Stafford	E-11
Staunton	F-8
Strasburg	D-9
Suffolk	I-12
Tangier	F-13
Tappahannock	F-11
Tazewell	H-4
Victoria	H-9
Virginia Beach	H-13
Warrenton	E-10
Waverly	H-11
Waynesboro	F-8
Williamsburg	H-12
Winchester	D-9
Wise	H-3
Woodbridge	E-11
Woodstock	D-9
Wytheville	H-5
Yorktown	H-12

West Virginia

Population:
1,810,400 (1/1/01 estimate)

Land Area: 24,087 sq. mi.

Capital: Charleston

Cities and Towns

Alderson	G-6
Ansted	F-5
Barboursville	E-3
Beckley	G-5
Belle	F-4
Bethlehem	B-6
Buckhannon	D-6
Charles Town	D-10
Charleston	E-4
Clarksburg	D-6
Clendenin	E-5
Dunbar	E-4
Elizabeth	D-5
Elkins	D-7
Fairmont	C-7
Franklin	E-8
Glenville	D-6
Grafton	C-7
Hamlin	F-3
Harpers Ferry	C-10
Harrisville	D-5
Hinton	G-5
Huntington	E-3
Keyser	C-8
Kingwood	C-7
Lewisburg	G-6
Logan	F-4
Madison	F-4
Mannington	C-6
Marlinton	F-7
Marmet	F-4
Martinsburg	C-10
Middlebourne	C-5
Milton	E-3
Moorefield	D-8
Morgantown	C-7
Moundsville	B-6
Mount Hope	F-5
Mullens	G-5
New Martinsville	C-6
Nitro	E-4
Oak Hill	F-5
Parkersburg	D-4
Parsons	D-7
Pennsboro	D-5
Petersburg	D-8
Philippi	D-7
Pineville	G-4
Princeton	G-5
Rand	F-4
Ravenswood	D-4
Richwood	F-6
Ripley	D-4
Romney	C-8
St. Albans	E-4
St. Marys	C-5
Salem	D-6
Shinnston	C-6
Sistersville	C-5
South Charleston	E-4
Spencer	E-5
Summersville	F-5
Sutton	E-6
Vienna	C-4
Wayne	F-3
Weirton	A-6
Welch	G-4
Wellsburg	B-6
Weston	D-6
Wheeling	B-6
White Sulphur Springs	G-6
Williamson	G-3
Winfield	E-4

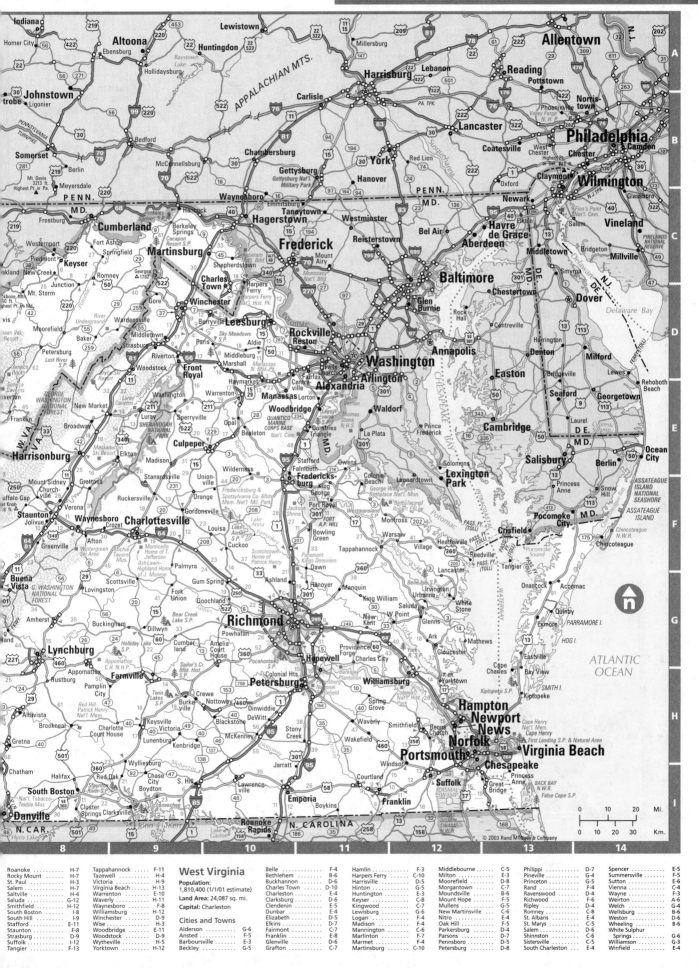

randmcnally.com
Express Access Code: UT

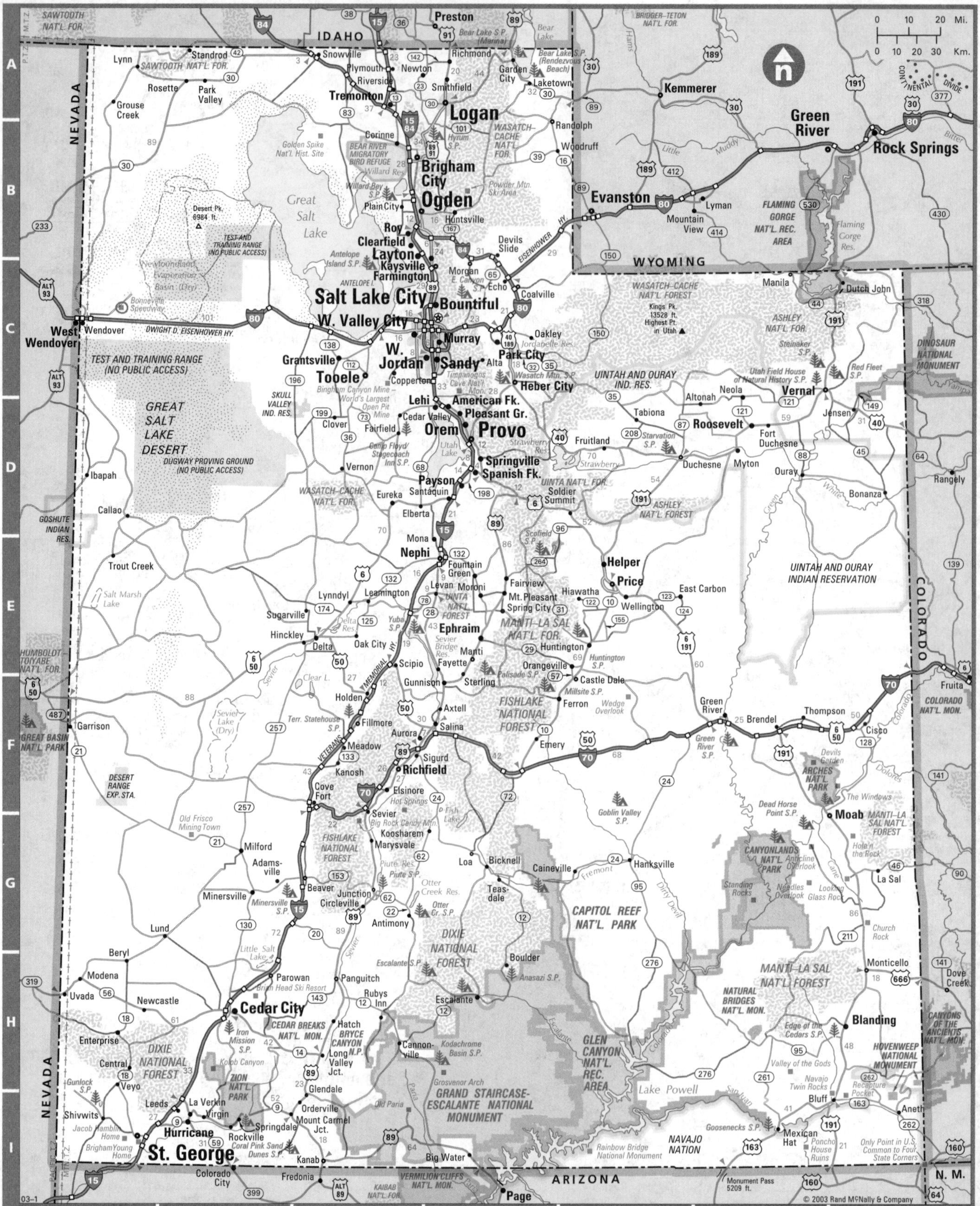

Utah

Population: 2,296,100 (1/1/01 estimate)
Land Area: 82,168 sq. mi.
Capital: Salt Lake City

Cities and Towns

American Fork	D-4
Antimony	G-3
Aurora	F-3
Beaver	G-3
Blanding	H-7
Bountiful	C-4
Brigham City	B-3
Castle Dale	F-5
Cedar City	H-2
Circleville	G-3
Clearfield	B-3
Coalville	C-4
Copperton	C-3
Delta	E-3
Duchesne	D-5
East Carbon	E-5
Elsinore	F-3
Enterprise	H-1
Ephraim	E-4
Escalante	H-4
Eureka	D-3
Fairview	E-4
Farmington	C-4
Ferron	F-4
Fillmore	F-3
Fort Duchesne	D-6
Fountain Green	E-4
Grantsville	C-3
Green River	F-6
Gunnison	F-4
Heber City	C-4
Helper	E-5
Hinckley	E-3
Holladay	C-4
Huntington	E-5
Huntsville	B-4
Hurricane	I-2
Junction	G-3
Kanab	I-3
Kaysville	B-4
La Verkin	I-2
Layton	B-3
Lehi	D-4
Loa	G-4
Logan	A-4
Manila	C-6
Manti	E-4
Milford	G-2
Minersville	G-2
Moab	F-6
Mona	E-4
Monticello	H-7
Morgan	C-4
Moroni	E-4
Mount Pleasant	E-4
Murray	C-4
Myton	D-6
Neola	C-6
Nephi	E-4
Newton	A-3
Oak City	E-3
Oakley	C-4
Ogden	B-3
Orangeville	E-5
Orem	D-4
Ouray	D-6
Panguitch	H-3
Park City	C-4
Parowan	H-2
Payson	D-4
Plain City	B-3
Pleasant Grove	D-4
Price	E-5
Provo	D-4
Randolph	B-4
Richfield	F-3
Richmond	A-4
Roosevelt	D-6
Roy	B-3
St. George	I-1
Salina	F-4
Salt Lake City	C-4
Sandy	C-4
Santaquin	D-4
Smithfield	A-4
Spanish Fork	D-4
Spring City	E-4
Springville	D-4
Tooele	C-3
Tremonton	A-3
Vernal	C-6
Virgin	I-2
Wellington	E-5
Wendover	C-1
West Jordan	C-4
W. Valley City	C-3

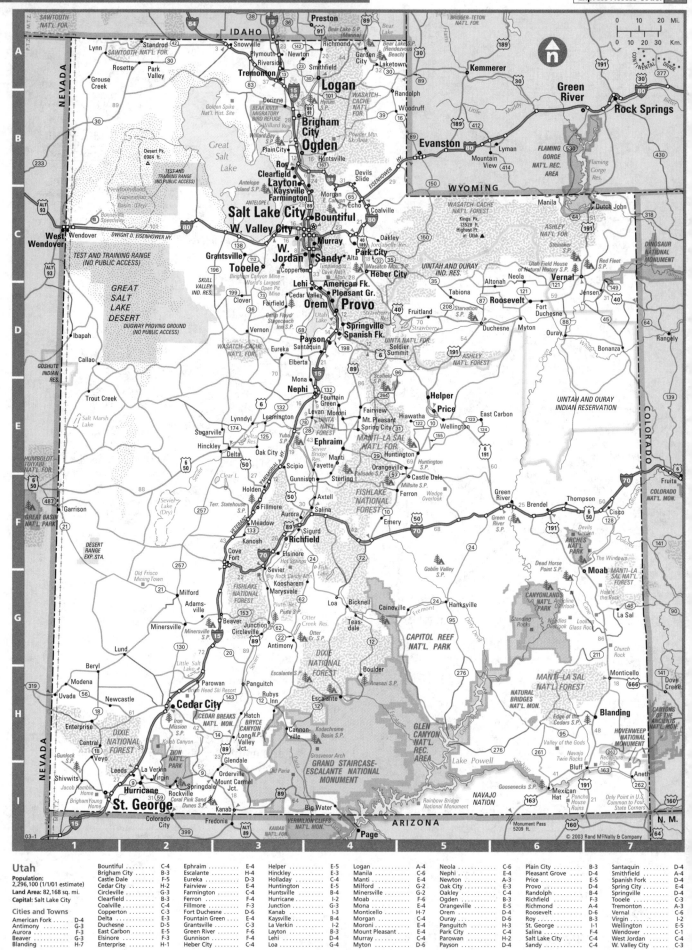

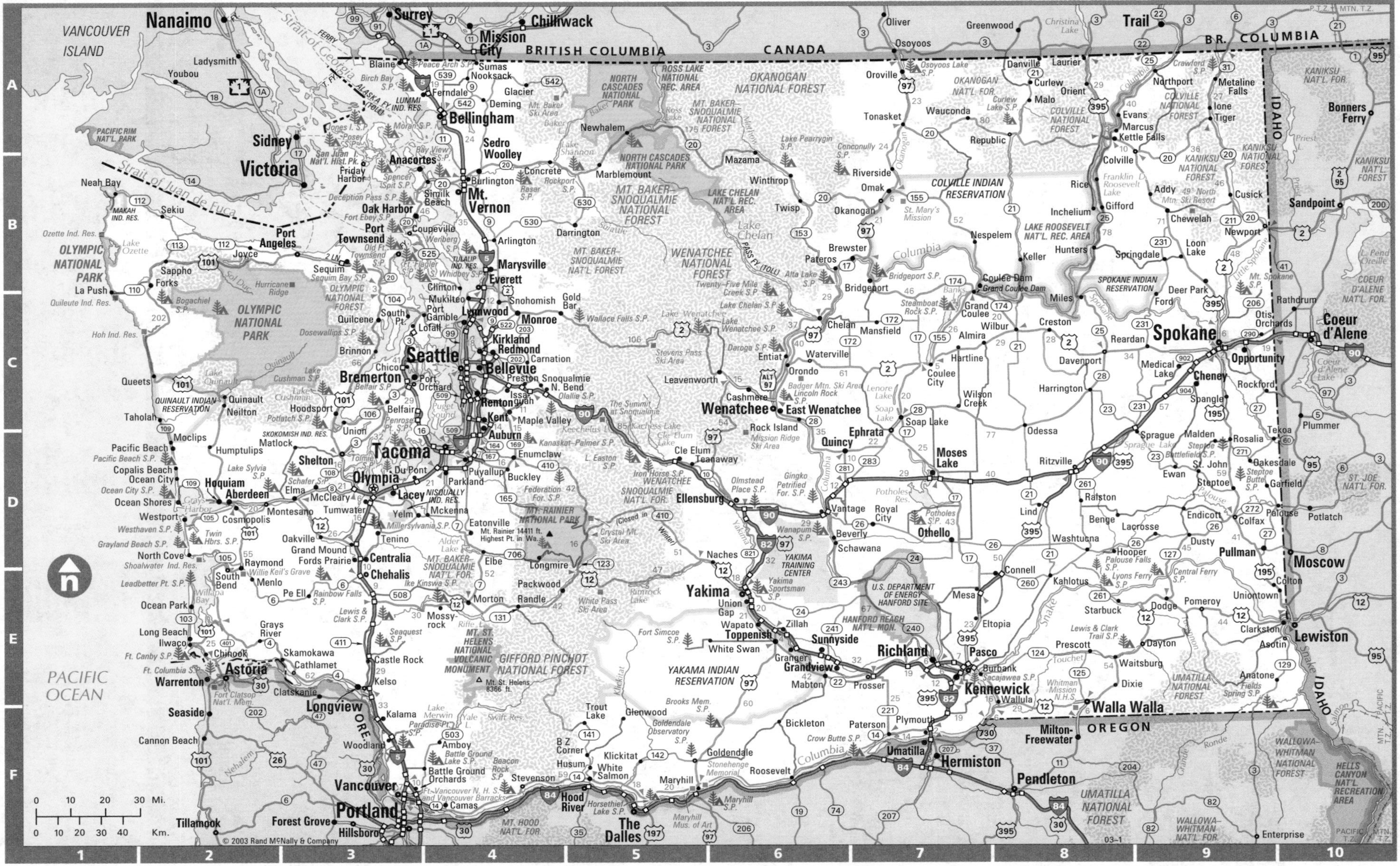

Washington

Population: 6,019,400 (1/1/01 estimate)

Land Area: 66,581 sq. mi.

Capital: Olympia

Cities and Towns

City	Grid
Aberdeen	D-2
Anacortes	B-3
Arlington	B-4
Asotin	E-10
Auburn	D-4
Battle Ground	F-4
Bellevue	C-4
Bellingham	A-4
Blaine	A-3
Bremerton	C-3
Brewster	B-7
Bridgeport	B-7
Buckley	D-4
Burlington	B-4
Camas	F-4
Carnation	C-4
Castle Rock	E-3
Cathlamet	E-3
Centralia	D-3
Chehalis	E-3
Chelan	C-6
Cheney	C-9
Chewelah	B-9
Clarkston	E-10
Cle Elum	D-5
Clinton	B-4
Colfax	D-9
Colville	B-9
Connell	E-8
Cosmopolis	D-2
Coulee Dam	B-7
Coupeville	B-3
Darrington	B-5
Davenport	C-8
Dayton	E-9
Deer Park	B-9
East Wenatchee	C-6
Eatonville	D-4
Ellensburg	D-6
Elma	D-3
Enumclaw	D-4
Ephrata	D-7
Everett	B-4
Ferndale	A-4
Forks	B-2
Friday Harbor	B-3
Gold Bar	C-4
Goldendale	F-5
Grand Coulee	C-7
Grandview	E-6
Granger	E-6
Hoodsport	C-3
Hoquiam	D-2
Issaquah	C-4
Kalama	F-3
Kelso	E-3
Kennewick	E-7
Kent	C-4
Kettle Falls	A-8
Kirkland	C-4
Lacey	D-3
Leavenworth	C-6
Long Beach	E-2
Longview	E-3
Lynnwood	C-4
Mabton	E-6
Maple Valley	C-4
Marysville	B-4
McCleary	D-3
Medical Lake	C-9
Monroe	C-4
Montesano	D-2
Morton	E-4
Moses Lake	D-7
Mount Vernon	B-4
Mukilteo	C-4
Neah Bay	B-1
Newport	B-9
North Bend	C-4
Oak Harbor	B-3
Ocean Park	E-2
Ocean Shores	D-2
Okanogan	B-7
Olympia	D-3
Omak	B-7
Opportunity	C-9
Orchards	F-3
Oroville	A-7
Othello	D-7
Otis Orchards	C-9
Pacific Beach	D-2
Packwood	E-4
Parkland	D-4
Pasco	E-7
Pomeroy	E-9
Port Angeles	B-3
Port Orchard	C-3
Port Townsend	B-3
Prosser	E-7
Pullman	D-9
Puyallup	D-4
Quilcene	C-3
Quincy	D-6
Raymond	D-2
Redmond	C-4
Renton	C-4
Republic	A-8
Richland	E-7
Ritzville	D-8
Royal City	D-7
Seattle	C-4
Sedro Woolley	B-4
Sequim	B-3
Shelton	D-3
Snohomish	C-4
Snoqualmie	C-4
Soap Lake	C-7
South Bend	E-2
Spokane	C-9
Stevenson	F-4
Sunnyside	E-6
Tacoma	D-4
Toppenish	E-6
Tumwater	D-3
Union Gap	E-6
Vancouver	F-3
Walla Walla	E-8
Wapato	E-6
Waterville	C-6
Wenatchee	C-6
Westport	D-2
White Salmon	F-5
Woodland	F-3
Yakima	E-6
Zillah	E-6

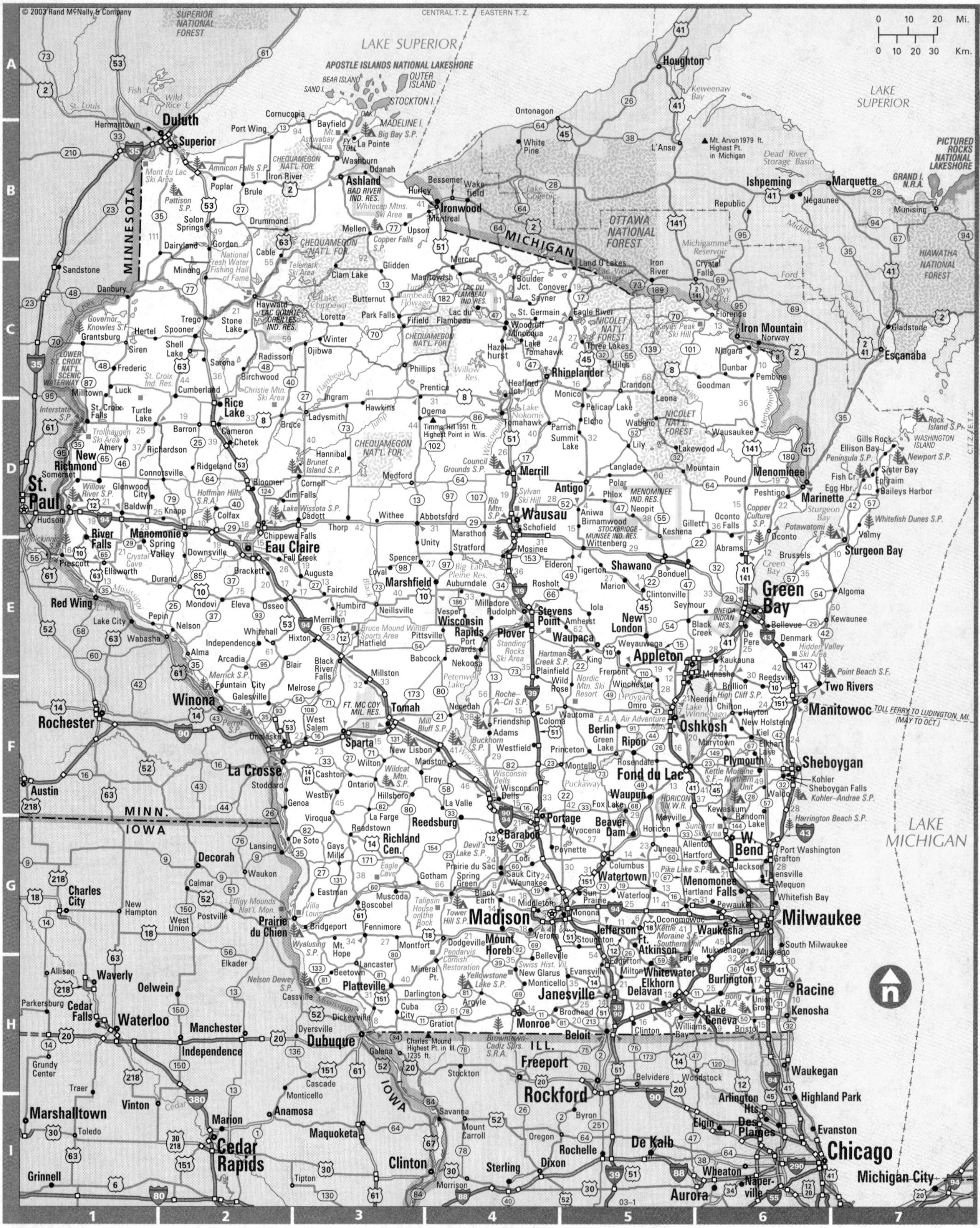

Wisconsin

Population: 5,419,800 (1/1/01 estimate)

Land Area: 54,314 sq. mi.

Capital: Madison

Cities and Towns

Antigo	D-5
Appleton	E-5
Ashland	B-3
Baraboo	G-4
Beaver Dam	G-5
Beloit	H-5
Berlin	F-5
Black River Falls	E-3
Burlington	H-6
Chilton	F-6
Chippewa Falls	D-2
Crandon	C-5
Darlington	H-4
Delavan	H-5
De Pere	E-6
Dodgeville	G-4
Eagle River	C-5
Eau Claire	E-2
Elkhorn	H-5
Fond du Lac	F-5
Fort Atkinson	G-5
Grafton	G-6
Green Bay	E-6
Hartford	G-6
Hayward	C-2
Hudson	D-1
Hurley	B-4
Janesville	H-5
Jefferson	G-5
Juneau	G-5
Kaukauna	E-6
Kenosha	H-6
Kewaunee	E-6
La Crosse	F-2
Ladysmith	D-3
Lake Geneva	H-6
Lancaster	H-3
Madison	G-4
Manitowoc	F-6
Marinette	D-6
Marshfield	E-4
Mauston	F-4
Medford	D-3
Menasha	E-5
Menomonee Falls	G-6
Menomonie	D-2
Mequon	G-6
Merrill	D-4
Middleton	G-4
Milwaukee	G-6
Monroe	H-4
Mount Horeb	G-4
Muskego	G-6
Neenah	F-5
New Glarus	H-4
Oconomowoc	G-5
Oconto	D-6
Onalaska	F-2
Oshkosh	F-5
Phillips	C-3
Platteville	H-3
Plover	E-4
Plymouth	F-6
Port Washington	G-6
Portage	F-4
Prairie du Chien	G-3
Racine	H-6
Rhinelander	C-4
Rice Lake	D-2
Richland Cen.	G-3
Ripon	F-5
River Falls	D-1
Shawano	E-5
Sheboygan	F-6
South Milwaukee	G-6
Sparta	F-3
Stevens Point	E-4
Stoughton	G-5
Sturgeon Bay	D-7
Sun Prairie	G-5
Superior	B-2
Tomah	F-3
Tomahawk	D-4
Two Rivers	F-6
Viroqua	F-3
Washburn	B-3
Watertown	G-5
Waukesha	G-6
Waupaca	E-5
Waupun	F-5
Wausau	D-4
Wautoma	F-5
West Bend	G-6
Whitefish Bay	G-6
Whitewater	H-5
Wisconsin Dells	F-4
Wisconsin Rapids	E-4

Wyoming

Population: 498,500 (1/1/01 estimate)
Land Area: 97,105 sq. mi.
Capital: Cheyenne

Cities and Towns

Afton	D-1
Albin	F-9
Alpine	C-1
Baggs	G-5
Bairoil	E-5
Bar Nunn	D-6
Basin	B-4
Big Horn	A-6
Big Piney	D-2
Bondurant	C-2
Buffalo	B-6
Burlington	B-4
Burns	F-9
Carpenter	G-9
Casper	D-6
Centennial	F-7
Cheyenne	F-8
Chugwater	F-8
Clearmont	A-6
Cody	A-3
Cokeville	E-1
Daniel	D-2
Dayton	A-5
Deaver	A-4
Devils Tower	A-8
Diamondville	F-2
Douglas	D-7
Dubois	C-3
Eden	E-3
Edgerton	C-6
Elk Mountain	F-6
Evanston	F-1
Evansville	D-6
Farson	E-3
Fort Bridger	F-2
Fort Laramie	E-8
Fort Washakie	D-4
Freedom	D-1
Gillette	B-7
Glendo	D-8
Glenrock	D-7
Granger	F-2
Green River	F-3
Greybull	A-4
Guernsey	E-8
Hanna	E-6
Horse Creek	F-8
Hudson	D-4
Hulett	A-8
Hyattville	B-5
Jackson	C-1
Jeffrey City	D-5
Kaycee	C-6
Kemmerer	E-2
Kinnear	C-4
La Barge	E-2
Lagrange	F-9
Lance Creek	D-8
Lander	D-4
Laramie	F-7
Linch	C-6
Lingle	E-9
Lovell	A-4
Lusk	D-8
Lyman	F-2
Manville	D-8
Marbleton	D-2
Medicine Bow	E-6
Meeteetse	B-4
Midwest	C-6
Moorcroft	B-8
Moose	C-2
Mountain View	F-2
Newcastle	B-9
Opal	F-2
Osage	B-8
Pavillion	C-4
Pine Bluffs	F-9
Pinedale	D-2
Powell	A-4
Ranchester	A-5
Rawlins	F-5
Riverton	D-4
Rock River	F-7
Rock Springs	F-3
Saratoga	F-6
Sheridan	A-6
Shoshoni	C-4
Sinclair	F-5
Smoot	D-1
Sundance	B-8
Superior	F-3
Ten Sleep	B-5
Teton Village	C-1
Thayne	D-1
Thermopolis	C-4
Torrington	E-9
Upton	B-8
Wamsutter	F-5
Wheatland	E-8
Worland	B-5
Wright	C-7
Yellowstone National Park	A-2

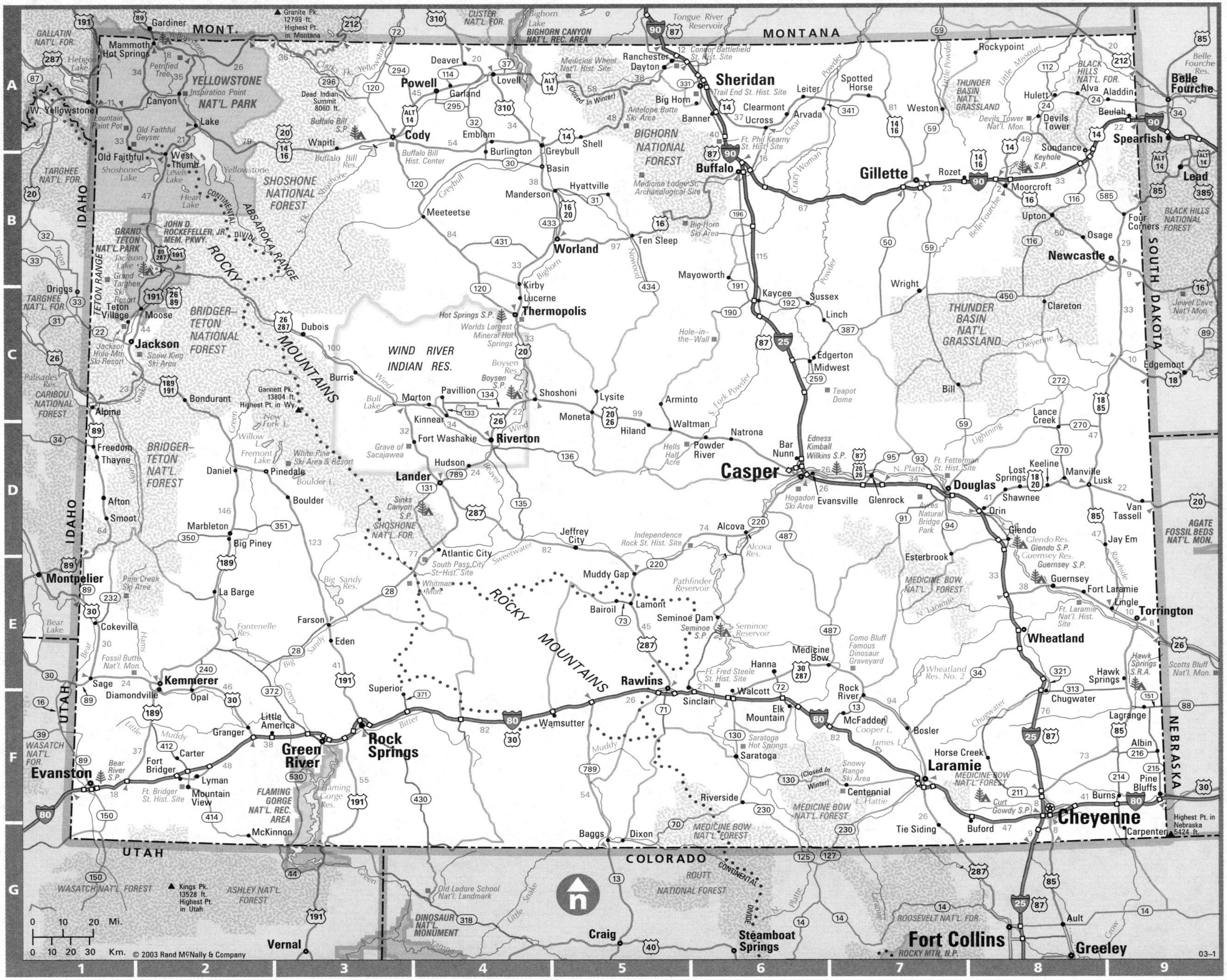

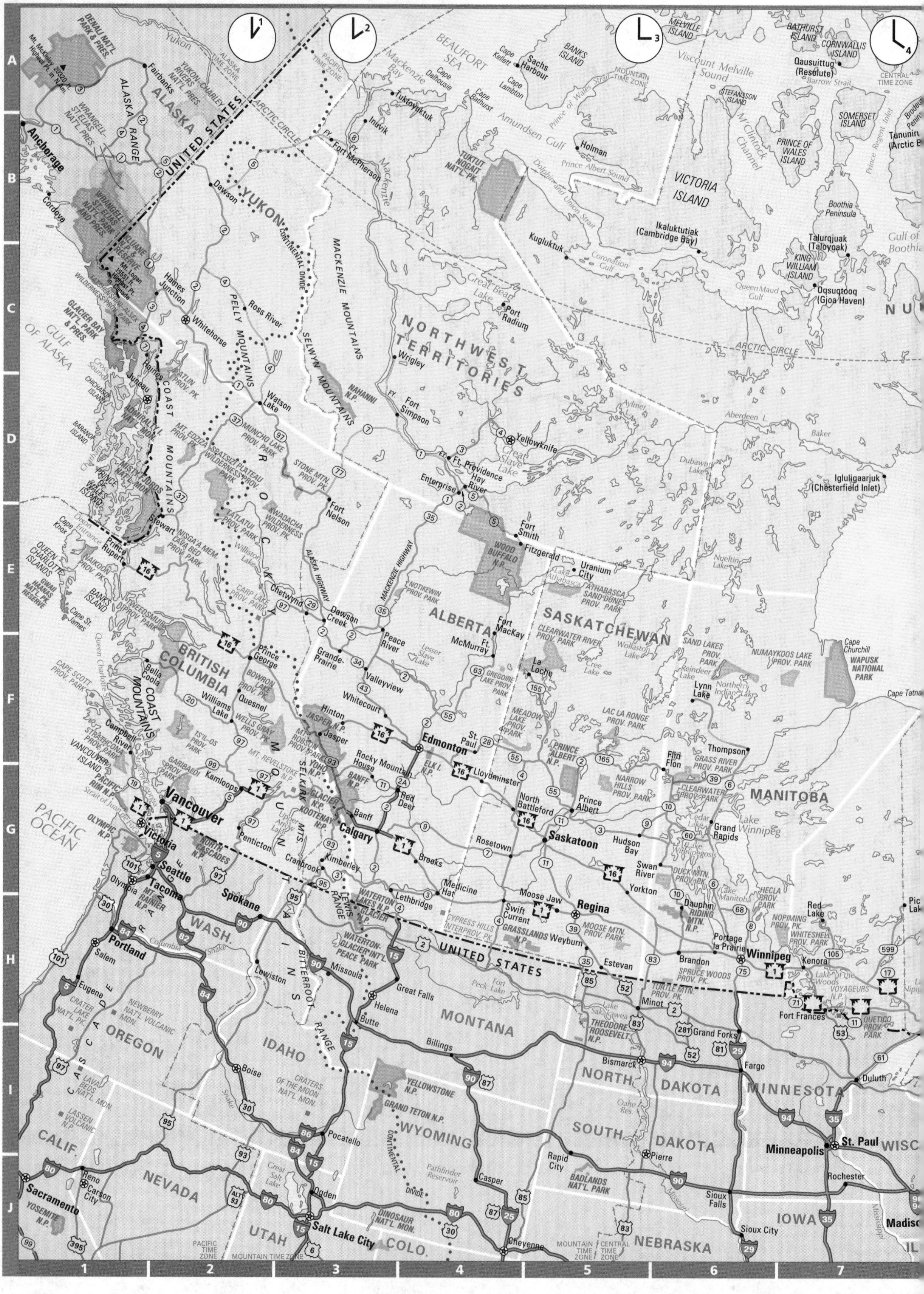

A
B
C
D
E
F
G
H
I
J
1
2
3
4
5
6
7
ALASKA TIME ZONE
PACIFIC TIME ZONE
MOUNTAIN TIME ZONE
CENTRAL TIME ZONE
BEAUFORT SEA
ARCTIC CIRCLE
ALASKA
UNITED STATES
YUKON
NORTHWEST TERRITORIES
NU
BRITISH COLUMBIA
ALBERTA
SASKATCHEWAN
MANITOBA
WASH.
OREGON
IDAHO
MONTANA
WYOMING
NORTH DAKOTA
SOUTH DAKOTA
MINNESOTA
NEBRASKA
IOWA
NEVADA
UTAH
COLO.
CALIF.
PACIFIC OCEAN
GULF OF ALASKA
DENALI NAT'L PARK & PRES.
Mt. McKinley 20320 ft. Highest Pt. in N. Am.
ALASKA RANGE
WRANGELL-ST. ELIAS NAT'L PRES.
WRANGELL-ST. ELIAS NAT'L PARK AND PRES.
YUKON-CHARLEY RIVERS NAT'L PRES.
KLUANE N.P. & RESERVE
Mt. Logan 19551 ft. Highest Pt. in Canada
GLACIER BAY NAT'L PARK & PRES.
Anchorage
Fairbanks
Cordova
Dawson
Haines Junction
Whitehorse
Haines
Juneau
Ross River
Watson Lake
Inuvik
Tuktoyaktuk
Fort McPherson
Mackenzie Bay
Cape Dalhousie
Cape Bathurst
Cape Kellett
Sachs Harbour
Cape Lambton
BANKS ISLAND
MELVILLE ISLAND
Viscount Melville Sound
Prince of Wales Strait
Amundsen Gulf
Holman
Prince Albert Sound
Dolphin and Union Strait
VICTORIA ISLAND
TUKTUT NOGAIT NAT'L PK.
Kugluktuk
Coronation Gulf
Ikaluktutiak (Cambridge Bay)
STEFANSSON ISLAND
M'Clintock Channel
PRINCE OF WALES ISLAND
SOMERSET ISLAND
BATHURST ISLAND
CORNWALLIS ISLAND
Qausuittuq (Resolute)
Barrow Strait
Boothia Peninsula
Taloyoak (Taloyoak)
KING WILLIAM ISLAND
Uqsuqtooq (Gjoa Haven)
Queen Maud Gulf
Gulf of Boothia
Great Bear Lake
Port Radium
MACKENZIE MOUNTAINS
SELWYN MOUNTAINS
PELLY MOUNTAINS
CONTINENTAL DIVIDE
Wrigley
Fort Simpson
NAHANNI N.P.
Yellowknife
Great Slave Lake
Ft. Providence
Hay River
Enterprise
Aylmer L.
Aberdeen L.
Baker L.
Dubawnt Lake
Igluligaarjuk (Chesterfield Inlet)
Nueltin Lake
Fort Smith
Fitzgerald
Uranium City
Lake Athabasca
ATHABASCA SAND DUNES PROV. PARK
WOOD BUFFALO N.P.
Fort Nelson
ALASKA HIGHWAY
MACKENZIE HIGHWAY
STONE MTN. PROV. PK.
MUNCHO LAKE PROV. PARK
KWADACHA WILDERNESS PROV. PK.
TATLATUI PROV. PARK
SPATSIZI PLATEAU WILDERNESS PARK
MT. EDZIZA PROV. PK.
ATLIN PROV. PK.
COAST MOUNTAINS
ROCKY MOUNTAINS
MISTY FIORDS NAT'L MON.
ADMIRALTY I. NAT'L MON.
CHICHAGOF ISLAND
BARANOF ISLAND
PRINCE OF WALES ISLAND
Stewart
Prince Rupert
NISGA'A MEM. LAVA BED PROV. PARK
Williston Lake
Dixon Entrance
Cape Knox
QUEEN CHARLOTTE ISLANDS
NAIKOON PROV. PK.
GWAII HAANAS PARK RESERVE
BANKS ISLAND
Cape St. James
Queen Charlotte Sound
CARP LAKE PROV. PARK
Chetwynd
Dawson Creek
Peace River
Grande Prairie
Lesser Slave Lake
Valleyview
Whitecourt
NOTIKEWIN PROV. PARK
Fort MacKay
Ft. McMurray
GREGOIRE LAKE PROV. PARK
La Loche
CLEARWATER RIVER PROV. PARK
Wollaston Lake
Cree Lake
SAND LAKES PROV. PARK
Reindeer Lake
Northern Indian Lake
Lynn Lake
NUMAYKOOS LAKE PROV. PARK
Cape Churchill
WAPUSK NATIONAL PARK
Cape Tatnam
TWEEDSMUIR PROV. PARK
Prince George
Bella Coola
Williams Lake
Quesnel
BOWRON LAKE PROV. PARK
WELLS GRAY PROV. PARK
CAPE SCOTT PROV. PARK
Campbell River
STRATHCONA PROV. PARK
VANCOUVER ISLAND
PACIFIC RIM N.P.
TS'IL-OS PROV. PARK
GARIBALDI PROV. PARK
Kamloops
Vancouver
Victoria
Strait of Juan de Fuca
OLYMPIC N.P.
Hinton
Jasper
JASPER N.P.
MT. ROBSON PROV. PARK
MT. REVELSTOKE N.P.
GLACIER N.P.
YOHO N.P.
BANFF N.P.
KOOTENAY N.P.
SELKIRK MTS.
Upper Arrow Lake
Rocky Mountain House
Red Deer
Banff
Calgary
Edmonton
ELK I. N.P.
St. Paul
Lloydminster
MEADOW LAKE PROV. PARK
LAC LA RONGE PROV. PARK
PRINCE ALBERT N.P.
North Battleford
Prince Albert
NARROW HILLS PROV. PARK
Flin Flon
GRASS RIVER PROV. PARK
Thompson
CLEARWATER PROV. PARK
Cedar Lake
Grand Rapids
Lake Winnipeg
Lake Winnipegosis
Saskatoon
Rosetown
Hudson Bay
Swan River
Yorkton
DUCK MTN. PROV. PARK
Lake Manitoba
HECLA PROV. PARK
Dauphin
RIDING MTN. N.P.
Penticton
Cranbrook
Kimberley
Brooks
Medicine Hat
Lethbridge
NORTH CASCADES N.P.
Seattle
Olympia
Tacoma
MT. RAINIER N.P.
Spokane
WATERTON LAKES N.P.
GLACIER N.P.
LEWIS RANGE
WATERTON-GLACIER INT'L PEACE PARK
CYPRESS HILLS INTERPROV. PK.
Swift Current
Moose Jaw
Regina
GRASSLANDS N.P.
MOOSE MTN. PROV. PARK
Weyburn
Estevan
Portage la Prairie
Brandon
Winnipeg
SPRUCE WOODS PROV. PK.
TURTLE MTN. PROV. PK.
NOPIMING PROV. PK.
WHITESHELL PROV. PARK
Red Lake
Kenora
Lake of the Woods
VOYAGEURS N.P.
Fort Frances
QUETICO PROV. PARK
Portland
Salem
Eugene
Columbia
Snake
Lewiston
BITTERROOT RANGE
Missoula
Helena
Great Falls
Butte
Billings
Peck Lake
Lake Sakakawea
Minot
THEODORE ROOSEVELT N.P.
Grand Forks
Fargo
Bismarck
Duluth
Oahe Res.
CRATER LAKE NAT'L PK.
NEWBERRY NAT'L VOLCANIC MON.
CASCADE RANGE
Boise
CRATERS OF THE MOON NAT'L MON.
YELLOWSTONE N.P.
GRAND TETON N.P.
Pocatello
LAVA BEDS NAT'L MON.
LASSEN VOLCANIC N.P.
Reno
Carson City
Sacramento
YOSEMITE N.P.
Great Salt Lake
Ogden
Salt Lake City
DINOSAUR NAT'L MON.
Pathfinder Reservoir
Casper
Cheyenne
Rapid City
BADLANDS NAT'L PARK
Pierre
Sioux Falls
Sioux City
Missouri
Minneapolis
St. Paul
Rochester
Mississippi
Madiso
WISC
PACIFIC TIME ZONE
MOUNTAIN TIME ZONE
MOUNTAIN TIME ZONE
CENTRAL TIME ZONE

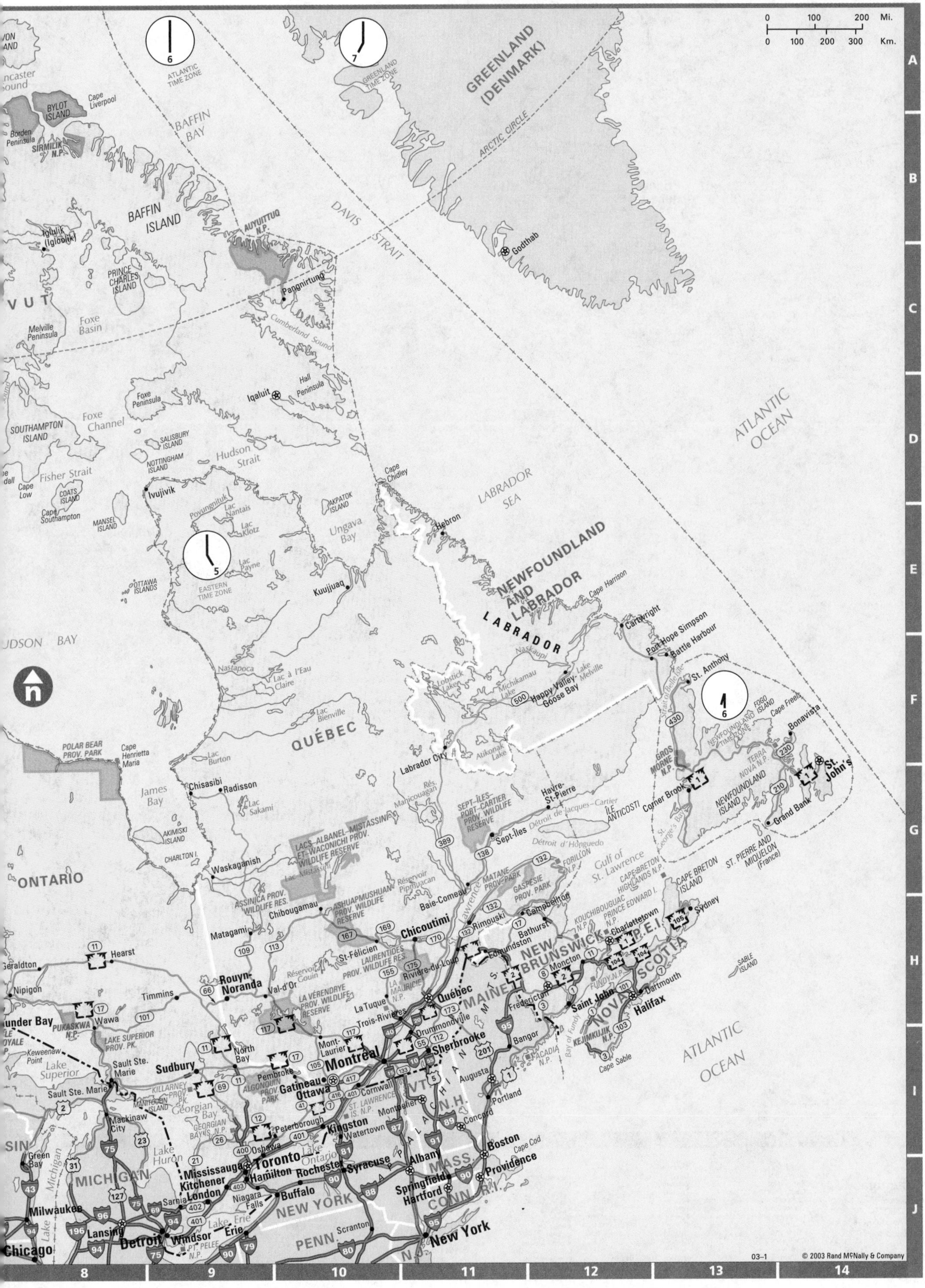
0 100 200 Mi.
0 100 200 300 Km.
A
B
C
D
E
F
G
H
I
J
8
9
10
11
12
13
14
ATLANTIC TIME ZONE
GREENLAND TIME ZONE
EASTERN TIME ZONE
GREENLAND (DENMARK)
ARCTIC CIRCLE
BAFFIN BAY
DAVIS STRAIT
Godthab
BYLOT ISLAND
Cape Liverpool
Borden Peninsula
SIRMILIK N.P.
BAFFIN ISLAND
AUYUITTUQ N.P.
Igloolik (Iglulik)
PRINCE CHARLES ISLAND
Pangnirtung
Cumberland Sound
Melville Peninsula
Foxe Basin
Foxe Peninsula
Iqaluit
Hall Peninsula
SOUTHAMPTON ISLAND
Foxe Channel
SALISBURY ISLAND
NOTTINGHAM ISLAND
Hudson Strait
Fisher Strait
Cape Low
COATS ISLAND
Cape Southampton
MANSEL ISLAND
Ivujivik
Cape Chidley
AKPATOK ISLAND
Ungava Bay
LABRADOR SEA
ATLANTIC OCEAN
Hebron
Lac Nantais
Lac Klotz
Lac Payne
OTTAWA ISLANDS
Kuujjuaq
NEWFOUNDLAND AND LABRADOR
LABRADOR
Cape Harrison
Cartwright
Port Hope Simpson
Battle Harbour
HUDSON BAY
Nastapoca
Lac à l'Eau Claire
Lac Bienville
Naskaupi
Lobstick Lake
Michikamau Lake
Happy Valley-Goose Bay
Lake Melville
500
St. Anthony
Strait of Belle Isle
QUÉBEC
POLAR BEAR PROV. PARK
Cape Henrietta Maria
Lac Burton
Labrador City
Atikonak Lake
James Bay
Chisasibi
Radisson
Lac Sakami
Manicouagan
Havre-St-Pierre
ÎLE ANTICOSTI
SEPT-ÎLES-PORT-CARTIER PROV. WILDLIFE RESERVE
Détroit de Jacques-Cartier
Détroit d'Honguedo
Sept-Îles
AKIMISKI ISLAND
CHARLTON I.
LACS-ALBANEL-MISTASSINI-ET-WACONICHI PROV. WILDLIFE RESERVE
Lac Mistassini
Waskaganish
389
138
FORILLON N.P.
Gulf of St. Lawrence
ONTARIO
ASSINICA PROV. WILDLIFE RES.
ASHUAPMUSHUAN PROV. WILDLIFE RESERVE
Réservoir Pipmuacan
Baie-Comeau
MATANE PROV. PARK
GASPÉSIE PROV. PARK
132
Chibougamau
Rimouski
Campbellton
Matagami
Chicoutimi
167
169
170
Bathurst
KOUCHIBOUGUAC N.P.
PRINCE EDWARD I.
CAPE BRETON HIGHLANDS N.P.
CAPE BRETON ISLAND
Sydney
105
Charlottetown
P.E.I.
NEW BRUNSWICK
Edmundston
Hearst
Geraldton
11
109
113
St-Félicien
LAURENTIDES PROV. RESERVE
Rivière-du-Loup
Réservoir Gouin
Rouyn-Noranda
Val-d'Or
66
Timmins
Nipigon
LA VÉRENDRYE PROV. WILDLIFE RESERVE
LA MAURICIE N.P.
La Tuque
Québec
Trois-Rivières
Drummondville
Thunder Bay
PUKASKWA N.P.
Wawa
17
101
LAKE SUPERIOR PROV. PK.
ISLE ROYALE N.P.
Keweenaw Point
Lake Superior
Sault Ste. Marie
North Bay
Sudbury
Pembroke
Mont-Laurier
Montréal
Sherbrooke
MAINE
Fredericton
Moncton
Saint John
FUNDY N.P.
Bay of Fundy
NOVA SCOTIA
Halifax
Dartmouth
KEJIMKUJIK N.P.
Cape Sable
SABLE ISLAND
ATLANTIC OCEAN
Bangor
ACADIA N.P.
Augusta
Portland
KILLARNEY PROV. PK.
MANITOULIN ISLAND
ALGONQUIN PROV. PARK
Gatineau
Ottawa
Cornwall
ST. LAWRENCE IS. N.P.
Montpelier
VT.
N.H.
Concord
Georgian Bay
GEORGIAN BAY IS. N.P.
Peterborough
Kingston
Watertown
Mackinaw City
Lake Huron
Oshawa
Toronto
Lake Ontario
Mississauga
Hamilton
Rochester
Syracuse
Albany
MASS.
Boston
Cape Cod
Providence
Green Bay
Lake Michigan
MICHIGAN
Kitchener
London
Sarnia
Niagara Falls
Buffalo
NEW YORK
Springfield
Hartford
CONN.
R.I.
Milwaukee
Lansing
Detroit
Windsor
Lake Erie
Erie
PT. PELEE N.P.
PENN.
Scranton
New York
N.J.
Chicago
GROS MORNE N.P.
Corner Brook
St. George's Bay
NEWFOUNDLAND ISLAND
NEWFOUNDLAND TIME ZONE
FOGO ISLAND
Cape Freels
Bonavista
TERRA NOVA N.P.
230
210
430
St. John's
Grand Bank
ST. PIERRE AND MIQUELON (France)
APPALACHIAN MTS.
03-1
© 2003 Rand McNally & Company

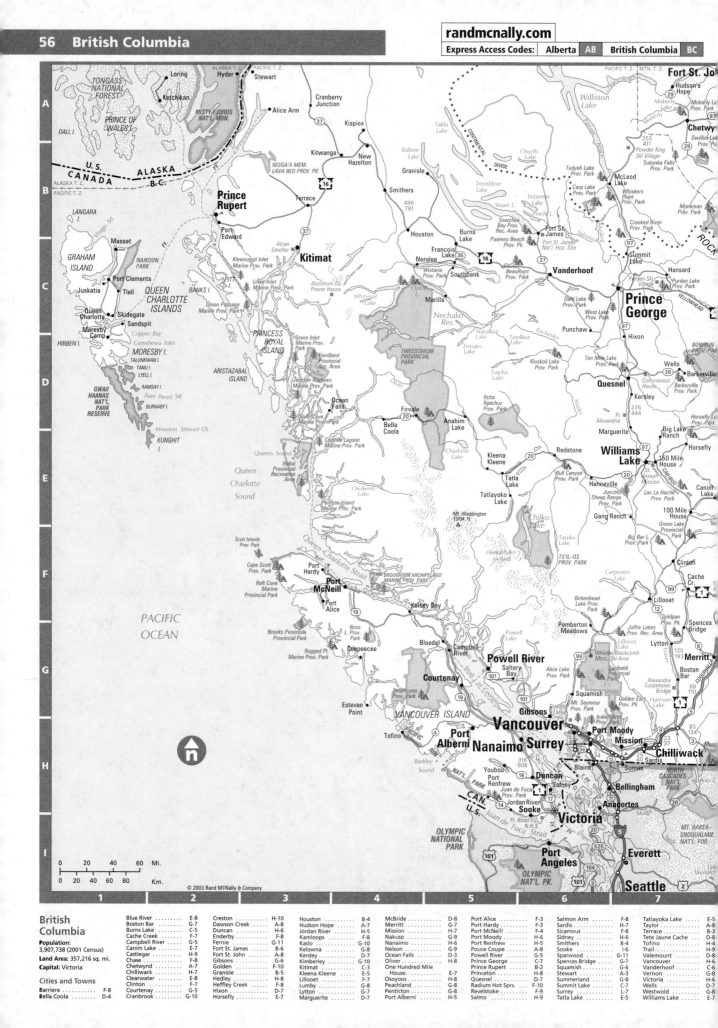

British Columbia

Population: 3,907,738 (2001 Census)

Land Area: 357,216 sq. mi.

Capital: Victoria

Cities and Towns

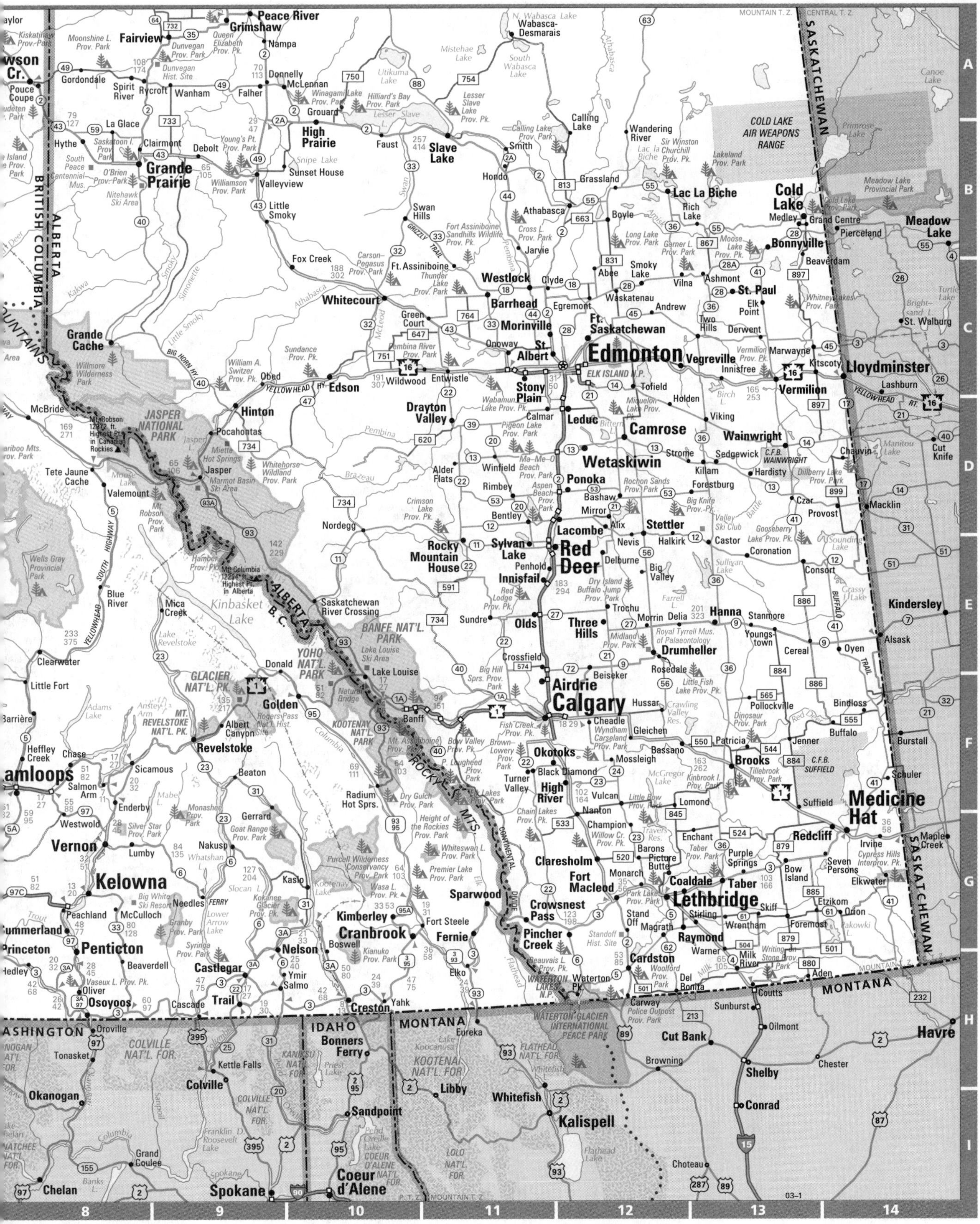
Peace River
Grimshaw
Fairview
Nampa
Dunvegan Hist. Site
Donnelly
McLennan
Falher
Spirit River
Rycroft
Wanham
Gordondale
Grouard
High Prairie
Faust
Slave Lake
Lesser Slave Lake
Wabasca-Desmarais
N. Wabasca Lake
South Wabasca Lake
Mistehae Lake
Utikuma Lake
Calling Lake
Smith
Hondo
Wandering River
Grassland
Lac La Biche
Rich Lake
Boyle
Athabasca
Jarvie
La Glace
Hythe
Clairmont
Debolt
Grande Prairie
Valleyview
Sunset House
Little Smoky
Swan Hills
Fox Creek
Whitecourt
Ft. Assiniboine
Westlock
Clyde
Barrhead
Egremont
Morinville
Abee
Smoky Lake
Vilna
Waskatenau
Ashmont
St. Paul
Elk Point
Andrew
Two Hills
Derwent
Cold Lake
Medley
Grand Centre
Bonnyville
Pierceland
Beaverdam
Meadow Lake
COLD LAKE AIR WEAPONS RANGE
SASKATCHEWAN
ALBERTA
BRITISH COLUMBIA
MOUNTAIN T. Z.
CENTRAL T. Z.
Grande Cache
Willmore Wilderness Park
Edson
Obed
Hinton
Wildwood
Entwistle
Green Court
Onoway
St. Albert
Edmonton
Ft. Saskatchewan
Vegreville
Innisfree
Vermilion
Marwayne
Kitscoty
Lloydminster
Lashburn
Stony Plain
Tofield
Holden
Viking
Drayton Valley
Calmar
Leduc
Camrose
Wainwright
Sedgewick
Hardisty
Chauvin
Cut Knife
McBride
JASPER NATIONAL PARK
Pocahontas
Jasper
Mt. Robson 12972 ft. Highest Pt. in Canadian Rockies
Tete Jaune Cache
Valemount
Alder Flats
Winfield
Rimbey
Ponoka
Wetaskiwin
Bashaw
Strome
Killam
Forestburg
Provost
Macklin
Nordegg
Bentley
Mirror
Lacombe
Alix
Stettler
Halkirk
Castor
Coronation
Rocky Mountain House
Sylvan Lake
Red Deer
Penhold
Innisfail
Delburne
Big Valley
Consort
Blue River
Mica Creek
Kinbasket Lake
Saskatchewan River Crossing
BANFF NAT'L. PARK
Sundre
Olds
Three Hills
Trochu
Morrin
Delia
Hanna
Stanmore
Youngstown
Cereal
Oyen
Kindersley
Alsask
Drumheller
Clearwater
Little Fort
Donald
YOHO NAT'L. PARK
GLACIER NAT'L. PK.
Lake Louise
Golden
Crossfield
Airdrie
Beiseker
Rosedale
Calgary
Hussar
Pollockville
Bindloss
Buffalo
Banff
Revelstoke
Albert Canyon
Cheadle
Gleichen
Bassano
Patricia
Jenner
Brooks
Burstall
Heffley Creek
Chase
Sicamous
Kamloops
Salmon Arm
Okotoks
Black Diamond
Turner Valley
High River
Mossleigh
Vulcan
Nanton
Lomond
Suffield
Medicine Hat
Schuler
Enderby
Westwold
Vernon
Radium Hot Sprs.
Champion
Enchant
Redcliff
Irvine
Claresholm
Barons
Picture Butte
Purple Springs
Bow Island
Seven Persons
Elkwater
Kelowna
Lumby
Nakusp
Kaslo
Sparwood
Fort Macleod
Monarch
Coaldale
Taber
Lethbridge
Skiff
Etzikom
Orion
Peachland
McCulloch
Needles
Kimberley
Crowsnest Pass
Stirling
Wrentham
Foremost
Summerland
Penticton
Fort Steele
Cranbrook
Fernie
Pincher Creek
Magrath
Raymond
Warner
Milk River
Princeton
Beaverdell
Castlegar
Nelson
Ymir
Salmo
Elko
Waterton
Cardston
Del Bonita
Aden
Coutts
Oliver
Osoyoos
Trail
Cascade
Creston
Yahk
Sunburst
Oilmont
WASHINGTON
IDAHO
MONTANA
Oroville
Eureka
Bonners Ferry
COLVILLE NAT'L. FOR.
Tonasket
Kettle Falls
Colville
Okanogan
KOOTENAI NAT'L. FOR.
Libby
Whitefish
Kalispell
Cut Bank
Browning
Shelby
Conrad
Chester
Havre
Sandpoint
WATERTON-GLACIER INTERNATIONAL PEACE PARK
Grand Coulee
Chelan
Spokane
Coeur d'Alene
LOLO NAT'L. FOR.
Flathead Lake
Choteau
03–1
A
B
C
D
E
F
G
H
I
8
9
10
11
12
13
14

Alberta

Population: 2,974,807 (2001 Census)

Land Area: 248,000 sq. mi.

Capital: Edmonton

Cities and Towns

Airdrie F-11
Alix D-12
Athabasca B-12
Banff F-10
Barrhead C-11
Bashaw D-12
Bassano F-12
Bentley D-11
Black Diamond F-11
Bonnyville B-13
Bow Island G-13
Boyle B-12
Brooks F-13
Calgary F-11
Calmar D-11
Camrose D-12
Cardston H-12
Castor E-13
Claresholm G-12
Coaldale G-12
Cold Lake B-13
Coronation E-13
Crossfield E-11
Crowsnest Pass G-11
Drayton Valley D-11
Drumheller E-12
Edmonton C-12
Edson C-10
Elk Point C-13
Fairview A-9
Falher A-9
Forestburg D-13
Fox Creek C-10
Fort Macleod G-12
Fort Saskatchewan C-12
Grand Centre B-13
Grande Cache C-8
Grande Prairie B-8
Grimshaw A-9
Hanna E-13
Hardisty D-13
High Prairie B-10
High River F-12
Hinton D-9
Innisfail E-11
Jasper D-9
Killam D-13
Lac la Biche B-12
Lacombe D-12
Lake Louise F-10
Lamont C-12
Leduc D-12
Lethbridge G-12
Lloydminster C-14
Magrath G-12
McLennan A-10
Medicine Hat G-14
Milk River H-13
Morinville C-11
Nanton G-12
Okotoks F-11
Olds E-11
Oyen E-14
Peace River A-9
Penhold E-11
Pincher Creek G-12
Ponoka D-12
Provost D-14
Raymond G-12
Red Deer E-12
Redcliff G-14
Rimbey D-11
Rocky Mountain House E-11
Rycroft A-8
St. Albert C-11
St. Paul C-13
Sedgewick D-13
Slave Lake B-11
Smoky lake C-12
Spirit River A-8
Stettler D-12
Stirling G-13
Stony Plain C-11
Sundre E-11
Swan Hills B-10
Sylvan Lake E-11
Taber G-13
Three Hills E-12
Tofield C-12
Trochu E-12
Turner Valley F-11
Two Hills C-13
Valleyview B-9
Vegreville C-12
Vermilion C-13
Viking D-13
Vulcan F-12
Wabasca-Desmarais A-11
Wainwright D-13
Westlock C-11
Wetaskiwin D-12
Whitecourt C-10

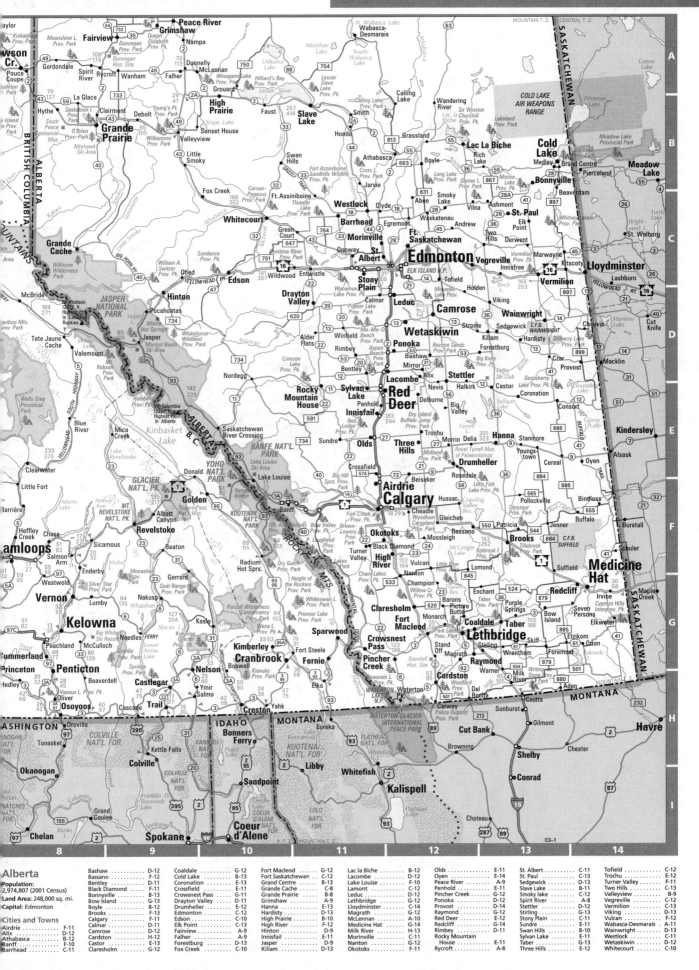

randmcnally.com
Express Access Codes: Saskatchewan SK Manitoba MB

Manitoba

Population:
1,119,583 (2001 census)
Land Area: 213,729 sq. mi.
Capital: Winnipeg

Cities and Towns

Amaranth	H-9
Angusville	H-7
Arborg	G-10
Ashern	G-10
Austin	I-9
Baldur	I-9
Beausejour	H-11
Belmont	I-9
Benito	F-7
Binscarth	H-7
Birch River	F-7
Birtle	H-7
Boissevain	I-8
Bowsman	F-7
Brandon	I-8
Camperville	F-8
Carberry	I-9
Carman	I-10
Cartwright	J-9
Clearwater	J-9
Cormorant	C-8
Cranberry Portage	C-7
Cross Lake	C-10
Crystal City	J-9
Darlingford	I-10
Dauphin	G-8
Deloraine	J-8
Douglas	I-9
Duck Bay	F-8
Easterville	E-8
Elkhorn	I-7
Elm Creek	I-10
Elphinstone	H-8
Emerson	J-11
Erickson	H-8
Eriksdale	G-10
Ethelbert	G-8
Fisher Branch	G-10
Flin Flon	C-7
Gilbert Plains	G-8
Gimli	H-11
Gladstone	H-9
Glenboro	I-9
Grand Rapids	E-9
Grandview	G-8
Gretna	J-10
Gypsumville	F-9
Hamiota	H-8
Hartney	I-8
Hodgson	G-10
Holland	I-9
Inglis	G-7
Kenville	F-7
Killarney	J-9
La Broquerie	I-11
Lac du Bonnet	H-11
Langruth	H-9
Letellier	J-10
Lockport	H-11
Lowe Farm	I-10
Lundar	H-10
MacGregor	I-9
Mafeking	E-7
Manigotagan	G-11
Manitou	I-9
McCreary	H-9
Melita	I-8
Miniota	H-7
Minitonas	F-7
Minnedosa	H-8
Minto	I-8
Moose Lake	D-8
Moosehorn	G-9
Morden	I-10
Morris	I-10
Neepawa	H-9
Newdale	H-8
Ninette	I-9
Niverville	I-11
Norway House	D-10
Oak River	H-8
Oakville	I-10
Ochre River	G-8
Petersfield	H-11
Pierson	J-7
Pilot Mound	I-9
Pine Falls	H-11
Pine River	H-8
Pipestone	I-8
Plum Coulee	I-10
Portage la Prairie	H-10
Rathwell	I-9
Rennie	I-12
Reston	I-7
Rivers	H-8
Riverton	G-11
Roblin	G-7
Roland	I-10
Rorketon	G-9
Rosenfeld	I-10
Rossburn	H-8
Russell	H-7
St. Georges	H-11
St. Jean Baptiste	I-10
St. Laurent	H-10
St. Malo	I-11
St. Pierre	I-11
Ste. Ann	I-11
Ste. Rose du Lac	G-9
Sanford	I-10
Selkirk	H-11
Shoal Lake	H-8
Snow Lake	B-8
Somerset	I-9
Souris	I-8
Sperling	I-10
Sprague	J-12
Steinbach	I-11
Swan River	F-7
Teulon	H-10
The Pas	D-7
Thompson	A-10
Tolstoi	J-11
Treherne	I-9
Tyndall	H-11
Virden	I-7
Vita	I-11
Wabowden	B-9
Wawanesa	I-9
Whitemouth	H-11
Winkler	I-10
Winnipeg	I-11
Winnipeg Beach	H-11
Winnipegosis	F-8
Woodlands	H-10
Woodridge	I-11

Saskatchewan

Population:
978,933 (2001 census)
Land Area: 228,445 sq. mi.
Capital: Regina

Cities and Towns

Alsask	F-1
Arborfield	E-6
Arcola	I-6
Asquith	F-3
Assiniboia	I-4
Avonlea	H-5
Balcarres	G-6
Battleford	E-2
Beauval	B-3
Bengough	I-5
Bienfait	J-6
Big River	D-3
Biggar	F-3
Blaine Lake	E-3
Bredenbury	G-7
Broadview	H-6
Buffalo Narrows	A-3
Burstall	G-1
Cabri	G-2
Canora	F-6
Carlyle	I-6
Carnduff	J-7
Carrot River	D-6
Central Butte	G-4
Choiceland	D-5
Coronach	J-4
Craik	G-4
Creighton	C-7
Cudworth	E-4
Cumberland House	D-7
Cupar	G-5
Cut Knife	E-2
Davidson	G-4
Delisle	F-3
Duck Lake	E-4
Dundurn	F-4
Eastend	I-2
Eatonia	G-1
Elrose	G-2
Esterhazy	H-7
Estevan	J-6
Eston	G-2
Foam Lake	F-6
Fort Qu'Appelle	H-5
Glaslyn	D-2
Gravelbourg	I-3
Green Lake	C-3
Grenfell	H-6
Gull Lake	H-2
Hafford	E-3
Hague	E-4
Herbert	H-3
Hudson Bay	E-6
Humboldt	F-5
Indian Head	H-6
Ituna	G-6
Kamsack	G-7
Kelvington	F-6
Kerrobert	F-2
Kindersley	F-2
Kinistino	E-5
Kyle	G-2
La Ronge	B-5
Lafleche	I-3
Langenburg	G-7
Lanigan	F-5
Lashburn	D-1
Leader	G-1
Lloydminster	D-1
Lumsden	H-5
Luseland	F-1
Macklin	E-1
Maidstone	D-2
Maple Creek	H-1
Martensville	F-4
Meadow Lake	C-2
Melfort	E-5
Melville	G-6
Midale	I-6
Milestone	H-5
Montmartre	H-6
Moose Jaw	H-4
Moosomin	H-7
Mossbank	H-4
North Battleford	E-2
Naicam	E-4
Nipawin	D-5
Nokomis	G-5
Norquay	F-7
Outlook	G-3
Oxbow	I-7
Pelican Narrows	B-6
Pense	H-5
Pierceland	C-2
Ponteix	I-3
Porcupine Plain	E-6
Preeceville	F-6
Prince Albert	D-4
Qu'Appelle	H-5
Quill Lake	F-5
Radisson	E-3
Raymore	G-5
Redvers	I-7
Regina	H-5
Regina Beach	G-5
Rocanville	H-7
Rockglen	I-4
Rose Valley	F-6
Rosetown	F-2
Rosthern	E-4
St. Louis	E-4
St. Walburg	D-2
Saskatoon	F-4
Shaunavon	I-2
Shellbrook	D-4
Southey	G-5
Spiritwood	D-3
Star City	E-5
Stoughton	I-6
Strasbourg	G-5
Sturgis	F-6
Swift Current	H-2
Theodore	G-6
Tisdale	E-5
Turtleford	D-2
Unity	E-2
Wadena	F-2
Wakaw	E-4
Waldheim	E-4
Watrous	F-4
Watson	F-5
Weyburn	I-5
Whitewood	H-6
Wilkie	E-2
Willow Bunch	I-4
Wolseley	H-6
Wynyard	F-5
Yellow Grass	I-5
Yorkton	G-6

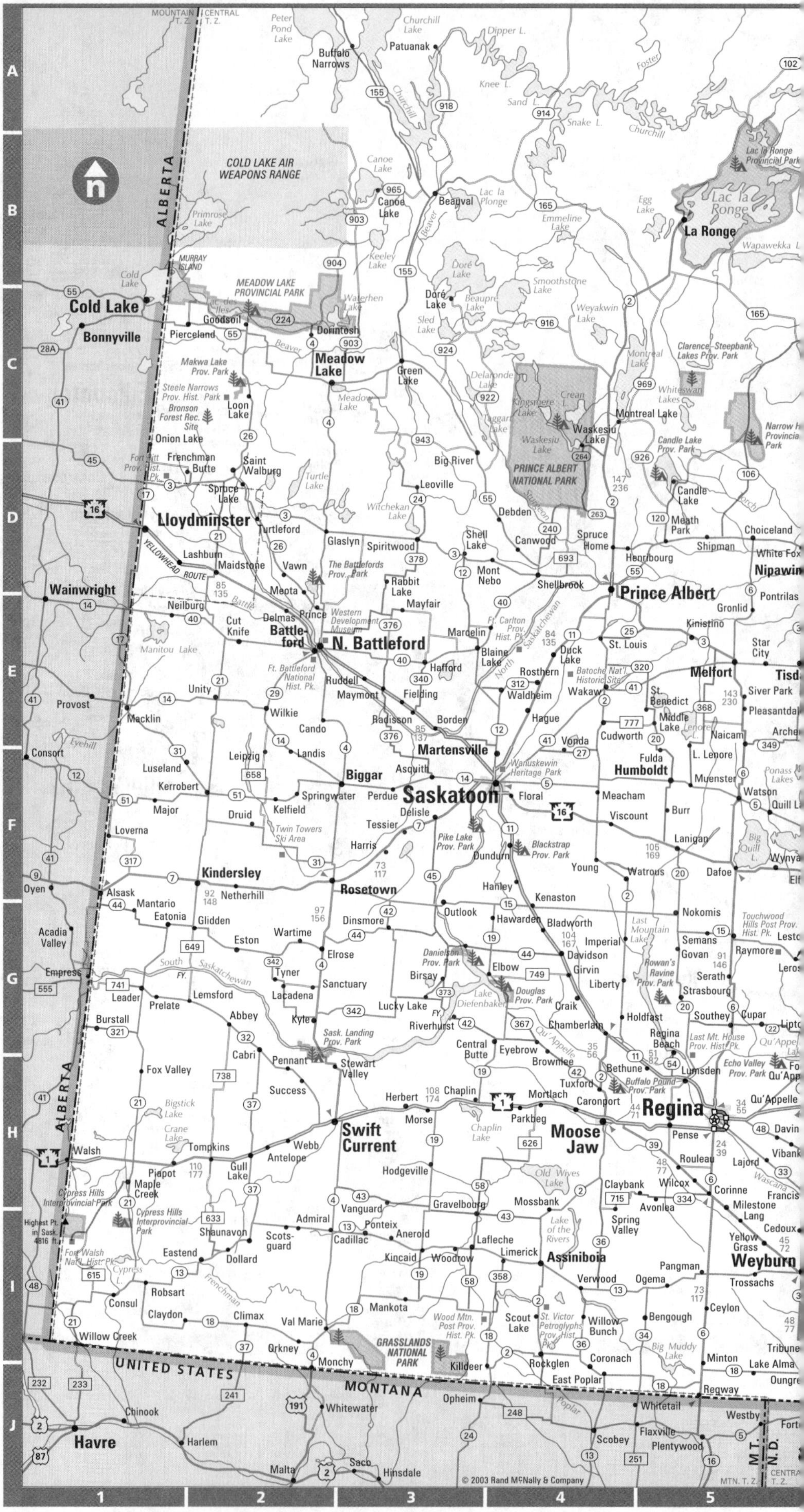

ALBERTA
COLD LAKE AIR WEAPONS RANGE
MEADOW LAKE PROVINCIAL PARK
PRINCE ALBERT NATIONAL PARK
GRASSLANDS NATIONAL PARK
UNITED STATES
MONTANA
Cold Lake
Bonnyville
Buffalo Narrows
Patuanak
Beauval
La Ronge
Meadow Lake
Green Lake
Lloydminster
Wainwright
N. Battleford
Battleford
Prince Albert
Melfort
Humboldt
Saskatoon
Kindersley
Rosetown
Biggar
Martensville
Swift Current
Moose Jaw
Regina
Weyburn
Assiniboia
Havre
Chinook
© 2003 Rand McNally & Company

0
20
40 Mi.
0
20
40
60
Km.
A
B
C
D
E
F
G
H
I
J
6
7
8
9
10
11
12
SASKATCHEWAN
MANITOBA
ONTARIO
UNITED STATES
N. DAK.
MINN.
Thompson
Flin Flon
Creighton
Channing
Cranberry Portage
Wekusko
Herb Lake
Herb Lake Landing
Tyrrell
Dunlop
Ponton
Wabowden
Pipun
Snow Lake
Cross Lake
Norway House
Warren Landing
Pelican Narrows
Sandy Bay
Cumberland House
The Pas
Prospector
Finger
Wanless
Cormorant
Moose Lake
Westray
Grand Rapids
Easterville
Overflowing River
Carrot River
Arborfield
Crooked River
Prairie River
Hudson Bay
Powell
Westgate
Mafeking
Novra
Birch River
Bjorkdale
Porcupine Plain
Somme
Bertwell
Usherville
Kelvington
Swan River
Lenswood
Bowsman
Minitonas
Duck Bay
Camperville
Skownan
Cowan
Kenville
Durban
Benito
Pine River
Okla
Preeceville
Sturgis
Norquay
Margo
Amsterdam
Pelly
Buchanan
Canora
Sheho
Foam Lake
Kamsack
Theodore
Gorlitz
San Clara
Ethelbert
Garland
Winnipegosis
Meadow Portage
Fork River
Toutes Aides
Steep Rock
Rorketon
Cayer
Reykjavik
Grahamdale
Moosehorn
Ashern
Gypsumville
Hilbre
Dallas
Hodgson
Fisher River
Pine Dock
Matheson Island
Jackhead
Dauphin River
Berens River
Bissett
Manigotagan
Fisher Branch
Riverton
Arborg
Hecla
Yorkton
Willowbrook
Jasmin
Roblin
Sifton
Ashville
Dauphin
Ste. Rose du Lac
Ochre River
Grandview
Gilbert Plains
Inglis
Bredenbury
Melville
Langenburg
Russell
Angusville
Rossburn
McCreary
Alonsa
Vogar
Eriksdale
Camper
Poplarfield
Chatfield
Deerhorn
Narcisse
Lundar
Clarkleigh
Amaranth
Glenella
Norgate
Wasagaming
Riding Mountain
Erickson
Elphinstone
Oakburn
Solsgirth
Binscarth
Shoal Lake
Stockholm
Esterhazy
Sintaluta
Grenfell
Rocanville
Whitewood
Broadview
Wolseley
Montmartre
Peebles
Moosomin
Birtle
Beulah
Miniota
Manson
Hamiota
Newdale
Minnedosa
Neepawa
Gladstone
Plumas
Langruth
Ogilvie
Woodside
Macdonald
Delta Beach
Portage la Prairie
Poplar Point
St. Laurent
Lake Francis
Woodlands
Teulon
Inwood
Petersfield
Gimli
Winnipeg Beach
Matlock
Libau
Selkirk
Clandeboye
Lockport
Grosse Isle
Winnipeg
Beausejour
Tyndall
Anola
Whitemouth
Rennie
Falcon Lake
Victoria Beach
Fraserwood
Grand Beach
Pine Falls
St. Georges
Great Falls
Lac du Bonnet
Seven Sisters Falls
Broken-head
Thalberg
Ft. Alexander
Werner Lake
Kennedy
Fillmore
Fairlight
Elkhorn
Hargrave
Virden
Crandall
Oak River
Rivers
Douglas
Brandon
Kemnay
Griswold
Souris
Wawanesa
Carberry
Austin
MacGregor
Oakville
Oak Bluff
Fannystelle
Elm Cr.
St. Claude
Holland
Treherne
Rathwell
Carman
Brunkild
Sanford
Sperling
Ste. Agathe
Lowe Farm
Roland
Dugald
Ste. Anne-des-Chênes
Grande Pointe
Ile des Chênes
Niverville
Richer
Hadashville
Steinbach
La Broquerie
St. Pierre-Jolys
La Rochelle
St. Malo
Woodridge
Stoughton
Griffin
Kisbey
Arcola
Carlyle
Redvers
Storthoaks
Reston
Pipestone
Sinclair
Halbrite
Midale
Benson
Macoun
Alameda
Oxbow
Hitchcock
Torquay
Estevan
Bienfait
Hirsch
Carnduff
Carievale
Northgate
N. Portal
Pierson
Melita
Hartney
Deloraine
Boissevain
Minto
Ninette
Baldur
Glenboro
Belmont
Killarney
Somerset
Pilot Mound
Crystal City
Clearwater
Rosebank
Manitou
Thornhill
Morden
Darlingford
Winkler
Plum Coulee
Morris
St. Jean Baptiste
Rosa
Letellier
Emerson
Tolstoi
Vita
Sundown
Piney
South Junction
Sprague
Warroad
Roseau
Badger
Greenbush
Karlstad
Donaldson
Hallock
St. Thomas
Lancaster
Humboldt
Pembina
Hamilton
Cavalier
Neche
Gretna
Walhalla
Mountain
Langdon
Munich
Rolla
Bocklake
Clyde
Dunseith
Bottineau
Westhope
Lena
Cartwright
Windygates
Antler
Sherwood
Mohall
Bowbells
Noonan
Crosby
LAKE WINNIPEG
Lake Winnipegosis
Lake Manitoba
Lake Winnipeg
Lake St. Martin
Lake St. George
Cedar Lake
Dawson Bay
Pelican Bay
Red Deer Lake
Swan Lake
Waterhen Lake
Sturgeon Bay
Kinwow Bay
HORSE ISLAND
ROSS ISLAND
REINDEER ISLAND
BERENS ISLAND
Long Pt.
Churchill
Burntwood
Nelson
Minago
Grass River Prov. Park
Paint Lake Provincial Park
Clearwater Lake Prov. Park
Cormorant Provincial Forest
Porcupine Provincial Forest
SWAN-PELICAN PROV. FOREST
Duck Mtn. Prov. Park
Duck Mtn. Prov. Forest
Asessippi Prov. Park
RIDING MOUNTAIN NATIONAL PARK
Spruce Woods Prov. Park
Spruce Woods Prov. Forest
Turtle Mtn. Prov. Park
Int'l. Peace Garden
Moose Mtn. Prov. Park
Cannington Manor Prov. Hist. Pk.
ATIKAKI PROVINCIAL PARK
Nopiming Provincial Park
Whiteshell Provincial Park
Sandilands Provincial Forest
Birds Hill Prov. Pk.
Hecla / Grindstone Prov. Park
Moose Creek Prov. Forest
Elk Island Prov. Pk.
Hnausa Beach Prov. Park
Grand Beach Prov. Park
St. Ambroise Prov. Park
Holiday Mtn. Ski Resort
Agassiz Ski Resort
Baldy Mtn. 2729 ft. Highest Pt. in Manitoba
Ketchum Hill 2500 ft.
Spirit Mtn. 2585 ft.
Wildcat Hill 2565 ft.
YELLOWHEAD ROUTE
Henry Kelsey Prov. Hist. Mon.
Cumberland House Prov. Hist. Park
Prehistoric Mounds
03-1

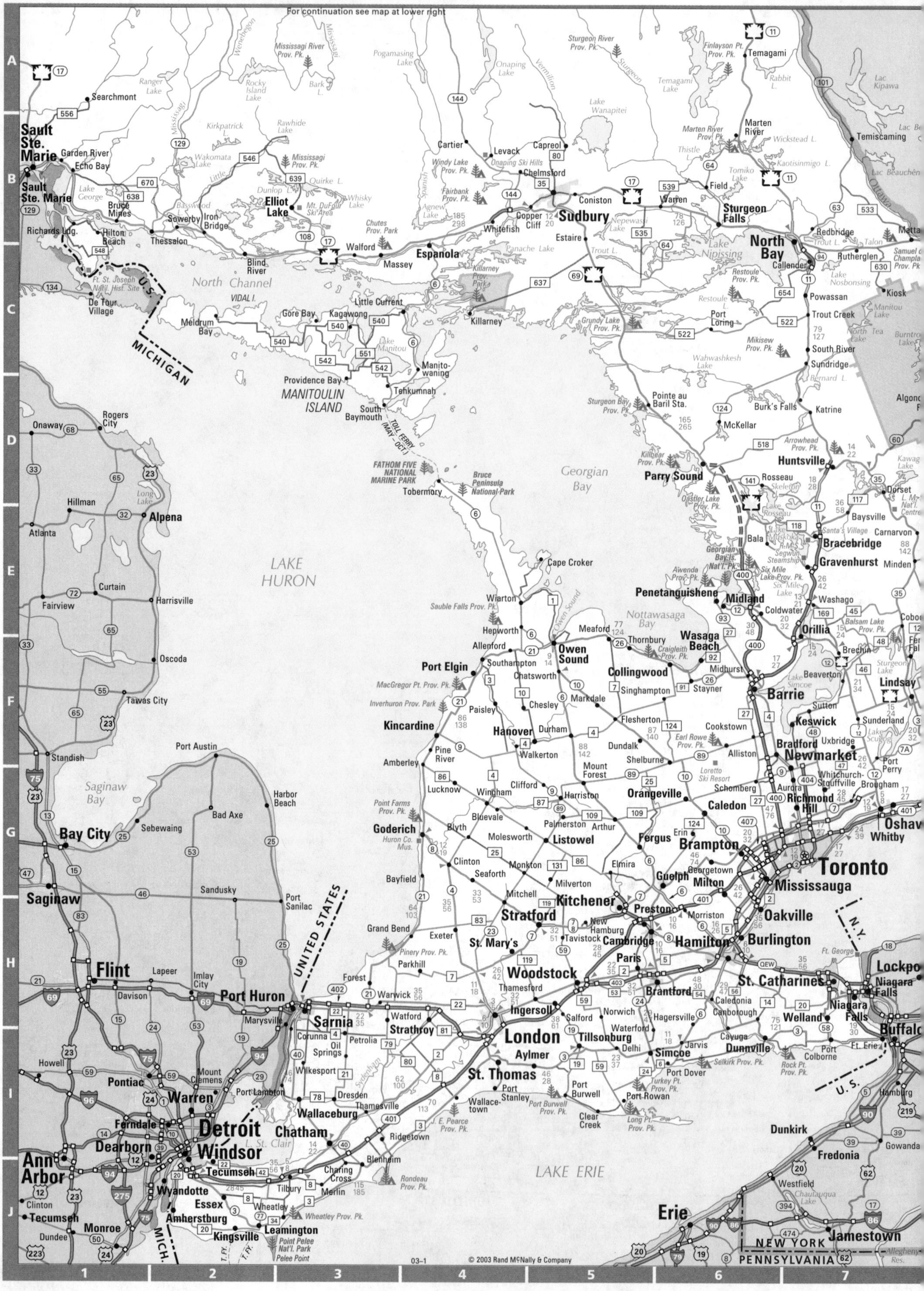
For continuation see map at lower right
Sault Ste. Marie
Searchmont
Garden River
Echo Bay
Bruce Mines
Richards Ldg.
Hilton Beach
Thessalon
Sowerby
Iron Bridge
Elliot Lake
Blind River
Walford
Massey
Espanola
Cartier
Levack
Capreol
Chelmsford
Sudbury
Coniston
Copper Cliff
Whitefish
Estaire
Warren
Sturgeon Falls
Field
Temagami
Marten River
Temiscaming
North Bay
Callender
Redbridge
Rutherglen
Mattawa
Powassan
Trout Creek
South River
Sundridge
Katrine
Burk's Falls
McKellar
Kiosk
Port Loring
Killarney
Little Current
Gore Bay
Kagawong
Meldrum Bay
Providence Bay
Manitowaning
Tehkummah
South Baymouth
MANITOULIN ISLAND
North Channel
De Tour Village
MICHIGAN
U.S.
Pointe au Baril Sta.
Parry Sound
Rosseau
Huntsville
Dorset
Baysville
Carnarvon
Bala
Bracebridge
Gravenhurst
Minden
Washago
Coldwater
Orillia
Midland
Penetanguishene
Georgian Bay
Tobermory
Cape Croker
Wiarton
Hepworth
Allenford
Southampton
Port Elgin
Owen Sound
Meaford
Thornbury
Collingwood
Wasaga Beach
Midhurst
Barrie
Stayner
Singhampton
Chatsworth
Chesley
Paisley
Markdale
Flesherton
Kincardine
Hanover
Durham
Walkerton
Dundalk
Shelburne
Mount Forest
Cookstown
Alliston
Bradford
Newmarket
Keswick
Sutton
Beaverton
Brechin
Lindsay
Sunderland
Uxbridge
Port Perry
Stouffville
Brougham
Aurora
Richmond Hill
Schomberg
Orangeville
Caledon
Amberley
Pine River
Lucknow
Wingham
Clifford
Harriston
Palmerston
Arthur
Listowel
Fergus
Erin
Brampton
Georgetown
Milton
Guelph
Elmira
Goderich
Blyth
Bluevale
Molesworth
Clinton
Seaforth
Monkton
Milverton
Mitchell
Kitchener
Preston
Stratford
Bayfield
Grand Bend
Exeter
St. Mary's
New Hamburg
Tavistock
Cambridge
Hamilton
Burlington
Oakville
Mississauga
Toronto
Whitby
Oshawa
Paris
Brantford
Woodstock
Thamesford
Ingersoll
Parkhill
Forest
Warwick
Sarnia
Watford
Strathroy
London
Salford
Norwich
Tillsonburg
Hagersville
Caledonia
Cayuga
Dunnville
Simcoe
Delhi
Aylmer
St. Thomas
Port Stanley
Port Burwell
Port Dover
Port Rowan
Clear Creek
St. Catharines
Niagara Falls
Welland
Port Colborne
Ft. Erie
Buffalo
Lockport
Corunna
Oil Springs
Petrolia
Wilkesport
Dresden
Thamesville
Wallaceburg
Chatham
Ridgetown
Blenheim
Charing Cross
Merlin
Tilbury
Wheatley
Leamington
Kingsville
Essex
Amherstburg
Tecumseh
Windsor
Detroit
Dearborn
Ferndale
Warren
Pontiac
Ann Arbor
Wyandotte
Monroe
Dundee
Clinton
Howell
Mount Clemens
Port Lambton
Marysville
Port Huron
Flint
Davison
Lapeer
Imlay City
Saginaw
Bay City
Sebewaing
Bad Axe
Harbor Beach
Port Austin
Sandusky
Port Sanilac
Standish
Saginaw Bay
Tawas City
Oscoda
Harrisville
Fairview
Curtain
Alpena
Hillman
Atlanta
Onaway
Rogers City
LAKE HURON
LAKE ERIE
L. St. Clair
UNITED STATES
Erie
Dunkirk
Fredonia
Westfield
Jamestown
Hamburg
Gowanda
NEW YORK
PENNSYLVANIA
N.Y.
MICH.
© 2003 Rand McNally & Company

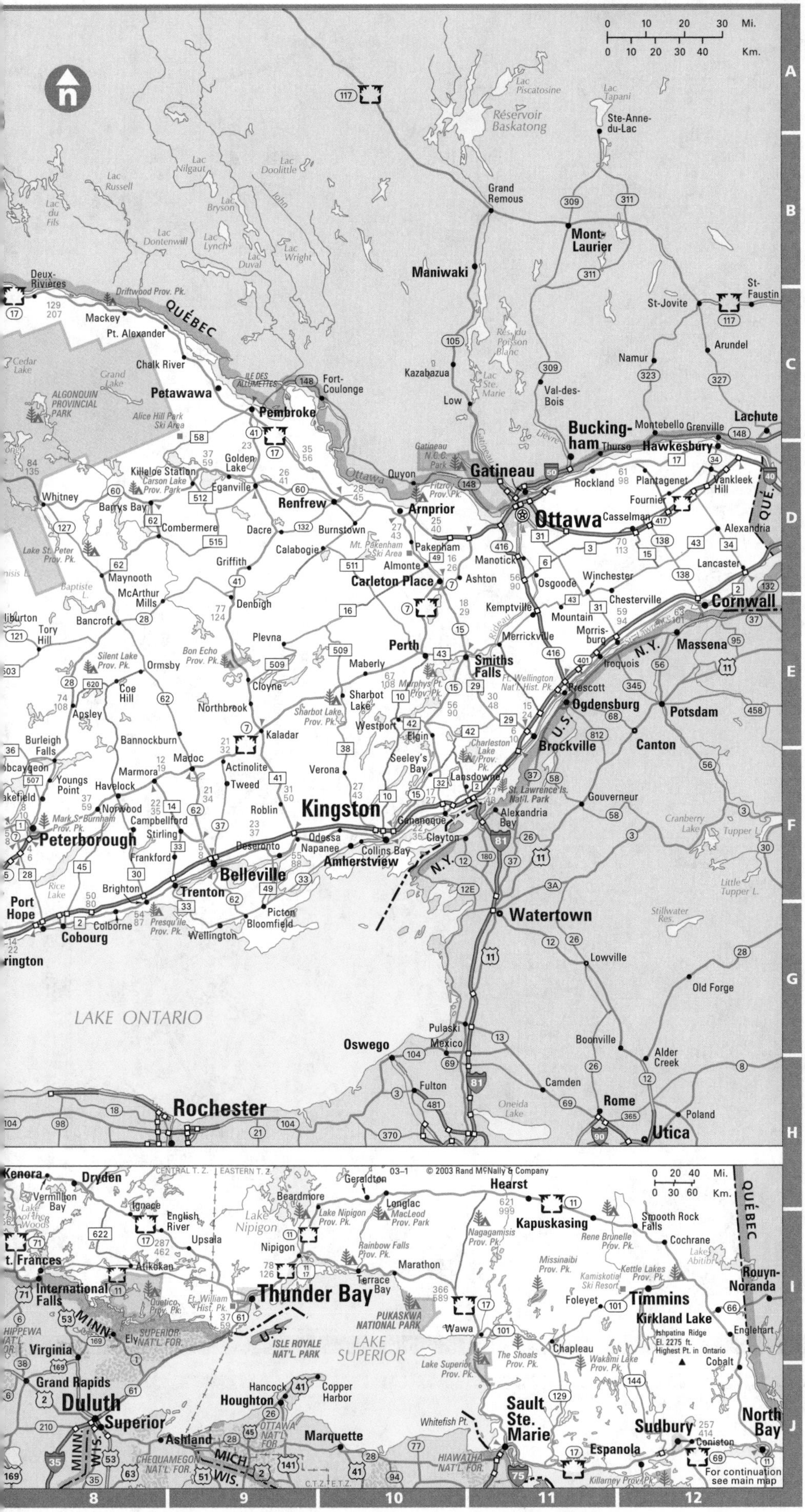

Ontario

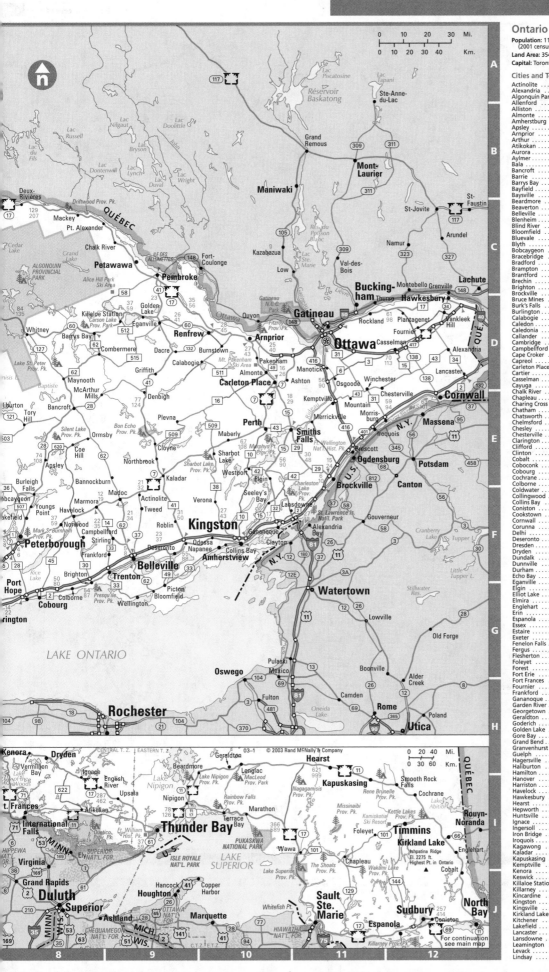

Population: 11,410,046 (2001 census)

Land Area: 354,342 sq. mi.

Capital: Toronto

Cities and Towns

randmcnally.com
Express Access Code: QC

Québec

Population: 7,237,479 (2001 census)
Land Area: 527,079 sq. mi.
Capital: Québec City

Cities and Towns

† Place keyed to Atlantic Provinces map

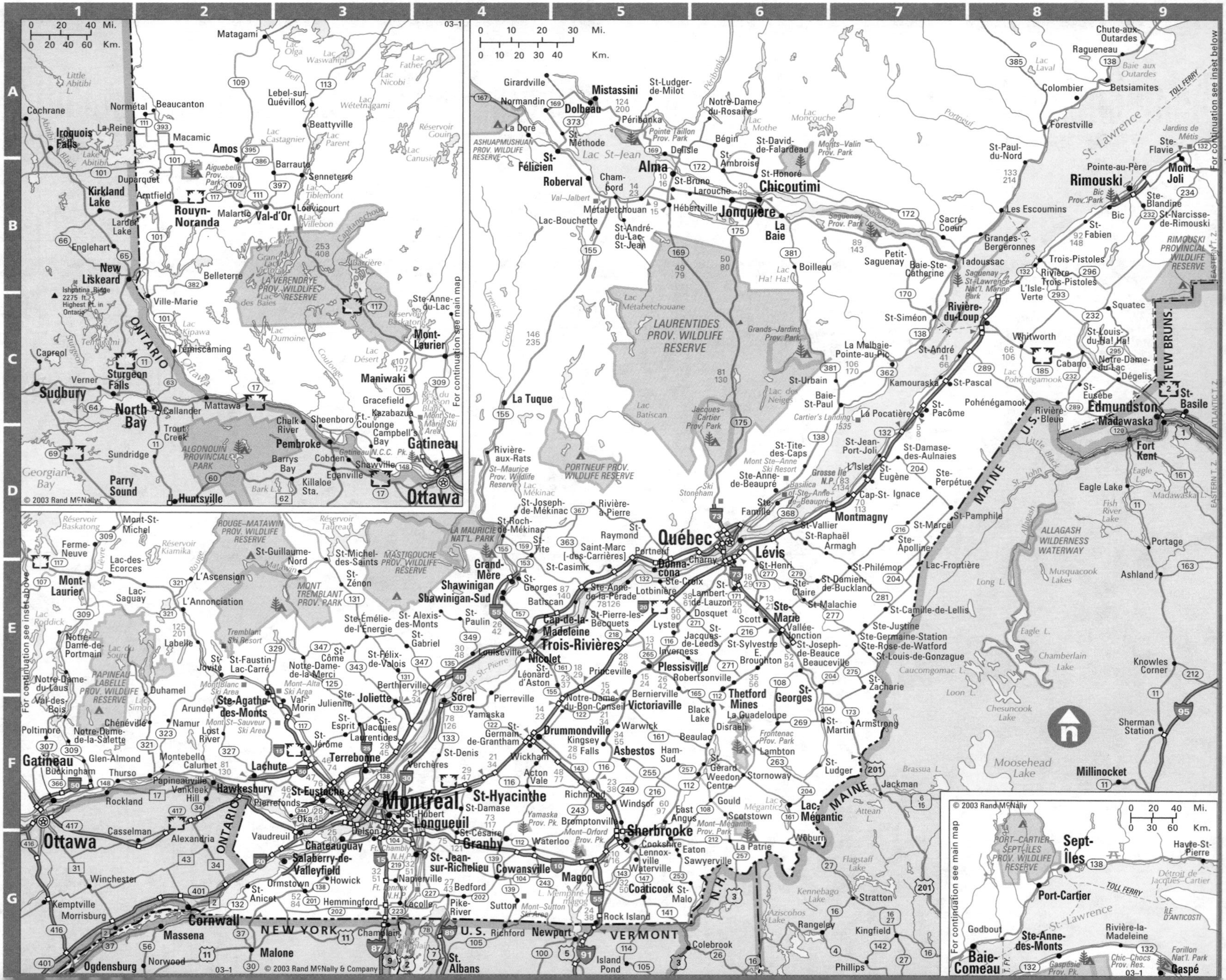

New Brunswick

Population:
729,498 (2001 census)
Land Area: 27,587 sq. mi.
Capital: Fredericton

Cities and Towns

Bathurst	B-4
Bouctouche	D-5
Campbellton	B-3
Caraquet	B-5
Chatham	C-4
Chipman	D-4
Dalhousie	B-4
Edmundston	C-2
Fredericton	D-3
Grand Falls/Grand Sault	C-2
Hampton	E-4
Kedgwick	B-3
Minto	D-4
Moncton	D-5
Newcastle	C-4
Oromocto	E-3
Sackville	D-5
St. John	E-4
St. Stephen	E-3
Shippagan	B-5
Sussex	E-4
Woodstock	D-3

Newfoundland and Labrador

Population:
512,930 (2001 census)
Land Area: 144,353 sq. mi.
Capital: St. John's

Cities and Towns

Bishop's Falls	B-8
Bonavista	B-9
Channel-Port-aux-Basques	B-7
Corner Brook	B-8
Gander	B-8
Grand Falls-Windsor	B-8
Harbour Breton	B-8
St. Anthony	A-8
St. John's	B-9

Nova Scotia

Population:
908,007 (2001 census)
Land Area: 20,594 sq. mi.
Capital: Halifax

Cities and Towns

Advocate Harbour	E-5
Amherst	E-5
Annapolis Royal	F-4
Antigonish	E-7
Bridgetown	F-4
Bridgewater	F-5
Canso	E-8
Chester	F-5
Chéticamp	D-8
Dartmouth	F-6
Digby	F-4
Glace Bay	D-9
Halifax	F-6
Ingonish	C-8
Inverness	D-8
Kentville	E-5
Liverpool	G-5
Louisbourg	D-9
Lunenburg	F-5
Mahone Bay	F-5
Middleton	F-5
New Germany	F-5
New Glasgow	E-7
New Waterford	D-9
North Sydney	D-9
Parrsboro	E-5
Pictou	E-7
Port Hawkesbury	E-8
Shelburne	G-4
Springhill	E-5
Sydney	D-9
Sydney Mines	D-9
Tatamagouche	E-6
Truro	E-6
Windsor	F-5
Wolfville	E-5
Yarmouth	G-4

Prince Edward Island

Population:
135,294 (2001 census)
Land Area: 2,185 sq. mi.
Capital: Charlottetown

Cities and Towns

Alberton	C-5
Charlottetown	D-6
Georgetown	D-7
Montague	D-7
Murray Harbour	D-7
Souris	D-7
Summerside	D-6
Tignish	C-6

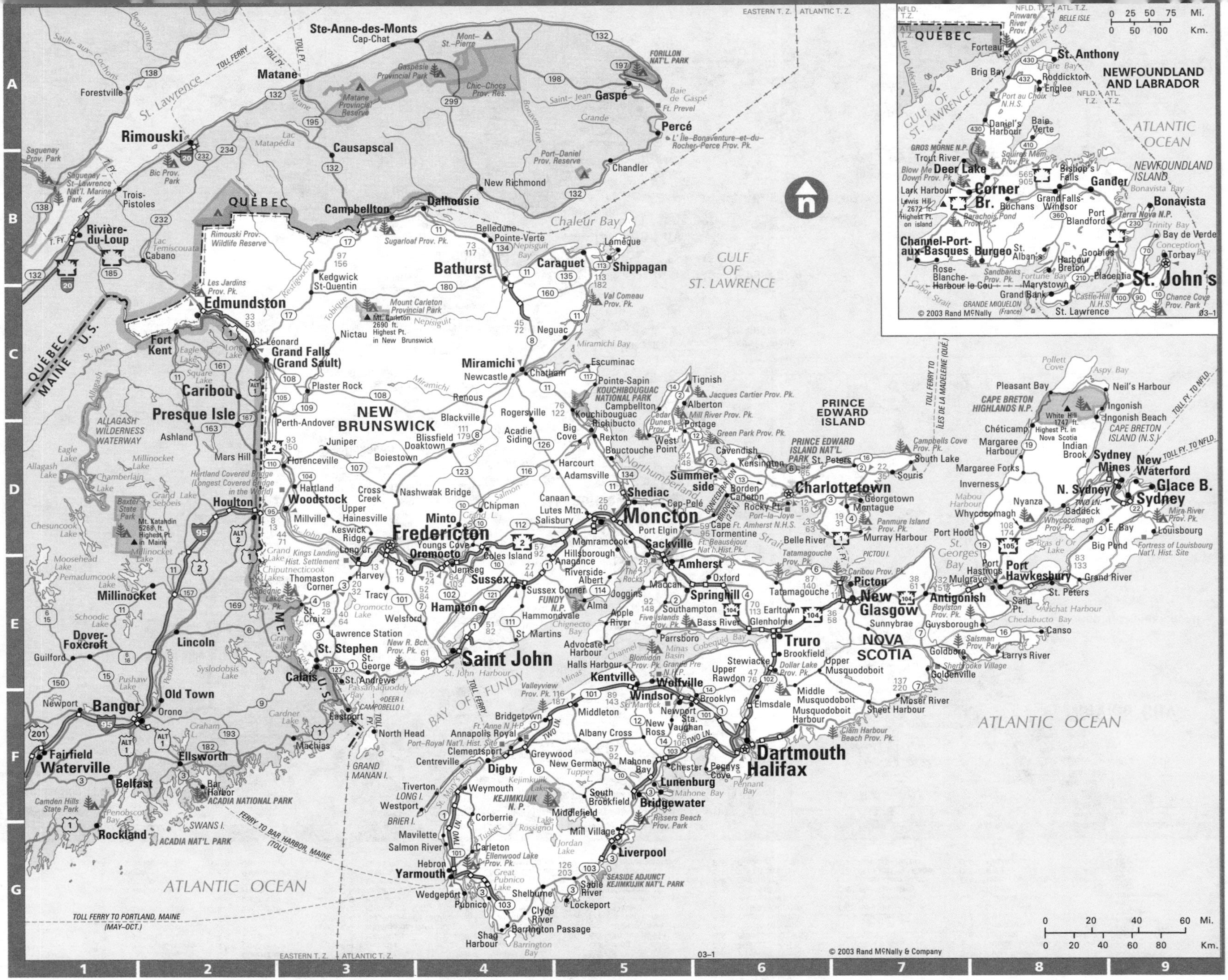

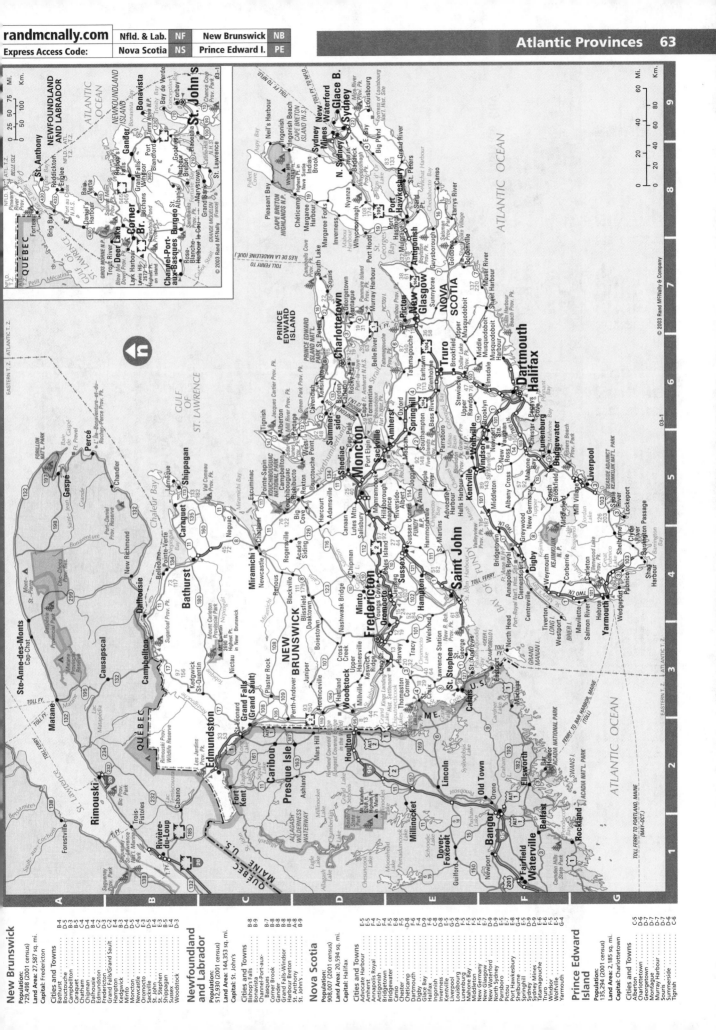

México

Population: 97,483,412 (2000 census)
Land Area: 758,450 sq. mi.
Capital: Mexico City

Cities and Towns

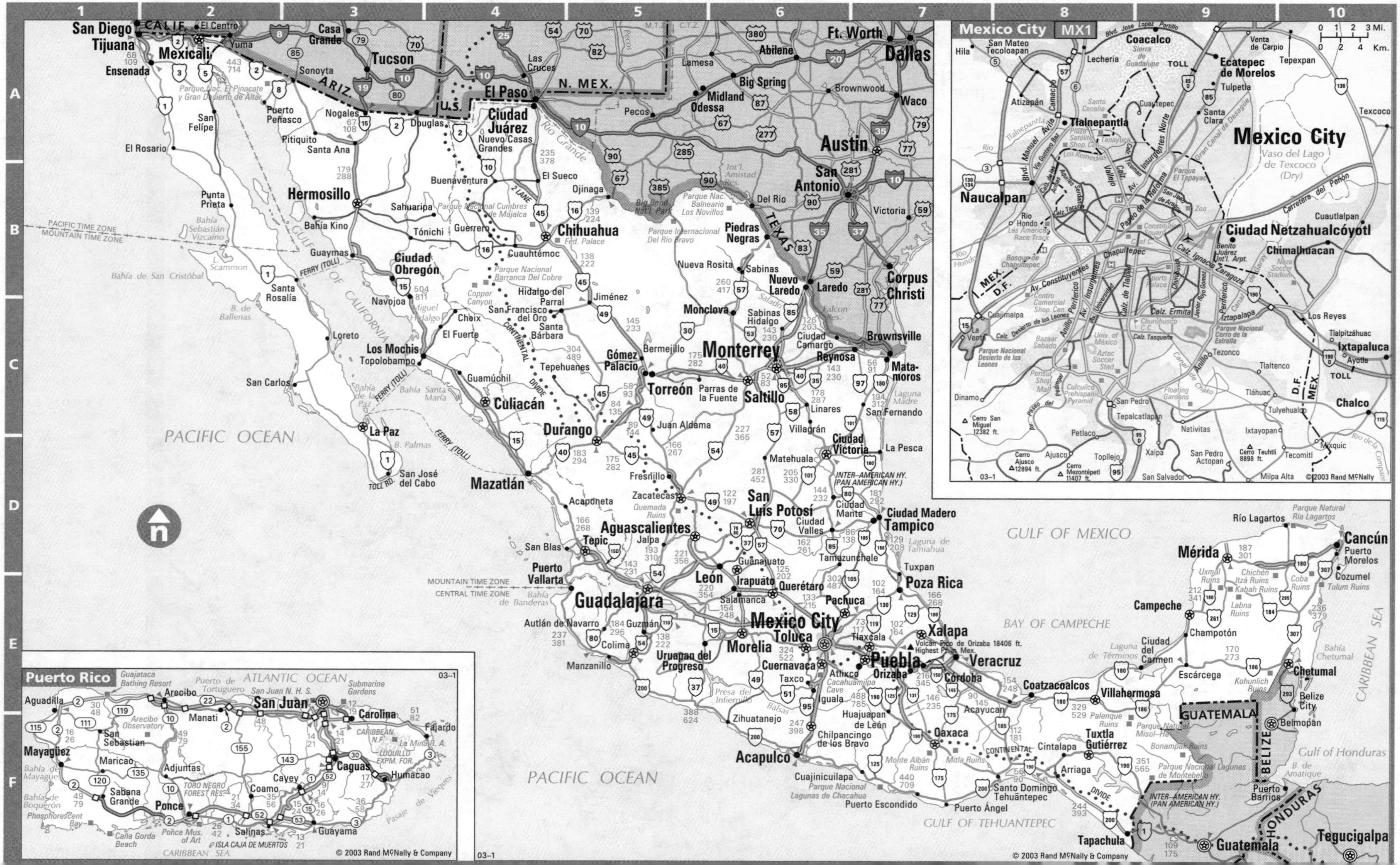

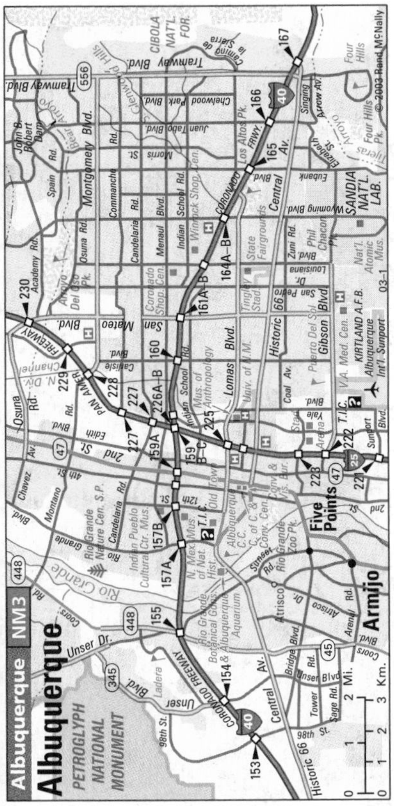
Albuquerque NM3
Albuquerque
PETROGLYPH NATIONAL MONUMENT
Rio Grande
Armijo
Five Points
CIBOLA NAT'L FOR.
SANDIA NAT'L LAB.
KIRTLAND A.F.B.
Albuquerque Int'l. Sunport
0 1 2 Mi.
0 1 2 3 Km.
© 2003 Rand McNally
03-1

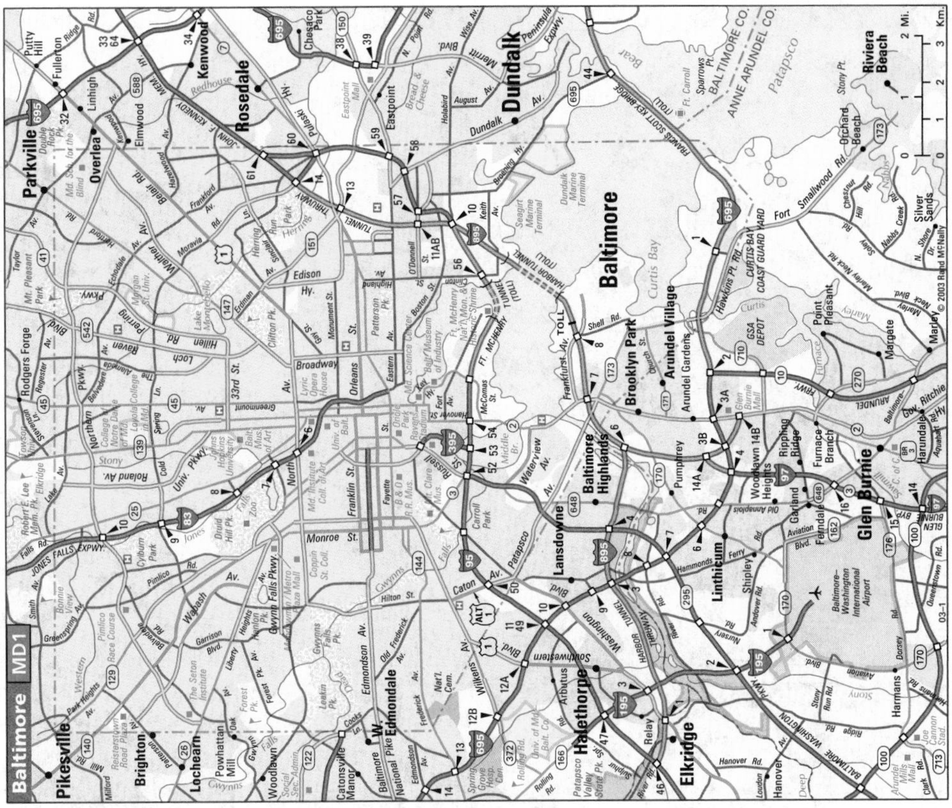
Baltimore MD1
Baltimore
Pikesville
Parkville
Overlea
Rosedale
Dundalk
Brooklyn Park
Arundel Village
Glen Burnie
Linthicum
Lansdowne
Baltimore Highlands
Halethorpe
Elkridge
Catonsville Manor
Woodlawn
Lochearn
Brighton
Riviera Beach
Baltimore-Washington International Airport
Patapsco
0 1 2 Mi.
0 1 2 3 Km.
© 2003 Rand McNally
03-1

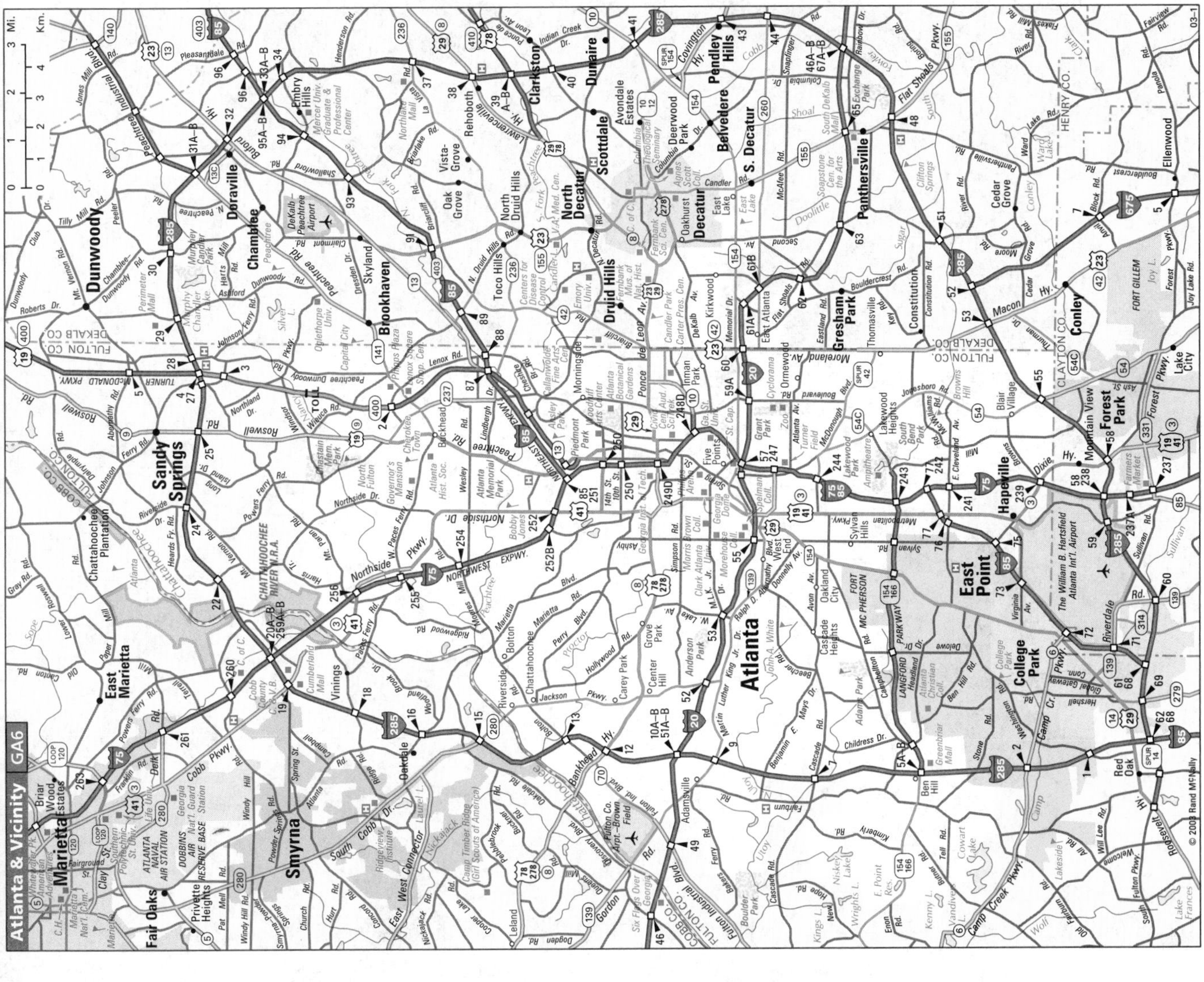
Atlanta & Vicinity GA6
Atlanta
Marietta
East Marietta
Smyrna
Fair Oaks
Sandy Springs
Dunwoody
Doraville
Chamblee
Brookhaven
Decatur
North Decatur
Druid Hills
Scottdale
Clarkston
Belvedere
Panthersville
Gresham Park
Conley
Forest Park
Hapeville
East Point
College Park
Lake City
Ellenwood
Red Oak
Adamsville
CHATTAHOOCHEE RIVER N.R.A.
DOBBINS AIR RESERVE BASE
FORT MC PHERSON
FORT GILLEM
The William B. Hartsfield Atlanta Int'l. Airport
FULTON CO.
DEKALB CO.
COBB CO.
CLAYTON CO.
HENRY CO.
0 1 2 3 Mi.
0 1 2 3 4 Km.
© 2003 Rand McNally
03-1

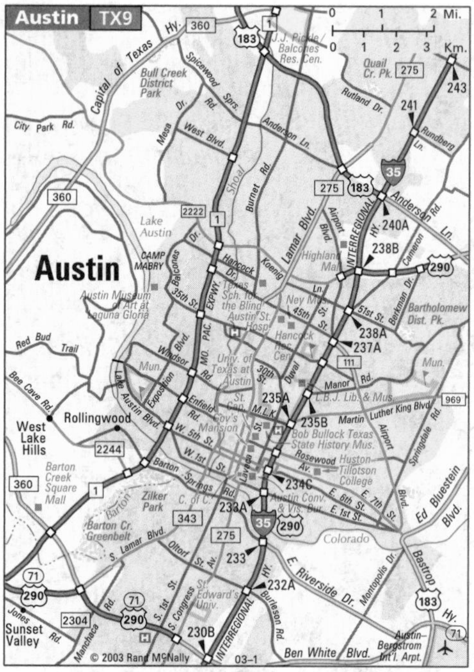
Austin TX9
0 1 2 Mi.
0 1 2 3 Km.
Austin
Lake Austin
Rollingwood
West Lake Hills
Sunset Valley
Zilker Park
Colorado
Capital of Texas Hy.
Lamar Blvd.
Burnet Rd.
Ben White Blvd.
Riverside Dr.
Austin-Bergstrom Int'l. Arpt.
© 2003 Rand McNally

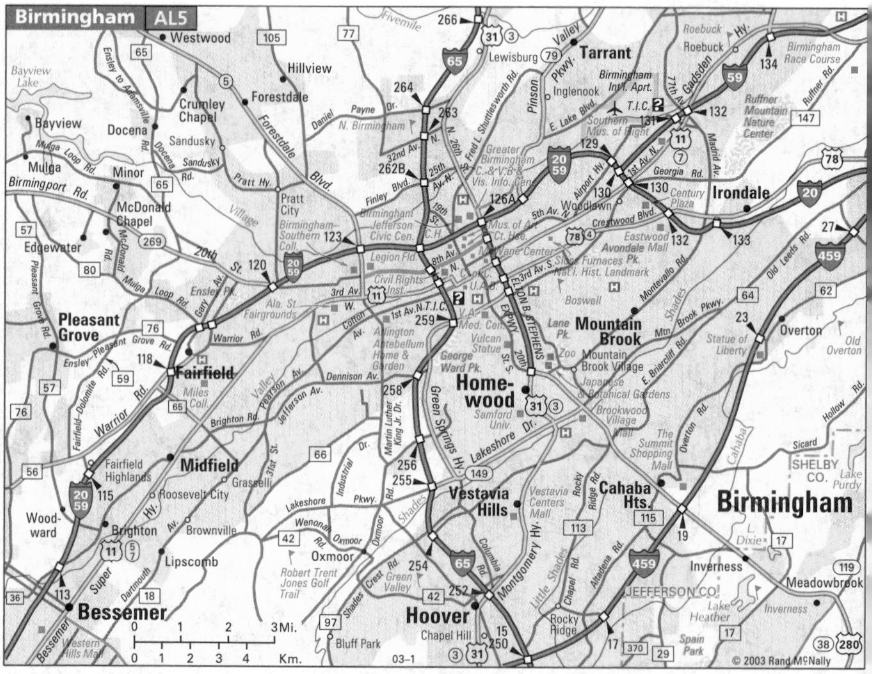
Birmingham AL5
Westwood
Hillview
Forestdale
Tarrant
Bayview
Docena
Crumley Chapel
Sandusky
Mulga
Minor
McDonald Chapel
Pratt City
Edgewater
Irondale
Pleasant Grove
Fairfield
Midfield
Mountain Brook
Homewood
Vestavia Hills
Cahaba Hts.
Birmingham
Wood-ward
Brighton
Lipscomb
Bessemer
Hoover
Inverness
Meadowbrook
Overton
0 1 2 3 Mi.
0 1 2 3 4 Km.
© 2003 Rand McNally

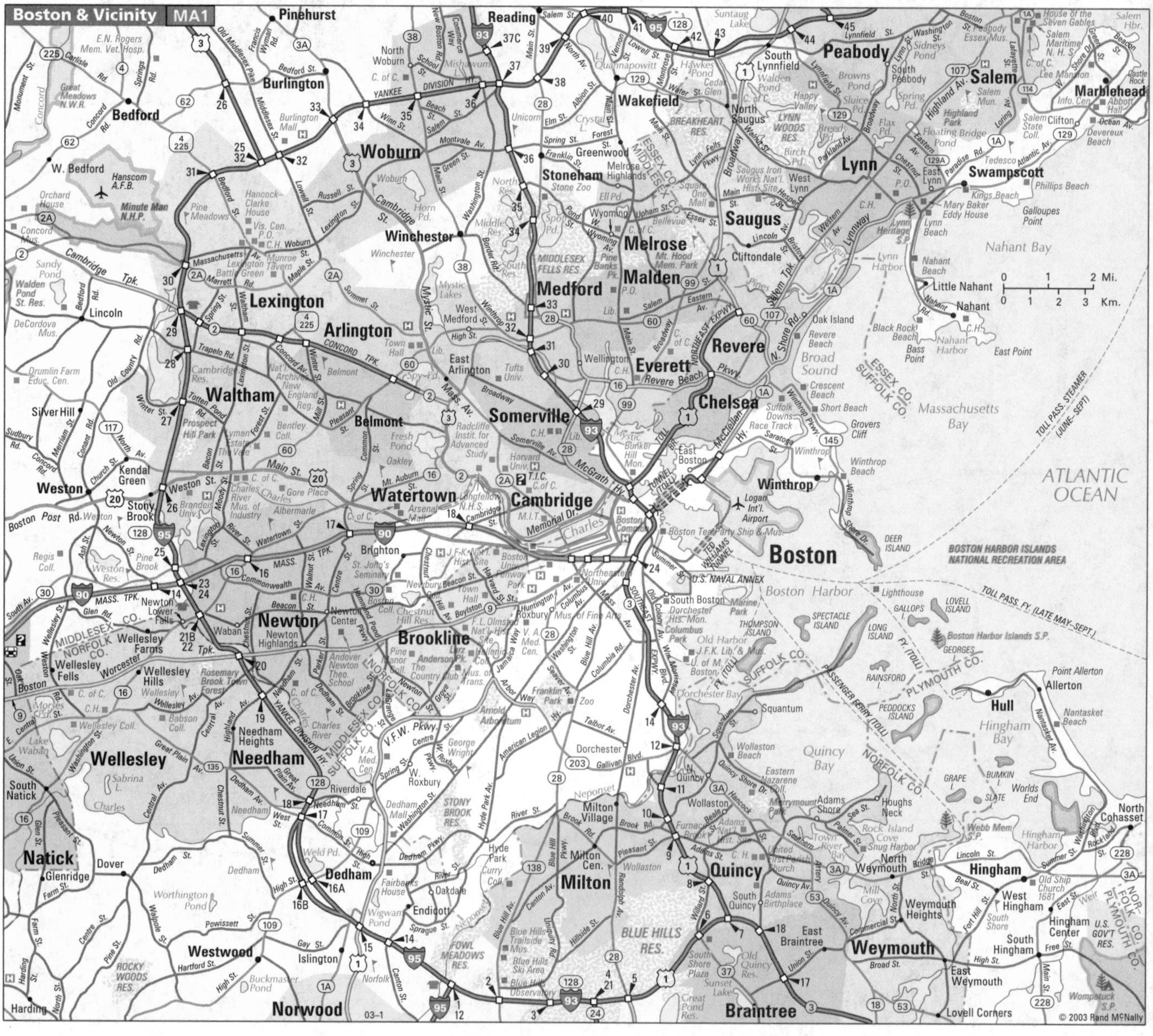
Boston & Vicinity MA1
Pinehurst
Reading
Burlington
Bedford
Peabody
Salem
Marblehead
Wakefield
Woburn
Stoneham
Lynn
Swampscott
Saugus
Winchester
Melrose
Malden
Medford
Revere
Lexington
Arlington
Everett
Chelsea
Waltham
Belmont
Somerville
Cambridge
Watertown
Winthrop
Weston
Boston
Newton
Brookline
Wellesley
Needham
Natick
Dedham
Milton
Quincy
Dover
Westwood
Norwood
Braintree
Weymouth
Hingham
Hull
Massachusetts Bay
ATLANTIC OCEAN
Nahant Bay
Boston Harbor
Quincy Bay
BOSTON HARBOR ISLANDS NATIONAL RECREATION AREA
0 1 2 Mi.
0 1 2 3 Km.
© 2003 Rand McNally

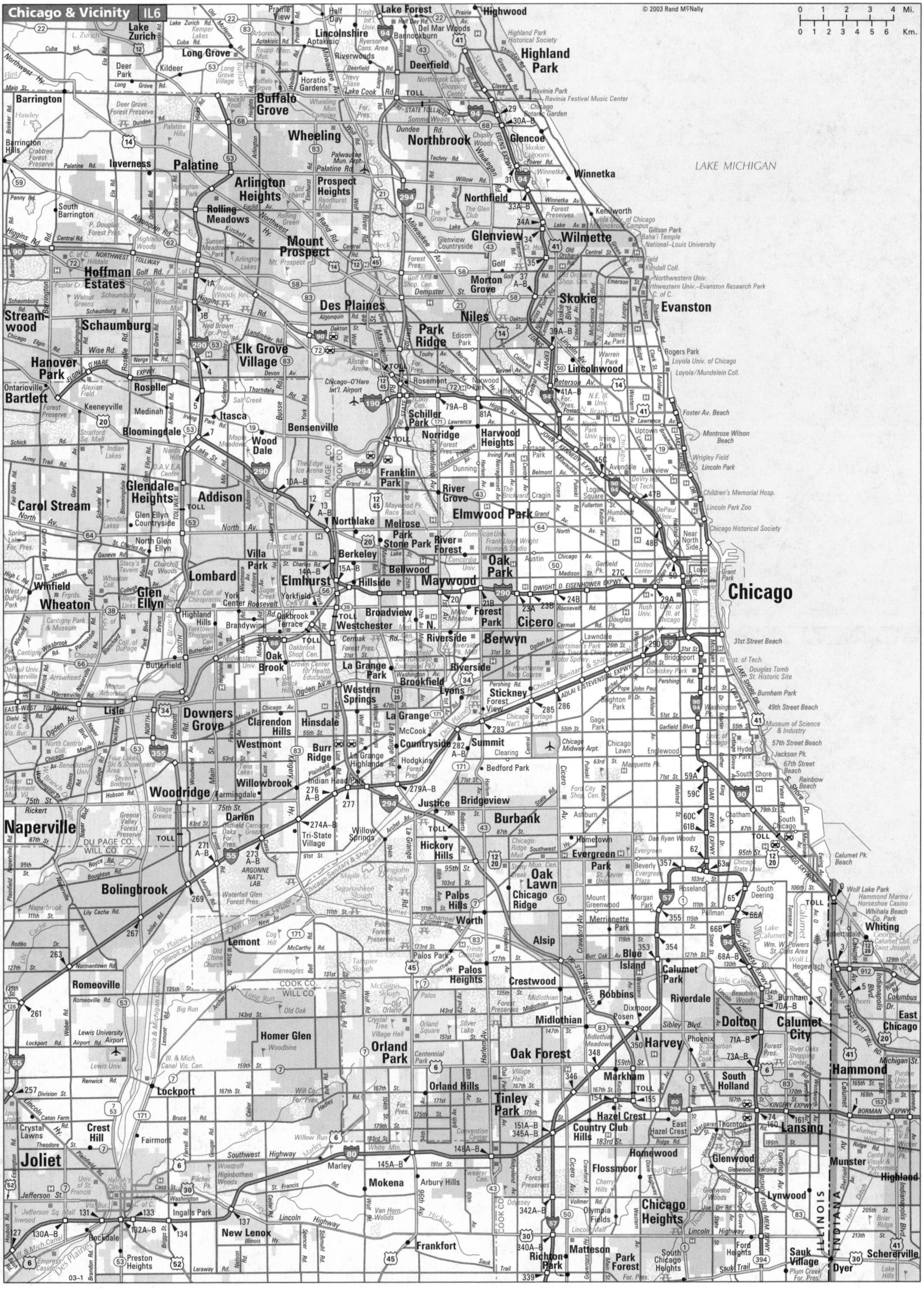
Chicago & Vicinity
IL6
© 2003 Rand McNally
0 1 2 3 4 Mi.
0 1 2 3 4 5 6 Km.
LAKE MICHIGAN
Chicago
Evanston
Skokie
Wilmette
Glenview
Northbrook
Highland Park
Deerfield
Lake Forest
Wheeling
Palatine
Arlington Heights
Mount Prospect
Des Plaines
Park Ridge
Niles
Schaumburg
Hoffman Estates
Elk Grove Village
Bensenville
Elmhurst
Oak Park
Cicero
Berwyn
Lombard
Wheaton
Glen Ellyn
Downers Grove
Naperville
Bolingbrook
Woodridge
Lisle
Hinsdale
Oak Lawn
Burbank
Harvey
Calumet City
Hammond
Joliet
Lockport
Orland Park
Tinley Park
Oak Forest
Chicago Heights
Lansing
Homer Glen
Romeoville
Lemont
ILLINOIS
INDIANA
03-1

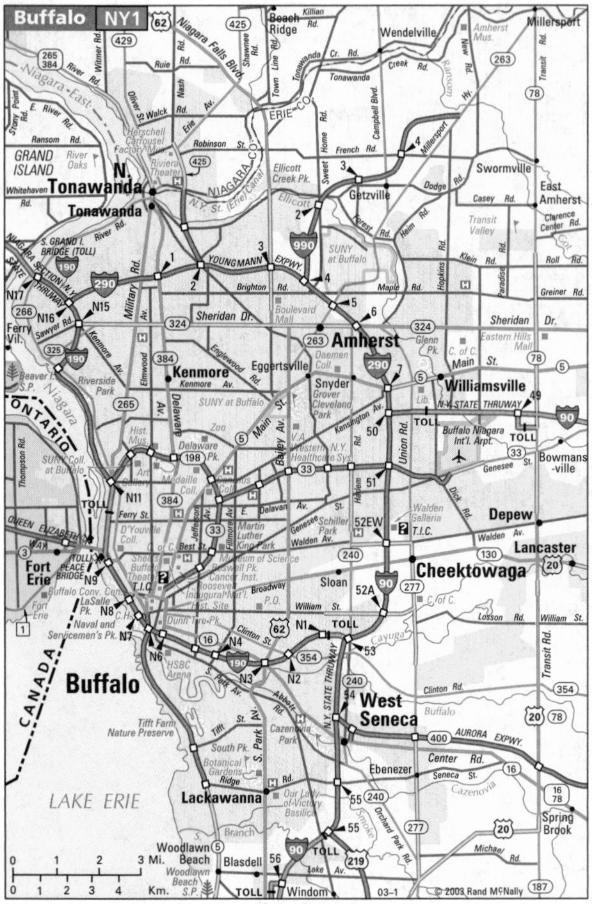
Buffalo NY1
N. Tonawanda
Tonawanda
Amherst
Kenmore
Williamsville
Cheektowaga
Depew
Lancaster
Buffalo
West Seneca
Lackawanna
Fort Erie
LAKE ERIE
CANADA
© 2003 Rand McNally

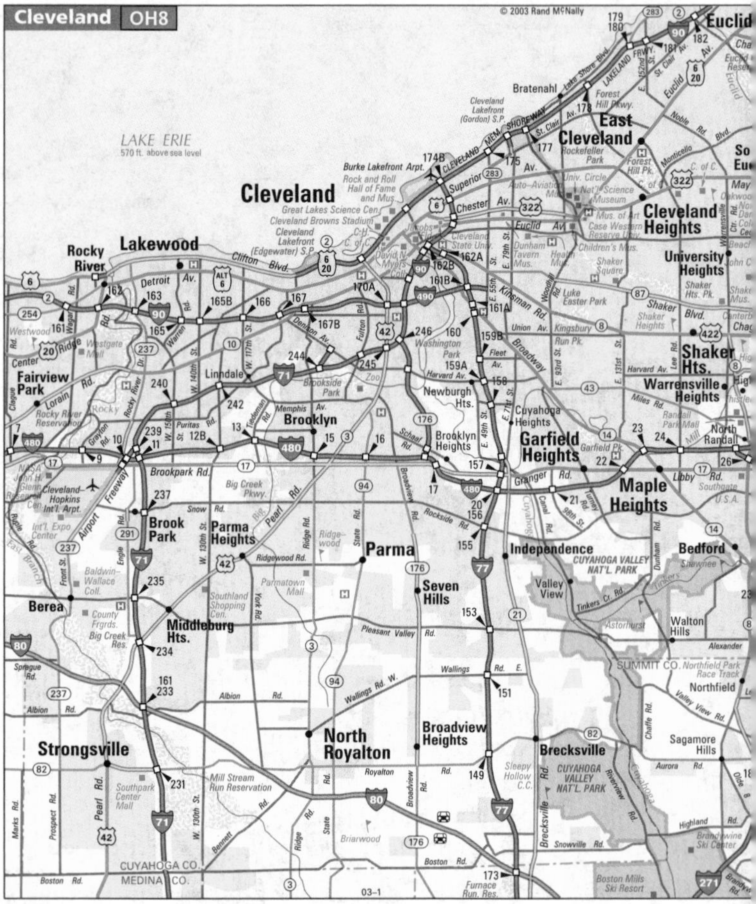
Cleveland OH8
© 2003 Rand McNally
LAKE ERIE
570 ft. above sea level
Cleveland
Lakewood
Rocky River
Euclid
East Cleveland
Cleveland Heights
University Heights
Shaker Hts.
Warrensville Heights
Fairview Park
Brooklyn
Garfield Heights
Maple Heights
Brook Park
Parma Heights
Parma
Independence
Bedford
Berea
Seven Hills
Middleburg Hts.
Strongsville
North Royalton
Broadview Heights
Brecksville
CUYAHOGA VALLEY NAT'L. PARK

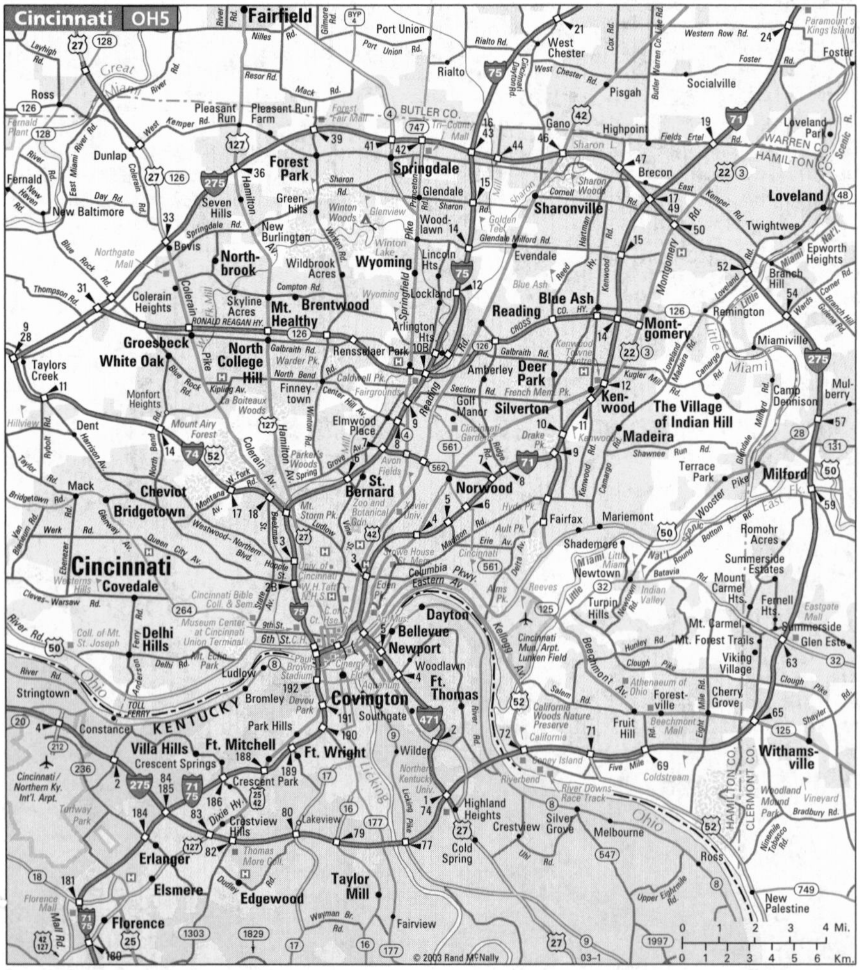
Cincinnati OH5
Fairfield
Forest Park
Springdale
Sharonville
Loveland
Wyoming
Blue Ash
Reading
Mt. Healthy
North College Hill
Deer Park
Kenwood
Silverton
Madeira
The Village of Indian Hill
Milford
Norwood
St. Bernard
Cheviot
Bridgetown
Cincinnati
Covedale
Delhi Hills
Newport
Covington
Ft. Thomas
Fort Mitchell
Ft. Wright
Erlanger
Elsmere
Edgewood
Taylor Mill
Florence
Withamsville
KENTUCKY
© 2003 Rand McNally

Dallas / Ft. Worth & Vicinity TX14
Newark
Haslet
Keller
Saginaw
Blue Mound
Lake Worth
Sansom Park
River Oaks
White Settlement
Westworth
Benbrook
Edgecliff
Haltom City
St. Francis Village

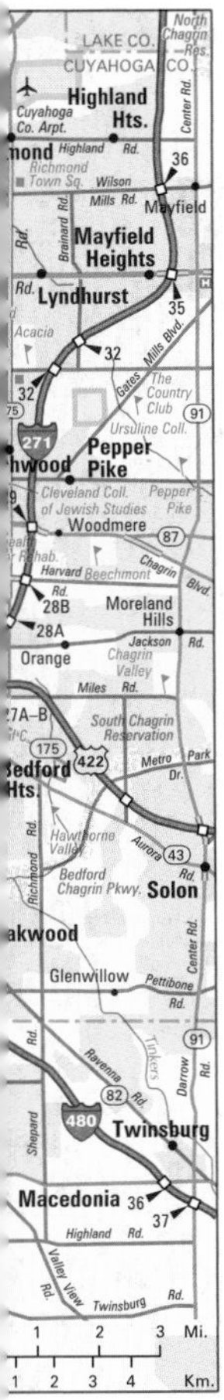

Highland Hts.
Mayfield Heights
Lyndhurst
Pepper Pike
Woodmere
Moreland Hills
Orange
Solon
Glenwillow
Twinsburg
Macedonia

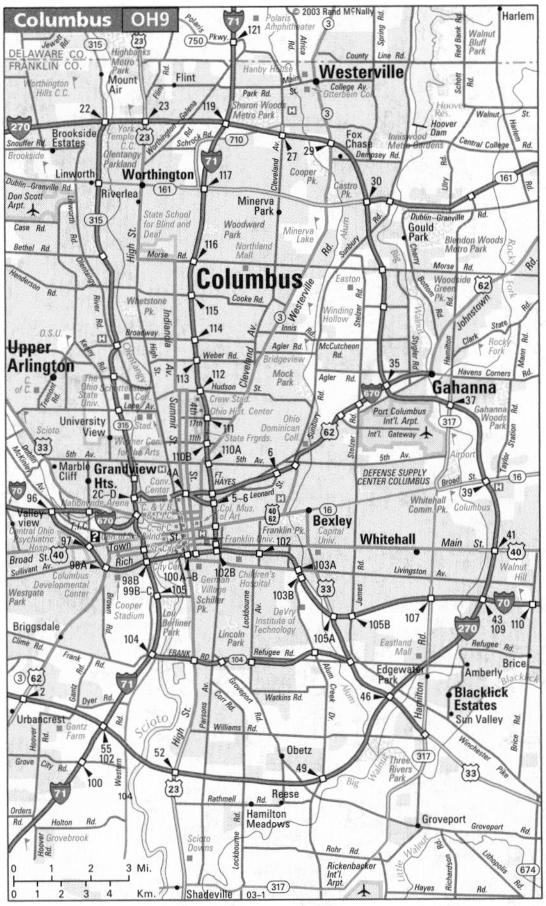

Columbus OH9
© 2003 Rand McNally
Westerville
Worthington
Upper Arlington
Columbus
Gahanna
Grandview Hts.
Bexley
Whitehall
Minerva Park
Gould Park
Blacklick Estates
Obetz
Groveport
Reese
Urbancrest
Shadeville

Denver & Vicinity CO5
Westminster
Thornton
Northglenn
Federal Hts.
Sherrelwood
Dupont
Commerce City
Arvada
Wheat Ridge
Edgewater
Mountain View
Lakewood
Denver
Aurora
Glendale
Sheridan
Englewood
Cherry Hills Village
Greenwood Village
Bow Mar
Littleton
Centennial
Columbine Valley
Highlands Ranch
Lone Tree
ROCKY MOUNTAIN ARSENAL NAT'L. WILDLIFE REFUGE
© 2003 Rand McNally

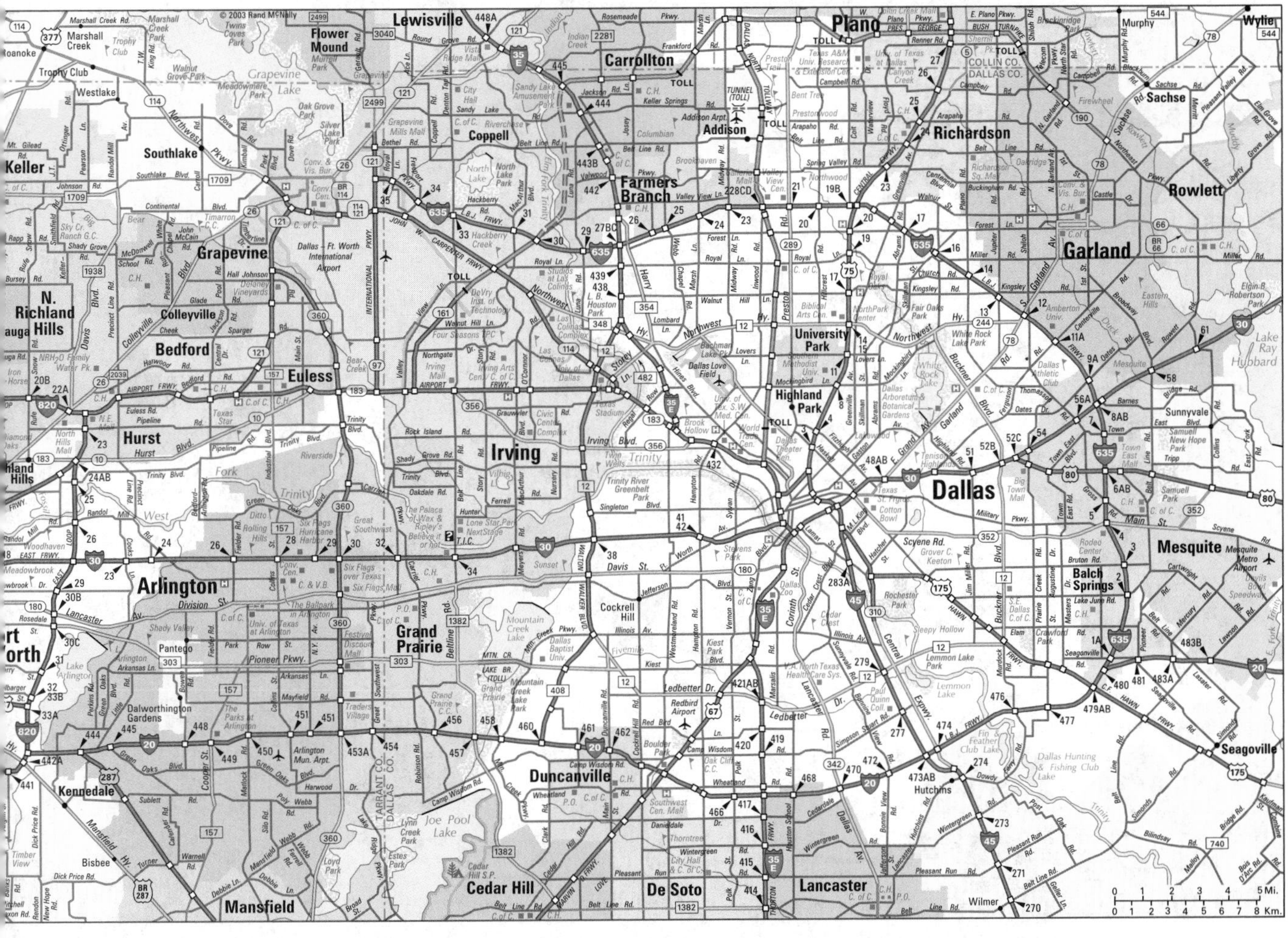

© 2003 Rand McNally
Lewisville
Flower Mound
Carrollton
Plano
Wylie
Murphy
Sachse
Coppell
Addison
Richardson
Southlake
Keller
Farmers Branch
Rowlett
Grapevine
Colleyville
N. Richland Hills
Bedford
Euless
Garland
University Park
Highland Park
Hurst
Irving
Dallas
Mesquite
Arlington
Grand Prairie
Balch Springs
Cockrell Hill
Hutchins
Seagoville
Duncanville
Kennedale
Cedar Hill
De Soto
Lancaster
Mansfield
Wilmer

Indianapolis
IN3
Lawrence
Speedway
Indianapolis
Beech Grove
Eagle Creek Park
Eagle Creek Reservoir
Castleton
Allisonville
Williams Creek
Meridian Hills
North Crows Nest
Crows Nest
Millersville
Wynnedale
Clermont
Chapel Hill
Ben Davis
Bridgeport
Indianapolis International Airport
Mars Hill
Maywood
Five Points
Wanamaker
Valley Mills
Sunshine Gardens
Augusta
New Augusta
Traders Point
Fort Harrison State Park
© 2003 Rand McNally

Los Angeles & Vicinity
CA12
Simi Valley
Chatsworth
Northridge
Canoga Park
Hidden Hills
Calabasas
Woodland Hills
Tarzana
Glenview
Sylvia Park
Topanga Park
SANTA MONICA MOUNTAINS
SANTA MONICA MTNS. NAT'L. REC. AREA
Topanga
Fernwood
Los Angeles
Pacific Palisades
Santa Monica
Santa Monica Bay
PACIFIC OCEAN
Malibu Pt.

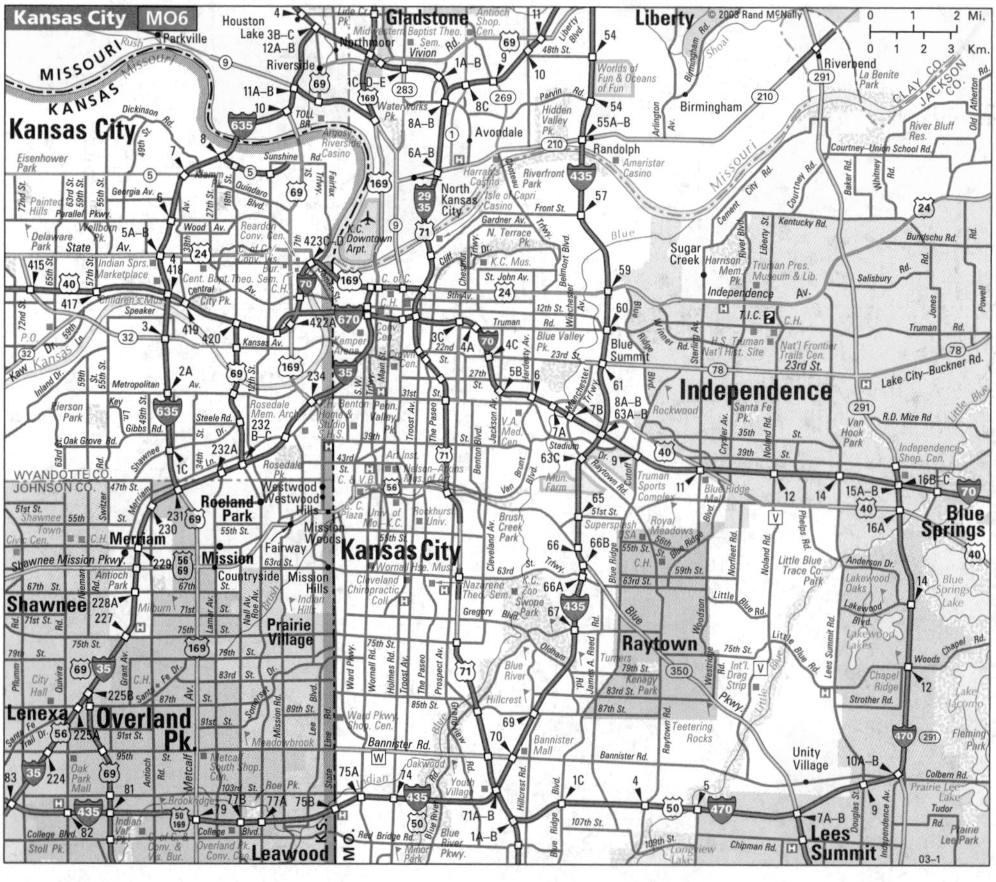
Kansas City
MO6
Gladstone
Liberty
Parkville
Houston Lake
Riverside
Northmoor
Kansas City
Avondale
Randolph
North Kansas City
Birmingham
Riverbend
Sugar Creek
Independence
Blue Summit
Raytown
Blue Springs
Roeland Park
Merriam
Mission
Mission Woods
Westwood
Westwood Hills
Fairway
Mission Hills
Prairie Village
Shawnee
Lenexa
Overland Pk.
Leawood
Lees Summit
Unity Village
Grandview
Kansas City
MISSOURI
KANSAS
© 2003 Rand McNally

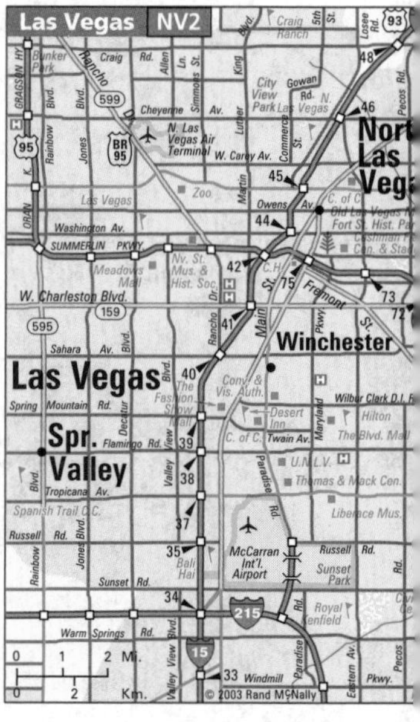
Las Vegas
NV2
North Las Vegas
Las Vegas
Winchester
Spr. Valley
McCarran Int'l. Airport
© 2003 Rand McNally

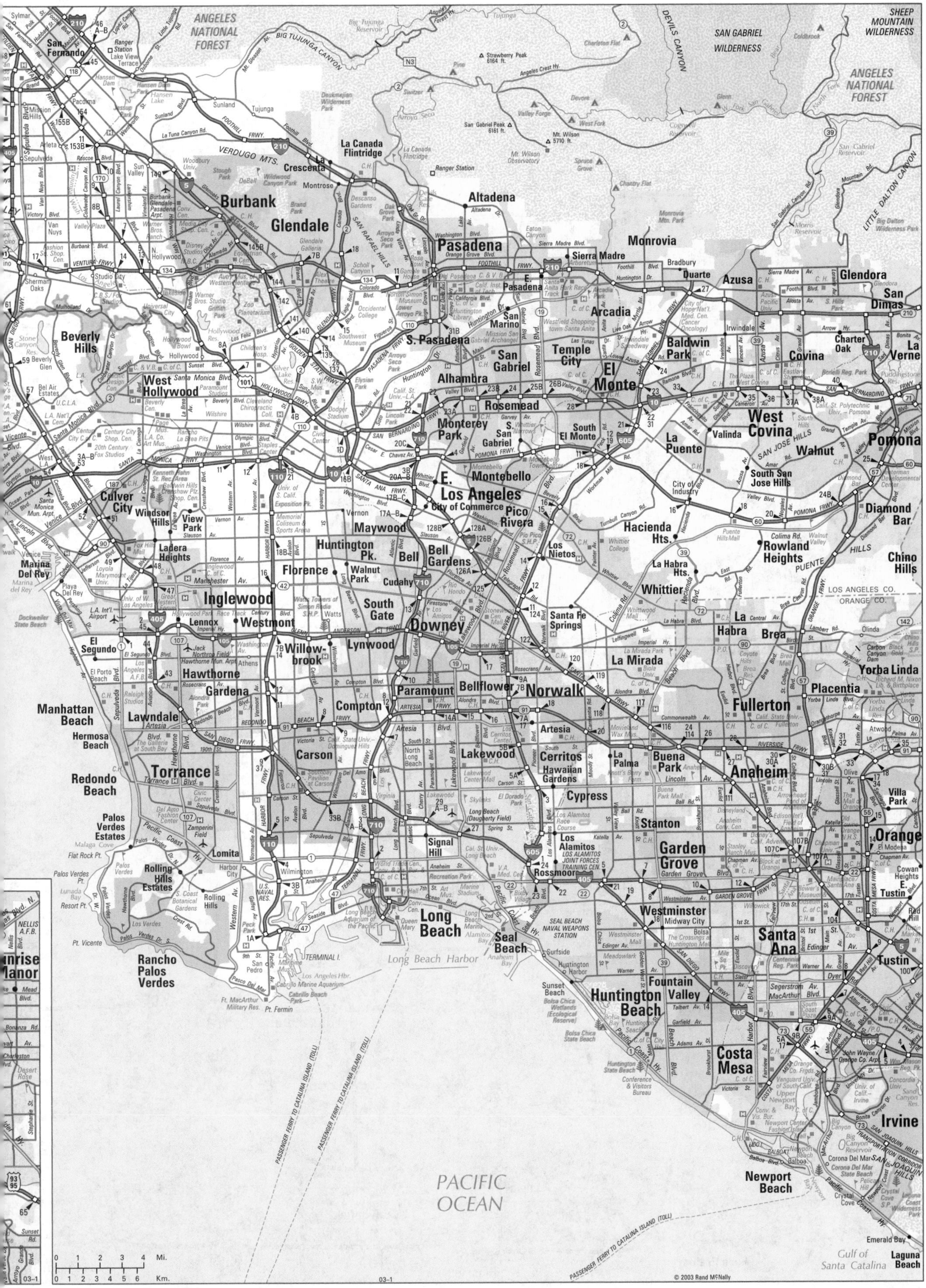
ANGELES NATIONAL FOREST
SAN GABRIEL WILDERNESS
SHEEP MOUNTAIN WILDERNESS
DEVILS CANYON
VERDUGO MTS.
Strawberry Peak 6164 ft.
San Gabriel Peak 6161 ft.
Mt. Wilson 5710 ft.
Sylmar
San Fernando
Pacoima
Sunland
Tujunga
La Canada Flintridge
La Crescenta
Burbank
Glendale
Altadena
Pasadena
Sierra Madre
Monrovia
Bradbury
Duarte
Azusa
Glendora
San Dimas
La Verne
Charter Oak
Covina
Irwindale
Baldwin Park
Arcadia
Temple City
San Marino
S. Pasadena
E. Pasadena
Alhambra
San Gabriel
Rosemead
El Monte
South El Monte
Monterey Park
West Covina
La Puente
Valinda
Walnut
Pomona
Diamond Bar
Rowland Heights
Hacienda Hts.
City of Industry
South San Jose Hills
Chino Hills
Van Nuys
Sherman Oaks
Studio City
North Hollywood
Beverly Hills
West Hollywood
Hollywood
Bel Air Estates
West Los Angeles
Culver City
Santa Monica
Venice
Marina Del Rey
Playa Del Rey
Ladera Heights
View Park
Windsor Hills
Inglewood
Westmont
Lennox
El Segundo
Hawthorne
Lawndale
Gardena
Manhattan Beach
Hermosa Beach
Redondo Beach
Torrance
Palos Verdes Estates
Rolling Hills
Rolling Hills Estates
Rancho Palos Verdes
Lomita
San Pedro
Wilmington
Carson
Compton
Willowbrook
Lynwood
South Gate
Florence
Huntington Pk.
Walnut Park
Maywood
Bell
Bell Gardens
Cudahy
E. Los Angeles
City of Commerce
Vernon
Montebello
Pico Rivera
Los Nietos
Whittier
La Habra Hts.
La Habra
Brea
Santa Fe Springs
Downey
Norwalk
La Mirada
Paramount
Bellflower
Lakewood
Artesia
Cerritos
Hawaiian Gardens
Fullerton
Placentia
Yorba Linda
Anaheim
Buena Park
La Palma
Cypress
Stanton
Los Alamitos
Rossmoor
Garden Grove
Orange
Villa Park
Long Beach
Signal Hill
Seal Beach
Westminster
Midway City
Santa Ana
Tustin
Fountain Valley
Huntington Beach
Costa Mesa
Newport Beach
Irvine
Laguna Beach
Emerald Bay
Long Beach Harbor
Los Angeles Hbr.
PACIFIC OCEAN
Gulf of Santa Catalina
PASSENGER FERRY TO CATALINA ISLAND (TOLL)
LOS ANGELES CO.
ORANGE CO.
L.A. Int'l. Airport
0 1 2 3 4 Mi.
0 1 2 3 4 5 6 Km.
© 2003 Rand McNally

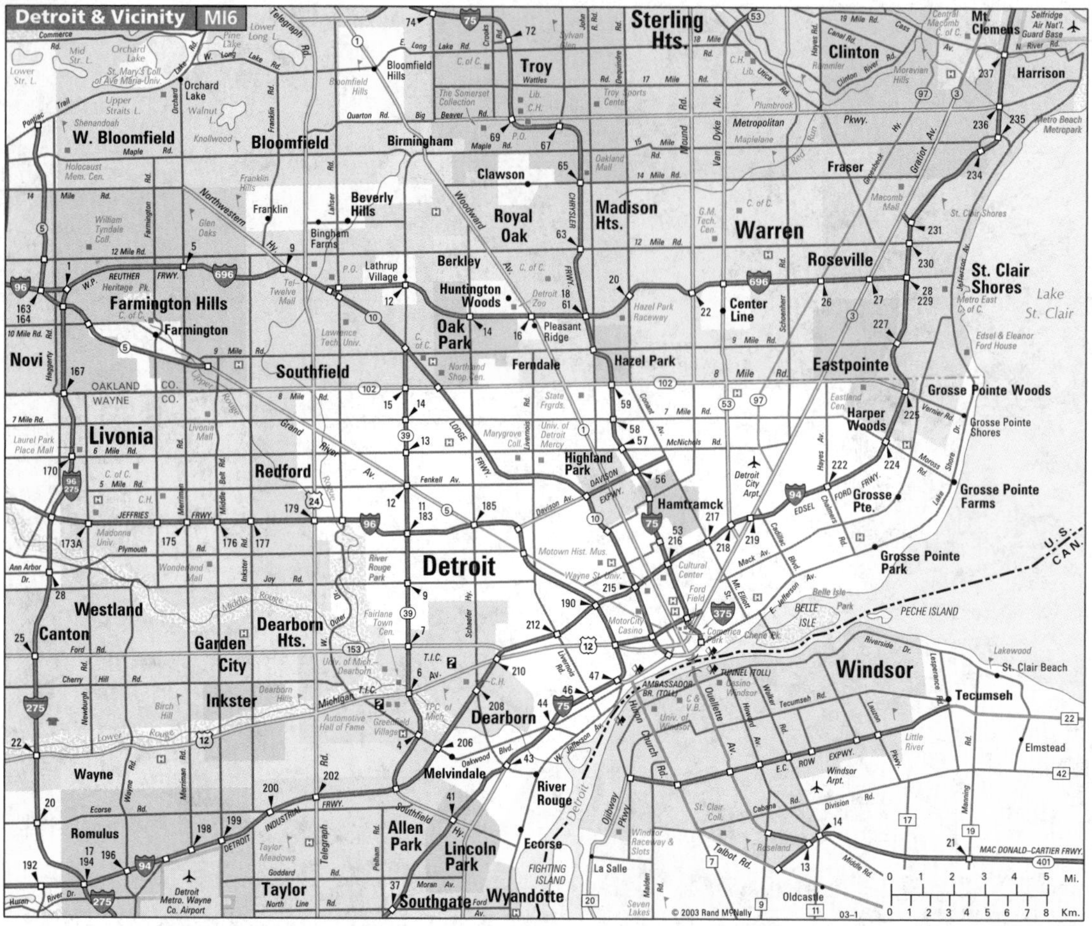
Detroit & Vicinity MI6
Sterling Hts.
Clinton
Troy
Harrison
W. Bloomfield
Bloomfield
Birmingham
Clawson
Fraser
Royal Oak
Madison Hts.
Warren
Roseville
St. Clair Shores
Farmington Hills
Farmington
Oak Park
Center Line
Novi
Southfield
Ferndale
Hazel Park
Eastpointe
Grosse Pointe Woods
Livonia
Redford
Highland Park
Hamtramck
Grosse Pte.
Grosse Pointe Farms
Grosse Pointe Park
Detroit
Westland
Canton
Dearborn Hts.
Garden City
Windsor
Tecumseh
Inkster
Dearborn
Wayne
Melvindale
River Rouge
Romulus
Allen Park
Lincoln Park
Ecorse
Taylor
Southgate
Wyandotte
© 2003 Rand McNally

Houston & Vicinity TX
Jersey Vill.
Spring Valley
Hedwig Village
Bunker Hill Village
Piney Point Village
Sugar Land
Stafford
Missouri City
© 2003 Rand McNally

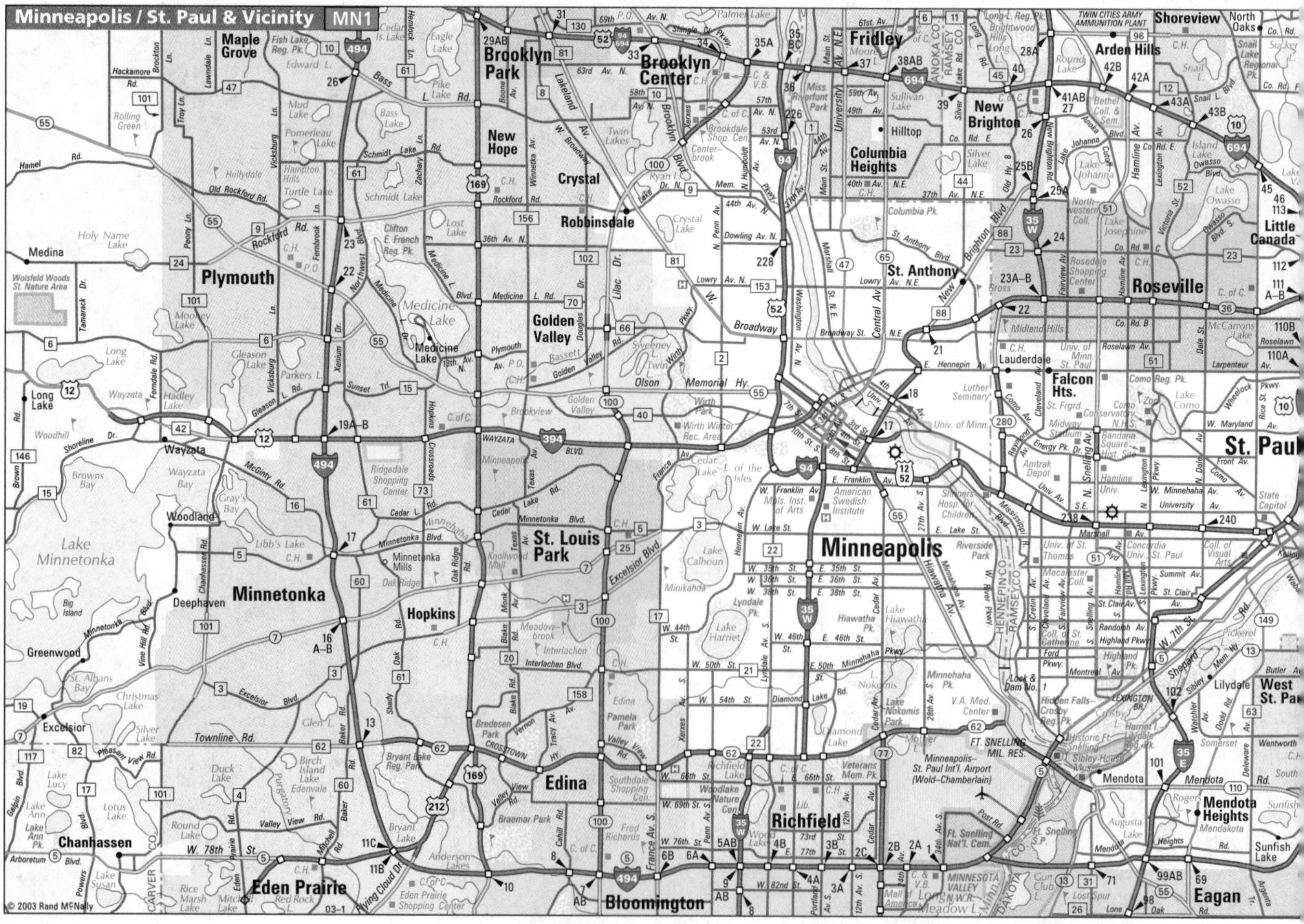
Minneapolis / St. Paul & Vicinity MN1
Maple Grove
Brooklyn Park
Brooklyn Center
Fridley
Shoreview
Arden Hills
New Brighton
New Hope
Crystal
Robbinsdale
Columbia Heights
Little Canada
Plymouth
St. Anthony
Roseville
Golden Valley
Lauderdale
Falcon Hts.
Long Lake
Wayzata
St. Paul
Woodland
St. Louis Park
Minneapolis
Deephaven
Minnetonka
Hopkins
Greenwood
West St. Paul
Lilydale
Excelsior
Edina
Richfield
Mendota
Mendota Heights
Chanhassen
Eden Prairie
Bloomington
Eagan
© 2003 Rand McNally

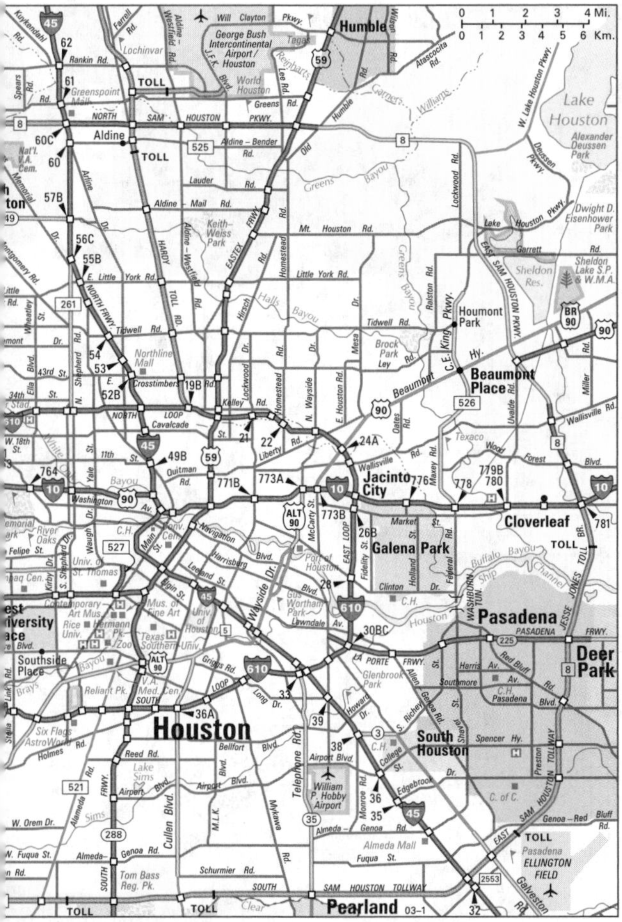

Houston
Humble
George Bush Intercontinental Airport / Houston
Lake Houston
Aldine
Pasadena
Deer Park
South Houston
Galena Park
Jacinto City
Cloverleaf
Beaumont Place
Houmont Park
Pearland
William P. Hobby Airport
Ellington Field
Southside Place
03-1

Mahtomedi
Grant
White Bear Lake
Birchwood Village
Willernie
Gem Lake
Pine Springs
Maplewood
North St. Paul
Lake Elmo
Oakdale
Landfall
Woodbury
South St. Paul
Newport
St. Paul Park
Inver Grove Heights
Cottage Grove

Miami & Vicinity FL4
Boynton Beach
Delray Beach
Boca Raton
Deerfield Beach
Arthur R. Marshall Loxahatchee National Wildlife Refuge
The Everglades
Palm Beach Co.
Broward Co.
Parkland
Coral Springs
Coconut Creek
Margate
North Lauderdale
Tamarac
Pompano Beach
Lauderdale Lakes
Sunrise
Oakland Park
Lauderhill
Fort Lauderdale
Plantation
Weston
Davie
Cooper City
Hollywood
Pembroke Pines
Miramar
Hallandale Beach
Carol City
Aventura
N. Miami Beach
Opa Locka
N. Miami
Hialeah
Hialeah Gardens
Miami Beach
Atlantic Ocean
Sweetwater
Miami
Coral Gables
Key Biscayne
Kendall
Pinecrest
Richmond Hts.
© 2003 Rand McNally
03-1

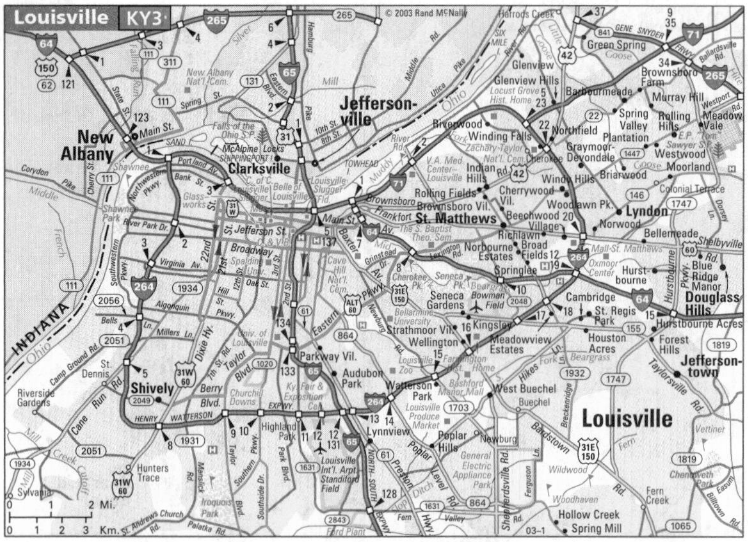
Louisville KY3
© 2003 Rand McNally
New Albany
Jefferson-ville
Clarksville
St. Matthews
Lyndon
Shively
Louisville
Jefferson-town
Douglass Hills
Hurstbourne
Middletown
INDIANA
Ohio
Louisville Int'l. Arpt.-Standiford Field
Fern Creek
Hollow Creek
Spring Mill
Hunters Trace
Sylvania
Riverside Gardens
0 1 2 Mi.
0 1 2 3 Km.
03-1

Milwaukee & Vicinity WI1
© 2003 Rand McNally
Shorewood
Brook-field
Wauwatosa
Milwaukee
West Allis
St. Francis
New Berlin
Greenfield
Greendale
Cudahy
Lake Michigan
Milwaukee Bay
Gen. Mitchell Air Nat'l Guard
General Mitchell Int'l. Airport
0 1 2 Mi.
0 1 2 3 Km.
03-1

Memphis TN3
Memphis
ARKANSAS
Mississippi
LOOSAHATCHIE BAR
MUD I.
Shelby Farms
West Junction
T.O. Fuller State Park
Chucalissa Archaeological Museum
Memphis Int'l. Arpt.
0 1 2 3 Mi.
0 1 2 3 4 Km.
03-1
© 2003 Rand McNally

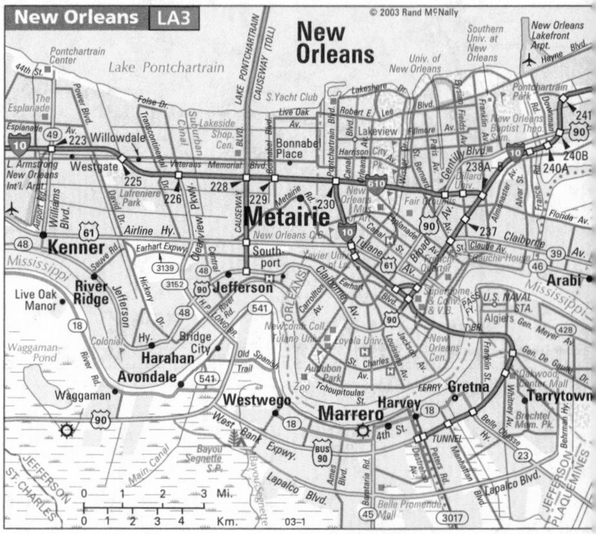
New Orleans LA3
© 2003 Rand McNally
New Orleans
Lake Pontchartrain
Metairie
Kenner
River Ridge
Jefferson
Harahan
Avondale
Westwego
Marrero
Harvey
Gretna
Terrytown
Arabi
Waggaman
Live Oak Manor
New Orleans Lakefront Arpt.
L. Armstrong New Orleans Int'l. Arpt.
JEFFERSON ST. CHARLES
JEFFERSON PLAQUEMINES
0 1 2 3 Mi.
0 1 2 3 4 Km.
03-1

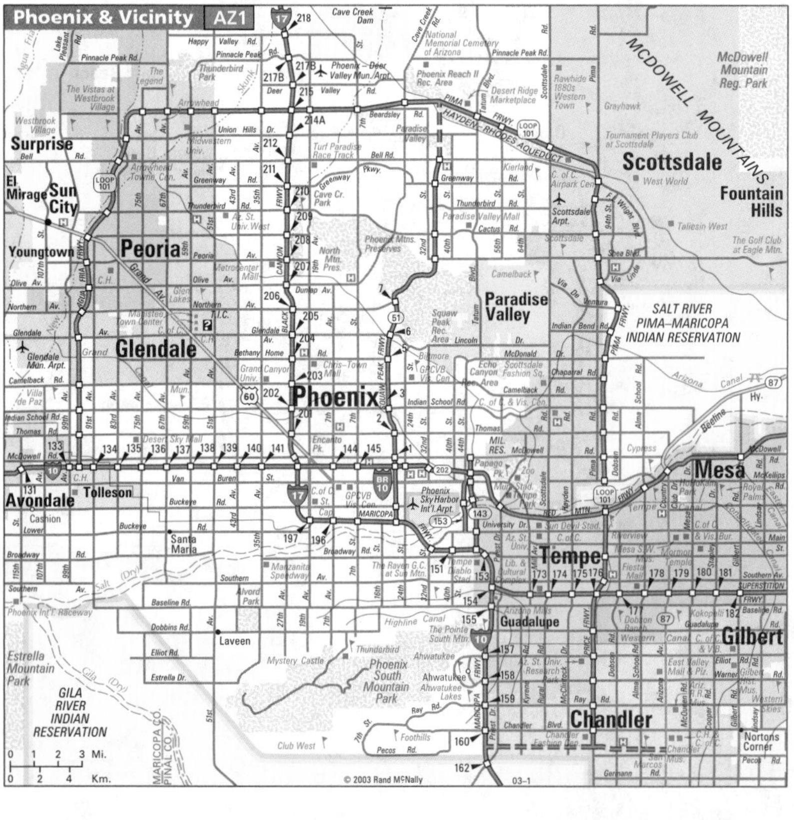
Phoenix & Vicinity AZ1
Cave Creek Dam
MCDOWELL MOUNTAINS
McDowell Mountain Reg. Park
Surprise
El Mirage
Sun City
Youngtown
Peoria
Glendale
Scottsdale
Fountain Hills
Paradise Valley
SALT RIVER PIMA-MARICOPA INDIAN RESERVATION
Phoenix
Avondale
Tolleson
Tempe
Mesa
Guadalupe
Gilbert
Chandler
Laveen
GILA RIVER INDIAN RESERVATION
MARICOPA CO. PINAL CO.
Estrella Mountain Park
Phoenix South Mountain Park
Phoenix Sky Harbor Int'l Airport
0 1 2 3 Mi.
0 2 4 Km.
© 2003 Rand McNally
03-1

Orlando FL8
Sweetwater Oaks
Longwood
Plymouth
Apopka
Wekiva Springs
Altamonte Springs
Casselberry
Winter Springs
Fern Park
Maitland
Lockhart
Eatonville
Winter Park
Lake Apopka
Orlando
Ocoee
Pine Hills
Winter Garden
Azalea Park
Orlo Vista
Conway
Belle Isle
Pine Castle
Sky Lake
Doctor Phillips
Windermere
Bay Hill
Williamsburg
Meadow Wood
Buena Ventura Lakes
Kissimmee
Orlando Int'l. Airport
WALT DISNEY WORLD RESORT COMPLEX
ORANGE CO. OSCEOLA CO.
0 1 2 3 Mi.
0 2 4 Km.
03-1
© 2003 Rand McNally

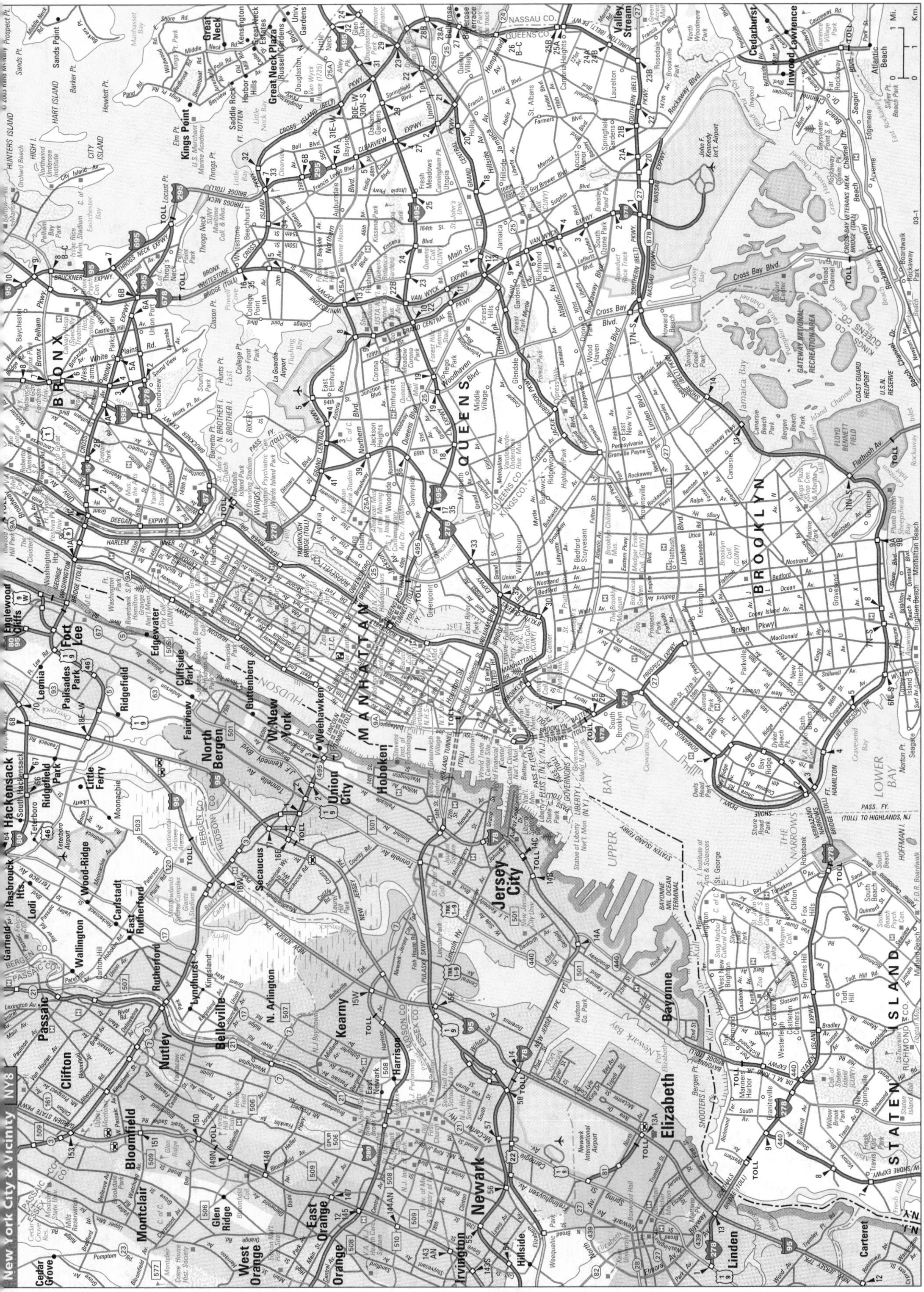
New York City & Vicinity NY8
© 2003 Rand McNally
BRONX
QUEENS
BROOKLYN
MANHATTAN
STATEN ISLAND
Newark
Jersey City
Hoboken
Union City
Bayonne
Elizabeth
North Bergen
Fort Lee
Englewood Cliffs
Hackensack
Secaucus
Kearny
Harrison
Belleville
Nutley
Bloomfield
Montclair
West Orange
East Orange
Orange
Irvington
Hillside
Linden
Carteret
Passaic
Clifton
Rutherford
Lyndhurst
Great Neck
Kings Point
Valley Stream
Cedarhurst
Inwood
Lawrence
Atlantic Beach
John F. Kennedy Int'l. Airport
La Guardia Airport
Newark International Airport
UPPER BAY
LOWER BAY
Jamaica Bay
Newark Bay
HUDSON
GATEWAY NATIONAL RECREATION AREA
FLOYD BENNETT FIELD
THE NARROWS
VERRAZANO NARROWS BRIDGE (TOLL)
STATEN ISLAND FERRY
Mi.
Km.
03-1

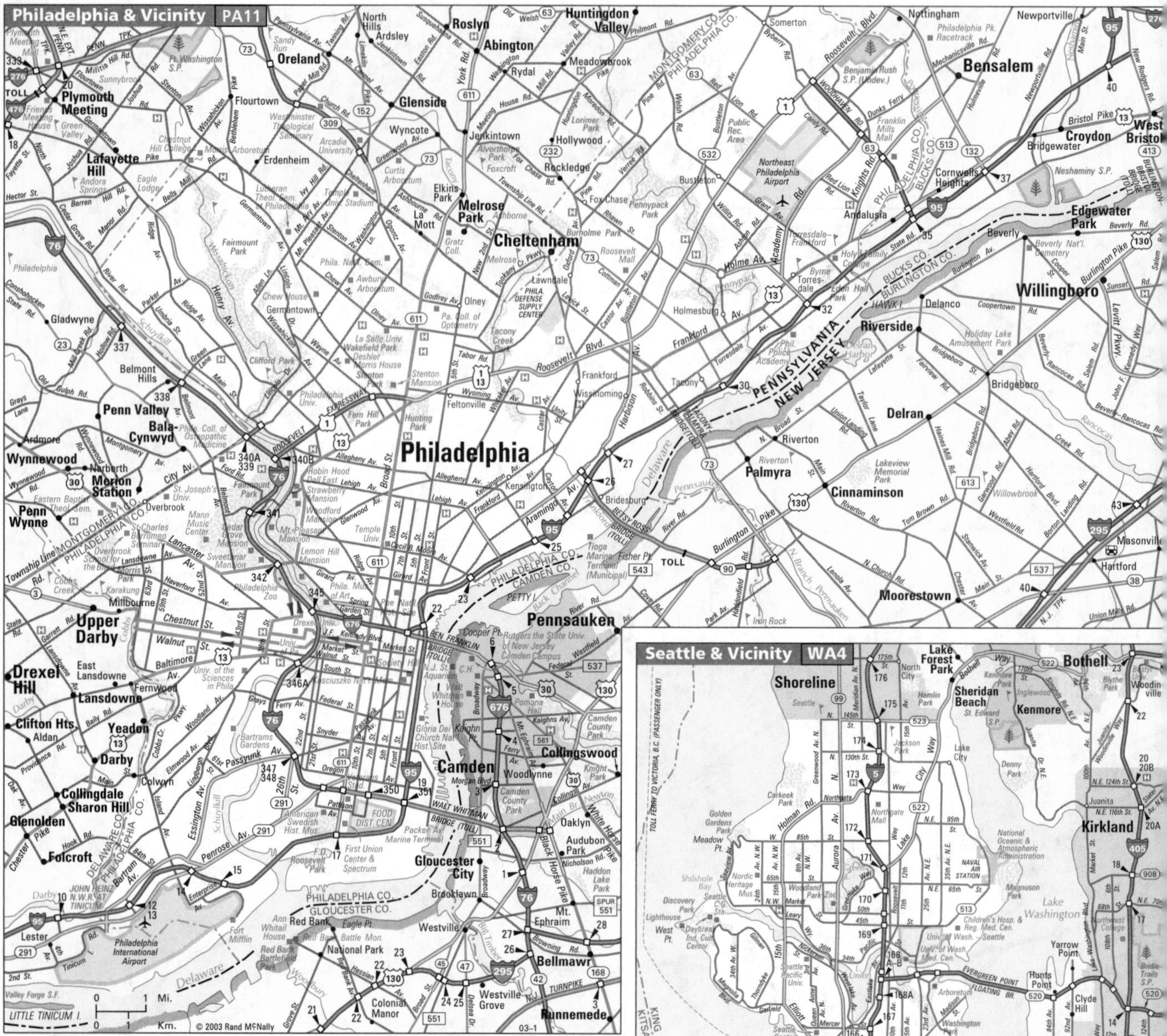
Philadelphia & Vicinity PA11
Philadelphia
Plymouth Meeting
Lafayette Hill
Oreland
Roslyn
Abington
Huntingdon Valley
Glenside
Jenkintown
Melrose Park
Cheltenham
Bensalem
Croydon
Cornwells Heights
Andalusia
Edgewater Park
Beverly
Willingboro
Riverside
Delanco
Delran
Riverton
Palmyra
Cinnaminson
Moorestown
Pennsauken
Camden
Collingswood
Gloucester City
Bellmawr
Runnemede
Westville
Upper Darby
Drexel Hill
Lansdowne
Yeadon
Darby
Collingdale
Sharon Hill
Glenolden
Folcroft
Penn Valley
Bala-Cynwyd
Wynnewood
Merion Station
Penn Wynne
Gladwyne
Philadelphia International Airport
PENNSYLVANIA
NEW JERSEY
© 2003 Rand McNally

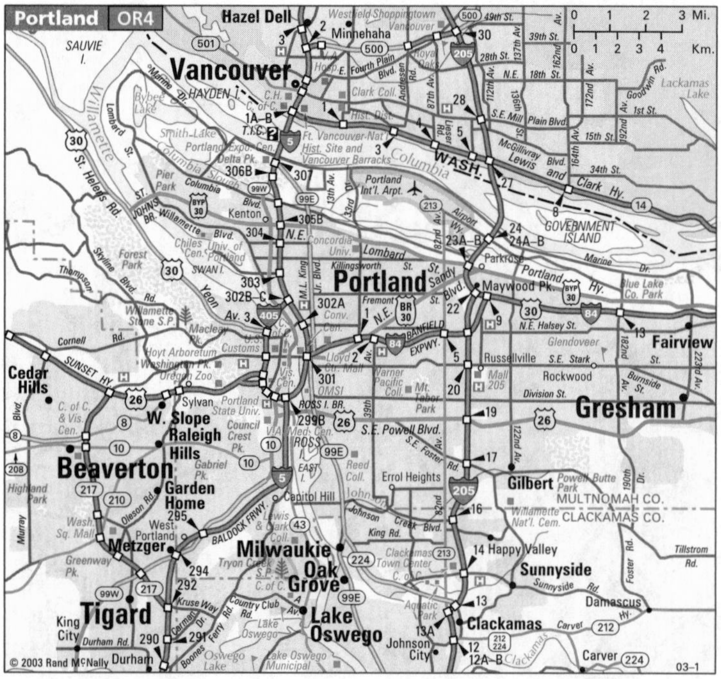
Portland OR4
Hazel Dell
Vancouver
Portland
Fairview
Gresham
Cedar Hills
W. Slope
Raleigh Hills
Beaverton
Garden Home
Metzger
Tigard
Milwaukie
Oak Grove
Lake Oswego
Gilbert
Sunnyside
Happy Valley
Clackamas
Damascus
Durham
King City
Johnson City
Portland Int'l. Arpt.
MULTNOMAH CO.
CLACKAMAS CO.
© 2003 Rand McNally

Seattle & Vicinity WA4
Shoreline
Lake Forest Park
Bothell
Kenmore
Sheridan Beach
Kirkland
Seattle
Bellevue
Mercer Island
Renton
Skyway
Tukwila
Burien
SeaTac
Riverton Hts.
White Center
Normandy Park
Des Moines
Kent
Puget Sound
Elliott Bay
VASHON ISLAND
Lake Washington
Seattle-Tacoma Int'l. Arpt.
© 2003 Rand McNally

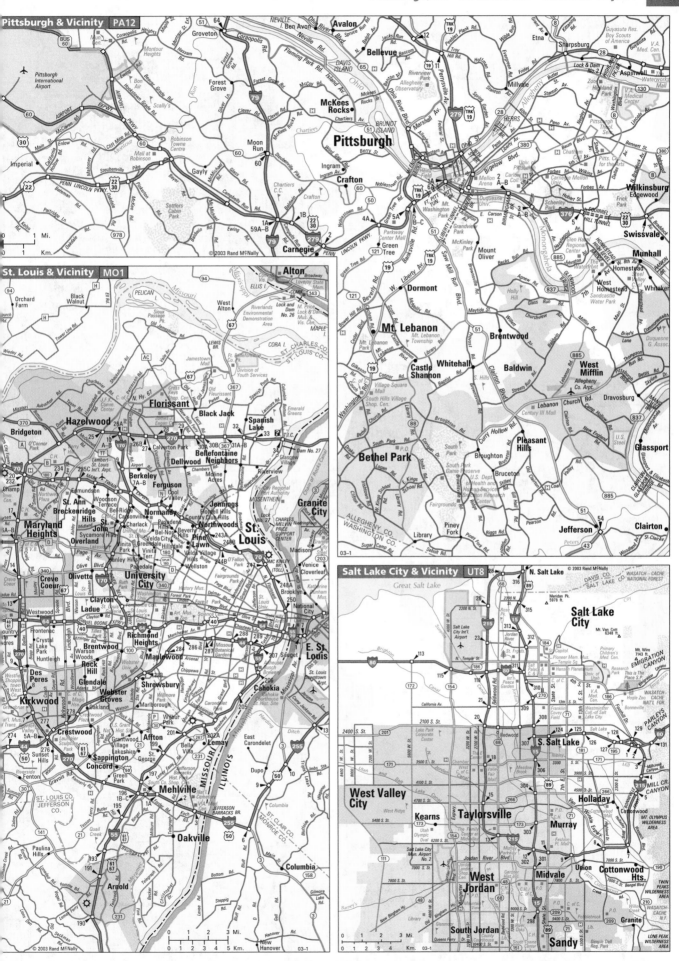

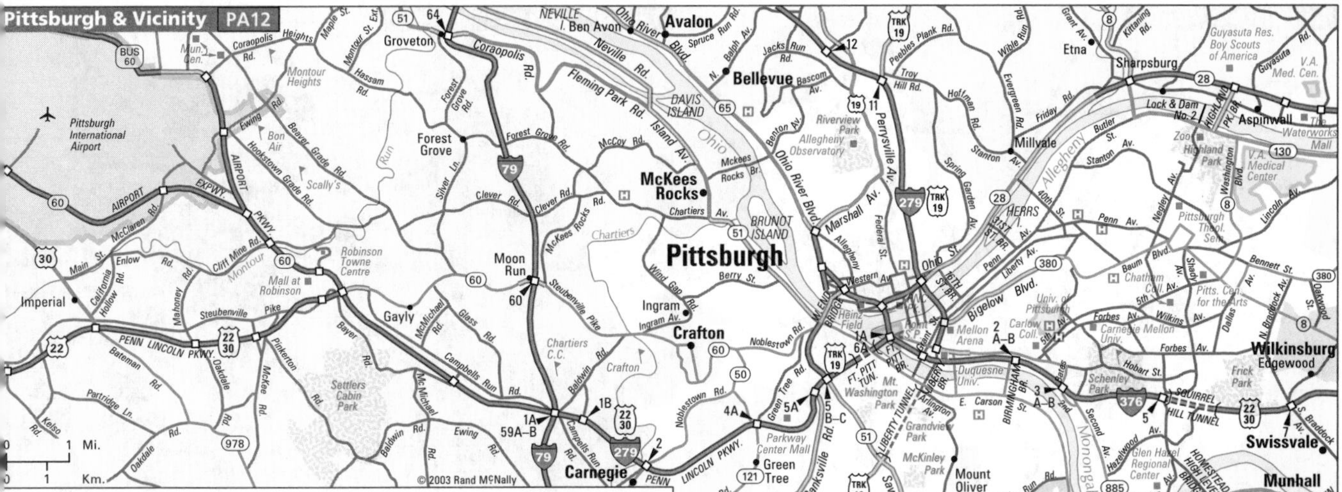
Pittsburgh & Vicinity PA12
Pittsburgh
Pittsburgh International Airport
Avalon
Bellevue
Etna
Sharpsburg
Aspinwall
Millvale
McKees Rocks
Forest Grove
Groveton
Imperial
Moon Run
Ingram
Crafton
Carnegie
Gayly
Wilkinsburg
Edgewood
Swissvale
Munhall
Homestead
West Homestead
Whitaker
Green Tree
Mount Oliver
© 2003 Rand McNally

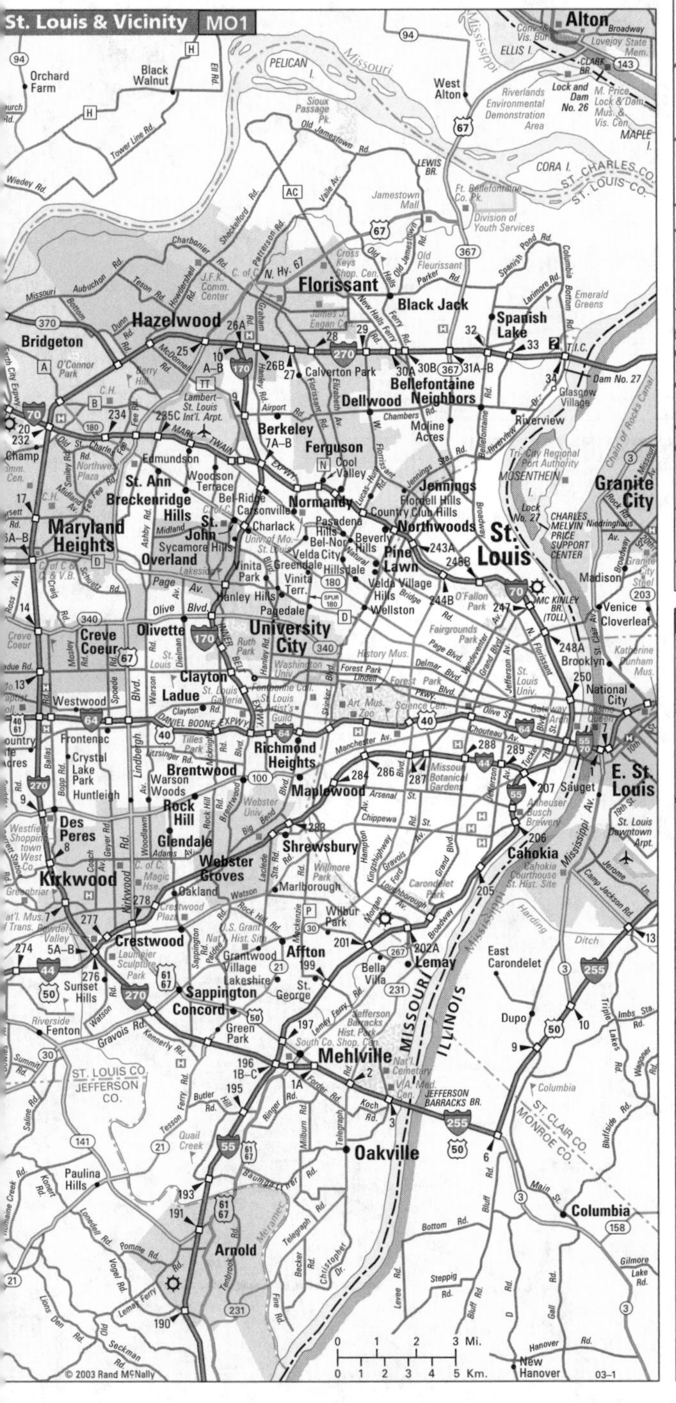
St. Louis & Vicinity MO1
St. Louis
Alton
West Alton
Florissant
Hazelwood
Bridgeton
Black Jack
Spanish Lake
Berkeley
Ferguson
Jennings
Granite City
Maryland Heights
Creve Coeur
Olivette
University City
Clayton
Ladue
Richmond Heights
Brentwood
Maplewood
Rock Hill
Glendale
Webster Groves
Shrewsbury
Kirkwood
Des Peres
Crestwood
Affton
Lemay
Sappington
Concord
Mehlville
Oakville
Arnold
E. St. Louis
Cahokia
Dupo
Columbia
ILLINOIS
MISSOURI
© 2003 Rand McNally

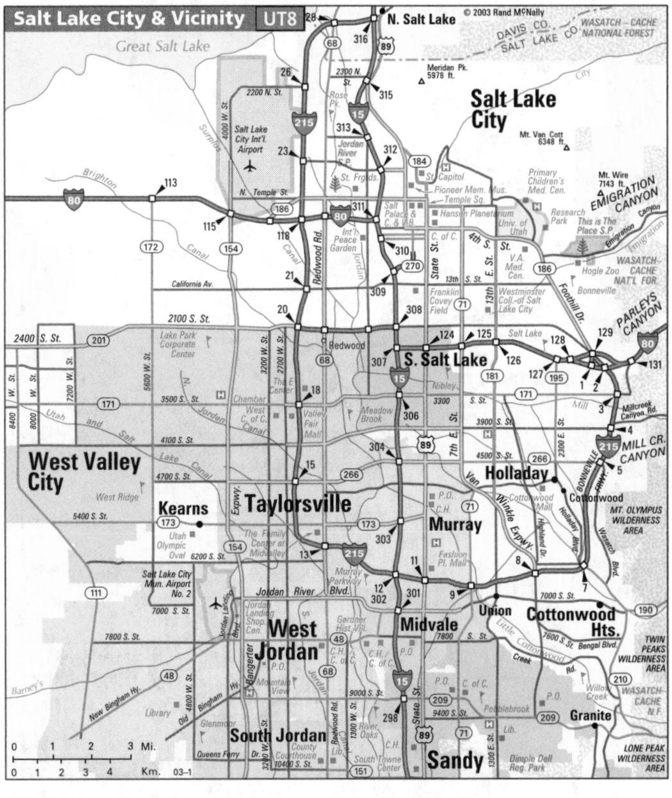
Salt Lake City & Vicinity UT8
Great Salt Lake
N. Salt Lake
Salt Lake City
S. Salt Lake
West Valley City
Kearns
Taylorsville
Holladay
Murray
Cottonwood Hts.
Midvale
West Jordan
South Jordan
Sandy
Granite
© 2003 Rand McNally

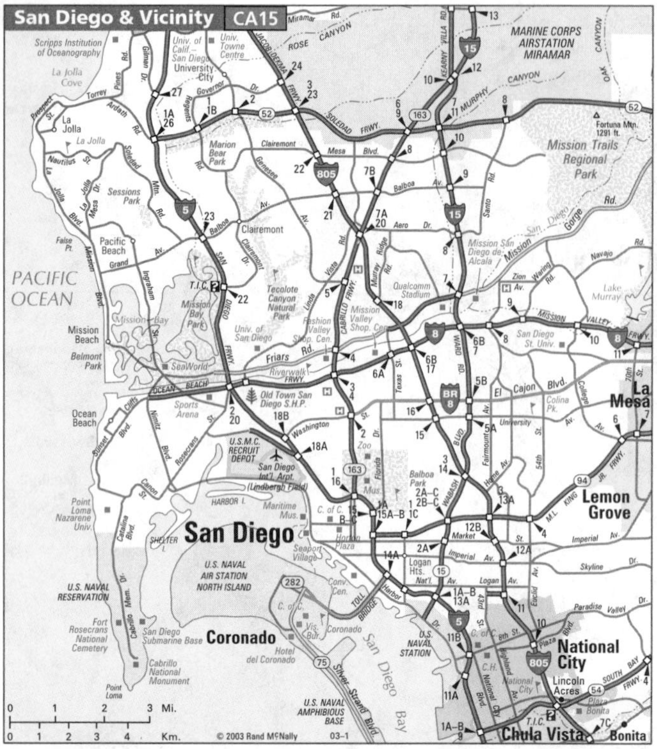
San Diego & Vicinity CA15
MARINE CORPS AIRSTATION MIRAMAR
Mission Trails Regional Park
PACIFIC OCEAN
La Jolla
Mission Beach
Ocean Beach
San Diego
Coronado
National City
Chula Vista
Bonita
Lemon Grove
La Mesa
U.S. NAVAL AIR STATION NORTH ISLAND
© 2003 Rand McNally
03-1

Tampa / St. Petersburg FL3
Lutz
Palm Hbr.
Oldsmar
Dunedin
Safety Hbr.
Carrollwood
Lake Magdalene
University West
Temple Terrace
Egypt Lake
Rocky Creek
Tampa
Brandon
Clearwater
Largo
High-point
Clair-Mel City
Seminole
Pinellas Park
Lealman
St. Petersburg
Treasure Island
S. Pasadena
St. Pete Beach
Gulfport
TAMPA BAY
Apollo Beach
Ruskin
Sun City Center
Sun City
GULF OF MEXICO
Anna Maria
Holmes Beach
Palma Sola
Bradenton
Memphis
Palmetto
Ellenton
West Bradenton
South Bradenton
Bradenton Beach
Cortez
Parrish
HILLSBOROUGH
MANATEE
© 2003 Rand McNally
03-1

Toronto ON1
Concord
Woodbridge
Malton
Mississauga
York
Toronto
LAKE ONTARIO
© 2003 Rand McNally
03-1

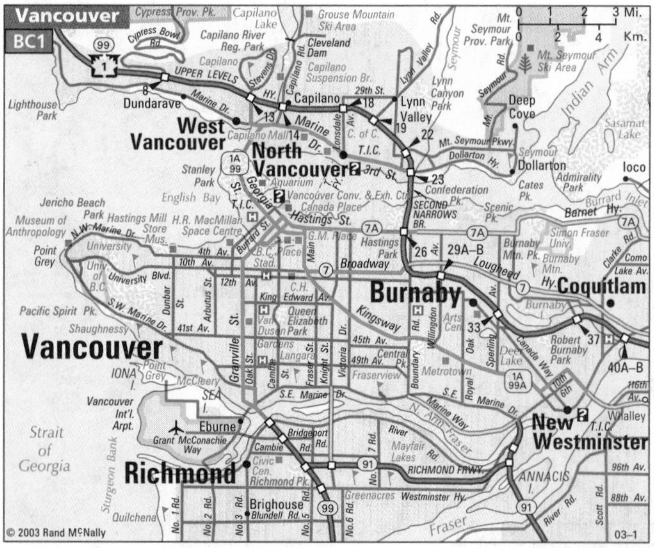
Vancouver BC1
West Vancouver
North Vancouver
Dundarave
Capilano
Lynn Valley
Deep Cove
Dollarton
Burnaby
Coquitlam
Vancouver
Richmond
New Westminster
Strait of Georgia
© 2003 Rand McNally
03-1

San Antonio TX13
CAMP BULLIS MIL. RES.
Shavano Park
Hollywood Park
Hill Country Village
Castle Hills
San Antonio
Leon Valley
Balcones Hts.
Olmos Park
Alamo Hts.
Terrell Hills
Kirby
Windcrest
LACKLAND A.F.B.
KELLY ANNEX
BROOKS A.F.B.
Von Ormy
Southton
© 2003 Rand McNally
03-1

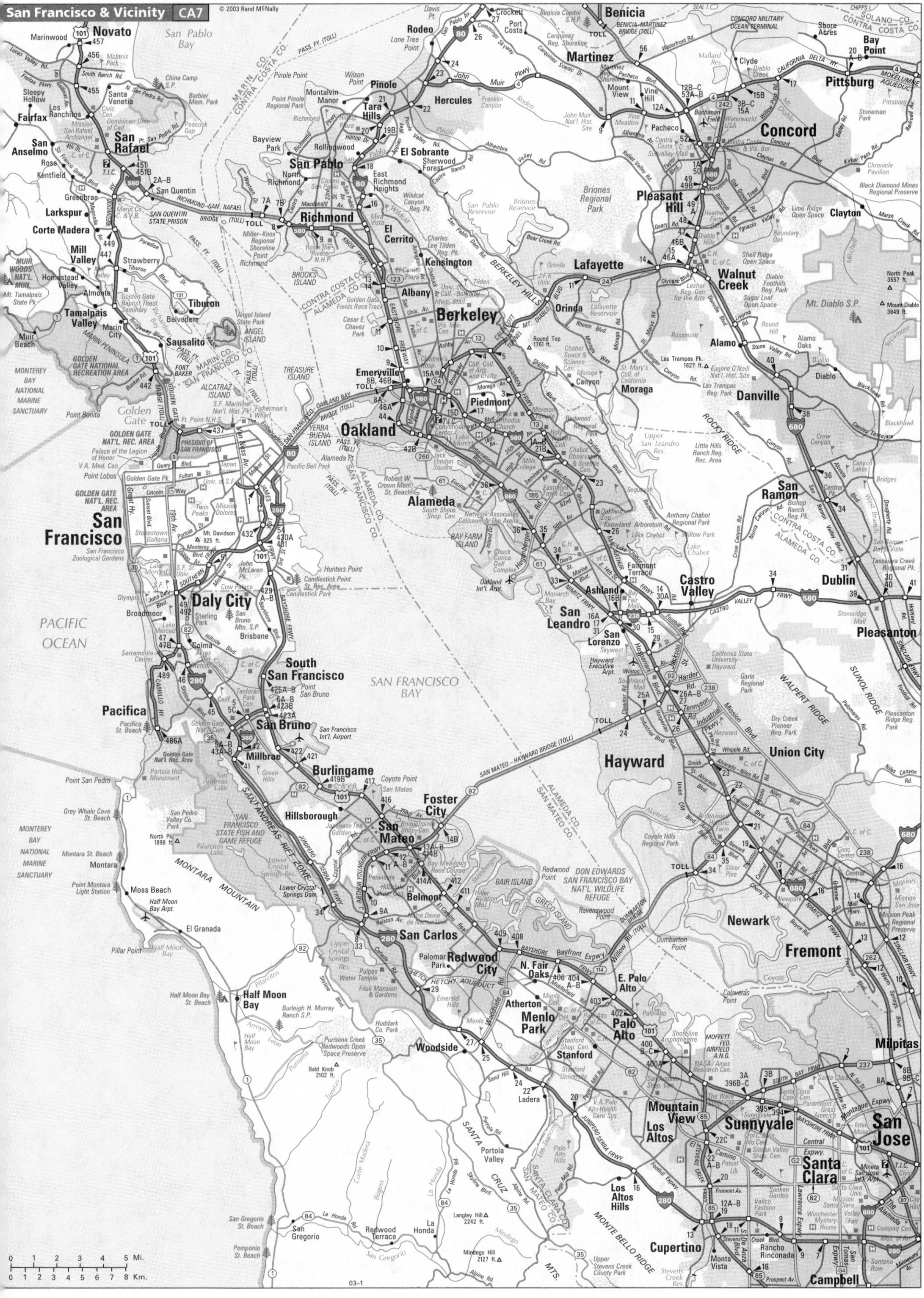
San Francisco & Vicinity CA7
© 2003 Rand McNally
San Pablo Bay
Novato
San Rafael
Richmond
San Pablo
Pinole
Hercules
Martinez
Benicia
Concord
Pittsburg
Pleasant Hill
Walnut Creek
Lafayette
Orinda
Berkeley
Albany
El Cerrito
Emeryville
Oakland
Piedmont
Alameda
San Leandro
Castro Valley
Dublin
Pleasanton
San Ramon
Danville
Hayward
Union City
Fremont
Newark
Milpitas
San Jose
Santa Clara
Sunnyvale
Mountain View
Los Altos
Cupertino
Campbell
Palo Alto
Menlo Park
Redwood City
San Carlos
Belmont
San Mateo
Foster City
Burlingame
Millbrae
San Bruno
South San Francisco
Daly City
Pacifica
Half Moon Bay
San Francisco
Sausalito
Mill Valley
Tiburon
PACIFIC OCEAN
SAN FRANCISCO BAY
Mt. Diablo S.P.
0 1 2 3 4 5 Mi.
0 1 2 3 4 5 6 7 8 Km.
03-1

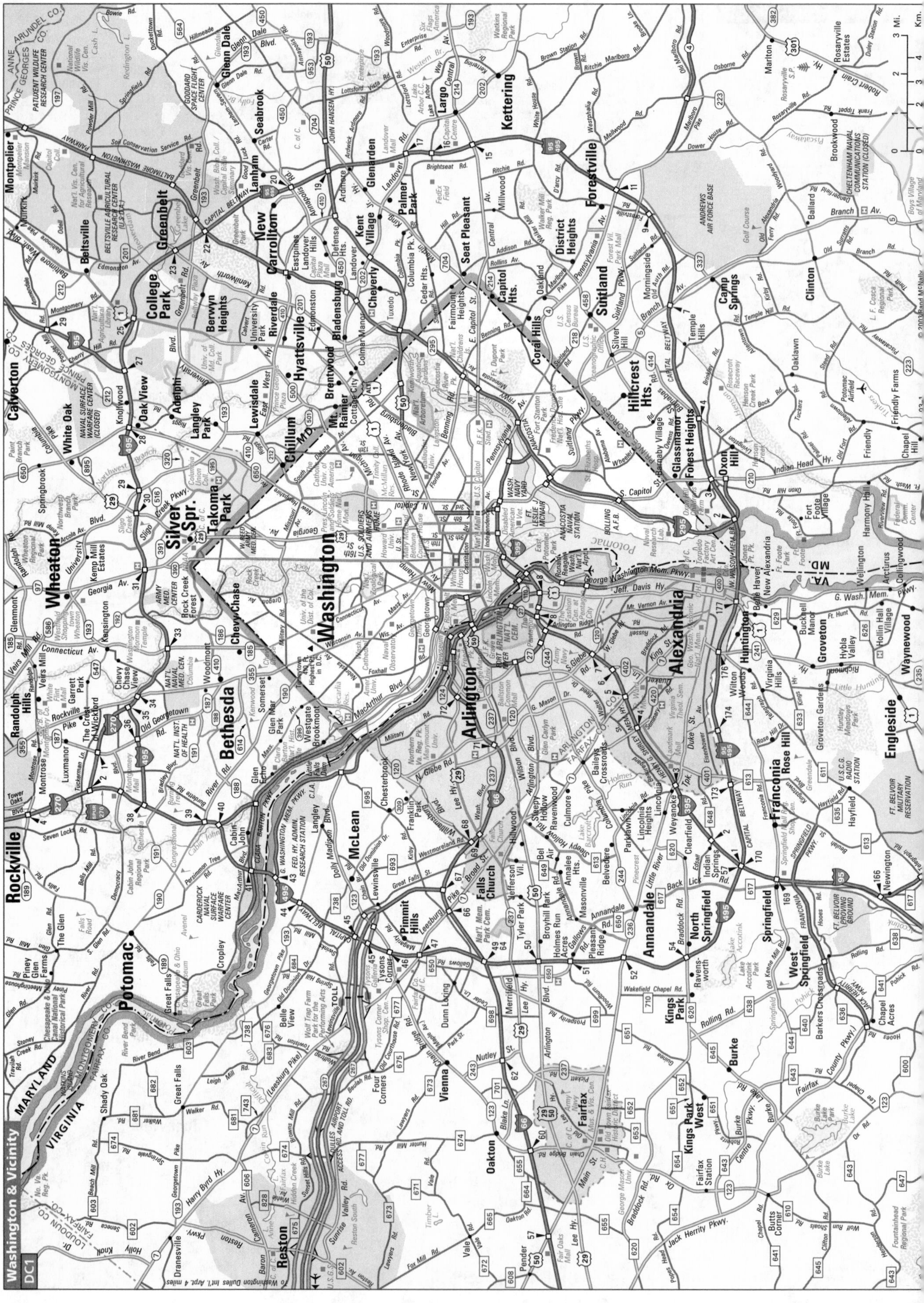
Washington & Vicinity
DC1
MARYLAND
VIRGINIA
Rockville
Wheaton
Silver Spr.
Takoma Park
Bethesda
Chevy Chase
Washington
Arlington
Alexandria
Falls Church
McLean
Potomac
Reston
Vienna
Oakton
Fairfax
Annandale
Springfield
West Springfield
Franconia
Rose Hill
Huntington
Groveton
Engleside
Burke
Kings Park
Kings Park West
Greenbelt
College Park
Hyattsville
Riverdale
Bladensburg
New Carrollton
Lanham
Seabrook
Glenn Dale
Largo
Kettering
Forestville
District Heights
Seat Pleasant
Capitol Hts.
Suitland
Coral Hills
Hillcrest Hts.
Camp Springs
Clinton
Oxon Hill
Glassmanor
Forest Heights
Beltsville
Calverton
White Oak
Montpelier
Chillum
Langley Park
Adelphi
Oak View
Mt. Rainier
Brentwood
Lewisdale
Cheverly
Landover
Glenarden
Palmer Park
Kent Village
Pimmit Hills
Tysons Corner
Great Falls
Dranesville
Merrifield
Dunn Loring
Fairfax Station
ANDREWS AIR FORCE BASE
FT. BELVOIR MILITARY RESERVATION
ARLINGTON NAT'L. CEM.
BOLLING A.F.B.
CAPITAL BELTWAY
George Washington Mem. Pkwy.
Potomac
Km. 0 1 2 3 4 5
0 1 2 3 Mi.
© 2003 Rand McNally

Tourism tools at your service

Not sure what to do on your last day in Pocatello, Idaho or Peculiar, Missouri? Don't fret — that's what this handy list of U.S. and Canadian tourism contacts is for.

But if you want a one-stop resource, we've got tons of great tourism information at **randmcnally.com**. From National Parks to hotels, restaurants, and thousands of points of interest, the resources at **randmcnally.com** help you make the most of your time on the road and when you get there.

United States

Alabama Bureau of Tourism & Travel
800/252-2262
www.touralabama.org

Alaska Tourism
907/929-2200
www.travelalaska.com

Arizona Office of Tourism
888/520-3433
www.arizonaguide.com

Arkansas Department of Parks & Tourism
800/828-8974
www.arkansas.com

California Division of Tourism
916/322-2881
www.visitcalifornia.com

Colorado Tourism Office
800/265-6723
www.colorado.com

Connecticut Office of Tourism
800/282-6863
www.ctbound.org

Delaware Tourism Office
866/284-7483
www.visitdelaware.net

Visit Florida
888/735-2872
www.flausa.com

Georgia Department of Industry, Trade & Tourism
800/847-4842
www.georgia.org

Hawaii Visitors & Convention Bureau
800/464-2924
www.gohawaii.com

Idaho Tourism
800/847-4843
www.visitid.org

Illinois Bureau of Tourism
800/226-6632
www.enjoyillinois.com

Indiana Tourism
888/365-6946
www.enjoyindiana.com

Iowa Division of Tourism
800/345-4692
www.traveliowa.com

Kansas Travel & Tourism Development Division
800/252-6727 *
785/296-2009
www.travelks.com

Kentucky Department of Travel
800/225-8747
www.kentuckytourism.com

Louisiana Office of Tourism
800/334-8626
www.louisianatravel.com

Maine Office of Tourism
888/624-6345
www.visitmaine.com

Maryland Office of Tourism
800/634-7386
www.mdisfun.org

Massachusetts Office of Travel & Tourism
800/227-6277
www.massvacation.com

Travel Michigan
888/784-7328
www.michigan.org

Minnesota Office of Tourism
800/657-3700
www.exploreminnesota.com

Mississippi Division of Tourism
800/927-6378
www.visitmississippi.org

Missouri Division of Tourism
800/519-2300 *
573/526-5900
www.visitmo.com

Travel Montana
800/847-4868
www.visitmt.com

Nebraska Division of Travel & Tourism
877/632-7275 *
800/228-4307
www.visitnebraska.org

Nevada Commission on Tourism
800/638-2328
www.travelnevada.com

New Hampshire Division of Travel & Tourism Development
800/386-4664 *
603/271-2665
www.visitnh.gov

New Jersey Office of Travel & Tourism
800/847-4865 *
609/292-2470
www.visitnj.org

New Mexico Department of Tourism
800/733-6396
www.newmexico.org

New York State Division of Tourism
800/225-5697
www.iloveny.state.ny.us

North Carolina Division of Tourism
800/847-4862
www.visitnc.com

North Dakota Tourism
800/435-5663
www.ndtourism.com

Ohio Division of Travel & Tourism
800/282-5393
www.ohiotourism.com

Oklahoma Tourism & Recreation Department
800/652-6552
www.travelok.com

Oregon Tourism Commission
800/547-7842
www.traveloregon.com

Pennsylvania Center for Travel & Marketing
800/847-4872 *
717/787-5453
www.experiencepa.com

Rhode Island Tourism Division
800/556-2484
401/222-2601
www.visitrhodeisland.com

South Carolina Department of Parks, Recreation, & Tourism
888/727-6453
803/734-1700
discoversouthcarolina.com

South Dakota Department of Tourism
800/732-5682
www.travelsd.com

Tennessee Department of Tourist Development
800/462-8366 *
615/741-2159
www.tnvacation.com

Texas Tourism Division
800/888-8839
www.traveltex.com

Utah Travel Council
800/200-1160
www.utah.com

Vermont Department of Tourism
800/837-6668
www.travel-vermont.com

Virginia Tourism Corporation
800/321-3244
804/786-4484
www.virginia.org

Washington Tourism
800/544-1800
360/725-5052
experiencewashington.com

Washington, D.C. Convention & Tourism Corporation
202/789-7000
www.washington.org

West Virginia Division of Tourism
800/225-5982
www.callwva.com

Wisconsin Department of Tourism
800/432-8747
www.travelwisconsin.com

Wyoming Division of Tourism & Travel
800/225-5996
www.wyomingtourism.org

Canada

Travel Alberta
800/661-8888
www.travelalberta.com

Tourism British Columbia
800/435-5622
www.hellobc.com

Travel Manitoba
866/626-4862
www.travelmanitoba.com

Tourism New Brunswick
800/561-0123
www.tourismnbcanada.com

Newfoundland & Labrador Department of Tourism
800/563-6353
www.gov.nf.ca/tourism

Tourism Nova Scotia
800/565-0000
explore.gov.ns.ca

Ontario Travel
800/668-2746
www.ontariotravel.net

Prince Edward Island Tourism
888/734-7529
www.peiplay.com

Tourisme Québec
877/266-5687
www.bonjourquebec.com

Tourism Saskatchewan
877/237-2273
www.sasktourism.com

** To request travel materials only*

Eat your way across the U.S.A.

30 cool and unusual food events for 2003 — *and Canada, too!*

1 National Date Festival

February 14-23, 2003
Indio, California *(p. 9, J-8)*

Sorry, lonely hearts, the date we're talking about here is the fibrous fruit, not the romantic rendezvous. Some 250,000 date palms sway over California's Coachella Valley, producing 35 million pounds of dates annually. Witness the ceremonial *Blessing of the Dates,* stroll through a shady date palm garden, check out elaborate date exhibits in the "Taj Mahal," and sample more than 50 varieties of dates, including sweet medjools, delicate deglet noors, and caramel-like amer hajjs. *800/811-3247, www.datefest.org*

2 Swamp Cabbage Festival

February 22-23, 2003
La Belle, Florida *(p. 14, G-4)*

As if regular cabbage wasn't bad enough, someone had to come up with swamp cabbage? Actually, this is just the local name for heart of palm. Tender, ivory-colored, and tasting somewhat like artichoke, it's harvested from the stem, or "heart," of Florida's state tree, the sabal palm. La Belle's festival honoring this delicacy features gospel music, armadillo races, and goods made by local Seminole Indians. And, of course, lots of swamp cabbage, served raw, stewed, or frittered. *863/675-1877, members.aol.com/browne/scf.html*

save your appetite for the catfish-eating contest

3 World Catfish Festival

April 5, 2003
Belzoni, Mississippi *(p. 27, D-3)*

With more than 30,000 acres of land under water and more catfish acreage than any other state, Humphreys County has earned the nickname "Catfish Capital of the World." What better place, then, for the world's largest catfish fry? Sample a genuine Southern midday dinner of fried catfish, hush puppies, and cole slaw. Or save your appetite for the catfish-eating contest: Entrants have 10 minutes to devour three pounds of hot catfish fillets. Watch out for those whiskers! *800/408-4838, www.catfishcapitalonline.com*

4 Vidalia Onion Festival

April 24-27, 2003*
Vidalia, Georgia *(p. 15, F-5)*

If the thought of biting into an onion brings tears to your eyes, you haven't tried a Vidalia. **Not just anyone can grow a Vidalia** — the Georgia legislature restricts production of this mild, sweet onion to a 20-county growing area. Munching on raw onions is common practice at this festival, but those who prefer 'em deep-fried can nosh on "blooming onions" and onion rings. There's also an onion cook-off and an onion-eating contest. BYOBM: Bring Your Own Breath Mints.
912/538-8687, www.vidaliaga.com

5 Stockton Asparagus Festival

April 25-27, 2003
Stockton, California *(p. 8, F-3)*

Stockton has asparagus to spare: Nearly 15 tons are cooked during this weekend extravaganza. Fried asparagus is the most popular dish, but asparagus nachos, asparagus pasta, and asparagus margaritas are also on the menu. Watch local celebrities hurl green projectiles through the air in the Spear Throwing Contest, then pose for pics with festival mascots Gus and Brit-Nee Spears.
800/350-1987, www.asparagusfest.com

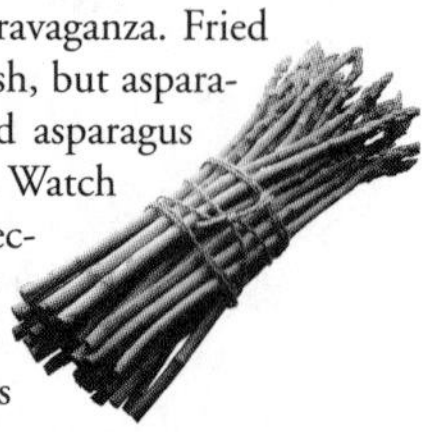

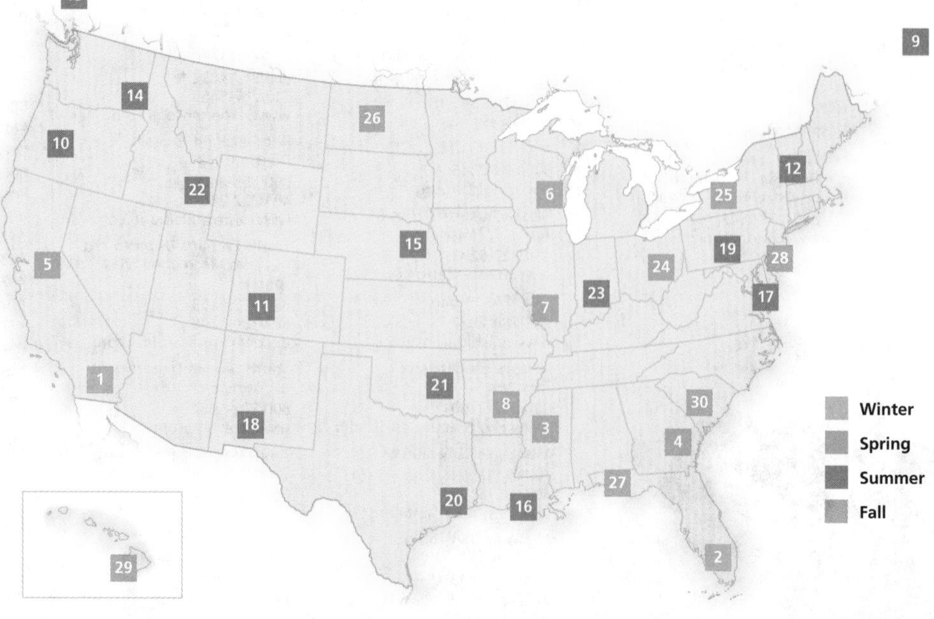

6 Great Wisconsin Cheese Festival

June 6-8, 2003
Little Chute, Wisconsin *(p. 52, E-6, near Kaukauna)*

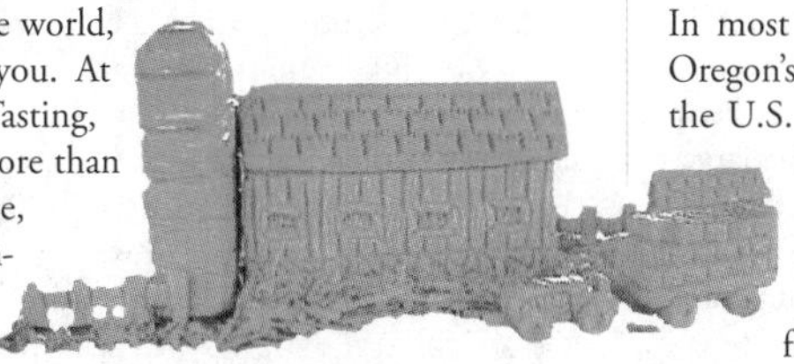

Cheeseheads of the world, this festival's for you. At the free Cheese Tasting, you can sample more than 30 types of cheese, including Wisconsin's native Colby. And no Dairy State experience would be complete without those peanut-sized munchies known as cheese curds. (Connoisseurs say they're best deep-fried.) Don't miss the cheese-carving demos, where barns, cows, and other sculptures take form out of behemoth blocks of cheddar. But please, don't eat the art! *920/788-7390, www.vil.little-chute.wi.us*

7 International Horseradish Festival

June 7-8, 2003
Collinsville, Illinois *(p. 17, G-3)*

Not only is Collinsville home to the world's largest ketchup bottle, it's also the Horseradish Capital of the World! The bottomlands of the Mississippi are fertile ground for the zesty root, producing more than 60 percent of the world's horseradish each year. This annual celebration features a Root Toss, a recipe contest *(mmm... horseradish apple pie!)*, and Root Golf, played with balls carved from horseradish. Pick up a jar of cranberry-horseradish relish or horseradish jelly to kick your next meal up a notch. *618/344-2884*

8 Pink Tomato Festival

June 13-14, 2003
Warren, Arkansas *(p. 7, F-5)*

Bradley County's prize produce might look a little underripe, but this is one case where a tomato is *supposed* to be pink. Unfortunately, the fruit isn't usually shipped because it bruises easily, so southern Arkansas might be the only place to sample what local folks call *"the world's tastiest tomato."* Taste them for yourself at Warren's festival, which features a tomato-eating contest, pink salsa competition, and an all-tomato luncheon ... tomato carrot cake, anyone? *870/226-5225, www.bradleycountychamberofcommerce.com*

9 Fish, Fun, and Folk Festival

July 23-27, 2003
Twillingate, Newfoundland and Labrador
(p. 63, B-8, near Gander)

There are many reasons to visit the tranquil village of Twillingate: the spectacular coastline, the towering blue icebergs that drift down from the Arctic, the humpback whales just offshore, the friendly people, and of course the annual Fish, Fun, and Folk Festival. This celebration of Newfoundland culture and heritage draws top folk musicians and dancers from throughout the province. When the fiddling stops, festivalgoers head to the dining hall for *traditional Newfoundland meals* of cod, salmon, and lobster. *709/884-2678, www.fishfunfolkfestival.com*

10 Springfield Filbert Festival

August 1-3, 2003
Springfield, Oregon *(p. 43, D-2)*

In most places they're known as hazelnuts, but here in Oregon's Willamette Valley — which grows 99 percent of the U.S. total — they're called filberts. When you get to Springfield, just look for Phil, the giant papier-mâché nut who watches over the celebration. Munch on spiced, roasted, or chocolate-covered filberts while the kids go nuts in the Nutty Kingdom play area. Then come out of your shell for an old-fashioned ice cream social and live music on two stages. *541/736-4044, www.springfieldfilbertfestival.com*

11 Olathe Sweet Corn Festival

August 2, 2003
Olathe, Colorado *(p. 12, E-2)*

Nothing says summer like fresh corn-on-the-cob, and in the tiny town of Olathe they've got plenty to give away on festival day (more than 70,000 free ears!). This isn't just any old corn either — it's Olathe Sweet, and *it's extra sweet.* This special strain grows best in the Uncompahgre Valley, where locals proclaim it "the best sweet corn on the planet." If you're an old pro at cleaning the cob, try chomping past the corn-eating contest record: 32 ears in 12 minutes. *800/858-6006, www.olathesweetcornfest.com*

12 Vermont State Zucchini Fest

August 16-17, 2003
Ludlow, Vermont *(p. 31, G-3)*

At festival time, Ludlow becomes a zucchini zoo. Kids zoom to the zucchini-carving, zucchini model car racing, and "Dress Your Zucchini Doll" contests, and green-thumbed locals produce their biggest produce for the squash weigh-in. At the "Taste of Zucchini," zuke zealots feast on dishes like zucchini-lemon sorbet and cold zucchini soup, while the less adventurous squash their appetites with fried zucchini and zucchini bread. So if you're zany for zucchini, Ludlow's the place to be this August. *802/228-5830, www.vacationinvermont.com/zucchini*

13 Blackberry Festival

August 16-22, 2003
Powell River, British Columbia *(p. 56, G-5)*

Blackberry vines are as ubiquitous in coastal British Columbia as kudzu in Mississippi. *Rubus armeniacus* is generally considered a thorny nuisance, but the people of Powell River celebrate its ***plump, sweet fruit*** each summer with a street party, music, clowns, and, of course, lots of blackberries. Dessert contests for amateur and professional chefs yield delectable dishes like blackberry crème brûlé and blackberry dessert pizza. Winning chefs can usually be persuaded to share their recipes. *604/485-6467, www.discoverpowellriver.com*

**Dates are tentative — please call ahead.*

(continued on the next page)

14 National Lentil Festival

August 22-23, 2003
Pullman, Washington (p. 51, D-9)

Having trouble getting the kids to eat their lentils? Treat them to some of the leguminous delicacies at this festival, and they'll never know what hit 'em. Lentil chocolate cake, lentil cookies, and lentil ice cream top the list of unusual creations offered in Pullman, heart of the largest U.S. lentil-producing region. Festival highlights include a parade led by mascot Tase T. Lentil, a lentil cook-off, and 250 gallons of free lentil chili. Don't forget to bring home a lentil dog biscuit for Spike.
800/365-6948, www.lentilfest.com

15 Norfolk Watermelon Festival

August 23-24, 2003
Norfolk, Nebraska (p. 30, C-8)

Sweet, juicy Norfolk watermelons just might be the best you'll ever taste. The sandy soil of northeastern Nebraska produces such an overabundance that no one feels melon-choly when green cannonballs splatter on the ground during this festival's watermelon catapult contest, or when seeds fly in the seed-spitting contest. Of course, everyone here knows that the best thing to do with a Norfolk watermelon is to eat it, and there are plenty of opportunities for that.
402/371-2932, www.norfolk.ne.us/tourism

16 Shrimp and Petroleum Festival

August 28-September 1, 2003
Morgan City, Louisiana (p. 23, F-6)

The name of this riverside blowout may conjure up images of dishes named "Shrimp Valdez," but have no fear: Cajun Country's two most important resources are kept separate at all times. Feast on shrimp cooked in so many ways it would "make Forrest Gump proud," then take in the Blessing of the Fleet and the Water Parade, where decorated shrimp trawlers and oil boats motor up and down the Atchafalaya River. *985/385-0703, www.shrimp-petrofest.org*

17 Hard Crab Derby and Fair

August 29-31, 2003
Crisfield, Maryland (p. 13, F-8)

Find a fast crab, because this event's all about pinching out the competition. About 350 of the clawed critters race down a wooden board, vying for trophies for their human cheerleaders. There's also a Governor's Cup race, where crabs representing all 50 states try to out-scuttle each other. (Winners are spared the pot.) A crab-picking contest and a crab-cooking contest round out the festivities. *800/782-3913, www.crisfield.org*

18 Hatch Chile Festival

August 30-31, 2003
Hatch, New Mexico (p. 33, G-3)

The "Chile Capital of the World" celebrates the harvest with a Chile Queen contest, a chile cook-off, and literally tons of the famous Hatch chiles. Jalapeños, anchos, serranos, and other varieties are served in tamales, enchiladas, empañadas, burritos, chile relleños, and chile con carne. If you can take the heat, head to Hatch for this fiery festival. It might take a few days, but the burning in your mouth will eventually fade away.
505/267-3638, www.zianet.com/snm/chilfest.htm

19 McClure Bean Soup Festival

September 9-13, 2003
McClure, Pennsylvania (p. 45, F-8)

Ever wondered what the Civil War tasted like? Find out at this festival, where ground beef, beans, and lard are slow-cooked in 35-gallon iron kettles just like they were back when the Blue fought the Gray. The festival began in 1891 when Civil War vets got together and cooked up their typical wartime fare at a public dinner. Today, descendants of those veterans and citizens of McClure stir the soup for more than 75,000 festivalgoers. Fireworks, parades, and Civil War reenactments top off the celebration.
800/338-7389, www.mcclurebeansoup.com

20 Texas Gator Fest

September 12-14, 2003
Anahuac, Texas (p. 47, F-11)

Does alligator really taste like chicken? Find out at this three-day celebration in the Alligator Capital of Texas, where gators outnumber people three to one. Food booths offer such reptilian fare as alligator sausage, fried alligator, grilled alligator legs, and alligator jerky. The festival also features airboat rides, live music, vendors selling alligator products, and the Great Texas Alligator Roundup, in which hunters compete to bring in the biggest gator. (The winners are often longer than 13 feet!)
409/267-4190, www.texasgatorfest.com

21 Okrafest

September 13, 2003*
Checotah, Oklahoma (p. 42, C-9)

Notoriously slimy, okra is one of those veggies people either love or hate. Lovers won't want to miss this, the only okra celebration in the United States. There's pickled okra, okra-dogs, okra gumbo, okra bread, and sometimes even okra ice cream. Sample free fried okra from the Okra Pot, which cooks more than 400 pounds of the pod. Then jump into line for the slime toss, where contestants try to catch balloons filled with the goo left over from boiled okra. No ponchos allowed.
918/473-4178

22 Idaho Spud Day

September 20, 2003
Shelley, Idaho (p. 16, H-5)

Bingham County is the top potato-growing county in the United States. So when harvest time comes around, there's good reason to celebrate — and to give out free baked potatoes. Spud Day isn't for couch potatoes. Competition is fierce in the Great Potato Games, which feature the World Spud-Picking Championships, **mashed potato wrestling,** and a Dutch oven cook-off. And then there's the Spud Tug: After a cement mixer fills a pit with mashed potatoes, tug-of-war teams try to pull each other into the glop. *208/357-7661*

23 Persimmon Festival

September 20-27, 2003
Mitchell, Indiana (p. 18, H-3)

If you've never eaten a persimmon, you can make up for lost time at this weeklong event. The people of Mitchell offer persimmon fudge, bread, cookies, cake, and ice cream, but the most popular dish is pudding. In fact, the Persimmon Pudding Contest grabs more attention than the midway rides, arts and crafts, and candlelight tours of Spring Mill State Park. When the festival's over and withdrawal sets in, don't get caught stealing persimmons from anyone's tree — around here, that's a serious crime. *800/580-1985, www.persimmonfestival.org*

24 Barnesville Pumpkin Festival

September 25-28, 2003
Barnesville, Ohio (p. 40, G-9)

Maybe you've rolled a pumpkin before, but have you ever rolled one uphill with sticks? At Barnesville's fall extravaganza, you can compete against other pumpkin-pushers on a tough 50-foot course. After the race, treat yourself to pumpkin pancakes, **pumpkin fudge,** or maybe even a pumpkin shake. Don't miss the King Pumpkin contest — winning pumpkins have tipped the scales at more than 1,000 pounds. And FYI, that enormous orange thing looming overhead isn't the Great Pumpkin — it's the town's water tower.
740/425-2593, www.pumpkinfestival.8k.com

25 Naples Grape Festival

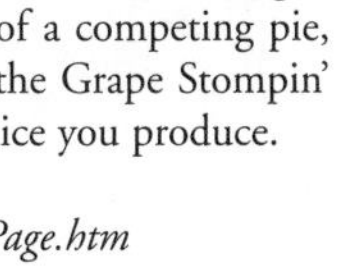

September 27-28, 2003
Naples, New York (p. 34, F-5)

Move over, apple pie. Festivalgoers can't get enough of the famous grape pies introduced in Naples in the 1960s. Over the years, entrants in the **World's Greatest Grape Pie Contest** have shocked traditionalists with new twists on Irene Bouchard's original recipe, introducing such radical additions as peanut butter and meringue (gasp!). After the judging, try a slice of a competing pie, then kick off your shoes and join in the Grape Stompin' Contest — it's all about how much juice you produce.
585/374-2240,
www.naplesvalleyny.com/GrapeFestivalPage.htm

26 Norsk Høstfest

October 7-11, 2003
Minot, North Dakota (p. 38, B-4)

North America's largest Scandinavian festival draws 60,000 people to Minot's sprawling All Seasons Arena, which is divided into separate halls representing Denmark, Finland, Iceland, Norway, and Sweden. Booths offer all things Norsk, from birch-bark boxes and baskets to rosemaling, runestones, and reindeer skins. On stage there are yodelers, folk dancers, and top-name entertainers. For those who can't stomach lutefisk (cod that's soaked in lye and then boiled), there are other Scandinavian specialties like lefse, Swedish meatballs, and Danish kringle. *701/852-2368, www.hostfest.com*

there are ***yodelers,*** *folk dancers, and top-name entertainers*

27 Boggy Bayou Mullet Festival

October 17-19, 2003
Niceville, Florida (p. 14, I-2, near Valparaiso)

Elsewhere it might be scorned as a trash fish, or "roadkill with fins," but the people who live along Boggy Bayou love the mullet. And they're out to make converts of the rest of us. They'll serve some 10 tons of the humble bottom feeder — oops, make that "algae eater" — during three days of mullet mania. If smoked or fried mullet doesn't tempt your taste buds, try other local specialties like crawfish bread, boiled peanuts, and alligator-on-a-stick. *850/729-4545, www.mulletfestival.com*

28 Chatsworth Cranberry Festival

October 18-19, 2003
Chatsworth, New Jersey (p. 32, G-4)

You could strap on your waders and jump into one of the dozens of cranberry bogs at the third-largest U.S. cranberry harvest. On second thought, stay on the festival tour bus, keep dry, and enjoy one of North America's only native fruits in another way. There's a **cornucopia of cranberry creations** to sample — from cranberry mustard and cranberry vinegar to cranberry ice cream and cranberry upside-down cake. Just the right blend of sweet and tart to satisfy any palate.
609/726-9237, www.cranfest.org

29 Kona Coffee Cultural Festival

November 1-9, 2003
Kailua Kona, Hawaii (p. 5, I-5)

There's enough joe here to give anyone the jitters. Hawaii is the only state where coffee is grown commercially, and the Big Island's Kona Coast is renowned for its **particularly potent bean.** Watch as local growers brew their best coffee at the Cupping Contest, then try your hand harvesting beans at the Kona-picking contest. Pooped after all that picking? Stay awake by sampling different island blends or indulging in a perked-up dessert at the Kona Coffee Recipe Contest.
808/326-7820, www.konacoffeefest.com

30 Chitlin' Strut

November 29, 2003
Salley, South Carolina (p. 36, G-5, near Neeses)

Chitlin' is Southern slang for "chitterling" — a cleaned hog intestine floured and deep-fried in peanut oil. Folks stand in long lines to get their hands on the delicacy, which connoisseurs say tastes similar to pork rinds and has an addictive texture — a crunch followed by a savory chew. Even avid chitlin'-eaters agree that the sizzling intestines smell something awful, yet more than 20,000 lbs. are devoured on festival day. After dinner, listen to the champs **serenade the swine** with their best "Sooooey!" at the hog-calling contest. *803/258-3485, www.chitlinstrut.com*

**Dates are tentative — please call ahead.*

What's down the road?

Road construction and road condition resources

Orange cones. Blizzards. Four lanes of traffic merging into one. Sometimes the highway can be an obstacle course of uncertainty. But don't panic — here are **a couple of ways** we can help you avoid those bulldozers, barricades, and bottlenecks:

1. Use the state and province websites and hotlines listed on the facing page for road construction and road condition information.
2. Check out **randmcnally.com** for current U.S. and Canadian road construction information. Just key in the **Express Access Code** for any map and click on the orange-striped barricade for the latest work-site details. Since some hotlines and websites are less helpful and up-to-date than others, it's great to know you can always get reliable construction reports at **randmcnally.com**.

Most of the hotlines and websites listed here offer information on both road construction and road conditions. For those that provide only one or the other, we've used an orange cone ▲ to indicate road construction information and a blue snowflake ❄ to indicate road condition information.

United States

Alabama
www.dot.state.al.us ▲

Alaska
800/478-7675 (in AK) ❄
907/456-7623 ❄
907/273-6037
www.dot.state.ak.us

Arizona
888/411-7623
www.azfms.com

Arkansas
800/245-1672 ❄
501/569-2374
501/569-2227 ▲
www.ahtd.state.ar.us

California
800/427-7623 (in CA) ▲
916/445-7623
www.dot.ca.gov

Colorado
877/315-7623 (in CO)
303/639-1111
www.cotrip.org

Connecticut
800/443-6817 (in CT) ❄
www.dot.state.ct.us

Delaware
800/652-5600 (in DE)
302/760-2080
www.deldot.net ▲

Florida
866/914-3838
305/914-3838 (Smartraveler for Miami-Dade, Palm Beach, and Broward Counties)
www11.myflorida.com ▲

Georgia
404/635-8000 ▲
www.dot.state.ga.us

Hawaii
808/536-6566 ▲
808/587-2345 (H-1 corridor) ▲
www.hawaii.gov/dot ▲

Idaho
888/432-7623 (in ID)
208/336-6600
www2.state.id.us/itd/ida-road/

Illinois
800/452-4368 ❄
312/368-4636
www.dot.state.il.us

Indiana
800/261-7623 ❄
www.in.gov/dot/

Iowa
515/288-1047 ❄
www.dot.state.ia.us

Kansas
800/585-7623 (in KS and area codes 214, 817, 903, 972, 806)
www.kanroad.org

Kentucky
800/459-7623
www.kytc.state.ky.us

Louisiana
www.dotd.state.la.us

Maine
207/624-3595 ❄
www.state.me.us/mdot/ ❄

Maryland
800/327-3125 ❄
www.chart.state.md.us

Massachusetts
617/374-1234 (Smartraveler)
www.state.ma.us/eotc/ ▲

Michigan
800/381-8477 ❄
888/305-7283 (for west and southwest MI) ▲
www.mdot.state.mi.us

Minnesota
800/542-0220 ❄
651/284-0511 ❄
www.dot.state.mn.us

Mississippi
601/359-7301 ▲
601/987-1211 ❄
www.mdot.state.ms.us

Missouri
800/222-6400 ❄
www.modot.state.mo.us

Montana
800/226-7623 ❄
www.mdt.state.mt.us/travinfo/

Nebraska
800/906-9069 ❄
402/471-4533 ❄
www.dor.state.ne.us

Nevada
877/687-6237 ❄
www.nevadadot.com

New Hampshire
800/918-9993 (in NH) ❄
603/271-6900 ❄
www.state.nh.us/dot/

New Jersey
Turnpike:
732/247-0900 ❄
www.state.nj.us/turnpike/ ▲
Garden State Parkway:
732/727-5929
All other roads:
www.njcommuter.com

New Mexico
800/432-4269 ❄
www.nmshtd.state.nm.us ▲

New York
Thruway:
800/847-8929 ❄
www.thruway.state.ny.us ▲
All other roads:
www.dot.state.ny.us ▲

North Carolina
www.ncsmartlink.org ▲

North Dakota
701/328-7623 ❄
www.state.nd.us/dot/

Ohio
Turnpike:
888/876-7453 ▲
440/234-2030 ❄
www.ohioturnpike.org
All other roads:
888/264-7623 (in OH)
614/644-7031 ❄
www.dot.state.oh.us

Oklahoma
405/425-2385 ❄
www.dps.state.ok.us ❄

Oregon
800/977-6368 (in OR)
503/588-2941
www.tripcheck.com

Pennsylvania
888/783-6783 (in PA)
www.dot.state.pa.us

Rhode Island
www.dot.state.ri.us ▲

South Carolina
www.dot.state.sc.us

South Dakota
605/367-5707 ❄
605/773-7515 ❄
www.sddot.com

Tennessee
800/342-3258 ❄
800/858-6349 ▲
www.tdot.state.tn.us

Texas
800/452-9292
www.dot.state.tx.us

Utah
800/492-2400 ❄
801/964-6000 ❄
www.dot.state.ut.us

Vermont
800/429-7623 (in VT)
www.aot.state.vt.us ❄

Virginia
800/367-7623 ❄
www.virginiadot.org

Washington
800/695-7623 ❄
www.wsdot.wa.gov/traveler

West Virginia
877/982-7623 ❄
www.wvdot.com

Wisconsin
800/762-3947
www.dot.state.wi.us

Wyoming
888/996-7623 (in WY)
307/772-0824
www.dot.state.wy.us

Canada

Alberta
403/246-5853 ❄
www.trans.gov.ab.ca

British Columbia
250/953-9000, then 7623 ❄
www.gov.bc.ca/tran/

Manitoba
877/627-6237 (in MB) ❄
204/945-3704 ❄
www.gov.mb.ca/roadinfo/

New Brunswick
800/561-4063 (in NB) ❄
www.gov.nb.ca/dot/

Newfoundland & Labrador
www.roads.gov.nf.ca

Nova Scotia
800/307-7669 (in NS) ❄
902/424-3933 ❄
www.gov.ns.ca/tran/

Ontario
800/668-2746, then 6
800/268-4686 (in ON) ❄
416/235-4686 ❄
www.mto.gov.on.ca

Prince Edward Island
902/368-4770 ❄
www.gov.pe.ca ❄

Québec
877/393-2363 (in QC) ❄
418/684-2363 (in Québec City) ❄
www.mtq.gouv.qc.ca

Saskatchewan
306/787-7623 ❄
www.highways.gov.sk.ca

avoid those ***bottlenecks*** *and barricades*

As the Odometer turns

Mileage chart

This handy chart offers more than 2,400 mileages covering 77 North American cities. Want more mileages? Just go to **www.randmcnally.com**, enter this page's Express Access Code (MC), then type in any two cities or addresses.

randmcnally.com
Express Access Code MC

Use Express Access Codes for quick access to online travel planning info, road construction updates, and more.

	Atlanta, GA	Billings, MT	Boston, MA	Charlotte, NC	Chicago, IL	Cincinnati, OH	Cleveland, OH	Dallas, TX	Denver, CO	Detroit, MI	Houston, TX	Indianapolis, IN	Kansas City, MO	Los Angeles, CA	Memphis, TN	Miami, FL	Milwaukee, WI	Minneapolis, MN	New Orleans, LA	New York, NY	Omaha, NE	Philadelphia, PA	Phoenix, AZ	Pittsburgh, PA	Portland, OR	St. Louis, MO	Salt Lake City, UT	San Francisco, CA	Seattle, WA	Tulsa, OK	Washington, D.C.	Wichita, KS
Albany, NY	1014	2076	166	777	820	727	478	1682	1814	648	1770	791	1287	2833	1230	1407	921	1236	1441	153	1274	238	2544	472	2927	1040	2206	2953	2899	1433	365	1477
Albuquerque, NM	1406	994	2247	1629	1341	1397	1606	644	439	1591	890	1290	783	799	1014	1960	1424	1222	1170	2019	979	1939	463	1649	1385	1041	626	1097	1456	650	1886	593
Amarillo, TX	1121	971	1962	1344	1056	1112	1321	359	424	1306	605	1005	604	1084	729	1675	1139	1043	885	1734	716	1654	748	1364	1666	756	911	1382	1737	365	1601	417
Atlanta, GA		1890	1100	243	712	463	715	791	1415	723	797	529	810	2205	393	661	811	1132	468	896	1000	816	1862	686	2604	556	1883	2503	2675	798	635	972
Baltimore, MD	673	1960	407	436	704	523	379	1366	1693	532	1454	592	1088	2681	914	1080	805	1120	1125	203	1158	102	2345	251	2811	841	2090	2837	2783	1234	38	1278
Billings, MT	1890		2242	2055	1247	1547	1598	1429	555	1534	1676	1433	1078	1239	1606	2551	1176	843	1954	2067	896	2017	1206	1716	891	1333	549	1179	821	1238	1961	1064
Birmingham, AL	148	1839	1185	391	661	467	719	647	1364	727	671	478	759	2058	246	783	760	1081	342	981	949	901	1722	753	2553	505	1832	2356	2624	651	743	825
Bismarck, ND	1558	417	1828	1610	833	1133	1184	1274	709	1120	1521	1019	790	1595	1318	2219	762	429	1709	1653	608	1603	1515	1302	1310	1045	927	1598	1240	1037	1547	802
Boise, ID	2184	621	2673	2349	1702	1959	2029	1704	830	1965	1951	1852	1372	846	1900	2845	1741	1466	2229	2498	1233	2448	995	2147	425	1627	338	648	496	1513	2392	1339
Boston, MA	1100	2242		863	986	893	644	1768	1980	814	1856	957	1453	2999	1316	1483	1087	1402	1527	211	1440	313	2710	586	3093	1206	2372	3119	3065	1599	441	1643
Buffalo, NY	896	1787	461	659	531	438	189	1376	1525	359	1495	502	998	2544	924	1381	632	947	1243	417	985	412	2255	216	2638	751	1917	2664	2610	1144	388	1188
Charleston, SC	321	2196	966	207	911	619	721	1112	1721	850	1113	730	1116	2526	714	580	1010	1325	784	762	1306	661	2183	654	2910	862	2189	2824	2981	1119	525	1306
Charlotte, NC	243	2055	863		770	478	516	1034	1580	645	1040	589	975	2428	617	724	869	1184	711	659	1165	534	2092	449	2769	721	2048	2726	2840	1021	398	1165
Cheyenne, WY	1450	455	1939	1615	968	1225	1295	974	100	1231	1221	1118	638	1102	1166	2111	1007	878	1499	1764	499	1714	906	1413	1155	893	434	1181	1226	783	1658	609
Chicago, IL	712	1247	986	770		293	342	933	1009	278	1089	179	529	2028	536	1373	92	407	927	811	469	761	1804	460	2122	300	1401	2148	2070	693	705	719
Cincinnati, OH	463	1547	893	478	293		252	938	1208	260	1057	112	603	2196	486	1124	392	707	805	660	726	580	1860	290	2379	356	1658	2405	2370	749	524	793
Cleveland, OH	715	1598	644	516	342	252		1190	1336	170	1309	316	812	2355	738	1238	443	758	1057	486	796	436	2069	135	2449	565	1728	2475	2421	958	380	1002
Columbus, OH	574	1606	783	433	352	111	142	1049	1276	204	1168	175	671	2264	597	1155	451	766	916	553	794	473	1928	183	2447	424	1726	2473	2429	817	417	861
Dallas, TX	791	1429	1768	1034	933	938	1190		882	1198	247	882	552	1440	454	1316	1016	991	526	1564	664	1484	1069	1228	2124	633	1403	1741	2195	262	1326	365
Davenport, IA	792	1166	1135	898	175	421	491	915	843	427	1095	314	363	1862	550	1453	214	359	941	960	303	910	1609	609	1956	266	1235	1982	1989	612	854	553
Denver, CO	1415	555	1980	1580	1009	1208	1336	882		1272	1129	1101	605	1022	1097	2076	1048	919	1407	1805	540	1750	809	1460	1250	858	529	1276	1321	691	1694	517
Des Moines, IA	961	997	1304	1067	333	590	660	746	674	596	926	483	194	1693	623	1622	372	243	1014	1129	134	1079	1440	778	1787	350	1066	1813	1820	443	1023	384
Detroit, MI	723	1534	814	645	278	260	170	1198	1272		1317	310	792	2291	746	1367	379	694	1065	639	732	589	2054	288	2385	550	1664	2411	2357	943	533	955
Duluth, MN	1189	861	1459	1241	464	764	815	1145	1073	751	1325	650	593	2092	965	1850	393	157	1356	1284	533	1234	1839	933	1754	681	1465	2042	1684	842	1178	783
El Paso, TX	1426	1178	2394	1669	1488	1544	1753	623	623	1738	753	1437	930	807	1087	1939	1571	1369	1100	2197	1016	2117	436	1796	1627	1188	868	1188	1698	797	1959	740
Fargo, ND	1369	607	1639	1421	644	944	995	1087	901	931	1334	830	603	1785	1131	2030	573	240	1522	1464	421	1414	1707	1113	1500	858	1117	1788	1430	850	1358	725
Flagstaff, AZ	1733	1070	2574	1956	1668	1724	1933	971	673	1918	1217	1617	1110	472	1341	2287	1751	1549	1497	2346	1210	2266	136	1976	1279	1368	520	770	1350	977	2213	920
Houston, TX	797	1676	1856	1040	1089	1057	1309	247	1129	1317		1025	732	1560	573	1190	1179	1171	351	1652	911	1572	1189	1347	2371	837	1650	1941	2442	505	1414	612
Indianapolis, IN	529	1433	957	589	179	112	316	882	1101	310	1025		496	2089	472	1190	278	593	816	729	619	649	1753	359	2272	249	1551	2298	2256	642	593	686
Jackson, MS	383	1817	1424	626	747	692	944	408	1225	952	442	683	737	1850	212	908	837	1119	180	1220	927	1140	1479	982	2467	495	1746	2149	2538	534	982	708
Jacksonville, FL	346	2236	1142	383	1058	795	897	1001	1761	1026	875	875	1156	2431	712	341	1157	1478	546	938	1346	837	2060	830	2950	902	2229	2742	3021	1117	701	1291
Kansas City, MO	810	1078	1453	975	529	603	812	552	605	792	732	496		1626	526	1471	568	439	917	1225	188	1145	1246	855	1792	253	1071	1818	1863	249	1089	190
Knoxville, TN	215	1826	928	229	542	250	502	840	1351	510	928	361	746	2199	388	876	641	956	599	724	936	644	1863	496	2540	492	1819	2497	2611	792	486	936
Las Vegas, NV	1982	966	2726	2205	1755	1956	2082	1220	749	2018	1466	1849	1353	275	1590	2536	1794	1665	1746	2551	1286	2498	292	2208	1021	1606	416	569	1122	1226	2462	1265
Lexington, KY	386	1669	935	401	375	83	335	874	1194	343	993	188	589	2175	422	1047	474	789	741	731	779	645	1839	373	2383	335	1662	2409	2454	728	543	779
Little Rock, AR	531	1513	1453	754	655	623	875	315	966	883	434	591	389	1682	139	1165	745	826	441	1249	577	1169	1346	913	2208	403	1487	1980	2279	275	1011	449
Los Angeles, CA	2205	1239	2999	2428	2028	2196	2355	1440	1022	2291	1560	2089	1626		1813	2746	2067	1938	1907	2824	1559	2738	371	2448	967	1840	689	381	1141	1449	2685	1392
Louisville, KY	415	1595	996	475	297	103	355	835	1120	363	954	114	515	2101	383	1076	396	711	702	763	705	683	1765	393	2309	261	1588	2335	2380	654	617	705
Memphis, TN	393	1606	1316	617	536	486	738	454	1097	746	573	472	526	1813		1027	626	908	392	1112	716	1032	1477	776	2320	284	1599	2111	2391	406	874	580
Miami, FL	661	2551	1483	724	1373	1124	1238	1316	2076	1367	1190	1190	1471	2746	1027		1472	1793	861	1279	1661	1178	2375	1171	3265	1217	2544	3057	3336	1432	1042	1606
Milwaukee, WI	811	1176	1087	869	92	392	443	1016	1048	379	1179	278	568	2067	626	1472		336	1017	912	508	862	1887	561	2069	383	1440	2187	1999	776	806	758
Minneapolis, MN	1132	843	1402	1184	407	707	758	991	919	694	1171	593	439	1938	908	1793	336		1299	1227	379	1177	1685	876	1736	624	1311	2058	1666	688	1121	629
Mobile, AL	329	2003	1429	572	920	726	978	598	1415	986	472	737	923	2028	398	718	1019	1305	143	1225	1113	1145	1657	1009	2657	681	1936	2339	2728	724	964	898
Montréal, QC	1227	1909	324	990	848	829	590	1767	1842	575	1886	879	1362	2861	1315	1632	949	1264	1654	384	1302	463	2632	617	2955	1128	2234	2981	2732	1521	590	1525
Nashville, TN	242	1650	1106	407	472	278	530	663	1175	538	782	289	570	2022	211	903	571	892	527	902	760	822	1686	568	2364	316	1643	2320	2435	615	664	760
New Orleans, LA	468	1954	1527	711	927	805	1057	526	1407	1065	351	816	917	1907	392	861	1017	1299		1323	1107	1243	1536	1095	2649	675	1928	2267	2720	679	1085	890
New York, NY	896	2067	211	659	811	660	486	1564	1805	639	1652	729	1225	2824	1112	1279	912	1227	1323		1265	109	2482	388	2918	978	2197	2944	2890	1371	237	1415
Norfolk, VA	557	2147	577	320	891	601	566	1348	1781	719	1384	713	1176	2729	918	948	992	1307	1055	373	1366	276	2393	438	2970	922	2249	2996	3041	1315	196	1366
Odessa, TX	1147	1204	2122	1390	1244	1292	1509	354	649	1494	546	1193	792	1088	808	1672	1327	1231	882	1918	904	1838	717	1552	1784	944	1025	1469	1855	553	1680	605
Oklahoma City, OK	862	1221	1702	1085	796	852	1061	208	674	1046	455	745	344	1343	470	1496	879	783	733	1474	456	1394	1007	1104	1916	496	1195	1641	1987	105	1342	157
Omaha, NE	1000	896	1440	1165	469	726	796	664	540	732	911	619	188	1559	716	1661	508	379	1107	1265		1215	1346	914	1653	443	932	1679	1724	435	1159	302
Orlando, FL	440	2330	1284	525	1152	903	1039	1095	1855	1163	969	969	1250	2525	806	229	1251	1572	640	1080	1440	979	2154	972	3044	996	2323	2836	3115	1211	843	1385
Philadelphia, PA	816	2017	313	534	761	580	436	1484	1750	589	1572	649	1145	2738	1032	1178	862	1177	1243	109	1215		2402	308	2868	898	2147	2894	2840	1291	136	1335
Phoenix, AZ	1862	1206	2710	2092	1804	1860	2069	1069	809	2054	1189	1753	1246	371	1477	2375	1887	1685	1536	2482	1346	2402		2112	1338	1504	656	752	1486	1113	2349	1056
Pittsburgh, PA	686	1716	586	449	460	290	135	1228	1460	288	1347	359	855	2448	776	1171	561	876	1095	388	914	308	2112		2567	608	1846	2593	2539	1001	252	1045
Portland, ME	1229	2343	117	964	1087	994	745	1897	2081	915	1985	1058	1554	3100	1445	1584	1188	1503	1656	312	1541	414	2811	687	3194	1307	2473	3220	3166	1700	542	1744
Portland, OR	2604	891	3093	2769	2122	2379	2449	2124	1250	2385	2371	2272	1792	967	2320	3265	2069	1736	2649	2918	1653	2868	1338	2567		2047	758	636	174	1933	2812	1759
Rapid City, SD	1521	373	1904	1686	909	1209	1260	1069	400	1196	1316	1095	709	1312	1237	2182	838	609	1628	1729	527	1679	1206	1378	1266	964	644	1391	1196	878	1623	704
Reno, NV	2406	955	2895	2571	1924	2181	2251	1665	1052	2187	1911	2074	1594	473	2122	3067	1963	1834	2193	2720	1455	2670	735	2369	578	1849	522	224	752	1735	2614	1561
Roanoke, VA	430	1917	678	193	663	370	429	1098	1550	558	1186	482	945	2457	646	915	762	1077	857	474	1135	394	2121	365	2739	691	2018	2765	2810	1050	236	1135
St. Louis, MO	556	1333	1206	721	300	356	565	633	858	550	837	249	253	1840	284	1217	383	624	675	978	443	898	1504	608	2047		1326	2073	2118	393	878	443
Salt Lake City, UT	1883	549	2372	2048	1401	1658	1728	1403	529	1664	1650	1551	1071	689	1599	2544	1440	1311	1928	2197	932	2147	656	1846	758	1326		746	829	1212	2091	1038
San Antonio, TX	992	1483	2051	1235	1210	1215	1467	277	936	1475	199	1159	817	1365	731	1385	1293	1256	546	1847	929	1767	994	1505	2100	910	1341	1746	2171	539	1609	630
San Diego, CA	2154	1299	3064	2397	2088	2214	2423	1361	1082	2351	1481	2107	1600	124	1831	2667	2127	1998	1828	2836	1619	2756	354	2466	1091	1858	749	505	1265	1467	2703	1410
San Francisco, CA	2503	1179	3119	2726	2148	2405	2475	1741	1276	2411	1941	2298	1818	381	2111	3057	2187	2058	2267	2944	1679	2894	752	2593	636	2073	746		810	1747	2838	1785
Sault Ste Marie, ON	1047	1282	943	960	452	584	506	1357	1446	350	1510	537	966	2465	957	1708	404	549	1347	939	906	925	2228	624	2175	724	1838	2585	2105	1117	869	1129
Seattle, WA	2675	821	3065	2840	2070	2370	2421	2195	1321	2357	2442	2256	1863	1141	2391	3336	1999	1666	2720	2890	1724	2840	1486	2539	174	2118	829	810		2004	2784	1830
Shreveport, LA	605	1614	1646	848	851	819	1071	186	1067	1079	239	787	566	1628	335	1130	941	1005	347	1442	752	1362	1257	1109	2309	599	1588	1927	2380	339	1204	550
Sioux Falls, SD	1177	717	1564	1342	569	876	920	849	654	856	1096	769	365	1673	893	1838	498	269	1284	1389	183	1339	1460	1038	1610	620	989	1736	1540	612	1283	487
Spokane, WA	2431	539	2783	2596	1788	2088	2139	1970	1096	2075	2217	1974	1619	1215	2147	3092	1717	1384	2495	2608	1437	2558	1377	2257	352	1874	720	885	282	1779	2502	1605
Springfield, MO	684	1247	1418	849	512	568	777	423	761	762	666	461	169	1630	283	1345	595	606	674	1190	357	1110	1294	820	1961	212	1240	1928	2032	183	1090	263
Tallahassee, FL	270	2143	1301	470	965	733	985	839	1668	993	713	782	1063	2269	550	478	1064	1385	384	1097	1253	996	1898	917	2857	809	2136	2580	2928	955	860	1129
Tampa, FL	458	2348	1340	581	1170	921	1095	1113	1873	1181	987	987	1268	2543	824	273	1269	1590	658	1136	1458	1035	2172	1028	3062	1014	2341	2854	3133	1229	899	1403
Toronto, ON	961	1773	566	766	517	498	296	1436	1511	244	1555	548	1031	2530	984	1488	618	933	1303	528	971	517	2301	323	2624	797	1903	2650	2596	1190	495	1194
Tulsa, OK	798	1238	1599	1021	693	749	958	262	691	943	505	642	249	1449	406	1432	776	688	679	1371	435	1291	1113	1001	1933	393	1212	1747	2004		1271	174
Washington, D.C.	635	1961	441	398	705	524	380	1326	1694	533	1414	593	1089	2685	874	1042	806	1121	1085	237	1159	136	2349	252	2812	878	2091	2838	2784	1271		1279
Wichita, KS	972	1064	1643	1165	719	793	1002	365	517	955	612	686	190	1392	580	1606	758	629	890	1415	302	1335	1056	1045	1759	443	1038	1785	1830	174	1279	

Mileages © 2003 Rand McNally-TDM, Inc.